The Washington High Bench

A Biographical History of
the State Supreme Court, 1889-1991

The Washington High Bench

A Biographical History of the State Supreme Court, 1889-1991

Charles H. Sheldon

Washington State University Press
Pullman, Washington

Washington State University Press, Pullman, Washington 99164-5910

©1992 by the Board of Regents of Washington State University
All rights reserved
First printing 1992

Library of Congress Cataloging-in-Publication Data
Sheldon, Charles H., 1929-
    The Washington high bench: a biographical history of the State Supreme Court, 1889-1991 / by Charles H. Sheldon.
        p. cm.
    Includes bibliographical references (p.   ) and index.
    ISBN 0-87422-080-7 (hardbound): $35.00.—ISBN 0-87422-076-9 (pbk.): $25.00
    1. Washington (State). Supreme Court—Biography. 2. Judges—Washington (State)—Biography. I. Title.
KFW512.S54   1992
347.797'03534—dc20
[B]
[347.97073534]   91-42576
[B]   CIP

To

Tiffany, Scott, Ryan, and Bryce
may their lives be blessed with justice

and

members of the Washington high bench, past and present, who have,
in their own ways, provided justice

Table of Contents

Foreword

by Justice Vernon R. Pearson

It has been a pleasure for me to read about the supreme court of Washington and the men and women who have been privileged to serve as its justices from statehood to the present.

Professor Sheldon is not only an eminent political scientist and historian, but has also over the years served the judiciary of the state in a variety of tasks which indicate his strong commitment to improving the administration of justice. He, with the assistance of many of his students, has done a remarkably accurate job of preparing biographies of the eighty lawyers who were either appointed or elected to the highest state judicial office. For the most part he stresses the positive rather than the negative aspects of our childhood, professional, and civic careers, but he does not hesitate to point out those things he believes may have influenced our judicial decision-making philosophies.

This publication also contains an accurate analysis of the shifting judicial selection process, with its emphasis on the continuing tension between accountability and independence, which is ever present in a state that elects its judiciary. Most unique in this publication is an incisive analysis of the collective decision-making process. As a former justice, I find all of these considerations accurate and fair; at least insofar as the decision-making process can be accurately portrayed by a statistical analysis.

An interesting historical fact shown by this book is that in the 102-year history of the supreme court, only eighty lawyers have had the opportunity to serve on that bench. This is more significant when one considers that more than 20,000 lawyers have served at the bar since statehood and are thus eligible as candidates for this highest judicial office. It is thus a rare privilege for the few fortunate who have served.

While my eight-year tenure on the court from 1982-1989 was relatively short, I was privileged to serve with thirteen of the eighty members. The oldest in terms of service was Hugh J. Rosellini who was elected to the court in 1955 and served until his death in 1984, less than a month prior to his planned retirement. It was also my privilege to have served with the first two women to sit on the supreme court, as well as the first non-caucasian justice.

All thirteen of these justices had certain unique, yet diverse talents. All had strong leadership qualities and were persons with strong and competitive personalities. All but one had served on one or more of the other levels within our court system. One had served on all four court levels. Four of the justices had been active in partisan politics and had served in the state legislature. Several had been experienced trial lawyers, and one had extensive experience in the executive branch of government. This diversity of background and experience made, in my opinion, for a strong court. We did not duck any of the tough societal or political issues of the day. In fact, the diversity meant that most societal points of view were brought to the decision-making process. This led to balanced decisions, as well as many concurring or dissenting opinions.

All of the justices I served with had one thing in common that is well documented in their biographies. All were or had been community leaders during their professional lives. Perhaps this commonalty is the most important reason why they were privileged to serve on the supreme court. It should be said also that most of the justices continued to be active in community affairs during their judicial tenure, at least to the extent ethically permitted by the *Code of Judicial Conduct.*

In this state the chief justice has very little administrative authority except as delegated by vote of a majority of the court. While this may be viewed as a weakness, it does have a positive side. During my term as chief justice it was never difficult to promote positive programs for improving the administration of justice if the members of the court were kept well informed of the plans and purposes of the programs. On the other hand, a majority of the court always had the ability to curb overly ambitious or expensive programs or ill-conceived pet projects of a particular chief. As chief justice, I welcomed a consensus approach to court management, and in my opinion this aspect strengthened rather than weakened the system.

The short two-year term for the chief justice has also been suggested as an administrative weakness. This may be true where a chief justice is chosen for his or her administrative ability. But where, as in Washington, the position is rotated by constitutional provision, it seems desirable to me that the term be short so that a chief justice of poor administrative ability will cause no undue harm during his or her tenure. Also, the court has a two year training period for the chief justice. As acting chief justice, the soon-to-be-chief has an opportunity to learn all the duties and responsibilities of the position. Among other things, the acting chief justice serves as chair of the important rules committee of the supreme court. This committee works with the Washington State Bar Association and the judicial council in processing and recommending to the court procedural rules and rule changes that affect all levels of the court system. The acting chief justice also serves on the Board for Judicial Administration (BJA), which has representation from the other court levels and from the state bar association. The BJA is the policy-recommending agency for the judicial branch of government. Thus, the acting chief justice has an opportunity to learn, before becoming chief justice, all that is going on within the entire court system. In my opinion, the acting chief justice diminishes the weakness which many perceive to be inherent in a short-term chief justice system.

Another thing should be stressed in this preface. The routine work of the supreme court changed dramatically in 1969 with the advent of the intermediate court of appeals. That court immediately became the repository of more than ninety-five percent of the cases that would have gone directly to the supreme court. Overnight, the supreme court shed the mantle of being a court of first and last appellate rcsort to a true court of last resort for all state criminal and civil matters.

As a court of last resort, the supreme court could select its issue agenda much as the United States Supreme Court does, with only a few items of direct review. These are (1) death penalty cases; (2) cases in which a trial court had determined a law to be unconstitutional; (3) mandates against state officials; and (4) a vague category where the issue is important statewide and requires a speedy and ultimate decision.

The court had to establish new procedures to decide which cases to review that already had been decided by the court of appeals. Also the court needed a mechanism to screen and decide which cases should be retained where direct review was sought from a trial court's decision. By the time I came to the supreme court, a commissioner's staff, with several staff attorneys, did the preconsideration workup in both these areas, making it possible for the court to decide which issues were significant enough to warrant direct review or a second review. This system worked well while I was on the court because of the excellent workups by the commissioner's office and because of conscientious prestudy by members of the court. Almost 100 of these matters were considered every month, in addition to the regular hearing calendar of the court. In many respects, the true philosophy of a court of last resort is determined by the issues that court chooses to decide. I thus considered these conferences to decide upon the cases we would review as some of the most important work of the court, equal in importance to the ultimate decisions. Most of the justices I served with shared my view on the importance of the monthly petitions-for-review calendar, and in my opinion an appropriate decision agenda was maintained.

Most citizens, including many lawyers, view the supreme court as primarily a decision-making court and judge its effectiveness solely from the number and quality of opinions it writes. This is much too narrow a view. When I came to the court I discovered that about forty percent of my time was related to the court's other functions. As the constitutional administrative head of the judicial branch of Washington, the supreme court performs both executive and legislative duties that require a considerable amount of time. Each justice serves on several committees to perform these functions. Much careful thought and study, and many hours of time, are required for these administrative matters. Among the executive-type functions are those involving regulation of the Washington

State Bar Association. During my time on the court there were many changes considered and implemented involving regulation of the legal profession, including the adoption of limited-practice procedures for non-attorney escrow agents; new admission and disciplinary procedures for lawyers; and adoption of a new code of professional conduct for lawyers. Numerous meetings and some hearings are required for every member of the court.

Equally as important and time-consuming is the court's legislative function. The supreme court is required by law to set the procedures that govern all levels of the court. At one time the court was involved in approving the fine schedule for traffic offenses and the support schedules for spouses in domestic relations cases.

The supreme court also has many executive or administrative responsibilities involving public relations, preparing and presenting court budgets to the legislature, and testifying on many legislative proposals that impact the administration of justice. Here again, all members of the court are involved in these matters and each justice devotes many hours beyond regular office time in dealing with them.

I also want to say with some pride that all this work could not be done without a creative and talented court staff, as well as an Office of the Administrator for the Courts (OAC). The OAC has done an outstanding job in assisting the courts in administering the judicial branch of government, and in seeing that all court levels are properly staffed, funded, educated, and informed. Most significantly, a statewide and integrated computer system has helped immeasurably in the prompt administration of justice in Washington state.

In conclusion, it is of vital importance that citizens of this state learn about the important work of the supreme court and the people who perform it. Professor Sheldon is to be thanked and congratulated by members of the bench and the public for this unique work he has now completed.

Gig Harbor, Washington
September 1991

Acknowledgements

I am indebted to many. The study would not have been possible without the cooperation of current and retired justices of the Washington Supreme Court. All were patient interviewees, frank respondents, and constructive critics throughout the research culminating in this volume. Grants from the American Philosophical Society (1977), the National Endowment for the Humanities (1978), the National Science Foundation – Law and Social Science Program (1982), and the Division of Archives and Records Management of the Washington Secretary of State's office (1988) eased the financial burdens involved in gathering data. Of course, the views expressed are those of the author, not the granting agencies. The office of the Dean of Social Sciences and Humanities and the Research and Arts Committee of Washington State University provided publication support.

Again, as with the first volume of this study – *A Century of Judging: A Political History of the Washington Supreme Court* (Seattle: University of Washington Press, 1988) – I extend thanks to my wife, Patricia Ann, who was my research collaborator, careful note-taker, critic, and archival "digger" throughout the fifteen years we have devoted to developing an understanding of the state's high bench.

A number of graduate and undergraduate students contributed through their initial data gathering for term papers and theses: Fran Bernat, Rick Carlson, Craig Curtis, Sandy Gallagher, Lynette Lee-Sammons, Kari A. Kisler, Michael Stohr-Gillmore, Todd Gay, Joe Homans, Kerry Radcliffe, Brian Hartnett, Kim Meyer, Robert Ingalls, Claudia Wade, Alan Gallagher, Orman Vertrees, Pat Youngblood, Mary Fagan, Danielle Darcy, Janet Foster, Melanie Ruta (Males), and Linda Zupan.

Professor Emeriti Jack Gabbert and Thor Swanson carefully edited the original manuscript and Keith Petersen of the Washington State University Press contributed substantially in preparing the final version.

Finally, I am indeed indebted to Bonnie Goodrich, who, beyond her impeccable typing of the manuscript, served as critic, editor, and leading wit on the "Honorables."

I hope I have provided the reader with various perspectives for researching the Washington high bench and with data to carry out that task. We are only beginning to understand the Washington Supreme Court's significant contributions to the state's history. This volume was designed to contribute to that understanding.

Introduction

The logic of this volume's organization is quite simple but unfortunately not self-evident; thus this brief introduction. The fundamental assumption underlying the work is that despite tradition, precedent, constitutions, and laws, it is the judges of Washington's high bench who have made a difference in the law, and to an important degree have made a difference in the history of the Evergreen State. Although we are said to have "a government of laws, not of men," in point of fact, the men and women of government shape that law. And, of course, the judges of the Washington Supreme Court are among those doing the shaping. To understand the eighty judges who have served on the state's court of last resort is, to a significant degree, to understand the role of the supreme court in state government.

However, these eighty jurists are themselves products of diverse backgrounds, training, and experience and each brings to the high bench a characteristic outlook on politics, economics, and the law. Within the often blurred but significant constraints of tradition, constitution, and the law, as well as the *Canons of Judicial Conduct,* these backgrounds go far in explaining why justices decide differently when confronted with the same facts, precedent, and law in any given case.

The logic of the book is first to confirm that the judges do important things; namely, exercise judicial review and thereby shape much of the state's law. Chapter One, "The Court as Policy Maker: The Evolution of Judicial Review with the Supreme Court," reviews the course of judicial review over the past century. State courts tended to mimic what transpired at the U. S. Supreme Court and in sister states. However, by the 1980s an independent path beckoned, luring jurists into a greater emphasis upon the often unique provisions of the state's own constitution and into an activist mode.

Indeed, the court does important things. But why were the eighty judges chosen and not the scores of others who coveted a seat on the high bench? Chapter Two, "A History of Selection to the State's High Bench," explains the process that winnowed high court aspirants from hundreds down to the eighty who finally donned the robes of office.

Beyond simply designating survivors, the election and appointment processes are responsible for creating an accommodation between the competing values of public accountability and judicial independence. The judges who affirm, make, or deny public policy through the exercise of judicial review must be held accountable for their policy decisions. Majoritarian democracy means no less. However, to render an objective decision based on law, and to protect the minority from the majority, judges must be independent from the pressures of public opinion and politics. The rule of law means no less. As Chapter Two shows, voter turnout and the extent of competition for seats on the bench affect the shifting balance between accountability and independence.

When the justices arrived at the temple of justice, how did they go about their business? The jurists—first five, then seven, and now nine—are obliged to produce a collective decision. Over the years, the court's deliberations varied as jurists experimented with decision-making procedures to accommodate not only the pressure of too-numerous appeals but also the often idiosyncratic preferences of individual justices. Chapter Three, "A Review of Supreme Court Decisional Processes," records those experiments in decision-making. Much like selection, decision-making swings between a collective and an individual mode, each pulling at the other for dominance. The ideal, of course, is to strike a balance between the competing modes. A comparison of the levels of unanimity and dissonance suggests whether the balance has been struck.

Chapter Four, "Judicial Profiles: The Uses of Biography," introduces the various dimensions of judicial biography. What background, training, and experience appear relevant to judicial review, selection, and decision-making procedures? The heart of the volume, of course, is the eighty judicial profiles that follow. Each attempts to record those factors that place the jurists within the context of information provided in the preceding chapters. The "profiles" are just that; sharp outlines without the shadings, shadows, and subtle reflections that constitute any person's character. The note on sources at the end of the volume will lead others to a deeper appraisal of these public servants.

That great supreme court justice, Oliver Wendell Holmes, Jr., was quite correct when he stated:

> The life of the law has not been logic; it has been experience. The felt necessities of the time, the prevalent moral and political theories, intuitions of public policy, avowed or unconscious, even the prejudices which judges share with their fellow men, have had a great deal more to do than syllogisms in determining the rules by which men should be governed.

Hopefully, this volume will contribute to an understanding of the "felt necessities of the time," for judges not only reflect these necessities, they shape them.

Members of the Washington Supreme Court 1889-1991

No.	Name	Term	Legal Training	Party Affiliation	Residence
1.	Thomas J. Anders	1889-1905	Michigan	R	Walla Walla
2.	Elmon Scott	1889-1899	Clerk	R	Pomeroy
3.	Ralph O. Dunbar	1889-1912	Clerk	R	Goldendale
4.	Theodore L. Stiles	1889-1895	Columbia	R	Tacoma
5.	John P. Hoyt	1889-1897	Union	R	Seattle
6.	Merritt J. Gordon	1895-1900	Clerk	R	Olympia
7.	James B. Reavis	1897-1903	Clerk	D	Yakima
8.	Mark A. Fullerton	1899-1931	Clerk	R	Colfax
9.	William H. White	*1900-1901 1901-1902	Clerk	D	Seattle
10.	Wallace Mount	1901-1921	Clerk	R	Spokane
11.	Hiram E. Hadley	*1901-1902 1903-1909	Northwestern	R	Bellingham
12.	Frank H. Rudkin	1905-1911	Washington & Lee	R	Yakima
13.	Milo A. Root	*1905-1908	Albany	R	Seattle
14.	Herman D. Crow	*1905-1915	Clerk	R	Spokane
15.	Stephen J. Chadwick	**1908-1909 1909-1919	Clerk	D	Colfax
16.	Mack F. Gose	*1909-1915	Clerk	R	Pomeroy
17.	George E. Morris	*1909-1918	Albany	R	Seattle
18.	Emmett N. Parker	*1909-1933	Cincinnati	R	Tacoma
19.	Overton G. Ellis	*1911-1918	Virginia	R	Seattle
20.	John F. Main	*1912-1942	Michigan	R	Seattle
21.	Oscar R. Holcomb	1915-1927 *1927-1939	Chicago-Kent	D	Ritzville
22.	Frederick Bausman	*1915-1916	Harvard	D	Seattle
23.	John Stanley Webster	**1916-1918	Michigan	R	Spokane
24.	Kenneth Mackintosh	*1918-1928	Columbia	R	Seattle
25.	John R. Mitchell	*1918-1937	Clerk	D	Olympia
26.	Warren W. Tolman	*1918-1937	Northwestern	D	Spokane
27.	Jessie B. Bridges	*1919-1927	Clerk	R	Aberdeen
28.	Chester R. Hovey	*1921-1923	Clerk	R	Ellensberg
29.	William H. Pemberton	1923-1925	Clerk	D	Bellingham
30.	William D. Askren	1925-1928	Clerk	R	Tacoma
31.	Walter M. French	1927-1930	Washington	D	Tacoma
32.	William J. Millard	*1928-1949 1956-1957	Georgetown	R	Olympia
33.	Walter B. Beals	1928-1946 1947-1951	Washington	R	Seattle

No. Name	Term	Legal Training	Party Affiliation	Residence
34. Adam Beeler	*1930-1932	George Washington	R	Seattle
35. Henry E. T. Herman	*1931-1932	Washington Univ.	R	Spokane
36. William J. Steinert	*1932-1949	Michigan	R	Seattle
37. Bruce Blake	1932-1946	Michigan	D	Spokane
38. James M. Geraghty	*1933-1940	Clerk-Georgetown	D	Spokane
39. John S. Robinson	1937-1951	Columbia	R	Seattle
40. George B. Simpson	*1937-1951	Willamette	D	Vancouver
41. Clyde G. Jeffers	1939-1949	Iowa	R	Ephrata
42. Samuel M. Driver	*1940-1942 1945-1946	Washington	D	Spokane
43. Joseph A. Mallery	**1942-1962	Washington	R	Tacoma
44. Thomas E. Grady	*1942-1945 1949-1955	Minnesota	R	Yakima
45. Edward M. Connelly	*1946-1947	Gonzaga	D	Spokane
46. E. W. Schwellenbach	**1946-1957	Wisconsin	D	Ephrata
47. Don G. Abel	*1946-1947	Washington	D	Chehalis
48. Matthew W. Hill	1947-1969	Washington	R	Seattle
49. Frederick G. Hamley	*1949-1956	Washington	R	Seattle
50. Charles T. Donworth	*1949-1967	Washington	R	Seattle
51. Robert C. Finley	1951-1976	Duke	D	Renton
52. Frank P. Weaver	*1951-1970	Washington	R	Spokane
53. Ralph O. Olson	*1952-1955	Minnesota	R	Bellingham
54. Hugh J. Rosellini	1955-1984	Washington	D	Tacoma
55. Richard B. Ott	*1955-1967	Idaho	R	Ritzville
56. Harry E. Foster	*1956 1957-1962	Washington	R	Olympia
57. Robert T. Hunter	*1957-1977	Washington	D	Ephrata
58. Orris L. Hamilton	*1962-1979	American	D	Prosser
59. Frank Hale	*1963-1975	Clerk	D	Tacoma
60. Marshall A. Neill	*1967-1972	Idaho	R	Pullman
61. Walter T. McGovern	*1968-1971	Washington	R	Seattle
62. Charles F. Stafford, Jr.	*1970-1984	Yale	R	Bellingham
63. Morell E. Sharp	*1970-1971 *1971	Northwestern	R	Seattle
64. Charles T. Wright	1971-1980	Clerk	R	Olympia
65. Robert F. Utter	*1971-	Washington	R	Seattle
66. Robert Brachtenbach	*1972-	Washington	R	Yakima
67. Charles Horowitz	1975-1980	Washington	D	Seattle
68. James M. Dolliver	*1976-	Washington	R	Olympia
69. Floyd V. Hicks	1977-1982	Washington	D	Tacoma
70. William H. Williams	1979-1985	Gonzaga	D	Spokane
71. Fred H. Dore	**1981-	Georgetown	D	Seattle
72. Carolyn R. Dimmick	*1981-1985	Washington	R	Seattle
73. Vernon R. Pearson	*1982-1989	Michigan	R	Tacoma

No.	Name	Term	Legal Training	Party Affiliation	Residence
74.	James A. Andersen	*1984-	Washington	R	Seattle
75.	Keith M. Callow	**1985-1991	Washington	R	Seattle
76.	William C. Goodloc	1985-1988	Washington	R	Seattle
77.	Barbara Durham	*1985-	Stanford	R	Seattle
78.	Charles Z. Smith	*1988-	Washington	R	Seattle
79.	Richard P. Guy	*1989-	Gonzaga	D	Spokane
80.	Charles W. Johnson	1991-	Puget Sound	D	Tacoma

*=appointed
**=appointed after being elected

Chapter One

The Court as Policy Maker: The Evolution of Judicial Review with the Supreme Court[1]

Jurists at the state and federal levels perform several essential governing functions, some that can be undertaken at least as well by others. The primary function of judging is to resolve disputes on the basis of predetermined rules. When conflicting claims are at issue between litigants, courts are called upon to settle those claims according to the law's dictates. Courts also confirm, reject, and set public policy. Often disputes involving the welfare of the community and issues of great interest to the public are brought before the courts. In the process of deciding between the contentions of two litigants in these kinds of issues, judges may be establishing a precedent for a considerable number — perhaps all — residents of a state or nation. For example, judges often establish definitions of pornography, eligibility for state aid, validity of a taxing program, or the make-up of curriculum for public education. When decided by a court of last resort, these decisions set precedent for resolving subsequent disputes and bind future generations. A court that purposefully determines policy is an activist court. However, within a democratic system based on majority rule and representative government, policy decisions ought to be made in legislative halls, not in courtrooms. Courts should respect the views of the people's representatives and accept a restraintist role.[2]

In addition to settling disputes and setting policy, courts perpetuate useful myths about governing that assist in maintaining the political system. For example, "a government of laws, not of men," "justice," or "constitutionalism," are terms and concepts often associated with courts and found referenced in judges' written opinions. Stable political systems rely upon such symbols to gain the support of the people and to enhance their legitimacy.

Judicial Review, Judges, and the Constitution

Constitutional governments are all products of a compact between governors and the governed. Popular consent clothes the agreement with legitimacy. Section 1 of Washington's Declaration of Rights states: "All political power is inherent

Olympia's Main Street, c. 1890, shortly after the first state supreme court met.

in the people, and governments derive their just powers from the consent of the governed, and are established to maintain and protect individual rights."

The compact designates public offices, defines officials' duties, and places authoritative limitations on those public officials. American constitutionalism, then, means limited government; but government nonetheless. Thus, constitutions grant power and place limits on the exercise of power. Over 175 years ago, Chief Justice John Marshall delineated this balance between power and its limits in the landmark case *Marbury v. Madison:*

> That the people have the original right to establish for their future government, such principles as, in their opinion, shall most conduce to their own happiness, is the basis upon which the whole American fabric has been erected. The exercise of this original right is a very great exertion; nor can it, nor ought it, to be frequently repeated. The principles, therefore, so established, are deemed fundamental; and...they are designed to be permanent...
>
> The powers of the legislature are defined and limited; and that those limits may not be mistaken, or forgotten, the constitution is written.[3]

Those assigned the duty of defining constitutional limits on power are therefore resolving fundamental public issues. Courts play this important role of judging the constitutional validity of governmental actions found in laws, ordinances, administrative rules, or executive orders that have been challenged in the legal system. Often, courts have the final say, and can overrule legislative or executive versions of constitutional limits. This power of judicial review, then, involves a potential for government by the judiciary.

State judicial review can take several forms, depending upon which governmental action is under scrutiny. Judges often weigh the consistency of actions of law enforcement and judicial agencies against fundamental law. Usually questions of "due process" arise when the actions of law enforcement (executive) officials are involved or when a trial court fails to exclude evidence that may have resulted from a tainted police search. This form of judicial review is generally accepted and appropriate for judges. But judicial review can also find judges confronting the actions of the governor, mayor, or county executive, as well as the administrative agencies under their control. Questions about the constitutionality of bureaucratic actions are then at issue and require resolution by third parties—the courts. Finally, the most controversial version of judicial review brings courts into direct confrontation with state legislatures, county commissions, and city councils. In these situations, courts decide whether laws or ordinances written by elected representatives are appropriate. It is generally this latter form of judicial review that involves the meshing of the courts' functions of resolving disputes, making public policy, and perpetuating myths. At these times the power of judges is at its greatest; however, it is also during these times that judges are the most vulnerable. As they exercise judicial review they may go beyond their constitutional boundaries. Suspicions are justly aroused when judges have the final word on who can do what according to the constitution.[4]

Although the power of judicial review contains the potential for government by the judiciary, several legal and political checks keep judges within constitutional limits. Jurists are products of a confining tradition. They are compelled to follow long-established procedures; they are dedicated to a professional code; they are limited by laws, precedent, and constitutions. Trial-judge decisions are reviewable by a higher court. At the appellate level a majority must agree on the results of their deliberations. And many judges are accountable to the public by means of elections. Ultimately, judicial versions of constitutional provisions can be undone by constitutional amendments, revised by subsequent courts, or simply ignored.

Tradition dictates that judges exchange their adversarial states of mind—learned from years of law-school training and practice as advocates—for more aloof, objective stances. Unlike advocates, judges must separate themselves from the interests of the parties in legal conflict. At the trial level, judges often share decisional responsibilities with juries. Further, courts are, in a sense, passive participants in the legal-political realms. Judges must wait for litigants to bring issues to them. Although jurists cannot seek problems they may wish to resolve, with a largely discretionary docket appellate judges can pick issues that intrigue them, and can solicit cases by the suggestions, if not outright invitations, recorded in court opinions. Traditionally, high-court jurists are confined to the facts and issues found in the record established by the trial courts and emphasized in the briefs and arguments attorneys present. *Stare decisis*, or following precedent, can be a compelling constraint. By training and tradition, judges look to prior court rulings before deciding.

The *Code of Judicial Conduct* directs judges to withdraw from the partisanship of politics and admonishes them to avoid even the appearance of succumbing to personal and partisan choices. Canon 1 reads: "Judges Should Uphold the Integrity and Independence of the Judiciary" and adds, "an independent and honorable judiciary is indispensable to justice in society." Canon 2 dictates that: "Judges Should Avoid Impropriety and the Appearance of Impropriety in All Their Activities." According to Canon 7: "Judges Should Refrain From Political Activity Inappropriate to Their Judicial Office."

Law, court rules, and provisions of the federal and state constitutions also limit jurists. For example, all states, through constitutional amendments or laws, have established commissions that investigate and recommend or enforce the provisions of a judicial code of conduct.[5] Judges usually have their own supervisory boards that lead, on occasion, to admonishments, reassignments, or persuasions. Constitutional clauses often dictate limits on judges. For example, the constitution of Washington forbids judges from running for other state offices while serving on a court. Article IV, Section 2 of the constitution further allows the legislature to impeach or remove errant justices through a joint resolution.[6] Even if a number of appellate court members disagree on the details of a particular decision, they must forge a majority in order to reach a final decision. Individual preferences must give way to a majority view. Staggered terms of office and interim appointments more often than not assure that at any given time, diverse interests will be represented on the court, thus reinforcing the restraining force of compromise on decision-making. In states that elect members to courts, an aroused electorate can force an incumbent judge into retirement.

Rarely, however, are incumbents voted out of office, although this may be changing.[7] Further, legislatures seldom threaten a judge with removal, and constitutional amendments to correct a court decision are seldom proposed or ratified. The judges of state courts, then, are left with substantial discretion. Precedent may not be available, may conflict with other precedents, or may be irrelevant to contemporary circumstances. The legislative intent behind statutes may be unclear, may be purely politically motivated, or may be undiscernible. The framers of the constitution may have been silent on particular matters or clearly outdated in their intent.[8] And yet, judicial decisions must be made. The presence of a number of dissents and separate concurring opinions throughout state court reports attests to the exercise of judicial choice. The importance of that choice is greatest when a state court of last resort exercises its power of judicial review.

Evolution of Judicial Review in the States

From the beginning of the republic, state courts, with the backing of their states' constitutions, have possessed the power to veto actions of other government agencies. Even before Chief Justice John Marshall's reaffirmation of the power of federal courts in *Marbury v. Madison* (1803), a number of state courts had negated acts of their legislatures.[9] At that time, however, judges often had to share review responsibilities with legislatures and councils of revision; their role as final arbiters of constitutional issues had not been universally accepted. After Marshall's assertion of power for federal courts, however, the practice of judicial review by state high courts became more acceptable, so that by 1818 every state except Rhode Island recognized the legitimacy of supervision of legislative acts by state judges.[10] Having the power and exercising it were two separate matters, however. Judicial review was "scarcely used before the Civil War . . . as an effective check upon legislative power," in large part because of the states' bad experiences with executives and judges in colonial times and, later, because the followers of Thomas Jefferson and Andrew Jackson emphasized the primacy of legislative authority.[11]

In the beginning, therefore, judicial review by state courts constituted little threat of creating a government by the judiciary. Judicial review simply meant that judges dealt most specifically with the acts and actions of other branches of government that infringed upon the prerogatives of courts. This is what Kermit L. Hall called the "departmental theory" of judicial review.[12] According to this theory, legislative action received priority in any conflict between branches of government. State courts concentrated on drawing and defending judicial boundaries in the separation of powers scheme rather than meddling in legislative or administrative matters. Judges viewed judicial review as a defensive mechanism to protect the judiciary from encroachments into judicial matters by the more political branches of government. Early courts also proved reluctant to invalidate legislative measures because many of the state founding fathers, who had written the constitutions, were accessible—in the legislature, the bar, and the courts—to remind judges of the document's true meaning. Legislatures were very willing to challenge judges should the judiciary stray too far from what legislators thought proper.[13] Furthermore, the kinds of disputes commonly appealed to state courts seldom involved constitutional questions, and only on rare occasions did they raise public interest or public policy issues.

However, as Francis Aumann noted, "It was not until after the Civil War . . . that the doctrine of the legislatively declared will of the people gave way before the doctrine of the supremacy of the law judicially interpreted."[14] Politically, the system had changed, and the types of disputes then being generated formed a strong challenge to the departmental version of judicial review. State courts had been generally recognized as exponents of the meaning of fundamental law. Further democratization of America and the lure of populism complicated state politics, and reformers and new immigrant groups challenged traditional values, fragmenting Americans' homogeneous outlook. The courts entered political contests, sometimes by default, as public trust in legislatures waned during the middle of the nineteenth century.

Both legislatures and courts were partly responsible for shifts in their respective roles. Taxpayers blamed legislators for a rising public debt, the interest on which they paid to outside creditors. Obvious corruption among the "people's representatives" as a result of growth in the power of organized interest groups also brought legislatures into disrepute. In response to increased suspicion surrounding state legislatures, the constitutions of new states contained detailed restrictions on the legislative body, thereby inviting court challenges and judicial intervention.[15] Further, citizen-legislatures, even if free from noxious influences, normally met only once every two years for a few days and could hardly cope with the demands of a rapidly expanding and urbanizing America. Citizen legislators lacked the technical skills needed to write laws unreceptive to legal challenges, and professional legislative staffs were nonexistent. But the courts were always open, available at the county seat or state capital, and proved increasingly receptive to citizen demands. Judges possessed the technical skills to understand and correct legislation. Also, judges were often elected, thus making them, like legislators, representatives of the public.[16] "As legislative prestige declined, judicial power expanded rapidly," stated Aumann.[17] Many judges embraced common law decision-making with impassioned enthusiasm, and judge-made decrees began to fill the books.

Under common law, judicial review inevitably became "interventionist." Judges dictated to lawmakers and administrators alike. James Willard Hurst summarized the first "golden age" of the judiciary:

> Actually, between 1820 and 1890 the judges were already taking the initiative in lawmaking. Far anticipating the leadership of the executive or administrative arms, the courts built upon the common law in the United States—a body of judge-made doctrine—to govern people's public and private affairs. At the same time the courts played a great role not only in declaring, but also in administering policy. For this they used particularly the flexible doctrines and remedies of Equity.[18]

Through injunctions and receiverships, courts also assumed regulatory roles. Activism replaced the defensive mode of departmentalism. Expansive judicial review became commonplace.

However, the idea of making law rather than discovering it made it necessary for judges to look for guidance from the community of which they were a part and product. According to Morton J. Horwitz:

> The process of common law decision making had taken on many of the qualities of legislation. As judges began to conceive of common law adjudication as a process of making and not merely discovering legal rules, they were led to frame general doctrines based on self-conscious considerations of social and economic policies. For the first time, lawyers and judges can be found with some regularity to reason about the social consequences of particular legal rules.[19]

"Public policy," or what judges considered to be in the "public interest," often became the measure of judicial limits.

In two respects, the common law decision-making process reinforced the outward-looking perspectives of judicial review. First, to ascertain public policy, one needed to appraise public desires. In 1853, one early critic of this requirement described the process:

> [Public policy] is a vague and unsatisfactory term, and calculated to lead to uncertainty and error, when applied to the decision of legal rights; it is capable of being understood in different senses; it may, and does, in its ordinary sense, mean "political expedience," or that which is best for the common good of the community... It is the province of the statesman, and not the lawyer, to discuss, and of the legislature to determine... It is the province of the judge to expound the law only...not to speculate upon what is best, in his opinion, for the advantage of the community.[20]

Second, much of the common law expressed in court decisions reflected community customs. Such practices usually involved business and property transactions. Judges had to look to the practices of the community to weigh public consequences of alternate solutions to constitutional disputes.

Debate over judicial review shifted from whether courts could exercise the power, to whether the results of such exercise were proper. Critics now disputed the results, not the process. The legitimacy of judicial review had been established. Judges were sufficiently comfortable with their role in constitutional adjudication to prompt one to contend:

> The right, and duty of this Court, to give judgement on the constitutional power of the Legislature in making statutes, [has been] established by so many elaborated opinions of this Court, and of the Supreme Court of the United States, and of our sister States, as to make further discussion or citation of authorities a useless attempt at a display of learning.[21]

However, this golden age of interventionist judicial review lasted only until about the turn of the twentieth century, at which time the common law, "with its cautious judicial etching out of the traditional law by interstitial lawmaking, lost favor in an impatient age [becoming] accustomed to instant communication, super-rapid transportation and government activities of the first moment."[22] Legislatures began to regain the initiative, courts came under suspicion, and statutes began competing with judge-made law. Pressures for change, though, did not come solely from outside the legal system.

In the late 1800s, Dean Christopher Columbus Langdell of Harvard Law School revolutionized legal education. Langdell believed that "law is a science;...all the available materials are contained in printed books."[23] Most important among these books were the *Reports* of appellate judges. Within a short time, the prevailing view of the law changed and with it, judicial review. The era of "scientific law" arrived with the installation of the case method at Harvard, and soon virtually all law schools of any consequence adopted it.

The new movement both strengthened and weakened the role of appellate judges. On the one hand, the emphasis placed upon the products of their toil—their published opinions—enhanced their positions. On the other hand, in seeking to resolve disputes, judges no longer had to weigh the consequences of their decisions on the public; they needed only to match facts and then apply former rulings to issues before them. Gone was the social creativity of the common law. Law became isolated from the society it sought to serve. It was, as Lawrence M. Friedman described, like "geology without rocks . . . astronomy without stars."[24]

This era of formalism profoundly affected judicial decision-making and, of course, judicial review:

> Formality was not only form, it was also a concept. Judges were not builders of law now, but protectors; they hid the power of the bench in a brier patch of legalism; they concealed their thought processes in jargon. First, it provided a screen of legitimacy. . . The judges did not decide cases out of exercise of free discretion; it was the law and only the law that determined results. The long string of precedents strung out in the case buttressed this fact. Second, formalism reinforced the judges' claim of sole and exclusive right to expound the law.[25]

Social, economic, and political events moved too rapidly for this scientific and isolated approach to adjust. While judges exercised judicial review by consulting the *Reports*, legislatures confronted society's real problems. Judicial review assumed a conservative stance, applying the past to new problems. This contradiction became evident in the confrontation between the United States Supreme Court and Franklin D. Roosevelt.[26]

The rigid formalism of the scientific period broke down in the federal arena in the late 1930s with the supreme court's withdrawal from rigid enforcement of constitutionally anchored "vested rights" or property rights.[27] State courts did not depart entirely from the field of economic regulation. As the nation's high court moved away from property and economic questions, state courts filled the void. However, there was less for them to review. Congress had preempted much supervision of the country's economic concerns under its and the U. S. Supreme Court's definition of "interstate commerce" and "due process."

But in another arena of constitutional law, the U. S. Supreme Court actively intervened, forcing state courts to follow. Beginning as early as 1925 in *Gitlow v. New York*, but gaining considerable momentum during Chief Justice Earl Warren's tenure (1953-1969), the court compelled states to observe the dictates of the federal Bill of Rights.[28] The court read the Fourteenth Amendment's due process clause to incorporate provisions of the Bill of Rights and used it effectively against state action. This was especially evident in the enforcement of procedural rights, such as search and seizure, right to counsel, and trial by jury. The high court also activated the equal protection clause of the Fourteenth Amendment to check state government excesses. As a consequence, state judges often became surrogates for U. S. Supreme Court justices, enforcing the Warren court's interpretations of the Fourteenth Amendment. State judges continued to invalidate state legislative enactments and criminal procedures, but now more often from fear of reversal in the nation's highest court than from any independent appraisal of a decision's impact on the community. The national public policy the Warren court set replaced state policy considerations by state courts.

After adhering to the U. S. Supreme Court's Bill of Rights dictates from the 1950s to the 1970s, state high courts began to scrutinize their own state declarations of rights for protections against threats to individual rights. In some cases, such study provided greater safeguards than those available under the federal constitution.

The constitutional principle of federalism, involving a dual system of courts responsible for separate jurisdictions, makes such state court independence possible. Although the U. S. Constitution is the supreme law of the land, a state judicial decision decided clearly on "adequate and independent" state grounds is usually unreviewable by the U. S. Supreme Court.[29] However, the state court's decision must meet or exceed, not fall below standards set by the federal high court. For example, state courts can place greater restrictions on police search and seizure if the state constitution permits, but they cannot ease these restrictions below the high court's dictates under the Fourth Amendment of the Bill of Rights.[30] Simply stated, state courts can avoid supreme court review by granting more but not fewer freedoms. Further, the state decision must rely wholly on state precedent and state constitutional provisions without reference to U. S. Supreme Court decisions, federal laws, or the federal constitution.

State judicial review appears to be undergoing a renaissance due in part to the Warren Burger and William Rehnquist courts' reluctance to extend Warren court rulings—especially in criminal procedures—and to recent administrations' desire for a new federalism and devolution of government power. Lawyers too, in their search for favorable forums, have turned to state benches, hoping to avoid the U. S. Supreme Court's apparent lack of receptivity to many civil rights issues. The caliber of state judges has also improved, and innovations in judicial administration have freed state appellate benches from the oppressive burden of case loads, permitting them to concentrate more on difficult constitutional issues. A majority of states now have intermediate courts of appeals that screen cases of little significance, leaving a few important appeals for the state courts of last resort. The public has also grown accustomed to a freer society, in no small way due to successful civil rights and anti-war protest movements and Warren court decisions.

Some argue that state judges are compelled by their constitutions to assume a more active stance regarding individual rights. Given the wording of the Washington Constitution's Article 1, Section 1—"governments . . . are established to protect and maintain individual rights," coupled with the dictate of Section 29—

"provisions of this Constitution are mandatory, unless by expressed words they are declared to be otherwise," it is difficult to argue that the Washington Supreme Court should ignore state legislation that may threaten individual rights. Perhaps an era of expansive review is in the offing.

To recapitulate, judicial review has evolved through five phases. In the early years of the republic, state courts adopted the narrow departmentalism approach, providing little opportunity for a debate concerning "government by the judiciary." The question of an activist judiciary searching for the public interest rarely arose. Next, state courts experienced the first "golden age" of interventionism under common law; activism became accepted practice. Formalism, with its built-in restraint, followed as the next phase and reflected the new "scientific" view of the law. Courts, however, became isolated from the public. Several decades of reactionism followed, involving forced compliance under the Fourteenth Amendment. In some measure as a reaction to the restraintist nature of the federal bench, and with a new emphasis on federalism, a second "golden age" under new federalism looms. State courts are becoming more activist.

This overview of judicial review by state high courts has not isolated precise periods of time because each change was gradual, and varied from state to state. However, a rough approximation of the phases in the evolution of state judicial review is possible:

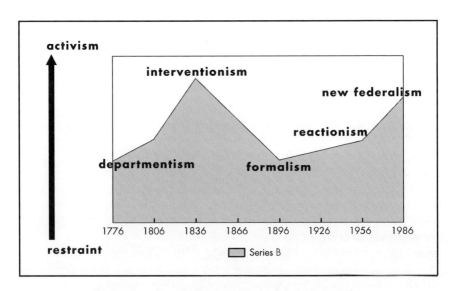

Figure One. State judicial review: activism vs. restraint

Washington's high court mirrored this depiction.

A Case Study: The Washington Supreme Court's Use of Judicial Review

Washington became a state in 1889 and missed some of the earlier trends in state judicial review. Nonetheless, a close look at the constitutional rulings of Washington's high court indicates that the justices did not stray far from the tendencies of other state tribunals.

Table One
Incidence of Judicial Review

Years	Number of Cases	Number Involving Judicial Review	Percent	Number Declared Unconstitutional	Percent
1890s (90,91,92)**	560	30	5.4	6	20.2
1900s (00,01,02)	876	36	4.1	8	22.2
1910s (10,11)	1,271	39	3.1	7	17.9
1920s (20,21)	1,019	37	3.6	5	13.5
1930s (30,31,35)	1,548	53	3.4	9	17.0
1940s (40,41,42)	955	47	4.9	13	27.7
1950s (50,51,55)	859	26	3.0	7	26.9
1960s (60,61,68)	844	38	4.5	8	21.1
1970s (70,71,73)	548	32	5.8	6	18.8
1980s (80,81,85)	487	42	8.6	16	38.1
Averages			4.6		22.3

** = years used for tabulation.

Table One reports the number of cases involving the exercise of judicial review by the Washington Supreme Court for selected years from 1890 through 1989.[31] The corresponding percentages indicate a low incidence of judicial review. When a constitutional issue is accepted, however, the court voids statutes in about one out of every four cases.

Washington Supreme Court justices infrequently invoked the power of judicial review largely because constitutional issues seldom arose. In only about four percent of the court's cases did it recognize a constitutional question. Initially, conflict between territorial law and the new constitution prompted a number of fundamental challenges. This, plus the expansive tendencies of common law interventionism during the period, helps to account for the comparatively high percentage of invalidated laws. The deferential tendencies evident between 1920 and 1930 appear to be a product of formalism. The more activist trend from 1935 to the early 1940s should be attributed to a concern over legislative intrusion into economic and property areas and reflects the dark shadow cast by the U. S. Supreme Court's activism. The lower incidence of state constitutional issues in the 1950s and 1960s suggests the state's high bench relied on Fourteenth Amendment provisions of the U. S. Constitution and only occasionally (about 3 percent of the time) referred to the state's fundamental law. Finally, the court's discretionary jurisdiction in the 1980s brought more problematic cases to the judges' attention, accounting for the increase in constitutional issues confronting the court and the expansionistic nature of judicial review. An analysis of the cases subject to judicial review during representative years can test these assertions.

The Tacoma Hall housed the supreme court from 1890 to 1891. *Susan Parish Collection.*©

Common Law Interventionism (1890-1910)

When the Washington State Supreme Court began to conduct judicial business after the 1889 elections, the judges enjoyed relatively unrestrained power of common law intervention. Judge Theodore L. Stiles, a leader of the Washington constitutional convention and activist on the five-member bench elected to the supreme court upon statehood, confirmed the prevailing view among judges in an address to the Washington State Bar Association:

> The courts are, and in the nature of things, must be the appellate body, and their power of review extends over the entire domain of public and private right. Once it is conceded, as it now is, universally, that a statute may be declared void as unconstitutional, there is no denying the proposition of judicial supremacy. Whenever the legislature enact a law it thereby assumes and asserts that it is constitutional; and whenever the court declares the contrary, the judgement of the court prevails, and there is no power except that of the people in constitutional convention that can reverse it.[32]

Stiles and some of his colleagues put this viewpoint into action. During its first full year of business in 1890, the high court decided 100 cases, considered issues of constitutionality in ten, and voided statutes in only three. Although the ten issues of constitutionality considered by the court constituted a high average, the 25 percent nullification rate was not unusual. Common law interventionist tradition would appear to compel jurists to focus on broad constitutional issues while, at the same time, the normal void rate of one-fourth suggests that perhaps the judges were abandoning the tradition. In part, the reluctance to take full advantage of their power under the common law tradition can be attributed to the fact that, in partisan contests between 1889 and 1896, only Republicans won election to the supreme court, at a time when the GOP also dominated both houses of the legislature. Thus, there would have been few occasions for the two branches to disagree over policy issues. A review of the 1890-1900 cases confirms that Washington's judges began to doubt the wisdom of common law interventionism. Also, high court jurists often apologized for doubting the wisdom of their political colleagues in the legislature.

In their first review case, *Kelly v. Stewart*, the judges, by a 4-1 vote, held unconstitutional a statute that would have allowed judicial courts, rather than the legislature, to create municipal corporations. The majority held that "a judicial court cannot exercise legislative functions and that the legislature cannot impose such power upon it." The judges displayed no reluctance to correct the legislative branch, especially when relying upon the long-accepted departmental tradition of judicial review. Even then, one judge found such impertinence unacceptable. Ever the restraintist, Judge Ralph Oregon Dunbar concurred in the results but not "in the opinion that the act of the legislature was unconstitutional."[33]

In the so-called "Opium Den" case, *Ah Lim v. Territory of Washington,* the court, by a 3-2 vote, upheld a territorial statute making the smoking of opium, even in the privacy of one's home, a misdemeanor. Dunbar, writing for a hesitant majority, used nine pages of a twelve-page opinion to explain why the court ought not intervene in legislative concerns. He repeatedly cautioned that judicial review "demands the most solemn, thoughtful and painstaking consideration." "[I]n view of the consequence to society from the annulling of law" made by the people's representatives, judicial review was "the gravest question" confronting judges. Courts should have nothing to do with "questions of policy or expediency." "Of course," he warned, "we do not pretend to argue that it is a responsibility which can at all times be obviated or avoided; but we insist that it must always be done with great caution and circumspection."[34] After urging restraint in issues involving judicial review, Dunbar turned to the merits of the case and quickly concluded that the legislature had acted within its power. Even with the cautious Dunbar, the broad common law responsibilities of judging still weighed heavily. He appeared almost apologetic for not invalidating the law.

The dissenters, Stiles and Elmon Scott, were not so apologetic. True to what Stiles asserted in his address to the bar, they argued that these were precisely the type of issues the court must consider. They quoted with approval from the U. S. Supreme Court case, *Mugler v. Kansas:*

> The courts are not bound by mere forms, nor are they to be misled by mere pretenses. They are at liberty—indeed, are under a solemn duty—to look at the substance of things, whenever they enter upon the inquiry whether the legislature has transcended the limits of its authority.[35]

Scott and Stiles viewed the opium law as an invasion of privacy, a violation of due process, and a denial of the "pursuit of happiness." They did not hesitate to condemn the legislation.

Ten years later, Judge William "War Horse" White, nicknamed for his oratorical skills and partisanship and never one to back away from political frays, apologized for the court's assertion of review in *Palmer v. Laberee,* but not until he and his colleagues declared the law void. White cautioned that courts "cannot correct what they deem excesses in legislation," but the legislative intent was "obnoxious to all constitutional restriction, and [the law] should not be upheld."[36]

These examples suggest that the Washington bench clearly understood its interventionist powers under the common law action of judicial review, but that the judges felt somewhat uneasy with that role. Furthermore, so long as Republicans dominated both the court and legislature, the judges proved reluctant to challenge the policies of legislative colleagues.

Formalism (1920-1930)

Using 1930 as a sample year, the court heard constitutional issues in sixteen of 503 cases (3.2 percent), but in only three of these (18.8 percent) did it disagree

The supreme court moved its offices to Talcott's Variety Store in 1891. *Susan Parish Collection.*©

with the legislature. These figures suggest that formalism pulled the judges back from their slightly activist stance of earlier years. The three cases in which the judges invalidated legislative acts covered a curious mix of subjects. In *Slotemaker v. International Fruit and Produce Company*,[37] the jurists simply used the legislative housekeeping provisions of Article II, Section 19 to invalidate the law. The title of the act was "not broad enough to cover" the subject of the law. This was hardly an issue of great moment, but it suggested the technical aspects of formalism.

In *Aberdeen Savings and Loan Association v. Chase,* the common law tradition's latent activism manifested itself. The court held that a tax on savings and loan institutions violated the equal protection clause of the Fourteenth Amendment of the U. S. Constitution, making it necessary to invoke Article VII, Sections 2 and 9 and Article XI, Section 12 of the state constitution. The special banks were being taxed unfairly when measured against taxes on similar corporations. For the majority, however, Judge Walter Beals wrote:

> Such a legislative declaration is to be carefully considered by the courts and due weight given thereto. Courts should, however, consider the true operation and effect of the law which must be dealt with on the basis of the practical results which follow its operation, and not alone by legislative declarations contained therein.[38]

Finally, in *Vincent v. Shields*[39] the legislature violated the due process clause of Article I, Section 3 of the state's fundamental law by allowing creation of special water districts without public hearings to determine boundaries and assessments. Again, this was not a resounding slap at the legislative body.

These three cases infer that the judges, although not completely taken with formalism's restraintist features, carefully exercised judicial review. Deference permeated the court's relations with the legislature, but deference only slightly more pronounced than in earlier years. For example, a challenge to an anti-gambling statute in 1930 prompted the judges to remind themselves, as much as their constituents, that:

> The courts cannot. . . ignore or set aside a plain mandate of the legislature. It can inquire into its constitutional power to pass the law, and can inquire into the procedure to ascertain whether the purported law is in fact a law, but they may not find the law invalid because of its severity unless it falls within that clause of the constitution which prohibits the infliction of cruel punishment, and this act we cannot say does this.[40]

The judges cautioned that "construction of a statute which would render it unconstitutional is to be avoided if at all possible."[41] Although the wisdom or politics of a law remained for the legislature to decide, the judges would not hesitate to invalidate a law "if it appeared from the testimony or upon the face of the law that it was clearly unreasonable."[42] Rarely did such testimony appear.

Formalism's greatest impact could readily be seen in opinion style. Many opinions were catalogues of citations, often simply paragraphs of referenced cases from a number of jurisdictions following an assertion. Citations came to replace explanation. Extensive quotations from prior opinions, usually from courts in other states or noted legal authorities, appeared necessary on many occasions when a listing of precedent seemed insufficient. The reasoning for any particular decision was rarely complete within the opinion; tedious research and many cited cases bolstered decisions. The style was "bombastic and repetitious: case reports were filled with strings of useless citations; barren logic and bad English abounded."[43]

This quick review of 1930 indicates formalism indeed permeated judicial decision-making and judicial review, largely in how the judges documented their decisions rather than in what they decided and why. The reluctance to invalidate a statute or ordinance could be attributed to confidence in the legislature, the formalistic training of the judges, a progressive political atmosphere in the state, and, of course, the outlook of the attorneys who researched and argued the cases before the high court.

Substantive Due Process and Equal Protection: Economic Reactionism (1930-1945)

The dislocation of the Great Depression prompted a flurry of legislative experiments. A Democrat-dominated legislature, with prodding from Democratic Governor Clarence D. Martin, boldly restricted heretofore largely unregulated businesses, much to the dismay of a Republican-dominated supreme court. Washington's constitution contained a due process clause susceptible to substantive application, and a "special privileges or immunities" clause equivalent to the Fourteenth Amendment's equal protection provision. In addition, the eminent domain section specifically required courts to supervise the "public use" character of any legislatively condemned lands. Other provisions limiting government (e. g., taxation) reflected the founders' suspicion of the legislature and provided a conservative court with the constitutional tools to strike down legislation threatening private property.

Typical of the court's reaction to regulation and revenue legislation was Judge O. R. Holcomb's condemnation of the 1935 attempt to regulate agricultural production. Holcomb's majority opinion reminded the legislature that it "is bound by the constitution when enacting legislation." Even when confronted with "dire financial and agricultural calamities, the constitution cannot be set aside."[44] Nonetheless, although economic issues prompted more constitutional questions, the rate of invalidations of state laws increased only slightly.

The U. S. Supreme Court had withdrawn from the economic field in 1937 and issued its *Carolene Products* footnote-four disclaimer a year later.[45] If courts were to continue intervening in the economy, it remained for state courts to do so. In 1940 the Washington Supreme Court heard eighteen opportunities for judicial review and found laws wanting in four of these cases. Although the percentages are not striking, the shift toward economic matters evident in 1935 continued in 1940. Economic questions were present in fourteen of the eighteen cases. The questions ranged from taxation to repossession of goods for nonpayment.

The court invoked the doctrine of substantive due process in four of the eighteen cases, with "reasonableness" being the standard of judgment. Equal protection, when used to challenge the application of allegedly discriminatory taxation or other arbitrary economic regulations, became an even more effective constitutional restraint. The justices relied upon the state version of equal protection in nine of the eighteen cases.

The four cases in which they invalidated ordinances or statutes showed that the judges still viewed judicial review favorably. They found an excise tax singling out fuel oil from solid fuel sources to violate Article I, Section 12. A Seattle ordinance requiring that all charitable organizations, except the Seattle Community Fund, obtain a license when soliciting contributions fell before the privileges clause in two cases. Finally, they held that a statute changing the term of office of appointed superior court judges violated provisions of Article IV, the judicial article. However, decisions upholding legislative regulations of business far exceeded in number and importance those striking down such statutes.

State v. Sears exemplified the more dominant restraintist or deferential review the court adopted. In a 5-4 decision, the majority upheld a "fair practices act" against a challenge that the act's exemption of motion picture theaters violated the privileges clause. According to Judge Clyde Jeffers, writing for the majority:

> We may or may not agree with the economic philosophy of the...act, but it is no part of the duty of this court to determine whether the policy embodied in a statute is wise or unwise. It is primarily a legislative, and not a judicial, function to determine economic policy.[46]

But the dissenters angrily disagreed: "personal rights and private property" cannot be arbitrarily invaded "under the guise of police regulations." The act "destroys the ideals of free enterprise which has been the dominant spirit of American progress." By upholding the law, the majority had acted "contrary to the wording and ideas contained in our state and national constitutions."[47] Unfortunately for the minority, the court failed to adopt the activist view of the constitution in crucial regulation cases. Only when exceptions singled out a business for special favors did the court invalidate the law.

Even though the Washington Constitution and other judicial doctrines permitted activism, throughout this period the high court behaved in a restraintist manner, deferring to the legislature. Thus, even though the Washington justices continued to review economic issues after 1937, in practice, like their national brethren, they left the economy largely to the people's representatives.

Incorporation of the Bill of Rights:
Procedural Due Process Reactionism (1950-1970)

Washington's court of last resort, like other state benches in the 1960s, actively engaged in judicial review, following the lead of the U. S. Supreme Court. Since 1833 (*Barron v. Baltimore*),[48] the federal Bill of Rights' protections had applied only to federal government actions. However, beginning in 1925 (*Gitlow v. New*

York),[49] the nation's supreme court interpreted the due process clause of the constitution's Fourteenth Amendment, which restricted state action, to include or incorporate many of the fundamental privileges of the Bill of Rights. People were now provided the same protection on a state government level as they were on the federal. As the Warren court rapidly expanded this "incorporation" doctrine to include nearly all of the procedural protections found primarily in the Fourth, Fifth, and Sixth Amendments of the Bill of Rights, the burden of enforcement fell on state courts. Justices ignored and sometimes overruled state constitutions while enforcing federal constitutional provisions in relevant state cases throughout the country, leading to a nationalization of the Bill of Rights.

Washington's judges were not always comfortable in this supporting role. For example, in *State v. Davis*, a case concerning whether police had properly applied the requirements of *Miranda v. Arizona* (1966),[50] liberal Judge Robert C. Finley wrote:

> I suppose it is rather superfluous to add that, were I free to choose, I would not follow the majority's decision... But I am not free to choose, for the Supreme Court has exercised ITS discretion... Any discretion or choice which I may have had has been preempted. Thus the majority opinion... aptly states the law, and I must fully, albeit unhappily, concur.[51]

Such statements by judges reluctantly admitting that U. S. Supreme Court rulings had prevailed were fairly common. In *Lally v. Gump* the majority wrote: "There is no dispute that the decision in this case rests upon the applicability of [the U. S. Supreme Court's opinion in] *Smith v. California.*"[52] Or, as conservative Judge Matt Hill more directly stated:

> I cannot agree with the majority that [the law] tends to unjustifiably restrict the freedom of expression. . . . I concur in the result solely because the Supreme Court of the United States says it does.[53]

However, as the more restraintist Burger and Rehnquist courts replaced the Warren court and the incorporation doctrine eased, the Washington bench, now composed of more moderate and liberal justices, began to emerge from the shadow of the nation's high bench.

New Judicial Federalism: Beyond Incorporation (1970-present)

Some recent activities of state courts suggest that a second golden age may be dawning. Reliance upon independent state grounds for decisions has allowed state high courts to avoid potentially adverse review by the U. S. Supreme Court. This "new federalism" has received a warm reception from some state benches. Ronald K. L. Collins has observed that

> since 1970 alone, state high courts have handed down over 250 published opinions holding that the constitutional minimums announced by the national supreme

court interpreting the federal constitution are insufficient to satisfy the more strin-
gent requirements of state law.[54]

In Washington, a plurality of the justices in *Alderwood Associates v. Washington Environmental Council* argued that the state constitution prohibits both state and private infringements of freedom of speech, holding that privately owned shopping centers cannot prevent orderly speech and petitioning activities on their premises. According to Justice Robert F. Utter, the plurality opinion's author:

> State courts are obliged to determine the scope of their state constitutions due to the structure of our government. . . When a state court neglects its duty to evaluate and apply its state constitution, it deprives the people of their "double security." It also removes from the people the ability to try "novel social and economic experiments" – which is another important justification for the federal system.[55]

Although agreeing with the plurality, Justice James Dolliver would have preferred to rely upon the state's police powers. His colleagues' audacity shocked him. The plurality, he scolded

> has made an unprecedented change in the application of this state's constitution. It interprets the constitution in a way which has never been done since that document was adopted in 1889. It does so without the slightest historical warrant: No case is cited, there is reference to no authority. The majority simply says, "We choose to follow [this] approach."[56]

Again, as in the 1890-1900 period, activism prevailed, but not without considerable skepticism from some high bench members. *Alderwood* was not the first application of the state's fundamental law to defy federal precedent, and the opinions clearly set forth the activism-versus-restraint issue of the new judicial federalism.

In *State v. Ringer,* a 1983 search and seizure case, the court construed the protections of Article I, Section 7 of the state Declaration of Rights to exceed the federal constitution's Fourth Amendment requirements. In choosing "to return to the protections of our own constitution," the majority found it necessary to overrule at least six previous decisions. "Constitutions are designed to endure through the years, and. . . should be interpreted to meet and cover changing conditions." The dissenters argued that the majority would handcuff the police: "Once again we have confounded the constabulary and, by picking and choosing between state and federal constitutions, changed the rules after the game has been played in good faith."[57]

The court returned to the state's fundamental law in a search and seizure issue in *State v. Chrisman.*[58] Upon remand from the U. S. Supreme Court, the majority overturned Chrisman's conviction, basing its decision on the state's Declaration of Rights despite the fact that the U. S. Supreme Court had upheld the trial judge. The "federal constitution only provides minimum protection of individual rights" and does not limit the authority of states "to accord. . . greater rights."[59] In this case, however, rather than arguing that this state privacy approach was wrong, the dissenters claimed the police were unreasonably hampered.

By 1986 the court had adopted the new federalism view regarding rights issues. For the first time anywhere, a state court established guidelines for determining when "to resort to independent state constitutional grounds to decide a case" and to ignore comparable provisions of federal fundamental law. Justice James A. Andersen, for a unanimous court in *State v. Gunwall*,[60] attempted to unite those who regarded the new judicial federalism as result-oriented "constitutional shopping" with those who viewed it as a "triumph of personal liberty," or "libertarian." The guidelines were aimed at:

(1) suggesting to counsel where briefing might appropriately be directed in cases wherein they are urging independent state constitutional grounds; and (2) helping to insure that if this court does use independent state constitutional grounds in a given situation, it will consider these criteria to the end that our decision will be made for well founded legal reasons and not by merely substituting our notion of justice for that of the duly elected legislative bodies or the United States Supreme Court.

To that end, the justices were careful to (1) appraise "the textual language of the state's constitution"; (2) isolate "significant differences in the texts of parallel provisions of the federal and state constitutions"; (3) review "state constitutional and common law history"; (4) search for "pre-existing state law"; (5) isolate, if possible, "difference in structure between the federal and state constitutions"; and (6) weigh "matters of particular interest or local concern."[61] Andersen proceeded to apply the new standards to the case before the court and persuasively accepted the privacy provisions of the state's Declaration of Rights over those of the U. S. Constitution's Fourth Amendment. He gave the new judicial federalism respectability. *Gunwall* encouraged counsel to argue on state grounds and provided security to justices desiring to depend upon state constitutional provisions.[62]

In *Witters v. Commission for the Blind*,[63] the court again displayed the power of the new federalism. The justices split 5-4, but nonetheless, relying on the state constitution, overturned a U. S. Supreme Court decision.

A blind student appealed a denial of state rehabilitation funds to study at a private religious college. In 1984 the state's high bench affirmed the denial of public funds to pursue a career in theology based on the federal constitution's First Amendment. In 1986 (*Witters v. Washington Department of Services for the Blind*)[64] the U. S. Supreme Court reversed the state supreme court, arguing that the case had not breached the First Amendment's establishment clause. The supreme court remanded the decision to the state bench, suggesting that "the state court is of course free to consider the applicability of the 'far stricter' dictates of the Washington State Constitution." This is exactly what the majority did.

Accepting the U. S. court's suggestion, Justice Andersen turned to the state's Declaration of Rights, and on these independent state grounds withheld Witters's public funds for religious training. Later, the U. S. Supreme Court refused to review the decision, apparently because of its reliance on adequate and independent state grounds.

Conclusion

Whatever the era, constitutional questions in the State of Washington seldom arose. Only about one of every twenty-five supreme court cases has involved a constitutional challenge to legislation. Nevertheless, when hearing such cases, the court has found nearly one out of four laws wanting—a fairly impressive invalidation rate. The constitutional questions raised in many of the cases, such as the adequacy of the title of a legislative act, were ordinarily of little consequence. If the legislature felt strongly enough about such reversals, it could easily correct the oversight. On rare occasions, however, the high court's judicial review had widespread consequences.

Because Washington statehood came relatively late in the expansion of the union, departmentalist judicial review played a minor role in the court's evolution. However, Washington experienced other forms of judicial review common to other states: common law, formalism, reactionism, and the new judicial federalism.

Heretofore, issues over judicial review focused on the proper role of the court within a system of separation of powers. Cases such as *Alderwood, Chrisman, Gunwall,* and *Witters,* however, pose questions about the role of courts in the system of federalism—an issue previously thought to be resolved with the selective incorporation of virtually all provisions of the federal Bill of Rights into the Fourteenth Amendment. Now, state courts are imposing their version of state constitutions on state governments and citizens despite, in some cases, U. S. Supreme Court rulings.[65] Will subsequent reactions again change the incidence and nature of judicial review?

In any event, Washington justices still show a sensitivity to tension between expansive and deferential judicial review. If that sensitivity, whether toward the separation of powers or federalism, becomes wanting, we should begin worrying about government by the judiciary.

Notes

1. This chapter is a revised version of an article entitled "Judicial Review and the Supreme Court of Washington, 1890-1986," which appeared in *Publius: The Journal of Federalism,* 17 (Winter 1987), pp. 69-90.
2. Karl Llewellyn, a noted authority on courts and the law, thought public policy was involved when judges had to think "in terms of prospective consequences of the rule under consideration." *The Common Law Tradition* (1960), p. 36.
3. *Marbury v. Madison,* 5 U. S. (1 Cranch) 137 (1803).
4. Roul Berger, *Government by Judiciary* (1977).
5. See amendment 71 of the Washington constitution, entitled "Judicial Qualifications Commission." In 1986 the agency's name was changed to "Commission on Judicial Conduct" to reflect more accurately its responsibility of enforcing the *Code of Judicial Conduct.*
6. The first and only attempt in Washington to remove a judge through the impeachment-resolution provisions of the constitution (Article 5 and Article 4, Section 9) was in 1891 when Superior Court Judge Morris B. Sachs survived a legislative resolution vote. Although the House voted 62-14 for removal, the Senate deadlocked on a 16-16 tie. See *Seattle Post-Intelligencer,* 5 Mar. 1891.
7. Voters are becoming more attentive to judicial elections. California witnessed a recent example when, in 1986, three members of the state's supreme court were removed from office in a retention election. See John Culver and John Wold, "The Defeat of California Justices: The Campaign, Electorate, and the Issue of Judicial Accountability," *Judicature,* 70 (1987), pp. 348-355. In Washington in the thirty-eight contested races throughout the state in the 1990 elections, only twenty-one incumbents retained their seats. Seventeen new judges were elected and nine of those defeated incumbents. One incumbent lost by four votes, and a write-in campaign placed a candidate for the Seattle municipal bench on the ballot, where she then garnered seventy-three percent of the vote.
8. The intent of the Washington constitutional framers becomes problematic because the record is unavailable. Edmond S. Meany recorded that "the convention engaged the best stenographers in the territory...to keep the records. A resolution was adopted requesting the legislature to appropriate money to pay the stenographers... The present writer introduced a bill to that effect in both the second and third legislatures but in each case it was defeated. Twelve years later the stenographers stated that they would no longer think of trying to transcribe their shorthand notes." *History of the State of Washington* (1924), p. 184.
9. See, for example, *Rutgers v. Waddington* (N.Y.C. Mayor's Ct., 1784); *Bayard v. Singleton* (1 Martin 42 N.C., 1787); *Cases of the Judges* (8 VA., 4 Call. 135, 1788); *Commonwealth v. Caton* (8 VA., 4 Call. 5, 1782); and *Holmes v. Walton* (N. J., 1780). "Between 1787 and 1803, state courts held void state laws in more than twenty instances," according to Alfred Kelly and Winfred Harrison, *The American Constitution* (1976), p. 94.
10. Francis R. Aumann, *The Changing American Legal System* (1969), p. 191.
11. Charles Haines, *The American Doctrine of Judicial Supremacy* (1932), p. 340.
12. Kermit L. Hall, *The Supreme Court and Judicial Review in American History* (1984).
13. Julius Goebel, Jr., *History of the Supreme Court of the United States* (1971), pp. 131-142.
14. Aumann, *Changing American Legal System,* p. 160.
15. This tradition of constitutional checks on the legislature can be found in the Washington document, especially in Article 2.

16. Kermit Hall, *The Magic Mirror* (1989), p. 231.
17. Aumann, *Changing American Legal System*, p. 161.
18. James W. Hurst, *The Growth of American Law* (1950), p. 84.
19. Morton J. Horwitz, *The Transformation of American Law* (1977), p. 2.
20. Justice Parke in *Egerton v. Earl Brownlow* 4 H. L. Ca. 1, 123 10 Eng. Rep. 359, 408-409 (1853). Quoted in Robert Brachtenbach, "Public Policy in Judicial Decisions," *Gonzaga Law Review*, 21 (1985-1986), p. 2.
21. Quoted in William Nelson, "Changing Conceptions of Judicial Review: The Evolution of Constitutional Theory in the States, 1760-1860," *University of Pennsylvania Law Review*, 120 (1972), pp. 1169-1170.
22. Aumann, *Changing American Legal System*, p. 215.
23. Hurst, *Growth of American Law*, p. 185.
24. Lawrence Friedman, *A History of American Law* (1973), p. 535.
25. Ibid., pp. 540-541.
26. See, for example, Leonard Baker, *Back to Back: The Duel Between FDR and the Supreme Court* (1967).
27. The "Switch in time that saved nine" from Roosevelt's court-packing plan was a Washington case— *West Coast Hotel v. Parrish*, 300 U. S. 379 (1937). The U. S. Supreme Court finally recognized the switch in famous footnote four of *U. S. v. Carolene Products*, 304 U. S. 144 (1938).
28. 268 U. S. 652 (1925).
29. See *Michigan v. Long*, 463 U. S. 1032 (1983).
30. See, for example, *State v. Boland*, 115 WN. 2nd 571 (1990).
31. Table One reports the incidence of judicial review on the court for each of the years reported. Data for every tenth year were recorded with interim years randomly selected in order to provide a representative picture of the court's activities. Only those cases posing questions of the consistency of legislative acts with the state constitution were tabulated. Municipal or county ordinances were included if authorized by a state statute. Review of administrative and lower court and police due process actions were excluded if not the products of legislation. Thus, the constitution was invoked and applied more than the table suggests. However, confrontations between the court and the legislature better represent the issues of activism versus restraint and judicial review versus democracy and, therefore, comprise the data for the table.
32. Theodore Stiles, "Legislative Encroachment Upon Private Right," *1899 Washington State Bar Association Proceedings*, p. 66. See also Charles Sheldon and Michael Stohr-Gillmore, "In the Beginning: The Washington Supreme Court a Century Ago," *University of Puget Sound Law Review*, 12 (1989), pp. 247-284.
33. 1 WASH. 98 (1890), p. 10.
34. 1 WASH. 156 (1890), pp. 159-160.
35. Ibid., p. 178.
36. 23 WASH. 409 (1900), pp. 413, 416.
37. 156 WASH. 574 (1930).
38. 157 WASH. 351 (1930), p. 364.
39. 158 WASH. 262 (1930).
40. *State v. Green*, 158 WASH. 574 (1930), p. 578.
41. *Tallyn v. Cowden*, 158 WASH. 335 (1930).
42. *Hardy v. Superior Court*, 155 WASH. 244 (1930), p. 251.
43. Friedman, *History of American Law*, p. 540.
44. *Uhden Inc. v. Greenough*, 181 WASH. 412 (1935), p. 428.

45. 304 U. S. 144 (1938). The footnote explained that the court would no longer concern itself with all economic issues but rather would begin looking more carefully at laws that discriminated against individuals and groups.
46. 4 WN. 2d 200 (1940), p. 207.
47. Ibid., p. 232.
48. 32 U. S. 243.
49. 268 U. S. 652.
50. 384 U. S. 436.
51. 73 WN. 2d 271 (1968), p. 297.
52. 361 U. S. 147 (1959).
53. 57 WN. 2d 244 (1960), pp. 228-229.
54. "Reliance on State Constitutions: Some Random Thoughts," in Bradley McGraw, ed., *Developments in State Constitutions* (1985), p. 2.
55. 96 WN. 2d 230 (1982), p. 238.
56. Ibid., p. 248.
57. 674 P. 2d 1240 (1984), p. 1248. Subsequently, the Ringer test of "totality of circumstances" permitting a police search was overruled in *State v. Stroud*, 106 WN. 2d 144 (1986). However, *Stroud* continued the primacy of the state constitution.
58. 676 P. 2d 419 (1984). See also Walfred Peterson, *Dormitory Drug Dens and Due Process* (1986).
59. *State v. Chrisman*, ibid., p. 422.
60. 106 WN. 2d 54 (1986).
61. Ibid., pp. 61-63.
62. For an analysis of *Gunwall* see Sheldon, " 'All Sail and No Anchor' in New Federalism Cases—Attempted Remedial Efforts by the Supreme Court of Washington," *State Constitutional Commentaries and Notes*, 1 (1990), pp. 8-13. Ironically, although *Gunwall* invites counsel to present historical analysis, the court continually rejects references to the case because no historical evidence is supplied by the lawyers for the parties to the dispute.
63. 112 WN. 2d 363 (1989).
64. 474 U. S. 481 (1986).
65. *State v. Boland*, 115 WN. 2d 571 (1990) is another recent new federalism case. In a 5-4 decision the majority opinion written by Justice James Dolliver concluded that Article I, Section 7 of the state constitution afforded more protections than the Fourth Amendment to the U. S. Constitution. Article I, Section 7 reads: "No person shall be disturbed in his private affairs or his home invaded, without authority of law." The Fourth Amendment reads in part: "The right of the people to be secure in their persons, houses, papers, and effects, against unreasonable searches and seizures, shall not be violated."

Chapter Two
A History of Selection to the State's High Bench

The high court's important, although infrequent, exercises of judicial review were outlined in Chapter One. Topics such as activism—when the court tests the validity of an enactment against the state's constitution, and in the extreme case invalidates the legislative or executive action—and restraint—when the court validates the efforts of other branches of government or avoids questions of constitutionality altogether—are decided by a full court.[1] Five or more justices are responsible for court decisions. In contrast, judicial selection affects individual justices. Chapter One analyzed decisions of the collective supreme court. This chapter concerns how selection molds the views of individual justices toward their proper role in government.

State judges are products of, and have an impact on, their environments. They can accurately reflect their environment by the often complex process that selects attorneys to serve on the high bench and by the kinds of cases brought to them for review. State judges are political creatures. They often serve in some political capacity prior to their judgeships. They behave like politicians while on the bench and, on occasion, make political decisions. They reflect the politics of their age, and also practice and define those politics.

That judges are politicians should not denigrate the judiciary nor tarnish the judges. As officials involved in making public policy decisions, judges, like other policy makers, ought to be part of the state's politics. Indeed, as explained in Chapter One, their role as final arbiter of constitutional issues places them in highly sensitive positions; as such, they should be accountable for their actions. Most often, accountability is achieved through the selection process. To understand the eighty jurists who, over the past century, have settled legal disputes and set public policy for the state, the elections and appointments of judges must be reviewed.[2]

The recruitment process involves various factors that voters weigh or that enter into a governor's considerations when he or she appoints someone to fill a supreme court vacancy: the evaluations of bar associations; the motivations of interested groups as they campaign for or against candidates; the voters' thoughts when they confirm high bench candidates; and, finally, the attitudes and actions of candidates who covet a high bench seat. All these factors narrow the field of judicial candidates. Recruitment screens aspirants who lack current requisites for the court. Thus, over the years, when the governor, interest groups, and the electorate applied different criteria for selection, candidates with divergent views of the law survived.

It must be remembered, however, that those chosen must render a collective decision in disputes appealed to them. The need to reach a group consensus, be it activist or restraintist, necessitates compromise, bargaining, and persuasion.[3] The biases, values, and beliefs a specific judge brings to the bench as a result of surviving the demands of selection must often be sacrificed, or at least softened, for the collectivity. Thus, in order to understand final decisions, not only must the recruitment sequence be clarified but, as explained in Chapter Three, the collective decision process of the high bench must also be reviewed.

Because of the central position of judges in the state's political system and because they sometimes remain largely hidden from or ignored by the public, those who help bring them to the high bench assume a heavy responsibility. Various motives, some selfish and some benign, underlie the selection of members to the state supreme court. These tend to reflect issues then at center stage of the political theater. Responsibility for recruiting supreme court justices has shifted over the years. Always, however, these changing fortunes of judicial selection bear directly on the satisfactory resolution of one of the fundamental contradictions of law in democracy.[4]

Public Accountability vs. Judicial Independence

In a democracy, officials responsible for determinations affecting the public are to be held accountable for their decisions.[5] The selection process is one of the most effective means of holding public servants accountable. Initial election or appointment, followed by periodic elections, should assure that politically sensitive persons arrive at the state's high bench and that they remain attuned to public needs and desires.

But judges also differ from other public officials. They are expected to remain free from politics in order to render objective and fair decisions. To enforce individual rights, judges must sometimes ignore angry outcries from the majority. People assume independence is part of judging. The contradiction of law in a democracy is between the need for judges to be accountable to the public (which is the essence of majoritarian democracy) while remaining independent from the public's demands (which is the essence of the rule of law). It is largely through the recruitment process that a balance is either struck or lost. The ideal system of judicial selection would bring to the state's high bench jurists able to resolve the contradiction.[6] How close has the selection process in Washington approximated this ideal? What indicators provide an answer to the question?

Olympia's Kneeland Building, or McKenny Block, housed the supreme court at the turn of the century. *Susan Parish Collection.*©

Measures of Accountability

Two leading, albeit imperfect, clues concerning the relative balance between accountability and independence are provided by voters and by candidates vying for a spot on the court, along with the supporters who bring them to the attention of those voters. As voter attention intensifies, public accountability heightens; as more challengers enter the race, political accountability increases. In contrast, as voters neglect judicial ballots and candidates go unchallenged, judges have the opportunity to exercise considerable independence. Thus, the measure of balance between accountability and independence depends upon the level of voter turnout for judicial races (roll-off) and the presence or absence of challengers on the ballot (contestedness).

Voter roll-off reflects the amount of attention paid less-visible races listed near the bottom of the election ballot – such as judicial contests. Roll-off refers to the percentage difference between those who vote for leading public offices on state ballots, such as president, senator, or governor, but do not vote for lesser offices, such as judges. For example, if 100,000 voters cast ballots for president but only 60,000 vote for a judicial position, the roll-off is forty percent. Under high roll-off conditions, voters seem apathetic about who sits on state benches and appear to make little effort to familiarize themselves with candidates and issues; jurists are shielded from close public scrutiny.[7] But the voter is not the only participant in the selection of judges. Others to whom judges may become accountable often have a stake in the outcome of judicial contests.

The number of challengers vying for an open seat suggests another dimension of accountability. Because of the high stakes in supreme court litigation, interest groups, factions within the legal profession, and political activists often encourage candidates. Contested supreme court races can be expensive. Consequently, support from well-financed groups often becomes necessary. A number of contested races suggests an intensified interest in who will sit on the high bench and encourages accountability. However, should positions go unchallenged, a low level of public concern about judicial office holders is indicated, and the jurist's independence is enhanced.

These two phenomena need not move in concert. Political accountability may thwart public accountability. Political parties and special interests have at times intervened between judges and the public, actually taking advantage of, if not encouraging, public inattention in order to bring sympathetic jurists to the state's high bench. Figure Two portrays the assumed relationship between accountability, roll-off, and contestedness.

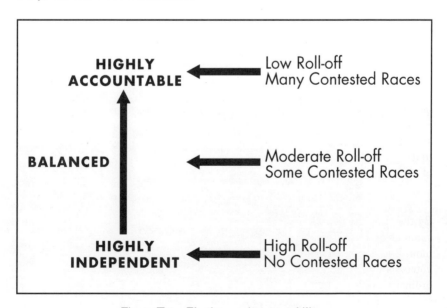

Figure Two. Elections and accountability.

Changes in the way judges were selected to the state's high bench have occurred over the past century. Possibly by isolating these shifts, the hypothesized relationship between accountability, roll-off, and contestedness can be confirmed.

Territorial Legacy

Washington territory enjoyed locally elected probate and justice courts.[8] But three judges appointed to four-year terms by the President of the United States, and confirmed by the senate, assumed the bulk of important judicial business. These three jurists conducted important trial work throughout a vast region extending from the Pacific Ocean to the Rocky Mountains. Once a year they assembled in the territorial capital at Olympia as a supreme court, hearing appeals from their own trial decisions rendered when they rode circuit as district judges. The government added a fourth judge in 1884 to allow a quorum of three when one judge felt compelled to withdraw from reviewing his own trial decision.

Of the twenty-eight jurists appointed to the territorial supreme court from 1853 until statehood, several lasted less than a year, while one served sixteen years.[9] Despite poor pay, inconvenient if not dangerous travel, uncomfortable working conditions, and often unappreciative and resentful residents, "they were seldom the hacks and derelicts described by [some historians]," according to Kermit Hall.[10]

The nucleus of the state's legal profession was drawn from those who practiced before these frontier judges. Further, the common law these pioneer jurists rendered constituted the foundation upon which the state built its legal system. And, of course, these judges provided the stabilizing effect of the law for the fledgling government.

Despite the sometimes commendable efforts of territorial judges, local residents resented these carpetbaggers who were often absent from the territory and not always attuned to the communities over which they presided. Such dissatisfaction with territorial justice was not the prime factor motivating citizens to seek statehood, but it clearly was important. Statehood would allow Washington to design its own judiciary and hold judges more accountable through a system of elections.

The Constitution and Accountability

By the time the Washington constitutional convention met in Olympia in the summer of 1889, recruiting judges through partisan elections was fairly common. Every state entering the union after 1846 elected judges. This reliance on voters can be attributed to several factors. Jacksonian democracy dictated that ordinary citizens select their leaders from among fellow citizens. This meant a state's electorate should choose judges. After enthusiasm for the Jacksonian movement waned, imitation explains the prevalence of an elected judiciary. For

Supreme court clerk's office in Kneeland Building, c. 1900. *Left to right:* Mr. Crandall, bailiff; C. S. Reinhart, clerk; Marion Patton, stenographer.

example, constitutional delegates in Olympia borrowed generously from other state constitutions, primarily California and Oregon.[11] They copied Article IV, the judicial article, nearly word for word from the California constitution. Since California elected its judiciary, delegates believed Washington should, too.

Unhappiness over appointed territorial judges encouraged the founders to favor voter selection. They believed judges would be an equal partner in the separation of powers scheme if they were elected on their own merits.[12]

Partisanship also dictated an elected judiciary. Republicans had controlled the territorial government. It was expected the GOP would also assume responsibility for the new state government, and an elected judiciary would assure it control of the courts.[13]

Delegates intended the appointment process – by which the governor could quickly fill a vacancy and keep the high bench at full capacity – to serve only as a backup for elections.[14] However, appointments came to dominate the selection process. Fifty-six of the state's eighty judges (sixty-six percent) were originally appointed.[15] However, all appointees must confirm their positions at the next general election following appointment. Of the fifty-six appointed jurists, only four have lost in their first election.[16] The appointment and electoral processes are mutually supportive. Because of the constitutional requirement of election after appointment, the concern for roll-off and contestedness applies equally to all jurists, whether they were initially elected or appointed.

The Inaugural Years: An Era of Public and Political Accountability (1890-1911)

In order to move ahead rapidly with state governance, the first election of state officials, including members of the supreme court, was held in conjunction with citizens' approval of the new constitution in October, 1889.[17] For the next twenty years, political partisans at party conventions nominated candidates.[18] The Democrat and Republican conventions selected a slate of candidates for the number of spots open on the high bench. Minority parties also occasionally placed nominees on the November ballot.[19] These judicial nominees carried partisan labels with them into their campaigns, which varied little from legislative or other highly political races.

The tradition of straight-party voting further enhanced the partisan nature of elections, especially in the days of ballots designed for slate voting. By simply marking the top of a political party's ballot, voters approved all those candidates listed under the party's name.[20] Supreme court candidates' fortunes followed that of their political parties.

Another feature of this inaugural period was the high level of registered voter participation in supreme court elections. Until 1912, when women voted for the first time Washington, only men entered voting booths.[21] Nonetheless, nearly all of them cast ballots for high court candidates. The roll-off percentage proved inconsequential between 1889 and 1908, at a time when nearly all seats were contested. The partisan nature of the elections and straight-party voting explain this low roll-off and the high number of court challenges. Public and political accountability dominated judicial as well as legislative and executive selection.

In these inaugural years, governors were limited to appointing persons to temporary or newly created positions under rules the legislature set. Of the twenty-two positions available, governors filled eleven. Six of these were temporary or new positions authorized by the legislature. The politics of endorsement shaped the governors' choices. Letters and petitions from the state's establishment filled the prospective appointees' files in the gubernatorial offices. State and local leaders, merchants, railroad officials, members of the legal elite, and newspaper editors registered support for various candidates. These petitions and endorsements played a crucial role in bringing to a governor's attention those aspiring to the high bench.

Partisanship prevailed; all but three of the eleven appointees were affiliated with the party of the governor. Governor John R. Rogers, a Democrat, crossed party lines because of a legislative mandate when he appointed Hiram Hadley in 1901. Republican Governor Albert E. Mead appointed Democrat Stephen J. Chadwick because the judge had already won election to the bench in 1908 and could conveniently fill a short-term vacancy until he qualified for his own elected seat. Republican Governor Marion E. Hay's appointment of Democrat Overton Ellis in 1911 remained the single exception to the political party rule, without extenuating circumstances.

In the inaugural years, from statehood until 1912, the destiny of judicial candidates depended upon the fate of political parties. If voters abandoned a party because of its policy stands, as in 1896, its judicial nominees suffered as well.[22] Public and political accountability through political parties and the ballot box held high-court nominees in check. They had to satisfy party regulars to capture the nomination, and then had to please the party faithful to prevail in the November elections. Voter roll-off proved nearly nonexistent, and court candidates could always count on opposition from other political parties.

The Years of Transition: Nonpartisanship Takes Over and Accountability Wanes (1912-1932)

In 1912 the direct primary and nonpartisan ballot permanently replaced political party conventions and straight-party tickets as the means of choosing high bench jurists.[23] Voters now lost the impetus to vote previously provided by party labels and loyalties. Court candidates now had to campaign on their own without benefit of party organizations. Other interest groups soon became drawn into the selection process.

Newspapers continued to editorially support or oppose supreme court aspirants. Interest groups, especially labor, began advocating certain candidates.[24] Surprisingly, not until 1924 did the legal profession get publicly involved. Previously, individual lawyers gave endorsements and signed petitions, but now the organized bar actively campaigned and provided funding.

In 1924 the Seattle Bar Association reacted adversely to a slate of candidates supported by left-leaning George F. Vanderveer, head of the legal bureau of the Seattle Central Labor Council.[25] He urged members of the letter carriers' union to support three candidates for the supreme court and to persuade those along their routes to vote for judges "friendly to the cause."[26]

For a time in the early 1900s the supreme court met in the Thurston County Courthouse.

Ads warning against the "Vanderveer ticket" appeared in newspapers over the names of more than 400 Seattle and King County attorneys. The Washington State Bar Association joined the political fray, and no Vanderveer candidate won. In 1926, voters again turned back William Pemberton, one of Vanderveer's candidates, in his rerun for the high court. The Seattle, Washington state, and many county bar associations actively opposed his election.[27]

The expansion of the electorate with woman suffrage in 1912 and the finality of primary elections (a majority vote in the primary meant a candidate's name appeared alone on the November ballot), encouraged high roll-off. During this period, election officials also separated the nonpartisan judicial ballot from the partisan ballot on voting machines. This required an added effort that many voters resented.

The transition years experienced a growing gubernatorial role in appointments. Endorsements gave way to a political process. The governor filled some vacancies as a reward for previous legal or political service or because he could gain some political advantage.[28] In recognition of the active role of bar associations, some appointments went to members of the legal elite.[29] Some gubernatorial selections were based on proven judicial and legal ability.[30] The appointment process became a separate force in the politics of selection involving a variety of legal and political considerations.

Because of the loss of the political party role in elections, voters' interest in judicial races deteriorated. The nonpartisan direct primary–with separate judicial ballots usually at the bottom of the voting form or separate from the voting machine–largely explains this abrupt change.

The Temple of Justice, which would become the supreme court's permanent home, neared completion at the time of this photo, c. 1919. *Susan Parish Collection.*©

Contestedness also leveled off by the 1930s. The organized bar, individual attorneys, and a few interest groups had shown some interest in judicial races now that the political parties no longer provided guidance to the average voter. Political accountability, as indicated by the fewer numbers of candidates filing for the supreme court, followed this loss of voter accountability.

The Early Modern Years: The Legal Profession and Independence (1933-1959)

Elected in 1932, Clarence D. Martin became the first Democrat to sit in the governor's chair in fifteen years. In August 1933 he appointed his close friend, Spokane city attorney James M. Geraghty, to the high bench, hoping to salvage business/occupation and income taxes from constitutional challenges.[31] Stung by criticisms for appointing a "crony" for a specific political purpose, confronted by a need to unify the state in its struggle with the Great Depression, and pressured by a unified legal profession, Governor Martin negotiated an agreement with the state bar that shaped his subsequent appointments. He agreed that he would make no other appointments without approval of the state bar's special judicial selection committee.

Martin's successor, Republican lawyer Arthur B. Langlie, continued the practice. Democratic Governor Mon Wallgren, however, ignored the bar's advice and selected three unendorsed people to the supreme court, much to the bar's disappointment.[32] In 1949 Langlie returned to the governor's chair and reinstated the arrangement with the bar. Two of the major participants in the selection of high bench jurists – the bar and the governor – had reached a system of sharing responsibilities, a collaboration that exists today.

In the 1940s the Washington State Bar Association, assured of a role in the appointment process, turned its attention to elections. In 1946 the supreme court had deadlocked 4-4, Judge Walter Beals being absent, in a case challenging the $135 million sale of Puget Sound Power and Light Company to the Skagit County public utility district. To break the tie, Chief Justice William Millard granted a rehearing, setting new arguments for early January, 1947. Upon becoming chief justice on January 13, Joseph Mallery added fuel to the flame by cancelling the rehearing and reinstating the 4-4 tie, which would have allowed the trial court's approval of the sale to stand. However, the full court rescinded his ruling and held the rehearing on January 30. By March, all judges but Millard had signed one of two draft opinions, resulting again in a 4-4 split. Three months later Millard still had not signed either opinion. Puget Power stock fluctuated on the New York Stock Exchange. The state Grange, which backed the sale, condemned the judges for their apparent procrastination. Five of the judges took the unprecedented step of publicizing a letter to Millard, holding him responsible for the delay.[33] Judge Millard voted immediately to void the sale and angrily accused his brethren, especially Mallery, of unethical behavior.[34]

Subsequently it was learned that Millard was heavily in debt, had borrowed from people indirectly involved in litigation before the high court, and had written several checks later returned for lack of funds. Rumors of bribes also circulated. Several investigations cleared Millard of criminal intent, with the exception of writing bad checks.

But Millard's behavior proved too much for the bar. Prior to the 1948 election, the Seattle Bar Association conducted the first bar preferential poll for supreme court candidates. Failing to convince voters to follow its lead, the Seattle bar conducted another poll of its membership before the November election. The poll again soundly thrashed Millard, and this time voters followed the bar's advice by giving victory to Millard's challenger, Judge Thomas Grady. For the next forty years the Seattle and state bars shared responsibility for polling lawyers before each contested election and publicizing the results.[35] With few exceptions, voters heeded the profession's advice.[36]

The bar associations and other interest groups, particularly labor and the Grange, had now supplanted political parties as a force in judicial elections. However, the governor, through appointments, still weighed partisan and political factors. All judges appointed during this period were political activists affiliated with the party of the governor. Governors also paid off a number of political debts by appointing judges from particular regions of the state.

The blanket primary, instituted in 1936, increased voter participation in primary elections but at the same time increased roll-off for judicial offices. The primary attracted more voters, but most ignored judicial races. The disruptions of World War II also contributed to high roll-off in the 1940s. Winning the war, not the concerns of law or politics at the state level, proved to be uppermost in voters' minds. Also, except for the organized bar's efforts to replace Justices Millard and Mallery for their involvement in the Puget Power case, contestedness remained low, indicating satisfaction with incumbents.

Judicial selection had recovered from the loss of partisanship. Now the selection of high court jurists involved efforts among several participants. A pluralistic system had evolved with a small number of competitive groups confronting one another. No group dominated. As an example of the fluidity of elections, a remnant of the past partisanship made a brief appearance in the late 1940s and early 1950s. With Republicans challenging New Deal Democrats throughout the state, judicial aspirants often welcomed partisan support. On occasion, candidates argued they were more anti-communist than their opponents. Because of the pluralistic nature of judicial selection, an unsteady balance between accountability and independence existed.

However, in this early modern period a trend developed. Although the governor and the state bar had reached a cooperative agreement as early as 1937, it remained tentative, with the bar acting somewhat cautiously. According to a member of the state bar's selection committee, the agreement with Governor Martin had worked well, but "other governors will be elected and it is quite possible ...that we will not have so happy a situation."[37] Nonetheless, the coalition remained in place for subsequent exploitation.

Late Modern Years: Independence Prevails (1960-1991)

Over the next thirty years cooperation replaced the previous era's balanced but fluid confrontation. Coordinated efforts became especially evident during the 1960s. The governor made all appointments from a list of names submitted by the state bar association's screening committee and board of governors. Voters retained all the appointees in office. Political accountability was at a low point, evidenced by the lack of challenges to appointees and incumbents. It was not until later in the period that cooperation momentarily broke down. Governor Daniel Evans appointed James Dolliver in 1976 without the approval—or disapproval—of the bar.

The bar associations continued to demonstrate their influence with voters during this period. Eighteen of twenty-five candidates endorsed by either the state or Seattle-King County bar defeated their opposition in September or November balloting.[38]

In 1968, the state's voters approved a constitutional amendment establishing an intermediate court of appeals composed of twelve judges located in three divisions, headquartered in Seattle, Tacoma, and Spokane.[39] The amendment, in essence, added a new requirement to the criteria for recruitment to the supreme court: eight of the nineteen jurists elected or appointed after 1969 served apprenticeships on the Court of Appeals, and, except for Justices James Dolliver, Robert Brachtenbach, and Charles Johnson, all justices have served on the superior court before elevation to the high bench. Prior judicial experience clearly became a prerequisite for the court.

As a consequence, the influence of bar associations was greatly enhanced. County bars dominated superior and district court appointments and elections, while the state bar controlled appellate appointments. The organized profession now had at least two opportunities to influence the selection of justices to the high bench: first by approving their initial lower court appointments or elections, and later when candidates were considered for the supreme court.

To a considerable extent, the mix of the governors' political considerations and the bars' professional concerns discouraged mainstream challenges to incumbents. On the few occasions when opponents mounted a challenge, it came from outside the political and legal establishment, with the outsider having little chance of winning.

The modern selection process is now complex, with the governor and the bar assuming leading roles and the electorate providing support. The bar tends to insulate justices from the pressures of politics and the passions of public opinion. For example, the *Judicial Canons* dictate:

> Judges Should Uphold the Integrity and Independence of the Judiciary. An independent and honorable judiciary is indispensable to justice in our society. Judges should participate in establishing, maintaining, and enforcing, and should themselves observe high standards of conduct so that the integrity and independence of the judiciary may be preserved.[40]

The electorate provides public accountability, although roll-off remains relatively high. Party affiliation, interest group endorsements, name familiarity, campaign issues, prior political activities and most important, incumbency, provide clues for the choices of judicial voters. But it is bar endorsement that often makes the difference.[41]

The governor's role provides a balance between the bar's insistence on independence and the electorate's demands for accountability. Appointments are based upon political, professional, and public considerations. The governor heeds the bar's advice, considers political party affiliation and activities, and weighs the ability of the appointee to win reelection. Judicial recruitment to the supreme court has, for the moment, stabilized. As indicated by roll-off and contestedness, and by a general glance at the last several decades, the confrontation between judicial independence and public accountability appears now to favor independence.

Roll-off, Contestedness, Judicial Review, and Accountability

Previously, it was hypothesized that roll-off and contestedness have an impact on the balance between accountability and independence. An increasing roll-off indicates that fewer voters are concerned with judicial races. As contestedness wanes, fewer candidates are tempted to challenge incumbents, indicating another lack of attention being paid the judiciary. Consequently, this condition of high roll-off coupled with low contestedness results in a highly independent bench. In contrast, low roll-off and high contestedness translates into a highly accountable court. How do the data match these assertions?

Tables Two and Three report the breakdown of these two important variables within the recruitment periods described above. Table Four tests the hypothesized relationship between accountability and roll-off and contestedness.

Table Two presents the average roll-off for the four periods.

Table Two

Roll-off Averages: 1889-1990

	Primary Elections	General Elections	Election Averages
Inaugural Years (1889-1911)	**	3.9%	3.9% (Low Roll-off)
Transition Years (1912-1932)	27.8%	49.9%	38.9%
Early Modern Years (1933-1959)	33.8%	49.6%	41.7% (High Roll-off)
Late Modern Years (1960-1990)	37.2%	44.5%	40.9%

**=No primaries held

The inaugural years represent the highest level of public accountability with very little roll-off evident. In contrast, the early modern and modern eras were most independent when roll-off was high. However, equally important to the measure of accountability is the degree of contestedness found in each of the selection periods.

The contestedness levels for each of the groupings of years is reported in Table Three. The inaugural era is also the most politically accountable with every position except a short-term spot in 1900 being contested. The modern period permitted the judges independence, as many candidates remained unopposed. The political world was apparently satisfied with the composition of the state's high bench, sponsoring few challengers. However, the question remains; how are these variations in roll-off and contestedness translated into accountable or independent judicial behavior?

One indication of the tug between accountability and independence is the court's exercise of judicial review. The contention is that a court concerned with

Table Three

Contestedness: 1889-1990

	Primary Elections	General Elections	Averages	
Inaugural Years				High
(1889-1911)	*	3.19**	3.19	Contestedness
Transition Years				
(1912-1932)	2.19	1.51	1.85	
Early Modern Years				
(1933-1959)	2.10	1.26	1.68	
Late Modern Years				Low
(1960-1990)	1.61	1.11	1.36	Contestedness

*=No primaries held
**=Average number of candidates per position

remaining accountable tends to resist the opportunity to question the constitutionality of laws. When the question cannot be avoided, every effort is made to validate those laws. Judicial restraint and accountability go hand-in-hand. We would expect to find that during low roll-off and high contestedness—the extreme in accountability (public and political)—the high court would be restraintist. Justices enjoying a situation of high roll-off and low contestedness would feel more at ease with confronting the constitutional issue and not altogether reluctant to invalidate the law. They would feel free to behave independently.

It is assumed that levels of roll-off and contestedness have an equal impact on the views of the justices toward accountability. For a simple statistical test of the hypothesis the two can be combined into a composite score and then compared with the incidence of judicial review. Table Four reports the association between those years representing the extremes in roll-off and contestedness (inaugural and later modern) and the incidence of judicial review.[42]

Table Four

Judicial Review and Accountability

Number of Cases	Number with Constitutional Questions	Number Declared Unconstitutional
Accountable: Inaugural Years – 1889-1911		
(Low Roll-off and High Contestedness)		
2707	105 (3.9%)	21 (20.0%)
Independent: Late Modern Years – 1960-1990		
(High Roll-off and Low Contestedness)		
1879	122 (6.5%)	30 (24.6%)

Source: Table One, Chapter One.

Table Four suggests that roll-off and contestedness affect levels of accountability. The accountable years (1889-1911) produced a lower incidence of judicial review when compared with the independent years (1960-1990). Not only did the court accept fewer constitutional cases, the justices were more reluctant to invalidate them. Selection apparently plays a role in shaping the outlook of judges.

The jurists may have retained or gained particular political or legal perspectives as a result of their selection experiences. Nonetheless, once on the high bench they are exposed to other forces that may impinge upon their judicial review perspectives. A decisional process within which all must work could reshape their views, possibly explaining the lack of a wider gap between the incidence of judicial review in the inaugural and late modern years.

Notes

1. The meanings attached to judicial activism and its antithesis, restraint, have been imprecise largely because of the numerous methods that claim to lead to activist or restraintist results. For example, the desegregation case of *Brown v. Board of Education* could be both an activist as well as a restraintist decision. See Lief Carter, *Contemporary Constitutional Lawmaking* (1985), p. 82. Also see Bradley Canon, "A Framework for the Analysis of Judicial Activism," in Stephen Halpern and Charles Lamb, eds., *Supreme Court Activism and Restraint* (1982), pp. 385-419; and Christopher Wolfe, *Judicial Activism: Bulwark of Freedom or Precarious Security?* (1991). The terms become more problematic when applied to state supreme courts simply because judges are usually elected to short terms. They are not protected by the "good behavior" provisions of the U. S. constitution. See Charles Sheldon, " 'We Feel Constraint to Hold': An Inquiry into the Basis for Decision in the Exercise of State Judicial Review," *Gonzaga Law Review*, 27 (1991), pp. 1-35.

2. For other discussions of judicial elections see Philip Dubois, *From Ballot to Bench* (1980); Herbert Jacob, "Judicial Insulation: Elections, Direct Participation, and Public Attention to the Courts in Wisconsin," *Wisconsin Law Review* (1966), pp. 801-819; David Adamany and Dubois, "Electing State Judges," *Wisconsin Law Review* (1976), pp. 731-779; Canon, "The Impact of Formal Selection Processes on the Characteristics of Judges – Reconsidered," *Land and Society Review*, 6 (1972), pp. 579-593; Herbert Jacob, "The Effects of Institutional Differences in the Recruitment Process: The Case of State Judges," *Journal of Public Law*, 13 (1964), pp. 104-119; Patrick Dunn, "Judicial Selection in the States: A Critical Study with Proposals for Reform," *Hofstra Law Review*, 4 (1976), pp. 267-353; and Jack Ladinski and Allen Silver, "Popular Democracy and Judicial Independence: Electorate and Elite Reactions to Two Wisconsin Supreme Court Elections," *Wisconsin Law Review* (1967), pp. 128-169. Appointments are discussed in John E. Crow, "Subterranean Politics: A Judge is Chosen," *Journal of Public Law*, 12 (1963), pp. 275-289; Stuart Nagel, *Comparing Elected and Appointed Judicial Systems* (1973); and Lamar Beman, *Election vs. Appointment of Judges* (1926). The role of the bar is reported in Edward Martin, *The Role of the Bar in Electing the Bench in Chicago* (1936); Richard Watson and Rondal Downing, *The Politics of the Bench and Bar* (1969). For references to Washington see Sheldon, "Influencing the Selection of Judges: The Variety and Effectiveness of State Bar Activities," *Western Political Quarterly*, 30 (1977), pp. 397-400; Sheldon, "The Washington Supreme Court: What it was Like Thirty Years Ago," *Gonzaga Law Review*, 19 (1983-1984), pp. 231-264; Nicholas Lovrich and Sheldon, "Voters in Contested Nonpartisan Elections: A Responsible Electorate or a Problematic Public?" *Western Political Quarterly*, 38 (1985), pp. 276-293; Sheldon and Lovrich, "Judicial Accountability vs. Responsibility: Balancing the Views of Voters and Judges," *Judicature*, 65 (1982), pp. 470-480; Sheldon and Lovrich, "Knowledge and Judicial Voting: The Oregon and Washington Experience," *Judicature*, 67 (1983), pp. 234-245; Sheldon and Lovrich, "Do Bar Pools Affect Voters?" *Seattle-King County Bar Bulletin* (1984), pp. 3-4; Sheldon and Lovrich, "Judicial Elections in Washington and Oregon: The Views of the Voters and the Judges (1980)," *Occasional Paper, Division of Governmental Studies and Services*, 1981; Sheldon, "The Composition and Selection of the Washington State Judiciary," *Washington State Minority and Justice Task Force, Final Report* (1990), pp. 77-99; Lovrich, Sheldon, and Eric Wasmann, "The Racial Factor in Nonpartisan Judicial Elections," *Western Political Quarterly*, 41 (1988), pp. 807-816; and Sheldon, "Representativeness of the Washington Judiciary: Ethnic and Gender Considerations," *Washington State Bar News*, 43 (1989), pp. 31-33.

3. Walter Murphy, *The Elements of Judicial Strategy* (1964).
4. Sheldon and Lovrich, "Judicial Accountability vs. Responsibility."
5. For a discussion of judicial accountability see Stephen Wasby, "Accountability of Courts," in Scott Greer, ed., *Accountability in Urban Society* (1978), pp. 143-168; and Dubois, *From Ballot to Bench.* As discussed in Chapter One, when a judge feels compelled to consider the consequences of his or her decision on the community, an issue of public policy is likely involved. Further, it could be argued that courts "resolve issues previously unsettled and thus...create law" or by their "supervision of the...court system" through their administrative and rule-making powers, they "exercise considerable policy-making responsibility." In such policy cases, accountability is a consideration. See, for example, *E.E.O.C. v. Massachusetts*, 858 F. 2d 52 (1988); *Chisom v. Roermer*, 917 F. 2d 187 (1991); and *Gregory v. Ashcroft*, 898 F 2d 598 (1990).
6. Sheldon and Lovrich, "State Judicial Selection," in John Gates and Charles Johnson, eds., *American Courts: A Critical Assessment* (1990), pp. 161-188.
7. Gubernatorial appointments account for nearly two-thirds of all initial selections to the supreme court. Obviously, an appointment may be motivated by a desire for a more independent or more accountable judge. Nonetheless, the roll-off results of the inevitable election still suggest how successful the governor was in his or her appointment. The voters may confirm the more accountable appointee with a low roll-off response or they may ignore the judicial ballot altogether and encourage independence.
8. See Earl Pomeroy, *The Territories and the United States: 1861-1890* (1947), pp. 58-60.
9. For a listing of the twenty-eight territorial judges see Edmund Meany, *History of the State of Washington* (1924), p. 370.
10. Kermit Hall, "Hacks and Derelicts Revisited: American Territorial Judiciary, 1789-1959," *Western Historical Quarterly*, 12 (1981), pp. 273-289.
11. Arthur Beardsley, "Sources of Washington Constitution," *Legislative Manual* (1985-1986), p. 355.
12. Hall, "Progressive Reform and the Decline of Democratic Accountability: The Popular Election of State Supreme Court Judges, 1850-1920," *American Bar Foundation Research Journal* (1984), pp. 345-369.
13. See Beverly Rosenow, ed., *The Journal of the Washington State Constitutional Convention,* 1889 (1962).
14. The final product of the delegates' deliberations, approved by a 40,152 to 11,879 vote of the electorate, contained the following provision in the judicial article: "The judge of the supreme court shall be elected by the qualified electors of the state at large at the general state election at the times and places at which state officers are elected...if a vacancy occurs in the office of a judge of the supreme court the governor shall appoint a person to hold the office until the election and qualification of a judge to fill the vacancy, which election shall take place at the next succeeding general election, and the judge so elected shall hold the office for the remainder of the unexpired term." Washington Constitution, Article IV, Section 3.
15. Five of the fifty-six were appointed to short terms on the bench after they had won a seat by election. Such short-term appointments permitted them to begin hearing cases prior to beginning their elected terms. The five were justices Chadwick (1908), Mallery (1942), Schwellenbach (1946), Dore (1981), and Callow (1984).
16. They were justices Hovey (1922), Herman (1932), Connelly (1946), and Sharp (1972).
17. Washington Constitution, Article IV, Section 3 states, "The first election of the judges of the supreme court shall be at the election which shall be held upon the adoption of this Constitution and the judges elected there at shall be classified by lot, so that two shall hold their office for the term of three years, two for the term of five years, and one for the term of seven years."

18. Election laws, 1889-1890, *Washington Laws* (1889), p. 419. A few special circumstances provided exceptions to full-party slates.
19. Minority parties such as Socialist, Socialist Labor, Prohibition, Peoples', and Social Democrats nominated candidates to the bench. However, only the Peoples' Party succeeded in winning a spot on the court. Reavis's victory as a Fusionist in 1896 was due to Democrat and dissident Republican support.
20. Chapter 13, *Session Laws*, 1889-1890.
21. Washington Constitution, Amendment V.
22. In 1896 a coalition of Free Silver Republicans, Democrats, and Peoples' Party followers formed the Fusion Party and swept all state offices.
23. The legislature first instituted nonpartisanship in judicial elections in 1908. However, fears of losing a supreme court seat in the 1910 elections prompted the Republican-dominated legislature to reinstate partisanship in the November balloting. After succeeding in electing its high-bench slate, the Republicans reenacted nonpartisanship in time for the 1912 elections.
24. *Seattle Daily Times*, 3 Sept. 1926 reported, "Members of Union Local #46, International Brotherhood of Electrical Workers, last night ratified the action of the Seattle Labor Council endorsing and recommending candidates for legislative, county and non-judiciary offices, and instructed their secretary to notify all members of the organization of the stand taken...Letters will be sent to the members."
25. Lowell Hawley and Ralph Potts, *Attorney for the Damned* (1953).
26. *Seattle Daily Times*, 29 Aug. 1924.
27. *Seattle Post-Intelligencer*, 21 Sept. 1926.
28. For example, Bausman had helped Governor Lister remove a rival from the Democrat's ballot in 1912 and Lister went on to become the eventual winner in the November elections. Mackintosh was appointed in order to create a superior court spot for a close ally of the governor. Adam Beeler was appointed as a reward for withdrawing from a Lieutenant Governor's race. Warren Tolman had backed the governor in an inter-party struggle. See Sheldon, *A Century of Judging: A Political History of the Washington Supreme Court* (1988).
29. Both Bridges and Hovey had been presidents of the state bar and Millard was the bar's executive secretary. However, Millard's appointment came as a surprise. Many felt the governor wanted a quick appointment to avoid the political pressures that inevitably build with a delay in filling a vacancy.
30. Holcomb had served with distinction on the supreme court for twelve years before his defeat in a reelection bid in 1926. Governor Hartley quickly returned him to the court in 1927. Beals and Steinert were popular and respected superior court judges appointed in part as a fence-mending tactic in King County.
31. The income tax lost on a 5-4 split on the court, but the justices upheld the business tax. See *Culliton v. Chase*, 174 WASH. 363 (1933); and *Steiner v. Yelle*, 174 WASH. 402 (1933).
32. Wallgren appointed Schwellenbach, Connelly, and Abel. Schwellenbach had already won election to the high court. Wallgren's appointment of him was to a short interim position. Connelly lost in his first election bid and Abel's appointment was to a temporary position.
33. For a description of the incident see Sheldon, *A Century of Judging*, pp. 117-123.
34. *P.U.D. District of Skagit v. Wylie*, 28 WASH. 2d 133 (1947).
35. Bar polls conducted by the state or Seattle bars before supreme court elections were discontinued after the 1984 elections. However, the Seattle-King County bar continues to rate candidates after screening by a special bar committee.

36. Candidates who won even though their opponents were more heavily endorsed by the Seattle or Washington State bar associations were Finley (1950); Rosellini (1954); Wright (1970, 1972); Hicks (1976); Williams (1978); Dore (1980); Goodloe (1984); and Johnson (1990). Only twelve of the eighty incumbents were subsequently rejected by the voters: Hoyt (term ending in 1897); Reavis (1903); Gose (1915); Holcomb (1927); Hovey (1923); Pemberton (1925); Millard (1949); Herman (1932); Simpson (1951); Connelly (1947); Sharp (1971); and Callow (1991).

37. "Report of Committee on Selection of Judges," *Washington Law Review and State Bar Journal,* 15 (1940), p. 200.

38. 1990 proved to be one of the seven exceptions. An unknown sole practitioner, Charles W. Johnson, filed against Chief Justice Keith Callow. Callow had the overwhelming support of leading newspapers and the organized bar, as evidenced by his high rating by the Seattle-King County bar screening committee. Neither candidate campaigned, leaving the voters with little information. Johnson prevailed in the September primary and became the eightieth justice to sit on the state's high bench.

39. Amendment L became Article IV, Section 29. The electorate approved the court of appeals by a vote of 650,025 to 37,059 in November 1968.

40. Rules of Court, *Code of Judicial Conduct,* Section 1.

41. Some evidence suggests that the more informed the voters, the more they will participate in judicial elections and the more they will understand the need for balance between independence and accountability. The judicial voter is perhaps more sophisticated than previously thought. See, for example, Lovrich and Sheldon, "Assessing Judicial Elections," *Western Political Quarterly,* 38 (1985), pp. 276-293; and Lovrich and Sheldon, "Voters in Judicial Elections: An Attentive Public or an Uninformed Electorate?" *Justice System Journal,* 9 (1984), pp. 23-39.

42. Assuming that both contestedness and roll-off have an equal affect on the level of accountability, the highest accountable and highest independent years can be determined by a logical manipulation of the averages reported in Tables Two and Three. First, in order to have the two variables working together rather than in opposition, the average percentage of roll-off for each recruitment period is subtracted from 100. Then, in order to give equal status to both variables, the remainder from the first manipulation is multiplied by the average contestedness figure for that period. The higher the results means more voters and more candidates and, thus, more accountability. The lower the total, the more independence. The inaugural years were most accountable with a total of 306.6 (100−3.9 = 96.1 x 3.19). The years of transition equal 113 (100−38.9 = 61.1 x 1.85). The early modern period totalled 97.9 (100−41.7 = 58.3 x 1.68). The modern years proved to be the most independent with a score of 80.4 (100−40.9 = 59.1 x 1.36). Assuming that both contestedness and roll-off have an equal effect on the level of accountability, the highest accountable and highest independence years can be determined by a simple manipulation of the totals reported in Tables Two and Three. First, roll-off is subtracted from 100 then multiplied by the contestedness figure for those particular years. For example, the years of transition roll-off for the primaries (27.8) is subtracted from 100, resulting in 72.2. This is then multiplied by the contestedness figure for that time (2.19 x 72.2) and then added to the totals for the same categories for the general elections (50.1 x 1.51 = 233.65). The inaugural years totalled 306.6, the early modern years is 202.5, and the later modern years totalled 174.9. Thus, the later modern years are the most independent while the inaugural years are the most accountable.

Chapter Three
A Review of
Supreme Court Decisional Processes

Although the shifting selection process brought attorneys with varied outlooks to the supreme court, those on the bench at any given time were exposed to the same confining decisional process. The confines of decision-making procedures may not have dictated the outcome of cases, but the procedures either encouraged singular contributions or enhanced compromise and agreement.[1]

As with judicial selection, the procedures served competing aims. A leading purpose was to arrive at a collective decision from a number of individual viewpoints. Because of the need to arrive at a final court decision involving at least a majority of the judges, jurists usually had to soften their particular views on contentious legal and policy issues. No member of the court was wholly free to follow his or her preferences. Each was a member of a collectivity, and consequently compelled to make his or her contribution to the collective decision.[2]

Yet procedures also encouraged individual contemplation of issues in each case. Nine separate minds attacking the legal puzzle from different perspectives were better than one or two like minds being applied to the issues. Failing to convince colleagues during group sessions, each justice was permitted to express individual disagreement. The judges applied their own experiences, training, and knowledge to resolve disputes. In short, the decision-making process, then as now, had both collective and individual elements.

Inaugural Court Deliberations (1890-1909)

The decisional process involved a reciprocal exchange between attorneys and judges. Each judge gave the twenty or so attorneys' briefs filed each week individual attention before the attorneys presented oral arguments. They decided a few appeals without oral arguments. On Fridays and Saturdays the judges met together in closed conference and debated, discussed, and voted on the tentative disposition of that week's cases.

Article IV, Section 2 of the state constitution dictated that, "all decisions of the court shall be given in writing and the grounds of the decision shall be stated." After the tentative conference vote, judges assigned cases to members of the majority for drafting opinions on a rotation basis, rather than relying upon a particular judge's preference or expertise. This system assured that each high bench member had responsibility for writing an equal number of opinions. Further, this was a court of last resort with general jurisdiction, responsible for all kinds of appeals. Each judge was expected to have an acquaintance with all aspects of the high bench's jurisdiction. Requiring each member to confront a variety of issues through the rotation method assured a collective expertise. It also guaranteed that no judge would monopolize a particular legal matter.

After assigning opinion-writing responsibility, the court's deliberations shifted from the collective back to the individual. The assigned judge researched and drafted the opinion, circulated it for review, and hoped other members agreed

Supreme court hearing room in the new Temple of Justice, c. 1919. *Susan Parish Collection.*©

with it. Because they had all been exposed to the case during oral arguments and conferences, most justices affixed their signatures to the draft promptly and agreeably.

Most of the cases followed this simple and fairly rapid route. However, if doubts arose or if justices could form no definite opinion from the briefs, oral arguments, and conference discussions, the individual and collective phases merged. The assigned judge examined the record again, researched precedent from other jurisdictions, and consulted informally with colleagues. If disagreement continued, the other judges examined the record for themselves, conducted their own individual research, and, again, discussed the issues with the others until differences were resolved. The assigned judge then circulated a revised draft, hoping that after this collective exchange it would pick up all the judges' signatures for a unanimous opinion. Of course, any individual judge who remained unconvinced could cast a dissenting vote, or in the extreme, file a dissenting opinion. If a judge agreed with the results but not the reasons expressed by the majority opinion, he could cast a concurring vote or write a concurring opinion.

The losing party in a case frequently filed a petition for rehearing. Each judge reviewed the request as time permitted. If denial seemed warranted, as was usually the case, the judge so indicated and passed the petition on to the other judges. When a majority indicated denial, they rejected the petition. A short *per curiam* opinion ended the matter.

As noted, the court's decision-making process was designed to lead to consensus while permitting individual contemplation of legal issues. Too much weight placed on the collective end of the decisional scale stifled the creative contribution of the diverse and individualistic minds on the high bench. Too much attention to the individual side of the scale prevented the united front necessary to instill a high degree of predictability and authority into the law. A balance was required.

"Two" Supreme Courts (1910-1939)

To deal with a crowded docket, the bench expanded from seven to nine members in 1909. The increase provided opportunity to divide the court into two five-judge departments, the chief justice presiding over both. In effect, this created two supreme courts. In order to remain in compliance with constitutional dictates of a single supreme court, the judges of each department reviewed the others' decisions. The chief justice had to assure that one panel's decision received adequate attention from the other. According to Judge O. G. Ellis, "There is constant and increasing effort on the part of the judges to make the work of each department the work of the entire court."[3] The chief could transfer a case to the other department, or to the full nine-member bench (*en banc*) if he felt the case warranted it. Transfers to *en banc* status were prompted mostly by a lack of panel consensus on the case.

Judges made opinion-drafting assignments in the department conference following oral arguments, rotating them to equalize work loads. If a majority of the five judges failed to accept the original opinion draft, a dissenting opinion might win enough votes to become the court's decision. If disagreement persisted, the chief justice reassigned the case to another judge, or transferred it to a full *en banc* hearing.

Written opinions relied on authorities and reasoning found in litigants' briefs, attorneys' oral presentations, responses to queries from the bench in open court, facts outlined in the abstract of the trial record filed with each brief, and from the discussions—formal and informal—among members of the departments.

Departmental decision-making permitted jurists to render a considerable number of decisions. But there were drawbacks, perhaps the most important being that each case received less than its deserved attention. Most decisions were the product of deliberations by a five-member department rather than a full nine-member court. Although both collective and individual phases remained under the departmental system, it appeared to some that the collective was most diluted.

The Reporting-Judge System (1940-1969)

In order to assure that each case received the thorough analysis some believed had been missing, the court of the 1940s instituted the "reporting-judge" system. Cases were assigned to each judge by lot at the beginning of each term. The assigned judge reviewed the briefs and trial record and researched the issues. By the 1950s each judge had a law clerk. With the clerk's assistance, the reporting judge wrote and circulated among his colleagues in the department a prehearing memorandum summarizing the issues and sometimes recommending a resolution. The reporting-judge process transferred greater responsibilities to the individual, as other members of the department usually accepted the recommendations of the prehearing memo.

Each attorney was allowed a half hour to present his or her case in open court, with the reporting judge taking the lead in questioning. As in the earlier courts, the judges adjourned to their conference or consultation room to discuss and take a tentative vote on the cases just heard. Being most conversant with the case, the reporting judge recited first, recommending a disposition. The judge sitting to the right of the reporting jurist recited next, indicating his vote, and so on around the table. The chief justice spoke last and announced the court's tentative vote. Each judge "voted" by agreeing or disagreeing with the reporting judge.

If a majority of the justice's colleagues agreed with the reporting judge, he was to draft the full opinion for the court. However, if his view did not prevail, three decisional alternatives were available. First, the judge who expressed the first or the strongest disagreement in conference could receive the drafting assignment. Second, and not infrequently, the reporting judge could concede to the majority and write the opinion according to their wishes. Third, if the reporter felt strongly about his view despite the majority, he could draft a dissenting opinion or cast a dissenting vote.

Most commonly, however, votes changed after the initial conference deliberations when the justices circulated dissent, concurring, and majority drafts. The passing sheets – the cover page on the majority opinion used for communication among the judges during the draft opinion circulation – contained comments like: "Judge Blake's dissent has shaken my view of this case"; "I am convinced of the correctness of the dissent"; or "The Chief Justice suggested that he was not in accord with the opinion. . . . I have made the following changes."[4] Of course, the final opinion or opinions were not ready for *Washington Reports* until all judges had signed one or another.

Another change in the court's deliberative system occurred earlier, although its full impact was not felt until the 1950s. In 1937 the court hired three young attorneys as its first law clerks. By the early 1950s each judge had one clerk to share decisional responsibilities, responsibilities determined by the judge's need and the clerk's abilities.[5] Some of the assistants received opinion-drafting assignments; others took primary responsibility for prehearing bench memos. Most clerks served as a sounding board for their judges, while a few acted as secretaries or chauffeurs.

Depending upon the law clerks' responsibilities, the balance between collective and individual modes of the decisional process shifted. On the one hand, relying on a loyal and devoted assistant enhanced the individual aspects of deliberations. The clerk assumed the detailed research and editing functions of opinion writing, leaving the judge to pursue his own legal reasoning.

On the other hand, the help of clerks resulted in more thorough consideration of draft opinions and bench memos, and allowed more time to research opinions. Both time and information were available to reach consensus. Communication between and among judges improved, with clerks serving as messengers. Most of the judges and clerks were University of Washington law graduates. Consequently, the clerks and justices analyzed similar authorities and had similar legal outlooks, enhancing collective decision-making.

Docket pressures continued to plague the high bench. The pressures encouraged the collective aspects of the deliberations, with less time available for individual judges to give full and creative attention to each case. The extra effort and time needed to draft a concurring or dissenting opinion meant less attention given other cases. A heavier reliance on the reporting judge's prehearing memo became evident. The "two court" department system and the assistance of the law clerks helped the judges, but more reform was needed. To address the problem, the judges successfully supported a constitutional amendment which would allow a majority of the supreme court members to commission retired or active

Washington State Law Library, Temple of Justice.

judges of courts of record to sit on the state's high bench as temporary but full participants in the decisional process.[6] On balance, the decisional process throughout the decades prior to the 1970s tended to enhance the collective contributions to decisions. Soon, however, the decisional process experienced a drastic change.

Contemporary Deliberations (1969-1991)

In 1968 the state's voters gave overwhelming approval to a constitutional amendment authorizing an intermediate court of appeals with separate divisions in Seattle, Tacoma, and Spokane.[7] This brought changes in the way the high court conducted its business. Nearly all appeals went to and were resolved by the new intermediate court. However, the court of appeals could be bypassed, with serious cases brought directly to the high bench.[8] No longer were cases the primary responsibility of departments. All but preliminary or minor procedural issues were heard by all nine justices *en banc*. For the first time, the justices became masters of their own docket. Now they gave full consideration to about 150 cases annually. In earlier times 300 to 400 full opinions were common. The new situation enhanced both individual and collective phases of the supreme court's deliberations, and the court's total effectiveness increased.

Petitions for review from attorneys for parties who had lost in a lower court first went to the court commissioner's staff attorneys for research and recommendation. The court commissioner's office, authorized in 1976, screened the hundreds of requests for review filed with the court. The commissioner's initial research permitted the justices more time to concentrate on both their individual and collective responsibilities. Again, each justice received assignments by lot for the research needed to confirm the commissioner's recommendations. The justices then met in departmental conference to determine whether to grant review. Only rarely did they overrule the commissioner's recommendations.

These preliminary departmental decisions were crucial, as many more requests for review were filed than could be granted. If the justices accepted an appeal for review, the case was reassigned by lot to a judge other than the one to whom it was initially assigned. The reassignment to another justice encouraged a different perspective when the case received a full hearing. Both the initial study of the petition by the assigned judge and his or her law clerk and the subsequent research of the reporting justice constituted significant individual phases of the decision-making process.

The conference deliberations, where discussions, debates, and tentative votes were recorded, were the most important collective decisional stage for the court. Although tentative, this initial decision shaped future actions. Only occasionally did the circulation of draft opinions after conference deliberations lead to changes.

Because of administrative tasks, the chief was not obligated to accept opinion assignments, although he usually carried his share of responsibilities. The chief also conducted preliminary hearings and often assumed responsibility for lawyer discipline appeals. When all signatures were accounted for, the legal issues in the majority opinion were classified or "headnoted" for easy reference in the official *Washington Reports* by the supreme court reporter, checked by the opinion writer, and returned to the chief, who released it with concurring or dissenting opinions.

Consequences of the Decisional Process

This review of major shifts in the decisional process over the past 100 years suggests that, with each major change, deliberations varied between the creative but divisive individual phase and the conciliatory collective phase of the process. What of the judicial results of the variations? Does it make a difference in the justices' behavior whether the decisional process is more collective than individual?

Indications of the movement along the collective-individual continuum are found in measurements of levels of agreement between and among the judges. These indications of the dynamic aspects of decision-making are portrayed in Figure Three.

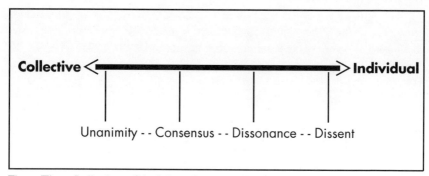

Figure Three. Indications of the balance between collective and individual decision-making.

As the decisional process shifts from collective to individual, the judges' responses fluctuate between unanimity/consensus and dissonance/dissent. Consensus results if a judge only rarely registers disagreement with his or her colleagues. Short of unanimity – the ultimate in collective decision-making – a judge may feel compelled to share his or her misgivings by means of an occasional dissent or concurring vote or opinion. This infrequent disagreement tends to shift among the judges, and general consensus remains. A state of dissonance results when concurrences and dissents characterize decisions.[9] The justices are more inclined to cast a concurring or dissenting vote rather than penning an angry minority opinion. Should a dissenting faction or an inflexible and persistent bloc form, resulting in a great number of split decisions and accusing opinions, dissent materializes.[10]

The collective phases of the decision-making process were designed to bring about agreement, while the individual phases were intended to showcase the creative skills of the single judge on the legal and policy problems confronting the high bench. Unanimity signifies the triumph of the collective phase, while dissent indicates the dominance of the individual phase. Ideally, the decision-making process should fluctuate between consensus and dissonance. How have these phases varied over the years?

Clues about the shifting fortunes of decision-making along the collective-individual continuum are supplied by comparing court opinions and votes during years representing a particular decisional process.

One of the causes of the dynamic shifting between unanimity and dissent can be attributed to a collective or an individual decisional process. Of course, these are all matters of degree and should be viewed as tendencies. As Table Five suggests, the inaugural decisional process encouraged unanimity and, consequently, relative to other courts, constituted a collective process. The five members of the court, all products of the partisan system dominated by Republicans, felt at ease with the collective phase of the court's deliberations. Also, the anti-dissenting tradition of the times constrained all courts, including the Washington

Table Five
Decisional Process Fluctuations: Unanimity or Dissent?[11]

Decision Process	Total Opinions	Unanimous Decisions	Concur Opinions	Dissent Votes	Dissent Opinions	% Disagree	Decisional Response
(Years)★							
Inaugural Court (1903-04)	310	298	8	6	10	3.8%	Unanimity
Two Courts (1939-40)	323	241	40	75	67	25.4%	Dissonance
Reporting Judge (1952-53)	258	208	33	33	46	19.4%	Consensus
Modern Court (1979-80)	176	112	55	82	50	36.7%	Dissent

★=Yearly average based on two years

high bench. Further, the leadership provided by the likes of Ralph Oregon Dunbar and Theodore Lamme Stiles tended to enhance collective aspects over individual ones.

The departmental system of dividing the nine justices into two panels encouraged dissonance. The individual judge played a more independent role within the five-judge panel system. The "two-court" system could avoid the collective pressures evident when a full court of nine had to work together. Apparently, the chief justice's role as mediator became diffused when he presided over both departments.

The reporting-judge deliberations tended to bring the court closer together in a moderate agreement or consensus mode. Disagreement continued, but not at the pace of earlier benches. The justices still made decisions primarily in departments, but a judge's prior research on a case, which he or she then shared, appeared to bring about a relative degree of consensus. Involving law clerks in the deliberations and in the communications network also seemed to bring more agreement. Likely, the pressures of crowded dockets compelled the judges to rely more on each other, question less, and dissent infrequently.

Finally, the modern court's manageable case load, its jurisdiction over only the contentious cases either unresolved by lower courts or requiring a definite decision, and *en banc* hearings, encouraged the court's individual deliberations. A relatively high rate of dissent resulted.

In Chapter Two, I suggested that judges of the Washington high bench are shaped by their selection experiences. Accountability, as measured by contestedness and roll-off, affects their responses to constitutional questions. This chapter demonstrates that all the judges serving at a particular time must observe the same decisional procedures. These procedures invariably interact with the effects of selection pressures. For example, a relatively accountable bench characterized the inaugural years. The inaugural decisional process was collective, a process that may enhance accountability. In contrast, an individual decisional process highlighted the independent years of the modern court, with its high roll-off and low contestedness. The creative characteristic of the individual decisional mode seems more in harmony with independently minded jurists. However, even with the importance of selection and decisional procedures, the portrait of the Washington high bench is not yet complete.

An examination of the personal background of each judge will provide a sharper image of his or her particular contribution to the rulings of the high bench. Each judge brings to the court a special background. And it is the mix of individual backgrounds, sharpened by the variations in selection but moderated by the decisional process, that gives to any court its special character.

Notes

1. For accounts of the court's decisional process see Charles Sheldon and Michael Stohr-Gillmore, "In the Beginning: The Washington Supreme Court a Century Ago," *University of Puget Sound Law Review*, 12 (1989), pp. 247-284; Frank Rudkin, "The Court's Work," *Washington State Bar Association Proceedings* (1906), pp. 170-171; Overton Ellis, "The Court's Work," *Washington State Bar Association Proceedings* (1914), pp. 179-180; *Seattle Daily Times*, 3 Sept. 1924; John Mitchell, "Address at State Prosecuting Attorneys Association," *Washington State Bar Association Proceedings* (1921), pp. 172-173; Sheldon, "The Washington Supreme Court: What it was Like Thirty Years Ago," *Gonzaga Law Review*, 19 (1983-1984), pp. 231-264; Robert Brachtenbach, "Mechanics of Supreme Court Decisionmaking," *Washington State Bar News*, 8 (1973), pp. 8-11; and Sheldon, "An Interpretation of the Judicial Process: The Washington Supreme Court as a Small Group," *Gonzaga Law Review*, 13 (1977), pp. 97-139.
2. Sheldon, *A Century of Judging: A Political History of the Washington Supreme Court* (1988), p. 241.
3. Ellis, "The Court's Work," p. 180.
4. From the passing sheets for *Thompson v. Mermer*, 1944; *Longview Co. v. Cowlitz*, 1944; and *Luellen v. Aberdeen*, 1944; all in Court Reporter's Office, Olympia. Also, according to the "assignment sheets" that record who had drawn the initial reporting assignments, in approximately 10 percent of the cases heard in 1950 the reporting judge either lost the vote or the opinion was reassigned.
5. Law clerks were first hired in 1937 when the judges brought in three personal assistants to help. By the 1950s each judge had his own law clerk and, today, two clerks per justice is the standard. See Sheldon, "Law Clerking with a State Supreme Court: View from the Perspective of the Personal Assistants to the Judges," *Justice System Journal*, 6 (1981), pp. 346-371; and Sheldon, "The Evolution of Law Clerking with the Washington Supreme Court: From 'Elbow Clerks' to 'Puisne Judges'," *Gonzaga Law Review*, 24 (1988-1989), pp. 45-84.
6. Amendment XXXVIII, approved by voters in November 1962, reads: "When necessary for the prompt and orderly administration of justice a majority of the supreme court is empowered to authorize judges or retired judges of courts of record of this state, to perform, temporarily, judicial duties in the supreme court." Washington Constitution, Article IV, Section 2a. Also see Sheldon and Frank Weaver, *Politicians, Judges and the People: A Study in Citizen's Participation* (1980).
7. Amendment L reads in part: *Court of Appeals* "In addition to the courts authorized in Section 1 of this Article, judicial power is vested in a court of appeals, which shall be established by statute. . . . The jurisdiction of the court of appeals shall be as provided by statute or by rules authorized by statute." Washington Constitution, Article IV, Section 30.
8. Original appellate jurisdiction was exercised in cases declaring a statute to be unconstitutional, death penalty convictions, overruling of prior cases by the supreme court and other conflicts of law, actions against state officials, and those cases "involving a fundamental and urgent issue of broad public import which requires prompt and ultimate determination." The court of appeals exercised discretionary review of the decisions unless the appeals bench reversal of a trial court's decision was not unanimous. In that event, the supreme court was required to review. See *Rules of Appellate Procedure* (RAP 4.2a).
9. Sheldon, *A Century of Judging*, pp. 246-251.
10. Steven Peterson, "Dissent in American Courts," *Journal of Politics*, 43 (1981), pp. 412-434.
11. See Sheldon, *A Century of Judging*, pp. 249-251

Chapter Four
Judicial Profiles: The Uses of Biography

When supreme court policy considerations mesh with judicial review, justices are governing. Learning about the judges' constitutional considerations, knowing how they were selected and how they undertook their deliberations are the first steps toward understanding the behavior of these governors in robes. The object now is to record and organize background biographical information on each of the eighty jurists who have filled eighty-eight seats on the state's court of last resort since 1889.[1]

One can only comprehend the effect of background on the judges' behavior by placing jurists in their appropriate context. The preceding chapters provided that context, and this one records noteworthy events in a judge's life, events that helped shape her or his perspectives of the law and politics.

Purposes of Judicial Biographies

Judicial biographies have a long and respected tradition in the literature on courts. These life stories are written for a variety of reasons. Persons who serve on appellate courts at the federal and state levels are not ordinary people; their lives provide encouragement and inspiration to others.[2] Biographies of political leaders are also written as a record of the past. Judges make decisions that impact society. A record of their personal views on those decisions supplies historians with documentation of important events.[3] Judicial biographies provide a means of holding judges accountable, although largely after-the-fact. As public officials, judges must not, in a democratic society, remain anonymous nor escape responsibility.[4] Accounts of past judicial records, good or bad, provide lessons for new generations of lawyers and judges, for, like everyone else, judges are products of their past. Knowing about that past helps people to understand the present and can guide future behavior.

Life histories can tell us much about the process of judging. Biographical accounts often reveal how decisions were made, the motives behind those decisions, and reactions to them.[5] Studies of a judge's life can also idealize and exonerate. Concern for a person's reputation often compels judges, or those who write about them, to justify a particular policy.[6] Of course, this form of biography is utilized by politicians generally.

The motivation behind this collection of brief accounts of supreme court judges, however, is to develop an understanding of the court. The enterprise

The 1911 supreme court. *Top row, left to right:* Mark Fullerton, Frank Rudkin, Herman Crow, and Emmett Parker. *Seated, left to right:* Mack Gose, Stephen Chadwick, Ralph Dunbar, Wallace Mount, and George Morris.

in which political scientists, legal scholars, and historians often engage attempts to describe, explain, and ultimately, predict. But first the information must be collected, organized, and recorded. The object here is to present the raw data within a historical context. Much of the explanation and all of the prediction will be left to others.

Approaches to Judicial Biographies

A volume devoted to judicial profiles lends itself to at least two approaches, both designed to develop an understanding of courts. It is generally assumed that a person's past life experiences will, to a great extent, condition future behavior. Judges' decisions are products not only of the law, precedents, or constitution being applied and interpreted, but also of the decision-makers' upbringing, education, and training. Thus, to have a thorough understanding of how judges decide, we must understand their backgrounds.[7] The more daring among us may attempt to use the backgrounds to predict judicial decisions.[8]

Two lines of inquiry dominate the traditional approach to biographical studies of judges. Political scientists have led scholarly efforts to explain courts by viewing the political and personal interactions between and among members of an appellate bench. For example, much of what transpired on the Warren court can be understood only if one studies the relations between Felix Frankfurter and Hugo Black or William O. Douglas. In turn, to understand these relations, the student must know the backgrounds of the justices involved.[9] Courts, such as the "Warren Court," the "Rehnquist Court," or the "Vinson Court" – collections of judges sitting together at one particular time – constitute the focus of these studies.[10]

Another approach to understanding judicial behavior is to study the background of individual judges. From Albert J. Beveridge's monumental work on John Marshall[11] to H. N. Hirsch's short but pithy study of Felix Frankfurter,[12] scholars have attempted to isolate the causes of one judge's motivations, attitudes, and behavior. In both these lines of inquiry researchers have provided rich descriptions, some explanations, and, on rare occasions, prediction.

A third approach may be taken with the type of information presented in this volume. Through time, a particular legal culture gathers around a court and produces a type of judge who tends to decide cases in predictable ways. As one team of scholars has noted, "[J]udicial background might be viewed as operating cumulatively, affecting the character and style of courts (not merely individual judges) and helping to explain how and why one court differs in spirit from another."[13] The Washington high bench appears to have enjoyed distinct "cultures" as a result of the patterns of selection, decisional procedures, and judicial review that have evolved over the past century. However, research results are mixed, largely because there have been few attempts to compare court cultures over the long time-span necessary.[14]

This volume is a beginning in that long-term comparison, providing materials to stimulate readers' curiosity, hopefully compelling some to pursue further: (1) the relationship between judges' backgrounds and their decisions; (2) the interactions among judges who served together at one particular time; or (3) the comparison of one group of judges with another group serving at a different time.

The behavioral aspects of Washington Supreme Court justices are reported in detail and analyzed in a companion volume, *A Century of Judging: A Political History of the Washington Supreme Court*.[15] The two volumes considered together may contribute to a better understanding of those sometimes brilliant, other times bumbling, but always influential policy makers among the jurists who have served on Washington's court of last resort.

A Biographical Summary

The background of any person, judge or not, to a significant degree determines his or her future. A part of this background relates to experiences beyond an individual's control, and part to the conscious choices a person makes. Generally, background experiences fall into three categories.[16] *Ascriptive* attributes are those personal characteristics with which a person is born. For example, one's ethnicity, race, and gender are givens, as are one's parents, place and time of birth, and social circumstances. *Acquired* characteristics are those experiences and training one gains throughout the course of a life. These attributes are, to a significant degree, a matter of choice. For judges, acquired characteristics likely to influence subsequent judicial careers would be educational experiences, legal practice, religion, and public offices held. *Affiliated* characteristics are also a matter of choice, such as experience gained through political organizations, fraternal groups, social clubs, and civic activities.

Ascribed, acquired, and affiliated characteristics tend to reinforce each other. For example, a man born into the working class who attends public schools while working and then joins the public defender's office will likely be a different sort of judge than one born into comfortable circumstances, educated at private schools, and selected to the bench from a lucrative law firm.

Over the past century, eighty justices have filled eighty-eight positions on the state's high bench. Those who have served on the supreme court have displayed a variety of backgrounds. Table Six summarizes these characteristics.

Table Six

Background Characteristics of Those Filling the Eighty-eight Positions

Ascribed Characteristics			
Birth Place			
	In-state	24	(27%)
	Out-of-state	64	(73%)
Upbringing			
	Rural	38	(43%)
	Urban	50	(57%)
Average age when appointed or elected		52 years	
Parents'			
Occupation	Farming	28	(32%)
	Working	14	(16%)
	Proprietary	6	(7%)
	Professional	10	(11%)
	Attorney	13	(15%)
	Other/Unknown	17	(19%)
Achieved Characteristics			
Precollege			
	Private	17	(20%)
	Public	66	(75%)
	Unknown	5	(5%)
College			
	In-state	22	(25%)
	Out-of-state	45	(51%)
	None	21	(24%)
	Private	34	(39%)
	Public	33	(38%)

Table Six (Continued)

Achieved Characteristics (Continued)			
Law School			
In-state		29	(33%)
U. of Washington		25	(86%)
Gonzaga		3	(10%)
U. of Puget Sound		1	(4%)
Out-of-state		40	(46%)
Top-flight law schools		14	(16%)
Private		31	(35%)
Public		38	(43%)
Office study (clerked)		19	(22%)
Professional Experience			
Law firm		37	(42%)
Sole practice		9	(10%)
Prosecutor		34	(39%)
Other		8	(9%)
Prior judicial experience		55	(63%)
Appointed		54	(62%)
Average years served		11 years	
Legislative experience		20	(23%)
Other public office		20	(23%)
Residence			
Seattle		28	(32%)
Spokane		11	(13%)
Tacoma		11	(13%)
Eastern Washington		20	(23%)
Western Washington		16	(19%)
Affiliated Characteristics			
Religion			
Protestant		67	(76%)
Catholic		8	(9%)
Jewish		1	(1%)
Unknown/None		12	(14%)
Political Party			
Republican		57	(65%)
Democrat		31	(35%)
Partisan activist		61	(70%)
Group Member			
Social		51	(59%)
Patriotic		19	(22%)
Civic		28	(32%)
Free Mason		40	(47%)

This data and the following profiles indicate that we still know comparatively little about our judges. Before time and memory obliterate the record, more historical materials should be collected and shared. Because Washingtonians are still close to their pioneer past, attorneys, family members, and other judges remember many of those who have sat on the high bench, making interviewing a worthwhile enterprise. Papers of judges are becoming available in several research repositories and can be used to expand the following essays.[17] The Washington Supreme Court is a public institution making public policy. The public ought to know more about it.

Notes

1. Although eighty people have been selected for the supreme court, several have served in two separate positions. Between 1890 and 1912, Judges White, Hadley, and Chadwick served twice on the court. Judge Holcomb was first elected in 1915, defeated in 1927, but returned immediately to the bench through gubernatorial appointment. Between 1933 and 1948 Judge Grady served in a temporary position and then was elected. Judge Millard served a second but short term in 1956, and Judge Foster was appointed to a short term and then elected to a full term the same year. In 1970 Judge Sharp was appointed, then defeated in an election, and subsequently reappointed in 1971. The statistics in Table Six account for these additional appointments or elections, bringing the total of positions filled to eighty-eight. Judges Webster, Mallery, Dore, Schwellenbach, and Callow were appointed to fill short-term vacancies before assuming the seats to which they were elected. They are not counted twice.
2. Hugo Black Jr., *My Father: A Remembrance* (1975); and Harry Ball, *The Vision and the Dream of Justice Hugo Black* (1975).
3. Earl Warren, *The Memoirs of Chief Justice Earl Warren* (1977); or Harlan B. Phillips, ed., *Felix Frankfurter Reminisces* (1960).
4. Bruce A. Murphy, *The Brandeis/Frankfurter Connection* (1982).
5. Carl B. Swisher, *Stephen J. Field: Craftsman of the Law* (1930); and Leonard Baker, *John Marshall* (1974).
6. G. Edward White, *Earl Warren, A Public Life* (1982).
7. C. Neal Tate, "Personal Attribute Models of the Voting Behavior of U. S. Supreme Court Justices," *American Political Science Review*, 75 (1981), pp. 355-367; and John Schmidhauser, *The Supreme Court: Its Politics, Personalities, and Procedures* (1961).
8. Charles Sheldon, *The American Judicial Process* (1974).
9. H. N. Hirsch, *The Enigma of Felix Frankfurter* (1981).
10. C. Herman Pritchett, *The Roosevelt Court: A Study in Judicial Politics and Values, 1937-47* (1948); and Pritchett, *Civil Liberties and The Vinson Court* (1954).
11. Albert Beveridge, *The Life of John Marshall* (1916).
12. Hirsch, *Enigma of Felix Frankfurter.*
13. Robert Kagen, Bobbie Infelise, and Robert Detlefsen, "American State Supreme Court Justices, 1900-1970," *American Bar Foundation Research Journal* (1984), pp. 371-407.
14. Christian G. Fritz, *Federal Justice: The California Court of Ogden Hoffman, 1851-1891* (1991).
15. Sheldon, *A Century of Judging: A Political History of the Washington Supreme Court* (1988).
16. Beverly Blair Cook, "Sentencing Behavior of Federal Judges: Draft Cases, 1972," *University of Cincinnati Law Review*, 42 (1973), pp. 597-633, 667-671.
17. The Manuscripts, Archives and Special Collections division of Holland Library, Washington State University, and the state archives in Olympia have extensive collections of oral histories, personal papers, research notes, and documents as a result of a supreme court archives project sponsored by the state archives and the secretary of state. These archives will hopefully be replenished by the donation of papers by other members of the supreme court.

Biographies

Donald George Abel
November 7, 1946-September 9, 1947

Born: December 23, 1894
Lincoln, Kansas
University of Washington (1917)
University of Washington School of Law,
LL.B. (1919)
Presbyterian
Died: July 8, 1980
Prosecuting Attorney (1922-1926)
State Director, Works Progress Administra-
tion (1936-1940)
Commissioner, State Department of Public
Service (1940-1942; 1956-1957)
State Liquor Control Board (1957-1967)
Democrat
Appointed

Donald G. Abel was born late in 1894 in Lincoln, a small central Kansas town. At age sixteen his family moved to Hoquiam, Washington, where his father— who later served fourteen years as Grays Harbor County Superior Court judge— opened a law office. Don graduated from Hoquiam High School in 1913 and enrolled at the University of Washington. His popularity among students was evident when his classmates elected him class president. He also lettered in varsity football in 1916 and 1917. During World War I he served with the Ninety-first Infantry Division, being cited for bravery in the Battle of Argonne Forest and promoted to the rank of captain. At the end of the war Abel returned to the University of Washington School of Law and graduated with an LL.B. in 1919. After admittance to the bar the same year he opened a law office in Chehalis.

In 1922 voters elected him prosecuting attorney of Lewis County and he served two terms, until 1926. His activities in Democratic party affairs increased. In 1932 he ran for the Democratic nomination to Congress in Washington's Third District, losing by more than 2,000 votes in the primary. The future judge served as special assistant attorney general attached to the 1935 legislature, where he helped draft legislation. In 1936 Abel became director of the Works Progress Administration for Washington state, a position he held until 1940. His appointment was based largely on patronage, but upon assuming his WPA responsibilities Abel announced that:

> The administrative employees of the W.P.A. will not take part in factional party politics. There will be no exceptions to this rule. Naturally, I expect the men and women of the staff to attend political meetings the same as they would attend church or go to the theatre. However, they will not belong to any political club which has for its object the advancement of the candidacy of any person seeking office during the coming primary campaign.

This statement was representative of Abel's public career. Although highly partisan, when appointed to an administrative position, he set partisanship aside.

Governor Clarence Martin appointed him commissioner of the state public service department immediately upon his resignation from the WPA. He had been anxious to give up his federal job and had considered returning to partisan politics either as a candidate for the U. S. Senate or governor. He became one of several candidates considered for appointment to the U. S. Senate when Louis B. Schwellenbach resigned to accept a federal judgeship.

After two years as head of the department of public service, Abel resigned to oppose Judge John Robinson for the state supreme court. Robinson handily won the September primary by nearly 34,000 votes. After his defeat, Abel returned to private practice in Chehalis.

In November 1946, when Walter Beals accepted temporary assignment as judge at the Nuremberg Trials, Governor Mon Wallgren appointed Abel to the temporary supreme court vacancy. In less than a year, Abel developed a reputation as a liberal-activist.

Upon leaving the state's high bench in 1947, Abel returned to Chehalis to private practice. His partisan activities still remained important to him. In 1952, party members elected him chairman of the state Democratic central committee, where he remained until 1955. The following year he served as state chairman for the gubernatorial campaign of Albert Rosellini, who rewarded his efforts by appointing him temporary chairman of the public service commission, a position he had held seventeen years earlier. In July 1957, Abel resigned from the commission to accept appointment as chairman of the state liquor control board which supervised the state monopoly of liquor sales and enforcement. Abel did not ask for the job, as the following newspaper account makes clear:

> Finding the proper man for the chairmanship turned out to be one of Rosellini's toughest problems. He finally located him right in his own Cabinet in Don G. Abel. . . This required a selling job. Abel didn't want the Liquor Control chairmanship, and probably isn't anxious even now to step into the position which required a keen ability to mix a measure of politics with the obligation to direct and maintain the liquor monopoly on a stable, profit-making basis where it will continue to inspire public confidence.

Abel began immediately to change board personnel, hiring new assistants and inspectors. In 1958, Rosellini reappointed him to a full nine-year board term.

Judge Abel maintained an effective and scandal-free board, although he frequently came under fire from the legislature and, later, from the governor, for his strict enforcement and close supervision. Some called him the "Czar" of the state monopoly, but church representatives, temperance groups, and alcohol rehabilitation agencies much admired him. His view of enforcement contained a moralistic if not religious element. By 1963 he had fallen out with his former benefactor, and the governor replaced him as chairman. However, he remained as one of the three commissioners until he retired in 1967.

Judge Abel married Marian Ross of Chehalis. They had three children, Donald, Jr., Margaret, and Janice. The son became a member of the Washington bar and was also prominent in state politics. Judge Abel actively participated in the American Legion and Veterans of Foreign Wars, serving twice as state commander of both organizations. He was president of the Chehalis Chamber of Commerce and an active Mason, Elk, and Eagle. He was several years a trustee of the Chehalis Presbyterian Church. His hobby was flower gardening. In 1980, Judge Abel died at the age of eighty-five.

Selected References

See *Seattle Times,* 27 May 1936, 23 Je. 1957, and 25 Mar. 1977; memorial services, *Washington Reports,* vol. 95, 2d (1981), pp. xxxvi-xlii; and Charles Sheldon, *A Century of Judging: A Political History of the Washington Supreme Court* (1988), p. 102.

Thomas Jefferson Anders
November 11, 1889-January 10, 1905

Born: April 4, 1838
Republic, Ohio
University of Michigan Law School, LL.B.
(1861)
Died: June 19, 1909
Prosecuting Attorney (1871-1890)
Walla Walla City Attorney (1878-1890)
Republican
Elected

Thomas Jefferson Anders was born April 4, 1838 in Seneca County near the towns of Republic and Bloomville in north-central Ohio. His father engaged in farming and lumbering. At age twelve Anders moved to Republic to attend public schools and the Seneca County Academy. After graduating from the academy he taught in local schools, became a member of the Republic school board at age seventeen, and soon joined the academy's faculty. He resigned in 1858 to attend the University of Michigan law department. Upon graduation in 1861 he taught school and practiced law in Wisconsin.

For health reasons he moved to Montana in 1864, driving an ox team. After regaining his health and accumulating some money from mining in Montana, Anders moved to Walla Walla, Washington Territory, and opened a law office in November, 1871. He successfully ran on the Republican ticket for prosecuting attorney of the eastern Washington district in 1872, and voters repeatedly reelected him. He served a total of eighteen years. He returned to private practice in Walla Walla, but was elected city attorney in 1878. He held this position for twelve years, concurrently with his prosecuting attorney post. In 1886 he was elected prosecuting attorney for Walla Walla County, an office he held until elected to the supreme court. Anders married Viola Hull in Walla Walla in December 1873, and the couple had six children.

Republicans nominated Anders to the supreme court in 1889 and he received 34,302 votes, the most of any of the judges running. He led the Republican judicial tickets again in 1892 and 1898. Upon the suggestion of Judge Elmon Scott, the youngest member of the new court, his colleagues unanimously selected Anders, the oldest member, as the state's first chief justice.

Judge Anders was a scholar of the law rather than a flamboyant politician. According to one early account:

> He is not possessed of a strong voice, or commanding presence but is tall and thin with a reserved, dignified, deliberate manner. He has a large head and intellectual face and his utterances, whether before a judge or jury or upon the rostrum, create a favorable impression.

Anders did not make hasty judicial decisions:

> Judge Anders was a very conscientious judge, so much so that it was hard for him to come to a decision. He was well grounded in the general principles of the law, but he would spend an inconceivable amount of time in looking up authorities in support of even fundamental principles. He seemed to be anxious to render his opinions satisfactory to the layman as to members of the bar.

An analysis of his voting record during the court's first five years confirms these appraisals. He wrote fewer opinions for the court than any of his colleagues. While he penned 181 majority opinions, the court average was 274. Ceremonial and administrative responsibilities might have been a burden, but even when Anders relinquished the chief's responsibilities to Ralph Dunbar in 1892, he continued to write fewer opinions than his colleagues.

Anders rarely cast a dissenting vote and wrote only five dissenting opinions. He maintained the lowest dissent rate of any judge on the court at that time. However, his opinions were persuasive. His carefully researched views were generally longer than those of his colleagues, and subsequent courts cited his opinions more than any of his fellow justices.

Anders provided a key swing vote in divisive cases that occasionally confronted the court. The first bench was divided between activist Theodore Stiles, one eager to exercise judicial review, and restraintists Elmon Scott and Ralph Dunbar, who gave the legislature the benefit of the doubt in constitutional issues. Moderates John P. Hoyt and Anders provided balance between the extremes in cases involving constitutional questions.

Judge Anders retired from the bench at the end of his second term in January, 1905. He was sixty-seven years old. By that time he had become somewhat isolated from his colleagues and his decisions tended to follow a relatively conservative line. He died at age seventy-one on June 19, 1909.

Selected References

See *Seattle Times,* 12 Sept. 1889; Washington State Bar Association *Proceedings* (1909), p. 197; C. S. Reinhart, *History of the Washington Supreme Court of the Territory and State of Washington* (n.d.), pp. 92, 100; and Charles Sheldon and Michael Stohr-Gillmore, "In the Beginning: The Washington Supreme Court a Century Ago," *University of Puget Sound Law Review,* vol. 12 (Winter 1989), p. 247.

James A. Andersen
July 25, 1984-

Born: September 21, 1924
Auburn, Washington
University of Washington, B.A. (1949)
University of Washington, LL.B. (1951)
Episcopalian
Deputy Prosecutor (1953-1957)
State House of Representatives (1959-1967)
State Senate (1968-1972)
Court of Appeals (1975-1984)
Republican
Appointed

A July, 1984 newspaper account of James A. Andersen's appointment to the state's
high court began with these words:

> A man who rose from South King County coal mines to become a state Senate
> Republican leader, and then a judge, was appointed to the Washington supreme
> court yesterday... [He] said he never thought his life would take such a presti-
> gious turn in the days when he worked in the Sunshine coal mine at Ravensdale.
> "Never in my wildest dreams."

It is unlikely that anyone who knew the young Andersen would have predicted
his future achievements. Nonetheless, he has remained true to coal mining beginnings: somewhat shy among strangers, not given to pretentiousness, always
going directly to the point, and often colorful in his responses. Yet he is at ease
among the politically powerful, confident in his views, and tough in the give-
and-take of judicial conference. The justice is a balanced mixture of worker, politician, and intellectual.

Justice Andersen's grandparents immigrated to the United States from Scan-
dinavia near the end of the last century. One grandfather, Christen Norgaard,
settled in Minnesota where he and wife Hansina farmed and raised a large family, the youngest child being the justice's mother, Margaret Cecilia Norgaard.
His other grandfather, Carl Andersen, mined coal in towns from Illinois and Montana to Washington. Carl and wife Lorena also raised a large family including
James Andersen, Sr., born in Newcastle, Washington, in 1909. Justice Andersen
was born in 1924 during the time his father worked the coal mines near
Ravensdale.

Young Andersen attended grade school in Seattle, and finished high school in Walla Walla in 1942. He returned to Seattle, enrolled at the University of Washington, and finished one quarter before running out of money. Then, like his father, he went to work in Ravensdale's mines. In 1943 he enlisted in the army, which sent him to the University of Nevada to train with a special engineering unit. But the army discontinued the training program and used members of his outfit to complete manpower requirements of divisions being sent overseas. It assigned Andersen to Company C, 63rd Armored Infantry Battalion of the 11th Armored Division of General George Patton's Third Army.

Andersen, gravely wounded in the Battle of the Bulge, suffered serious shrapnel wounds in his knee and thigh. Out of 250 men in his company only about fifty survived an intensive campaign against General Von Rundstedt's elite armored and Waffen SS troops; most were wounded or killed. Andersen was one of the lucky ones. His battlefield experiences had a profound effect on him. "We were so very, very young," he recalled, "and we expected to live forever. We had not yet discovered that death knows no age limits. We learned otherwise in that bloody battle, however; where there were estimated 81,000 American casualties and 100,000 German casualties." He adds that "when it became irrefutably clear to me that I was not immortal, it came as one hell of a jolt. And nothing so educates a person as shock. I expect that was the moment of my growing up." He remembered, "It was about then that I started thinking about how I spend whatever additional time on earth, if any, that God might see fit to grant me."

After being hospitalized for his injuries for most of a year, first in Europe and then in the United States, he obtained a disability discharge from the army. "I was a disabled veteran at the ripe old age of twenty-one years and a few days," he remembered. "Where once I looked forward to being a track star, I was now doing well to walk."

After the war, Andersen drifted for a while, angry and confused:

> I have never before nor since met anybody who even approached me in the depths of my bitterness... I had killed many people. I had lost every friend I had. I bummed around the country, riding my thumb, through the Midwest, starting out for Arizona. I wanted to go somewhere where there was sunshine. I got drunk in Los Angeles, ran out of money, and got a job at the terminal island shipyards, very lonely, very lost.

It was another turning point. Until then his dream of a job was to work indoors, perhaps with a men's clothing store. But now he decided there had to be something better for him, so he took advantage of the G. I. Bill, quit his job at Terminal Island, returned to Seattle, and enrolled at the University of Washington.

As an undergraduate Andersen was erratic, doing exceptionally well in courses that interested him and barely passing in those that appeared to be irrelevant to his career interests. In 1949 he received a degree in political science and went to law school. Andersen graduated with an LL.B in 1951 and, as he put it, "conned my way into" the King County Prosecutor's Office under Charles O. Carroll. He knew no lawyers, had no experience, and had not been politically active. He simply talked Carroll into giving him a chance. In a few years with the prosecutor's office, Andersen compiled one of its best records. He prosecuted many of the office's most important cases involving murder, bribery, robbery, and rape. Prosecutor Carroll remarked when Andersen left after three-and-a-half years, "Jimmy was one of the hardest working young attorneys I've had in my office. He lost only two cases."

In 1956 Andersen resigned from the prosecutor's staff and filed for election to the office of Washington State Attorney General, his first political campaign. He was thirty-one. Had he won he would have been the youngest attorney general in state history. He received the Republican nomination but lost the general election to John J. O'Connell, the Democratic candidate. He nevertheless polled more votes than all but one other statewide candidate of his party. Although he personally opposed it, a right to work measure had the practical effect of defeating him. The initiative attracted many Democrats to the polls, leading to the defeat of the entire Republican slate for statewide office. This was his only election defeat, but as he recalled, "It was a real blessing, though well concealed at the time. I learned in a way calculated to stay in mind that people were the ones running things."

Andersen learned his lesson well, defeating an incumbent Republican legislator in the 1958 election and serving with distinction for fourteen years in the state legislature, first in the house then the senate. Each time he ran for reelection he received the nonpartisan Seattle-King County Municipal League's highest rating. He also has the distinction of receiving more votes than any other Republican representative in state history.

"That was in the last days of the real 'citizens' legislature' " he recalled, "when if your neighbors paid you the honor of electing you, you closed up your store, office, or left the farm for sixty days or so every two years. Then you went to Olympia, decided on a state budget, passed some bills, and returned home. Those days are gone forever in this state, and it has now become virtually a full-time job. It was when the legislature turned that corner that I had no real choice but to leave."

Columnist Adele Ferguson commented that Andersen

went into politics and stayed there 15 years, plugging away at filling loopholes in laws on law enforcement, like granting immunity to private citizens aiding a police officer, making it a crime to mutilate or trample on the American flag, creating a statewide criminal identification bureau, preventing pawnbrokers who received stolen goods from making the rightful owner pay to get their property back. And who tried again and again to get mandatory sentences for drug pushers. It was his bill that set up Medic I, and it was his bill that established Seattle, Bellevue and Edmonds Community Colleges.

A conflict between his law practice and legislative duties prompted Andersen to resign from the lawmaking body. There was not enough time to serve his legal clients and also perform the leadership roles his legislative colleagues assigned him. He had to make a choice, and the law won over politics.

Until late 1974, when Governor Daniel Evans appointed him to the Washington Court of Appeals Division One in Seattle, Andersen committed himself to his law practice, winning most of his cases and earning a respectable living. He won because of his thoroughness. As he worded it, he "put a little bit of myself" into each case. This strain, as well as missing public service, prompted Andersen to accept Governor Evans's offer, and he assumed his position on the court of appeals in January 1975. In standing for election to the appeals bench a short time later, Judge Andersen won overwhelmingly, garnering approximately seventy percent of the popular vote against an experienced candidate. Part of his success can be attributed to his eighty-one percent favorable vote from attorneys in the bar poll.

After almost ten years on the court of appeals, Republican Governor John D. Spellman appointed Andersen to the supreme court. In so doing, he filled the vacancy created by the death of Justice Charles Stafford.

Justice Andersen regards himself as a judicial restraintist. He is not "one who believes that the judiciary is the fountain of all . . . knowledge in this world." For him, "there has to be a good reason to change the law . . . Give power to those elected to govern." At the same time, Andersen is concerned about the lack of balance, as he sees it, between the rights of the accused and those of victims: "I spent enough years as a prosecutor sitting with the victims of crime to understand what crime really is and what it does to people." The justice has tended to align himself with those on the bench who take a moderate-to-conservative view regarding criminal law. At the same time, he has remained a staunch protector of First Amendment principles. He is considered by most to be the staunchest advocate on the court for freedom of the press.

Justice Andersen has written more than his share of majority opinions, garnering a better-than-average number of votes from his colleagues. His reluctance to dissent confirms him as a strong believer in the court "team concept." A sample of nearly 500 opinions show that Andersen filed only nine dissenting opinions. He recognizes that he does not dissent often but rather tries "to work it out" with the other justices.

Writing for a unanimous court in *State v. Gunwall*, Justice Andersen, in a straightforward style that separates each topic into sections and subsections, established standards for applying state constitutional provisions to issues before the court. Although he accepted liberal provisions of the state constitution, Andersen limited those provisions by insisting they be applied only in accordance with well-defined and strict standards. In *Gunwall* Andersen brought together those critics who regarded the new emphasis upon the state constitution as "constitution shopping" and "all sail and no anchor" with those who viewed state constitutions as the "triumph of personal liberty" or a means to "adapt our law . . . to changing civilization." Politics is the art of the possible, accomplished by compromise. The *Gunwall* opinion is an example of that art. By applying carefully defined standards to state constitutional provisions, the justice imposed a degree of accountability on the activism of judicial new federalism.

Justice Andersen has two children, Tia Louise and James Blair. He is divorced, and readily admits that he is a "workaholic" and that his work is his hobby.

Selected References

Andersen's oral history interview is part of the supreme court collection, Washington State Archives. Also see *Bellingham Times*, 7 Oct. 1987; *Spokane Spokesman-Review*, 10 Jy. 1984; *Bellevue American*, 12 Jan. 1972; and supreme court "Induction Ceremony Program," 24 Jy. 1984.

William David Askren
January 12, 1925-December 1, 1928

Born: October 1, 1885
Mount Ayr, Iowa
Presbyterian
Died: October 21, 1964
Deputy and Chief Prosecutor (1913-1914;
    1919-1920)
Superior Court (1921-1924)
Republican
Elected

William David Askren, son of William Wirt and Nettie Eleanor (Lawhead) Askren, was born in southern Iowa only a few miles from the Missouri border. He attended public schools in the small farming community of Mount Ayr until the age of fourteen when the family went to Oklahoma. In 1902 Askren moved to Tacoma. His first employment there was as a hotel bellhop; later he clerked in a pawn shop. In the evenings and during spare time Askren studied the law. In 1908 the future jurist took the bar exam and was admitted to practice in Washington at the age of twenty-three. After five years in private practice Askren was appointed deputy prosecuting attorney for Pierce County, serving until 1915. After another stint of private practice he successfully campaigned for Pierce County Prosecutor, defeating his opponent by more than 2,000 votes. Fears of Industrial Workers of the World (IWW) insurrection focused attention on prosecutors, and in 1920, following the Centralia massacre, he prosecuted thirty-six members of the IWW under a new anti-syndicalism law. The jury found all guilty of "publishing and circulating seditious literature" and of "criminal syndicalism."

In April 1920 Askren received considerable attention when Mrs. Julia Smith, whom he had recently prosecuted, shot him. She drove to Askren's home in an automobile owned by an attorney for whom she worked. Attired in men's clothes, she shot the judge point-blank as he opened his door. The bullet narrowly missed his heart, but he remained near death for weeks. He recovered completely, however, and in September voters elected him to the Pierce County Superior Court. He benefitted both from the publicity surrounding the shooting and from his success as a prosecutor.

In 1922 William H. Pemberton, Whatcom County Superior Court Judge, unseated incumbent Chester Hovey for a two-year term on the high bench. He had strong backing from both farm and labor organizations. Pemberton's plans to seek a full term in 1924 caused concern among the state bar leaders who considered him to represent the extreme left. At their urging, William Askren filed for the supreme court and narrowly defeated Pemberton after a hard and bitter campaign. It was the first time the state bar association publicly endorsed a supreme court candidate.

"Billy" Askren served only three years of his full term on the supreme court, resigning December 1, 1928 to return to private practice. In explaining his resignation the judge announced:

> It has been a pleasure to serve the people of the state, and I have enjoyed to the full the association with my colleagues on the bench. Mrs. Askren and I regret to leave Olympia, but both our daughters are attending the University of Washington and we feel that it will add to the happiness of the family if we all live in the same city.

The judge joined the new law firm of Allen, Froude, Hilen, and Askren in Seattle. Four years later he formed a new partnership with noted attorney John E. Ryan. In the meantime, Askren's daughter Marian graduated from the University of Washington School of Law and passed the bar exam in 1931.

Askren became active in bar association and civic affairs in Seattle. In 1938 the mayor appointed him to the city library board, and reappointed him in 1940, 1945, and 1950. Problems in the Seattle police department in 1943 prompted Mayor Art Devin to select Askren as part of a three-man police advisory council to investigate the situation. Askren remained active in Republican party affairs as well, campaigning frequently for Republican candidates. While playing golf at the Seattle Golf and Country Club in November 1964, Judge Askren collapsed and died.

Askren married Bessie Frances Caldwell of Tacoma in 1907. They had two daughters, Kathryn Marie and Marian Eleanor. Judge Askren received a divorce in 1939 when the court declared Bessie incurably insane. In February 1940 he married Margaret Unger Hubbard, the ceremony performed in the temple of justice, in the chambers of Askren's former colleague, Justice John F. Main. The judge was active in Phi Delta Phi, the Masons, Elks, Rainier Club, and the Seattle Golf Club. He was an accomplished amateur magician, a member of the Pacific Coast Association of Magicians, the Society of American Magicians, and the Seattle Magic Ring, which he served as president.

In addition to his long tenure as a trustee of the Seattle Public Library, he was a charter member of the American Heritage Foundation, the Seattle Foundation, and twice a member of the Governor's Safety Conference.

Judge Matthew W. Hill recalled William Askren's years as judge and attorney on occasion of the court's memorial services in 1965:

His keen power of analysis; his capacity for clear logical thinking; his talent for terse, lucid and exact expression; his continued ability to function notwithstanding the exacting, continuous and ever urgent nature of the work; his understanding cooperation with the other judges; and his sound knowledge of fundamental legal principles were some of the qualities which contributed to his notable success on both the Superior and the Supreme Court.

His patience sometimes wore a bit thin, when it seemed to him that counsel was wasting the court's time on peripheral issues, and his infrequent questions from the bench were usually calculated to bring the errant advocate back to a consideration of decisive issues.

Although his record on both the trial and appellate bench was outstanding, the lure of advocacy brought him back to the legal arena where for 36 years he actively and successfully engaged in the practice of his profession.

In 1935, I had the privilege of assisting him in a minor role in the preparation of his brief in one of our landmark cases in labor law: *Safeway Stores, Inc. v. Retail Clerks Union Local 148.* I could not help but be impressed with his thoroughness, his exactness, and his ability to condense three pages of my discussion to a single paragraph; nor shall I ever forget his closing comment in the oral argument of that case, when the Chief Justice admonished him that he had used all of his time—he, with that characteristic smile said, "Your Honor, time goes a lot faster down here than it does up there." Which may well be the explanation of why he left the bench—he wanted to be where the time went faster.

Selected References

C. W. Taylor, *Eminent Judges and Lawyers of the Northwest* (1954), p. 118; W. P. Bonney, *History of Pierce County, Washington,* vol. 2 (1927), pp. 729-730; *Seattle Times,* 14 Oct. 1924; and memorial services, *Washington Reports,* vol. 65, 2d (1965), pp. xxi-xxvii.

Frederick Bausman
October 26, 1915-November 20, 1916

Born: March 23, 1861
Pittsburgh, Pennsylvania
University of Pittsburgh, A.B. (1881)
Harvard Law School, LL.B. (1883)
Protestant
Died: June 19, 1931
Seattle Charter Commission (1894-1896)
Democrat
Appointed

Judge Bausman's early life is relatively unknown. He received his undergraduate degree from the University of Pittsburgh in 1881, then went to Harvard Law School, graduating in 1883. Bausman did literary research in New York City and traveled extensively in Europe before moving to Olympia in 1886.

In Olympia he served as private secretary to Territorial Governor Eugene Sample (1887-1888), and as a member of the Territorial Code Commission in 1888. The commission had the charge of collecting and organizing the laws of the territory. In 1891 he entered Seattle's legal, social, and political life. He was, successively, a partner in the law firms of Bausman and Kelleher, and Bausman, Oldham, and Eggerman. As a member of the Seattle Charter Commission, Bausman helped write the Seattle city charter in 1896.

Bausman gained considerable attention for his defense of Seattle Mayor Hiram C. Gill in his recall election in 1911. He successfully challenged the Democratic nomination of Judge W. W. Black for governor in 1912. As a sitting judge, Black was ineligible to run for other state offices. This permitted Ernest Lister's name to be placed on the November ballot. Lister went on to win the governorship. In appreciation, Lister's first supreme court appointment went to Bausman, a move nearly everyone praised. One observer commented: "Frederick Bausman possesses enough brain and legal ability to supply three or four ordinary lawyers." Bausman's skills as a defense attorney and his knowledge of criminal law proved valuable contributions to the work of the court. Yet, apparently both Lister and Bausman regarded the appointment as temporary. Bausman possessed a "nervous, energetic personality" and soon grew bored with Olympia. Even his former supporters began to criticize him:

His career on the bench has not been startling, or created any demand for a monument prior to his demise. He is, in temperament, unfitted for the judiciary, and his appointment proved to be as unfortunate as some others of the governor... Come home Freddy. Your usefulness on the bench never happened. Give the state a chance to retrieve its loss.

In August 1916, Bausman announced he would not seek election to the supreme court, allowing the position to be openly contested in the September primaries. J. Stanley Webster won the primary and Governor Lister appointed him to complete the last few weeks in Bausman's term. Bausman returned to Seattle to practice with his old law firm, now named Bausman, Oldham, and Walkinshaw.

Bausman and his firm represented banks, irrigation companies, *The Seattle Times*, large estates, and "individual capitalists." Following the First World War, Bausman became alarmed at what he regarded as a propaganda effort on the part of Great Britain to beguile America back under its subjection. He viewed himself as a Paul Revere sounding a message about the English menace throughout the United States. After his wife died in 1929, Bausman left Seattle, and eventually the United States, to travel extensively in Europe. His concern for the continent and his pro-German stance came out in his books, *Let France Explain* (1923) and *Facing Europe* (1926). Writing was not new for the judge. He had started a literary career with the 1908 publication of *Adventures of a Nice Young Man*, written under the pen name "Aix."

Bausman married Adelaide Holmes of California in 1894. They had no children. He was a member of the University Club, Rainier Club, and Seattle Golf and Country Club. Although a staunch Democrat, Bausman was not especially active in partisan affairs following his supreme court resignation. He devoted himself to his law practice and to writing and lecturing about post-World War I Europe. He had been relatively active in bar association activities prior to his appointment to the bench, but only minimally concerned with organizational affairs after 1916.

In an address to the Washington State Bar Association after he left the bench, Bausman set forth his concept of judging:

Public opinion is a temporary public policy, and public policy is a permanent public opinion. It would be a dangerous judiciary that should yield at all to the one, but a stiff and needlessly narrow judiciary that should never accept the other. Public policy is the sum of the experience of a people, represents their morals and customs; indicates their national growth and silently distributes their offices and their power. Judges and legislators rather expound than create it, for while it is sometimes given a direction by statutes and decisions, it generally precedes them. Indeed, it is an interesting speculation whether all law did not originally come from public policy alone.

Our own jurisprudence, too stiff with precedent, is not so much to enrich itself from this source as, perhaps, could be wished...

I would say of public policy generally that, to my mind, it is the stream by which a fruitful jurisprudence is watered and renewed. By sudden inundation it is sometimes permitted to devastate, but in the bounty of its natural flow it continually revives and nourishes the fields of law.

Frederick Bausman was ahead of his times in his particular perception of the course of law.

Selected References

Seattle Times, 20 Oct. 1927 and 19 Je. 1931; and C. S. Reinhart, *The History of the Supreme Court of Washington Territory and State* (n.d.), pp. 80-81.

Walter Burges Beals

April 16, 1928-October 1, 1946;
September 10, 1947-September 10, 1951

Born: July 21, 1876
St. Paul, Minnesota
University of Washington School of Law,
LL.B. (1901)
Died: September 18, 1960
U. S. Army (1917-1919; 1946-1947)
Seattle Corporate Counsel (1923-1926)
Superior Court (1926-1928)
Republican
Appointed

Walter Beals was the son of James Burrill and Katherine (McMillan) Beals and a descendant of Roger Williams, founder of Rhode Island Colony. His family also included a chief justice of Rhode Island's supreme court, a chief justice of Minnesota's high court, and a senator from that state. Beals attended public schools in St. Paul, graduating from high school in 1895. He began law studies under an attorney's supervision, but ill health prompted his move to Bellingham, Washington. Within a year he became strong enough to work in a saw mill as a shingle weaver. In 1899 he entered the first law class at the University of Washington, graduating with a bachelor of laws degree in 1901. His first law practice was in partnership with Fred Rice Power. Upon the latter's death, Beals continued to practice in Seattle. He became active in Republican affairs but did not seek public office.

Walter married Othilia Gertrude Carroll in 1904, a classmate at the University of Washington School of Law. She was the first woman graduate in the school's first graduating class. She entered practice with her father and brother in Seattle, but resigned from practice when she married. However, during World War I she replaced her brother as Seattle justice of the peace when he went into the armed services. She resigned when her brother returned from the war. Active in civic affairs, she helped found the Seattle Milk Fund, served on the board of the Seattle Girl Scout Council, was state president and national vice president of the American Legion Auxiliary, and was active in the Red Cross. The couple had no children.

A member of the Washington National Guard from 1909, Walter Beals rose from an infantry private to the rank of major. He entered the U. S. Army in

August 1917, serving in the judge advocate's division. Beals spent sixteen months in France and saw action in the Meuse-Argonne offensive with American expeditionary forces. Promoted to lieutenant colonel and decorated with the Legion of Honor by France, he became one of the founders of the American Legion. Fluent in French, he remained in Europe for several months after the armistice as a liaison officer with the French government. Returning to Washington, Beals announced his intention to run for the state supreme court. In the September primary he failed to unseat any of the three incumbents, falling short by more than 30,000 votes.

In 1923 the Seattle city council appointed him first assistant corporate counsel. Three years later Governor Roland H. Hartley appointed him to the King County Superior Court, fulfilling a life-long ambition for the judge. Beals had earlier announced his intention to file against one of Hartley's appointees on the King County bench, but when another incumbent resigned, the governor appointed Beals. Two years later, in April 1928, Hartley promoted Beals to the state's high bench, an appointment widely praised. Beals received token opposition only once in his four reelection campaigns.

In October 1946 the Army ordered Judge Beals, a colonel in the reserves, into active duty as presiding judge in the trial of twenty-three Nazi doctors. On December 6, 1946, the trial opened in the musty, dark Nuremberg courtroom where the first major war crimes trials led to the conviction of Hermann Goering and other top Nazis. The twenty-three doctors charged with crimes against humanity had undertaken experiments involving sterilization, abortions, freezing, use of pressure chambers, and other torturous and fatal acts. The court found sixteen of the defendants guilty, sentencing seven to death while acquitting seven others. Of his experience at Nuremberg, Judge Beals reported:

> I think the trials have been a healthy thing. The section of the court reserved for Germans was well filled throughout the trial, to a large extent by classes of high school and college students. The German lawyers especially like the American court procedure we followed. We went upon the principle that defendants were presumed to be innocent until proven guilty.

Europe's 1946 winter was one of the worst on record. His cold, damp hotel, late hours, and a heavy workload took a toll on the judge, an ordeal from which he never completely recovered. Nonetheless, he was back on the bench when the state court's term opened in September, 1947. In August 1951 Judge Beals announced his retirement after twenty-three years on the high bench.

One of his colleagues later recalled of Beals:

> He was a great one to lobby for his opinions. On one occasion he reached my office before his opinion reached me via circulation.
>
> Walter had one bad habit as a judge: his format for writing opinions resulted in opinions of great length which caused lawyers to groan. Instead of stating the general problem on appeal and then discussing and deciding the assignments of

error on appeal, he started with a detailed analysis of the pleadings and the evidence, then an analysis of the judge's memo opinion and the facts and judgment entered or of all the instructions given. By the time he got to the [issues] on appeal, they seemed almost inconsequential. He was clearly a great man and a fair-to-good judge.

The judge assumed a moderate-to-conservative stance in his opinions and often provided the swing vote on close decisions. He proved fairly reluctant to confront public policy issues, preferring to leave such decisions to the political branches of government.

Judge Beals served as state commander of the Military Order of the Loyal Legion, and state president of the Sons of the American Revolution. He was a thirty-second degree Mason, a member of the Scottish Rite, and the Nile Temple of the Shrine. Over the years he accumulated a valuable collection of rare books and manuscripts, his Bible collection being one of the most complete held in private hands. He also had prized stamp, coin, and autograph collections. Cataloguing, displaying, and studying his collections occupied many of the judge's hours during retirement. On September 18, 1960, Judge Beals died at his home in Olympia at the age of eighty-three. Othilia Beals passed away in May 1970 at age ninety-four.

Selected References

C. S. Reinhart, *The History of the Supreme Court of the Territory and State of Washington* (n.d.), p. 81; Lloyd Spencer and Lancaster Pollard, *A History of the State of Washington,* vol. 4 (1937), p. 526; memorial services, *Washington Reports,* vol. 58, 2d (1961), pp. xvii-xxiv; and *Seattle Times,* 10 Aug. 1952.

Adam Beeler
September 30, 1930-May 23, 1932

Born: October 11, 1882
Wells County, Indiana
Indiana University
George Washington University, LL.B. (1906)
Died: March 25, 1947
State Legislature (1921-1928)
Superior Court (1928-1930)
Republican
Appointed

Adam Beeler was born on a farm near Bluffton, Indiana, the county seat of Wells County, northeastern Indiana. His father, Peter Beeler, a German immigrant, labored on a small farm to support Adam's mother, Mary Elizabeth, and their nine children. Adam was the fourth child. All the children helped on the farm and attended public schools in the county. Apparently Adam always wanted to be a lawyer:

> His sister, Ada... likes to tell of the young Adam, who would line his tiny brothers and sisters along the rocky fence rows of the Indiana farm and speak to them, not as the brother, nor the teacher, but as the orator, with his audience in the palm of his hand. Adam's speeches consisted of any and every subject, but as he said, "Some day I shall be a famous lawyer, and some day a judge."

It should be added that Adam also had a strong desire to enter politics.

At seventeen, Adam attended Indiana University, working his way through school by waiting tables, selling books, and doing odd jobs. After completing a three-year course, Adam made the first of many attempts at public office, running for the Indiana state legislature. As a Republican in a predominantly Democratic area, Beeler lost. With law school as his goal, he taught for two years, saving money to enroll at the George Washington University law department in Washington, D. C. Although not an outstanding student, his forensic talents and charm placed him among the class leaders. He graduated with a bachelor of laws degree in 1906.

Adam arrived in Seattle in 1908 with "his education, a suit of clothes, a few books, and fifty cents in his pocket." He began a law practice that year, partnering with Robert Grass. His practice began flourishing in 1909 when he joined John J. Sullivan in the firm of Beeler and Sullivan.

Beeler served four years, 1921-1925, in the Washington House of Representatives and two years, 1927-1928, in the senate. He sponsored and steered to passage the innovative Anti-Narcotic Act in 1923, which became a model for other states. He staunchly supported Governor Roland H. Hartley and actively worked for Republicans in King County. In 1924 Beeler made an unsuccessful run for lieutenant governor. He and another west-side candidate split the King County vote, allowing Colville's Lon Johnson to win. In 1928 it appeared the same scenario might develop when Beeler showed signs of organizing another campaign for lieutenant governor. Another avowed supporter of Governor Hartley, Paul W. Houser, announced his intention of running for the same office. The west-side vote might split again, allowing an anti-Hartley candidate to gain the Republican nomination. The resignation of supreme court Judge Kenneth Mackintosh allowed the governor to appoint superior court Judge Walter Beals to the high bench and select Adam Beeler to fill Beals's vacancy. These actions freed Houser to run for lieutenant governor. On April 16, 1928, Beeler donned the robes of judicial office, being elected to the superior court post without opposition that fall.

On September 13, 1930, supreme court Judge Walter M. French died. Governor Hartley quickly appointed Beeler to the vacancy. It was not altogether clear, however, if the appointment would continue until the end of French's term in 1932 or if a special election would be necessary in November 1930 to fill the vacancy. The issue was further complicated because French died after the September primary, preventing any candidates from proceeding through the required nominating process before the November election.

The supreme court resolved the issue by ruling that Beeler's appointment lasted only until the winner of a November special election could be certified. The court also held that a primary election was unnecessary before such an election. Because of the special nature of the election, and because of the lack of time, a ballot was not printed and Beeler and three other announced candidates conducted a sticker, or write-in, campaign, the second such judicial election in state history. (John F. Main won a write-in race in 1912). Beeler gathered 78,178 votes, defeating his closest rival by nearly 10,000 votes. The victory permitted him to complete the remaining two years in French's term.

Walter Beals, who served with Beeler on the state's high bench, recalled Beeler's judicial character:

> During his service as a Judge of this Court, he further demonstrated his ability as a sound lawyer; and those of us whose good fortune it was to serve with him will never forget his cheerful and efficient cooperation, his willingness to discuss with the other Judges his own and their problems, and his never failing desire to declare the law in accordance with the careful exercise of his sincere opinion.

Near the end of his term in 1932, Judge Beeler announced his resignation to join in a law partnership with Seattle mayor-elect John F. Dore and Louis Haven. He really resigned, however, to challenge U. S. Senator Wesley L. Jones in the Republican primary in September. Beeler's campaign centered on the failures of prohibition, calling for a resubmission of the question to the voters. Beeler opposed the World Court and the League of Nations. He advocated more government efficiency by consolidating several federal bureaus. His attack on Jones focused on what Beeler characterized as the senator's disregard for the state and the economy. Despite a spirited campaign, Beeler was handily defeated.

Although Beeler remained active in Republican politics, the senate run was his last political campaign. In 1934 the law firm of Beeler, Haven, and Dore dissolved and the former judge practiced alone until 1941 when he formed a partnership with Edward Merges. On March 25, 1947, Beeler suffered a fatal heart attack in his Seattle home.

On April 9, 1909, Adam Beeler married Florence Scott, an accomplished concert musician and vocalist. Both she and the judge participated in social and civic affairs. Judge Beeler was a member of the Eagles, Elks, Masons, Delta Tau Delta, Washington Athletic Club, Woodmen of the World, Ancient Order of United Workmen, Metropolitan Club, and the Seattle Commercial Club. Florence Beeler belonged to the Seattle Music and Art Association and the Seattle Symphony League. She sang the lead in several Seattle civic opera productions. The Beelers had three children, Madison Scott, Betty Sue, and Virginia.

Selected References

Lloyd Spencer and Lancaster Pollard, *A History of the State of Washington,* vol. 4 (1937), pp. 735-736; C. S. Reinhart, *The History of the Supreme Court of the Territory and State of Washington* (n.d.), pp. 122-123; *Seattle Times,* 7 Mar. 1928; *Seattle Post-Intelligencer,* 19 Sept. 1930; memorial services, *Washington Reports,* vol. 36, 2d (1950), pp. xvii-xix.

Bruce Richard Blake

December 1, 1932-August 31, 1946

Born: February 17, 1881
Danville, Indiana
University of Chicago
University of Michigan, LL.B. (1905)
Died: January 6, 1957
Spokane Assistant Corporate Counsel
(1909; 1912)
Superior Court (1912-1932)
Democrat
Elected

Bruce Blake, born in in Danville, Indiana, in 1881, moved to Spokane with his parents, Richard B. and Antoinette (Moore) Blake, when he was seven. Richard was a lawyer and, in 1889, after only a year in the region, voters elected him superior court judge for Spokane and Stevens counties. After serving three years of his four-year term, Judge Blake resigned and with Frank T. Post formed a partnership that soon became one of the area's prominent law offices.

Bruce determined to follow in his father's path. After public education in Spokane he spent two years at the University of Chicago and three years at the University of Michigan School of Law where William Steinert, another future Washington supreme court jurist, was a classmate. Blake returned to Spokane after graduation to join the new law firm of Graves, Kizer, and Graves. The following year, 1907, he co-founded the firm of Dalameter and Blake, which expanded into Cohn, Dalameter, and Blake in 1909.

Blake served as assistant corporation counsel for Spokane for three years beginning in 1909. In 1910 he married Mary E. Emery of Jacksonville, Florida. They had two daughters, Antoinette Emery and Helen May.

Blake won election to the Spokane County Superior Court in 1912, a position his father first held twenty-three years earlier. He was then only thirty-one, the youngest judge yet to sit on the Spokane bench. Judge Blake remained on the trial bench for twenty years until elected to the supreme court in 1932, defeating the appointed incumbent, and his friend, Henry E. T. Herman in the September primary. Blake's family name, his many years on the trial bench, and his two previous unsuccessful supreme court campaigns in 1924 and 1928 gave him the recognition necessary to unseat Herman.

Blake had been fairly active in Democratic politics prior to his election to the Spokane court. He carried his liberal beliefs, if not his politics, with him to the bench. For example, his former law partner Benjamin H. Kizer observed:

> He had a deep sympathy with the underprivileged that caused him to be a liberal in his political convictions, and a strong desire to see their wrongs righted, helping wherever he could, no less in the field of politics, where, as judge, he could not take an active part, than in the halls of justice where he pled their cause, first as a lawyer, then as jurist, with the deepest earnestness and conviction.

As a former trial judge, Blake only reluctantly overturned jury verdicts. But he did not hesitate to strike down legislative acts that threatened individual rights, nor was he reluctant to overrule outmoded decisions. Harry Ellsworth Foster, who argued cases before the judge, explained Blake's view in these words:

> It would be fair to say that he did not agree fully with the orthodox constitutional views of Chief Justice John Marshall that the judicial branch of the government could veto a legislative act but was inclined to the British view that the legislature was omnipotent unless the bill of rights was transgressed...
>
> He found himself frequently in dissent, but he never dissented for dissent alone and never without clearly stating his reasons. He held many unorthodox views, for, in fact, he was an iconoclast, but was exceedingly tolerant of those who did not share his views.

Blake saw his role as a supreme court judge to be neutral: neither activism nor restraint were appropriate judicial stances. For Blake, the law was not logic but experience.

Mary Blake died in 1927 and the judge married state librarian Mildred H. Pope in 1934. Judge Blake belonged to Beta Theta Pi, Delta Chi, and Phi Alpha Delta fraternities, the Elks, Masons, Moose, and the Tacoma Golf and Country Club.

After Mildred died in 1955, Judge Blake's health rapidly declined and his daughter, Antoinette, took him to her home in Washington, D. C., to care for him. He passed away on January 6, 1957.

Selected References

Charles Sheldon, *A Century of Judging: A Political History of the Washington Supreme Court* (1988), pp. 69, 85-87, 279-288, 320; and memorial services, *Washington Reports*, vol. 50, 2d (1957), pp. xxii-xxx.

Robert F. Brachtenbach
November 20, 1972-

Born: January 28, 1931
Sidney, Nebraska
Yakima Valley College, A.A. (1950)
University of Washington, B.A. (1953)
University of Washington, LL.B. (1954)
Selah School Board (1960-1972)
Washington House of Representatives
   (1962-1966)
Trustee, Eastern Washington University
   (1966-1968)
Republican
Appointed

In 1972 Governor Daniel J. Evans appointed Yakima attorney Robert F. Brachtenbach to the vacancy created by Justice Marshall Neill's elevation to the federal district court bench. The governor and attorney were friends and colleagues, serving together in the state legislature in the 1960s. Over the years the governor had appointed Brachtenbach to important study commissions and had consulted him on Republican party matters. The justice described his relationship with Governor Evans in these words:

> The Governor and I had served together in the legislature. When he became Governor, I was our party's whip in the House and worked closely with him throughout the legislative session. After I left the legislature, I served as his appointee to a college board of trustees, I was chairman of his Conference on Education and was appointed as one of his representatives to the Special Levy Study Commission. In addition, I worked with him for some years at the county, state and national level of political matters. In view of the foregoing, the Governor had had ample opportunity to form his own evaluations of my abilities. That was the most important factor in his appointment of me to the Supreme Court.

The governor had considered Brachtenbach for an earlier appointment to the court when Morell Sharp resigned to move to the federal bench, but Evans chose King County Superior Court Judge Robert Utter, largely because he wanted to balance geographical representation on the state's high bench. In 1968 Brachtenbach turned down an Evans offer to join the newly created court of appeals. Soon, however, he "became more frustrated in practicing law simply because of the volume and the pressures and all the private practice problems" and he reconsidered a judgeship. Assured of support from the bar association, Brachtenbach contacted the governor and informed him that he was now eager to don judicial robes: "I'll take it if it's on the supreme court." Anticipating Judge Neill's resignation, Governor Evans looked for an eastern Washingtonian to replace the Pullman native. Geography, which had worked against Brachtenbach earlier, assured his selection this time.

Evans's office announced the appointment on September 5, but Neill delayed his resignation to complete writing assigned opinions. Neill finally resigned on November 16, and the Yakima attorney took his oath of office on the twentieth. At age forty-one, the new judge became one of the youngest to serve on the court.

Evans and Brachtenbach had also wanted to postpone the swearing-in for political reasons. If they delayed until after the filing deadlines for the 1972 elections, Brachtenbach would not have to face the voters until 1974. Ironically, the legislature changed the law, requiring Brachtenbach to run for his post in 1973, when he handily defeated Auburn attorney Dale Sawyer. In 1976, 1982, and 1988 the justice ran unopposed.

Little in Brachtenbach's background suggested he was destined for the judiciary. Born in Sidney, Nebraska, on January 28, 1931, he was the youngest of three sons. His parents, Henry and Elizabeth, were wheat farmers. Victims of the dust bowl and the depression, they sought work in Washington. Robert attended public schools in Wishram on the Columbia River in Klickitat County and in Yakima, graduating from Yakima High School in 1948, and from Yakima Valley College in 1950. He crossed the Cascades and enrolled at the University of Washington, graduating with a B.S. degree in 1953 and an LL.B. from the law school in 1954.

Chance played a role in his becoming a lawyer. He and a high school friend, Phillip Trautman, later a law professor at the University of Washington, were assigned an English class essay on their future aspirations. Robert had thought of becoming a pharmacist, but Trautman suggested writing about being an attorney. The study of law sounded "more complicated" and if both wrote on it they could help each other. The research apparently convinced Robert that law held more promise than pharmacy.

Following graduation from law school, Brachtenbach taught legal research and writing at the University of California Law School for a year. In 1955 he returned to Selah, near Yakima, to begin private practice. Real estate, banking, the legal concerns of farming cooperatives, and commercial trial work constituted the bulk of his practice. He also became a specialist on the commercial code.

Republican politics attracted Brachtenbach. He attended a number of state conventions, serving as parliamentarian and a member of the rules committee. In 1962 voters elected him to the Washington House of Representatives, where he served two terms. He became a legislative leader, serving as Republican whip in his second term. Because of his hectic legal practice, he did not stand for reelection in 1966. He served as a Richard Nixon delegate at the Republican presidential nominating convention in 1968.

Brachtenbach's political background, although relatively short, explains to a great extent the course he followed on the supreme court. A satisfying political experience required compromise, a broad search for guides to public policy, and a smooth working relationship with colleagues. To a great extent, Brachtenbach carried these legislative attributes with him to the court.

The justice regards himself as a moderate in most matters that come before the state's high bench. In criminal appeals, however, he is conservative. He prefers to leave the resolution of policy issues to the legislature, but understands the need for judicial intervention in some public policy matters. Judges, he feels, have a special responsibility to keep the common law viable and consistent with contemporary economic and social developments. He expressed this creative cross-fertilization of politics and judging in the following way:

> Public policy, whatever its changing perimeters, has been and is and should continue to be a fundamental, vital, and persuasive element of jurisprudential philosophy and technique. Otherwise, ours would be a rigid and sterile judiciary deprived of the societal values inherent in public policy considerations... Indeed, public policy is an unruly horse but appellate courts are astride it.

Justice Robert Finley served as Brachtenbach's role model on the court. Although Finley tended to be more liberal and activist, Brachtenbach admired his decisional style and realism. To both judges, the policy role of the state's court of last resort had to be recognized. Like Finley, Brachtenbach believes that:

> Some policy views do in fact emanate from the collective experiences and values of the members of the court. Integrity of the process demands that we admit value judgments are inherent in the decisional structure. We need to concur with Holmes that "[t]he life of the law has not been logic; it has been experience."

Once having admitted that, Brachtenbach feels judges could then act more responsibly. On policy questions they should consult the work of scholars outside the legal field — exercising care in the use of facts that may not stand the test of the adversary process — and must "identify the goal to be achieved by application of a perceived public policy." Blaming policy decisions on the law or on the constitution rather than on their own perspectives is not the path to a responsive and responsible judiciary.

According to the results of a survey of former law clerks and experienced appellate attorneys, Brachtenbach is slightly liberal regarding economic and civil rights issues, and middle of the road concerning whether an activist or restraintist role is proper, despite his recognition of the need to keep the law contemporary by referring to public policy.

Although claiming he is not reluctant to write dissents, Brachtenbach seldom files them, preferring, when in disagreement, to cast a concurring or dissenting vote. He is usually motivated to write a dissenting opinion only if a possibility for persuading four others to join him exists. On occasion he will draft a dissent to "improve the majority opinion," but often does not file the draft. The justice is reluctant to use the dissent simply to provide a forum for minority views. Winning over the majority is important, and Brachtenbach's low dissent rate fails to reflect those occasions when he picked up enough votes to become the majority, or compelled the majority to make changes. His views of dissent clearly suggest a collective rather than individual orientation.

His commitment to the Court as an institution also is an important factor in his behavior. The court, according to Brachtenbach, should not appear too divided too often:

> After you have been around here for a while, you begin to get a sense of an institution. You really do. You realize that you walk out of the [conference] room and in two days of hearings...you're all over the place in terms of philosophy. You argue with your best friend and your best friend challenges you and your next best friend etc.... Pretty soon you realize that it is important that we carry on this thing, that we do get the job done. Conversations are very heavy in there.
> Sometimes I walk out of there so proud of that court. People will just go to the floor on issues, and walk out of there as friends. "Ok, let's put this together. Let's do it cohesively."

Compromise, consultation, and persuasion, learned from his legislative days, characterize his style. Several of his former law clerks remembered that Brachtenbach believed the important concerns of the other members of the bench were to be written into his opinions. He does not lobby for his views, but often consults with other members of the bench on wording, emphasis, or interpretation. As one clerk put it, "He works and thinks individually, but once he has reached his own conclusions, he seeks the opinions of others." While serving as chief justice, Brachtenbach became even more concerned with compromise and persuasion.

In conference, the justice takes one of three approaches. First, when sure of his viewpoint:

> I don't ordinarily talk very long in conference. I'm confident that people know I've done my home work and therefore it will go or not...I just want the collective judgment. Occasionally, I'll say "the issue is very simple. It's a 'yes' or a 'no' question and frankly in my own mind I can't write it 'no.' I've got to write it 'yes.' "

However, many times cases are simply not exciting: "You look at it and this isn't going to impact the law... We're not going to make any new law." The justice remains largely uncommitted in such cases. The best cases, requiring collective deliberations,

> are those that we . . . go back and forth. . . .as we try to make some kind [of] logical solution. Lots of our problems up here are insoluble. They really are. We shouldn't be in the business. It should be across the street [with the legislature].

Justice Brachtenbach has an open relationship with his law clerks. They are included in important aspects of his deliberations. When he first arrived at the court, he drafted nearly all of his opinions alone. But later, as confidence in his clerks increased and as pressures on his time intensified, a sharing of responsibility evolved. The law clerks now draft the first version of roughly half of the justice's assignments. Then a give-and-take process follows, with both the clerks and the justice researching, revising, and editing, resulting in a collective final product.

Brachtenbach's decisional standards reinforce his consensual style. The views of the other justices rate highest among his decision references. The work of the reporting judge is also significant, while the briefs and oral arguments of the attorneys, although important, rank low as sources. Interestingly, he ranked socioeconomic and political factors last despite his attitude regarding the role of public policy.

Brachtenbach served as chief justice from 1981 to 1983. He established the first Board of Judicial Administration to create a cohesive policy group for all levels of the court and radically revised the procedures by which the court adopted rules. Observers of the inner workings of the court regarded his term as chief as innovative and effective.

For eight years he headed the statewide project of computerizing court records. His work is evidenced in Washington's high ranking among the states in rationalizing docket data and utilizing computers, which facilitate the keeping of accurate records and speed the judicial process.

Justice Brachtenbach has been variously described as "spirited," "restless," and "independent." The pipe-smoking jurist is an enthusiastic conversationalist, an entertaining storyteller, an engaging master of ceremonies, and an avid reader. He fills his spare hours with painting, photography, sailing, writing, rock collecting, and wood sculpting. Many of his photos, oils, and watercolors now hang in his Temple of Justice chambers. He also designed his office furnishings, from the desk to an inlaid hardwood floor. The justice has a home on the beach near Ocean Shores and spends many off-bench hours doing homework away from the hectic environment of the temple.

Brachtenbach married Nancy R. Clark, daughter of Yakima attorney George E. Clark, in 1951 and they became parents of five sons. They divorced in 1975. The judge married Marilyn Hammond, then serving as staff director of the senate Republican caucus, in 1977. A psychologist, she was the first woman to serve as deputy secretary of the state senate.

Although people have occasionally urged Brachtenbach to return to the political arena, he has grown to appreciate the important role of the state's high court and is satisfied being a member of that bench. The challenge of achieving the proper balance between political and legal considerations in the court's deliberations attracted him to the judiciary in the first place and continues to hold his interest.

Selected References

Brachtenbach's oral history is in the supreme court collection, Washington State Archives. Also see *Seattle Post-Intelligencer*, 11 Jan. 1981; news release, Governor Daniel Evans's office, 5 Sept. 1972; Washington Supreme Court "Induction Ceremony Program," 20 Nov. 1972; and Charles Sheldon, "An Interpretation of the Judicial Process: The Washington Supreme Court as a Small Group," *Gonzaga Law Review*, 13 (1977), pp. 97-139.

Jessie B. Bridges
June 1, 1919-April 14, 1927

Born: November 10, 1862
Putnam County, Indiana
DePauw University, A.B. (1885)
Universalist
Died: April 14, 1927
Prosecuting Attorney (1896-1898)
President, Washington State Bar Association
   (1908)
Republican
Appointed

Jessie B. Bridges's father, James, a Kentucky native, moved north to a farm near Greencastle, Indiana. His mother, Mary (Darnell) Bridges, grew up in Indiana. Jessie was born on the family farm, where he spent his boyhood days. He graduated from DePauw University in 1885 and began studying law in the office of a respected Indianapolis lawyer, Major Jonathan W. Gordon. In 1888 the Indiana bar admitted Bridges and he practiced in Indianapolis. In 1890 he moved to Tacoma, remaining there for six months before opening an office in Montesano in southwestern Washington. He soon joined in the law partnership of Lind, McKinley, and Bridges. Elected Grays Harbor Prosecuting Attorney in 1895 as a Republican, he served one term, then opened an office in Aberdeen with Judge Mason Irwin. In 1902 the partnership dissolved and Bridges practiced alone for four years until he formed a partnership with T. B. Bruener, "one of the strongest legal organizations in southwestern Washington." Bridges developed a strong reputation as a lawyer for business concerns, and actively participated in professional affairs. In 1908 the fledgling Washington State Bar Association elected him president.

    Bridges's knowledge of corporate law and his acumen in business affairs led to his appointment as president of the Electric Service and Supply Company, first vice president and counsel for Grays Harbor Railway and Light Company, vice president of the Big Creek Timber Company, and director of Olympia National Bank. Perhaps the accomplishment bringing him the greatest statewide attention, aside from the presidency of the state bar, was his drafting of the state probate code that the legislature adopted in 1917.

When Judge Stephen Chadwick resigned from the supreme court in 1919, acting Governor Louis F. Hart turned to Jessie Bridges to fill the vacancy. Although Bridges had a very lucrative practice, his belief in public service compelled him to accept the governor's offer. Bridges had not been active in Republican politics; the governor had no commitment to achieve or maintain geographical balance on the court and had no political debts to pay. He chose Bridges because of his legal abilities and his stature in the profession.

Bridges had no difficulty turning back his opposition in the 1920 election, achieving victory with an absolute majority in the primary. In the 1926 primary contest against William Pemberton he garnered 10,000 more votes than his opponent and won the general election by nearly 50,000 ballots. Both the state and the Seattle bar associations, as well as nearly all county bars, supported his re-election in 1926, not only because of his judicial competence but also because of concern about Pemberton's "radicalism."

Judge Bridges provided many of the "swing" votes in cases that divided the court during his tenure. As a moderate, he held the balance between conservatives and liberals on the bench, especially during his earlier years. His colleagues often rewarded him with opinion-drafting assignments for the court majority.

One of Bridges's special interests was legal training. Although he had read law himself, he became a strong advocate of formal law school education. In his 1908 presidential address to the state bar he revealed what many then felt about the differences between studying law with an attorney and attending a law school:

> Of late years I have become a most thorough and earnest advocate of the law school and law school education. I will be suffered to more freely express my opinion because I am not of such schools. I have had the honor to be for several years a member of the State Board of Examiners for admission to the Bar. There, as elsewhere in my profession, have I been converted to the law schools. Eight times out of ten can the examiner tell, by reading the answers to the first half dozen questions, whether the applicant is a law graduate or not. If he is his answers will show that he is grounded: that he is familiar with the fundamental principles of law; that he has unlocked the door of and boldly entered into the solemn temple where law resides. It is most beautiful and satisfactory, to see the young mind arrive at a correct answer, not because he has seen or read the answer, but because he knows the fundamental principles, and from them, by reason and logic, reaches the correct conclusion...
>
> It has been argued that the self-made lawyer gets earlier into the profession: that he gains by experience what the other gains from his teachers. To some great minds this argument applies, but it does not to the average mind. With as much reason may we advise the child to teach himself the law. One is as much a child as the other. The self educated lawyer builds his house on the sands, while the other builds on the rock. The first must always protect himself against every legal storm and every tide of battle, while the other lives in full confidence of the security of his foundation.

Judge Bridges married Mary L. Smith of Hoquiam, member of one of Grays Harbor's pioneer families and the daughter of a successful banker. They had no children. The judge was an avid golfer, a charter member of the Grays Harbor Country Club, and a member of the Olympia Country Club. He also joined the Elks and Woodmen of the World.

In March 1926, Judge Bridges received a seventy-five day leave to take an ocean voyage to regain his health. He never fully recovered and, after two major operations for stomach cancer, succumbed to the illness in April 1927.

Selected References

William Prosser, *History of the Puget Sound Country,* vol. 2 (1903), pp. 404-405; H. James Boswell, *American Blue Book: Western Washington* (1922), p. 48; *Seattle Times* 15 Apr. 1927; and Washington State Bar Association *Proceedings* (1927), pp. 69-70.

Keith McLean Callow
January 2, 1985-January 7, 1991

Born: January 11, 1925
Seattle, Washington
University of Washington, B.A. (1949)
University of Washington, J.D. (1952)
Methodist
U. S. Army
Assistant Attorney General (1952)
Law Clerk (1953)
Deputy Prosecutor (1954-1956)
Superior Court (1969-1972)
Court of Appeals (1972-1984)
Republican
Elected/Appointed

Although the historical record indicates the governor initially appointed Justice Keith Callow to the state's court of last resort, his selection followed a hard-fought election campaign for the seat. He was appointed on January 2, 1985 to fill the twelve-day vacancy caused by Justice Hugh Rosellini's death, and he began his elected six-year term on January 14. He started twelve days early for two reasons. The sooner he arrived at the Temple of Justice, the sooner he could help with the court's backlog. And accepting the short-term appointment gave him seniority over Justice William Goodloe, also elected for a full term in 1984.

Justice Callow unsuccessfully campaigned two prior times for the supreme court. In 1976 he lost to former Congressman Floyd Hicks in the primary. Similarly, in 1978 Callow ran behind William Williams and Francis Holman. In all his races, Callow had overwhelming support from the Washington and Seattle-King County bar associations. He also ran well-financed campaigns. He spent $30,105 in 1976; $44,038 in 1978; and $114,688 in the 1984 winning effort against Edward Heavey, who set the record for a supreme court race by spending $139,971.

Callow learned much from his two early runs for the court: how to raise funds, use television, and get his name before voters. He began his last campaign two years before the 1984 election, introducing himself around the state, gaining pledges of support and funding, accepting speaking engagements, and gaining press coverage. Former clients—including insurance companies and businesses—as well as law enforcement officials, prosecutors, and leaders in the bar all encouraged him to run. But, as he observed, despite support from an impressive list of notables, "you still need the energy and desire yourself. You can't do it unless you want to." Callow's motivations for going through three exhausting campaigns can be simply stated: he wanted to sit on the state's high court.

But he was not without a program. One issue Callow emphasized in all his campaigns was the judicial system's backlog. The problem of congestion, which he confronted as chief judge of the court of appeals, called for action. He also believed justices should write more concise opinions to provide precise guidelines to lower courts and lawyers. He was concerned about how decisions were implemented by the high court. He was sensitive to the need for striking a proper balance between the rights of the accused and victims. "You don't want to have a police state...in which people are not treated respectfully and civilly by law enforcement officers," he wrote, but courts must foster an atmosphere that allows the "police to do their work."

Justice Callow was a restraintist, concerned with the court's law-making tendencies: "When the legislature sets forth law in [a] plain and understandable way it is not for the judge to say, 'I know better,' or to second guess the legislature. You've got to follow what the legislature says."

If the legislature does not anticipate a problem, or if situations change, a judge should be an interpreter and "to a great extent follow what the legislative intent was." If the law does not cover the occasion, then the judge turns to the common law—judge-made law. Here and only here, according to the justice, can a jurist change the law, since judges made it in the first place.

Callow was concerned with unanimity on the bench. He took extensive notes on conference discussions and debates in order "to have a feel for what the court is saying as a consensus." Thus, the justice adopted a collective approach to deliberations:

> I try to be a person who senses what the appropriate consensus is and why it is there...and if it's a matter of principle once in a while I would...maybe add a little individualism there but I'll still work...[with the others].

His view of dissent supported his consensus approach. Even if a justice has questions about the majority opinion, he or she must "subvert...pride and look for unison." The authority of the court depends upon as little factionalism as possible. Callow's dissent rate indicates that he practiced what he advocated. He wrote only eleven dissents from 1985-1988, below the court average of nineteen, and voted with other dissenters twenty-three times, again below the court average of twenty-nine. "Squabbling people who can't make up their minds" detract from the public image of the supreme court, Callow asserted.

Another indication of Callow's effort to reach consensus was his "swing vote" record. He ranked third on the court in terms of supplying the crucial swing vote that often made the difference between an opinion becoming the majority or remaining the minority view.

During his campaigns Callow reminded his audiences that judges could not discuss many interesting aspects of the law for fear of violating the *Judicial Canons.* However, he readily talked about his restraintist perspective of the law and judging. His favorite speech, entitled "Humor in the Courts," poked fun at himself, the judiciary, and the legal profession generally. Apart from being an attractive campaign speech, this approach reflected the justice's personality. His sense of humor could be counted on to lighten otherwise solemn occasions. This trait stood him in good stead on the court, in conference, and in informal associations with the other judges. His ability to achieve consensus may in part be attributed to his personality.

Justice Callow was born in Seattle on January 11, 1925, the second son of Russell and Dollie Callow. His father farmed near Little Skookum Creek in western Washington where his family had settled in the 1890s. Russell "Rusty" Callow graduated from the University of Washington in 1916 where he rowed on the university crew team and served as student body president. In 1922, the University of Washington hired him as crew coach. He moved to the University of Pennsylvania in 1927 and then in 1950 to the U. S. Naval Academy, where he coached the winning crew at the 1952 Olympics. Keith Callow's mother, Dollie, had taught school at Chehalis before marriage.

Keith graduated from Lower Merion High School in Philadelphia in 1943, was drafted, and went to a special training program for engineering officers at New York's Alfred University and at the City College of New York. When the program phased out, the army assigned Callow to the Seventy-fifth Infantry Division for combat in Europe. After discharge with a purple heart citation, Callow enrolled in Biarritz American University. As a sophomore he returned to the University of Washington, majoring in business and English. In 1949 he, with his brother Gordon, began law school at the university. Callow graduated in 1952 with law review honors.

His first law job was with Washington Attorney General Smith Troy. After six months, Justice Matt Hill of the state supreme court hired him as a law clerk. From 1954 through 1956 Callow served as deputy prosecutor under Charles O. Carroll in King County. Next, the future judge joined Little, LeSourd, Palmer, Scott, and Slemmons, the third largest law firm in Seattle. In 1962 he formed his own partnership with Ed Taylor, a firm later known as Barker, Day, Callow, and Taylor, where he remained until his appointment to the superior court in 1969. Among his clients were insurance companies, credit unions, and other businesses. He handled personal injury cases and did probate and trial work.

Justice Callow's family actively engaged in politics. An uncle had been a legislator; a great uncle was mayor of Charleston, near Bremerton. Callow's father served as sergeant-at-arms at the 1940 Republican national convention. But Keith showed little interest in politics until he joined the staff of King County Prosecutor Carroll, who urged all of his deputies to become involved in Republican politics. Callow became a precinct committeeman, co-leader of the Forty-sixth District Republicans, and president of the Young Men's Republican Club. Nonetheless, the practice of law remained his main concern; politics were clearly secondary.

He did not know Governor Dan Evans well, but attended law school and later served on the supreme court with the governor's administrative assistant, James Dolliver. Dolliver advised the governor on judicial appointments and brought Callow to his attention. After seventeen years of private practice, Callow was ready to consider a career change and accepted an appointment to the King County Superior Court in 1969. In 1972 Evans appointed him to the Washington Court of Appeals, Division One, in Seattle. In 1974 he easily turned back the challenge of Marie Donohue in the September primary election to remain in that post.

He married Evelyn Ann Case from Waterville, Washington—whom he had met at the University of Washington—just before he began law school. They had three children. The justice actively participated in both Girl and Boy Scout programs and the Evergreen Safety Council, receiving the Council's Governor's Award "for outstanding public service in the field of accident prevention." In recognition of his service on both the trial and appellate benches, the Washington State Trial Lawyers Association awarded him the Brandeis Judge of the Year honor in 1984. He co-founded the Council of Chief Judges of Courts of Appeal, a national organization devoted to studying problems of court backlog and appellate reform, and remains active in American Bar Association affairs.

In January 1989, he assumed the responsibilities of chief justice of the Washington Supreme Court. During his two years as the judiciary's administrative head he worked to unify the bench, to preserve an independent judiciary, and to reduce the backlog in trial courts. Although little evidence suggests that consensus on the high bench increased during his tenure as chief justice, Callow moved forward on trial court reform. For example, soon after assuming his responsibilities as chief, he appointed a special task force to study and recommend remedies for attacking the state's overburdened superior courts. In recognition of his interests, U. S. Supreme Court Chief Justice William Rehnquist appointed Callow to a fifteen-member federal courts study commission, the only state judge to receive an appointment.

Because of time constraints, some minor health problems, and an assumption he would easily win reelection, Callow chose to focus on his many court and administrative responsibilities rather than campaigning against his challenger in the September 18, 1990 primary election. Charles W. Johnson, a thirty-nine year old Gig Harbor lawyer paid the $893 filing fee, spent less than that on a few campaign materials, and avoided virtually all opportunities to inform voters of his qualifications. To everyone's surprise—including his own—he became only the second person in the state's 100 years to defeat an incumbent chief justice

(James B. Reavis had defeated John P. Hoyt in 1896), and one of only twelve to successfully challenge incumbents.

In retrospect, Callow's defeat can be attributed to three factors. First, he, as others, failed to take Johnson's challenge seriously, and consequently did not campaign actively. Second, the news media, after heavily endorsing Callow, failed to draw out either candidate and inform voters of their qualifications. Third, with virtually no information to guide them, voters had to rely on name recognition. Consequently, they may have confused Charles W. Johnson, little-known candidate for the supreme court, with Charles Johnson, a popular television news anchor at Tacoma's KSTW, the only statewide TV channel; or with Charles V. Johnson, a respected presiding judge of the King County Superior Court. After twenty-one years as a member of the state's judiciary, Keith Callow retired his black robe. But he did not give up his judicial activities. He remains a leader in court reform at the national level, and in January 1991 he joined Judicial Arbitration and Mediation Services, serving as a mediator and arbitrator.

Selected References

Callow's oral history is in the supreme court collection, Washington State Archives. Also see Seattle-King County Bar Association *Bar Bulletin* (Nov. 1984), p. 6 and Mar. 1989, p. 1; *Seattle Post-Intelligencer,* 24 Oct. 1984 and 2 Apr. 1989; *Seattle Times,* 9 Jan. 1989; and *Washington State Bar News* (Jan. 1990), pp. 19-23 and Je. 1990, pp. 40-41.

Stephen James Chadwick
December 3, 1908-June 1, 1919

Born: April 28, 1863
Roseburg, Oregon
University of Oregon, B.A.
Episcopalian
Died: November 19, 1931
Colfax Mayor (1891-1893)
State Land Commissioner (1894-1897)
Superior Court (1900-1908)
President, Washington State Bar Association
  (1924)
Democrat
Elected/Appointed

Stephen J. Chadwick was the son of Stephen Fowler and Jane Ann (Smith) Chadwick. His father, a member of a party of early pioneers, entered Oregon in 1851 by way of steamer from New York, mule train across the Panama Isthmus, and another steamer to San Francisco and Portland. With many others of that group, Chadwick's forebears played prominent roles in early Oregon history. Stephen's maternal grandfather had been a judge. His father was an attorney who later served as secretary of state and governor of Oregon. Stephen grew up in the company of prominent lawyers and politicians.

The future jurist attended the juvenile department of Willamette University and then the University of Oregon. He tried newspaper work for a time but soon returned to the study of law. Chadwick was admitted to the bar in 1885, and with his friend Mark Fullerton crossed into Washington Territory to open an office in Colfax in southeastern Washington. In 1891 voters elected him mayor of Colfax, and he then served on the State Board of Land Commissioners from 1894 to 1897. In 1900 Whitman County residents elected the Democrat to the first of two terms on the county's superior court. In 1908 he became only the second Democrat to win election to the supreme court, joining his old friend and law partner, Mark Fullerton. Judge Milo Root had resigned his court position late in 1908 and Governor Albert E. Mead appointed the already-elected Chadwick to complete the few remaining weeks of Root's term.

Chadwick had a traditional view of the court's role and proved reluctant to intervene in legislative concerns. For example, in *Webster v. Superior Court* in 1912 he wrote:

We have no power to negative [*sic*] the will of the legislature because we do not like the law. Within the limits of its constitutional warrant, the legislature is supreme;...for us to hold the public utilities act obnoxious to the constitution or as offensive to our own notions of governmental policy, would make this court the law-making body, in defiance of the will of the people to enact their own laws in legislative assemblies duly convened.

In 1913 Chadwick appeared to be in line for an appointment to the federal district court. Although called to Washington, D. C., to confer with President Woodrow Wilson, the appointment never materialized. Nonetheless, Chadwick was not content to remain in the relative obscurity of the state's high bench. He resigned in 1919 to join the prestigious law firm of Hughes, McMicken, Ramsey, and Rupp in Seattle. He apparently chose Seattle in order to build a political following on the west side of the state. It was rumored that he planned to run for the U. S. Senate in 1920, although he did not. He waited out the 1926 campaign while his son, Stephen F. Chadwick, campaigned unsuccessfully for Congress. In 1928 the judge made a valiant run for the Democratic nomination for governor, missing by 7,000 votes. He relied too heavily on his west-side acquaintances, but in the words of one reporter, "hadn't renewed them and hadn't catered to new ones." Chadwick served on the state Democratic council, was president of the state bar in 1924, grand master of the Masons of Washington, a member of the Washington Historical Society, the American Geographical Society, and the American Legion. He also chaired the state development committee of the chamber of commerce.

Judge Chadwick married Emma Plummer of Portland, Oregon, on March 2, 1887, and they became parents of four children: Claire Leslie, Harriet Jane, Stephen Fowler, and Elizabeth. The judge practiced law with his son in Seattle from 1929 until his death in 1931.

Judge Chadwick delivered an address to the Oregon Historical Society in 1930 in which he recalled his childhood. The talk sheds light on his personality and the early influences on his life:

I was born of pioneer parents, in the then village of Roseburg, Oregon, in 1863. My father was a pioneer of 1851. In that year several groups of people took passage on the steamer *Empire City* at New York, bound for the West Coast. When under way, it was ascertained that there were twenty-one of the number bound for Oregon. Among others was Samuel R. Thurston, first member of Congress from Oregon; Thomas Nelson, who had been appointed by President Fillmore as Chief Justice of Oregon; John B. Preston, Surveyor General, also appointed by President Fillmore; my father, A. C. Gibbs, and Zenas F. Moody, [all] of whom were afterwards governors of Oregon...

The party landed in Portland and scattered from there. My father first settled at Scottsburg where he became associated with Addison C. Gibbs... My father was the first postmaster of Scottsburg. When Roseburg was established, he moved to that place. He was the first County Judge of Umpqua County and was later a delegate to the Constitutional Convention in 1864 and 1868, in which year he carried the vote of the state for Horatio Seymour to Washington, D. C. My mother was the daughter of Judge Richard Smith and Patsy Ann Pitzer... She was born in Covington, Virginia.

After we moved to Salem, I was about the State House a great deal, and my father seems to have made it a point to introduce me to men, so that it was my privilege to know all of the men who had been governor of the State of Oregon and some who had been governor of the Territory, and all the judges and a great many of the prominent men in professional and business life. But of all the men I was privileged to meet, I believe that Joe Meek, the famous mountain man, made the deepest impression upon me. I must have been about nine or ten years of age. I had read some of the Beadle's Dime Novels. This I had to do out in the barn or behind the wood pile – how innocent they seem now in the light of some of the filth that is current literature in these days. I had heard something of Joe Meek; he was a fascinating character. He won my heart, for he patted me on the head, saying, "Stephen, did you ever kill a bar?" I told him I had not. He said, "Some day we will go out and kill a bar." The day never came, but Joe Meek became my hero.

Selected References

See Stephen F. Chadwick, "The Recollections of Stephen James Chadwick," *Pacific Northwest Quarterly* (July 1964), pp. 11-18; *Seattle Legal News,* 7 Sept. 1929; C. W. Taylor, *Eminent Judges and Lawyers of the Northwest* (1954), p. 113; H. James Boswell, *American Blue Book: Western Washington* (1922), p. 17; Washington State Bar Association *Proceedings* (1911), pp. 107-118; Lloyd Spencer and Lancaster Pollard, *A History of the State of Washington,* vol. 3 (1937), p. 48.

Edward Michael Connelly
April 22, 1946-January 13, 1947

Born: September 8, 1892
Bellingham, Washington
Gonzaga, B.A. (1912); M.A. (1914)
Gonzaga, LL.B. (1915)
Catholic
Died: August 31, 1947
Deputy Prosecutor (1920-1921; 1924-1928)
U. S. Attorney (1942-1946)
Democrat
Appointed

Ed Connelly, regarded as one of the best criminal lawyers that Gonzaga Law School produced, learned his trade in the front lines of the prosecutor's office against such masters of the adversary process as George Vanderveer and Richard Nuzum. When the challenge of the trial brought his skill together with his enthusiasm, he proved a formidable opponent. According to an old acquaintance, Connelly found

> Office practice... a necessary but drab routine and something to do between trials, for trial work was his first love... His sharp cross-examinations, based upon thorough preparation and ready flow of beautiful English before juries and courts, his resonant voice, his apparent enjoyment of the work... will not be soon forgotten. To him, every trial was a drama.

Connelly, born on September 8, 1892 in Bellingham, Washington, of pioneer parents Patrick Edward and Elizabeth (Murphy) Connelly—who arrived in Whatcom County in the 1870s—was one of three brothers. After public schooling in Bellingham, Connelly attended Gonzaga College, earning a B.A. in 1912 and an M.A. in 1914. A member of the first graduating class of the Gonzaga Law School in 1915, Connelly taught in the Gonzaga grade school while attending classes.

After graduation he became secretary to newly appointed supreme court Judge J. Stanley Webster, one of his instructors at Gonzaga Law School. When Judge Webster resigned to run for Congress, Connelly moved to Raymond as city attorney and deputy prosecutor for Pacific County for the years 1920-1921.

He married Grace Ellsworth of Olympia in 1920. They had two sons, Ellsworth and James, who studied law and established successful practices in Spokane and Tacoma.

In 1924 Connelly returned to Spokane as chief assistant prosecutor for Spokane County, where he remained until 1928 when he joined with Judge George Turner and Richard Nuzum to form one of the most effective partnerships in Spokane, known especially for its trial work. He also taught at the law school throughout his Spokane residency. In 1942 Judge Louis Schwellenbach appointed him U. S. Attorney, and he served four years. Over many years of practice, Connelly was admitted to the bars of the federal district courts in Washington, Idaho, and Oregon, and to the Ninth Circuit Court of Appeals in San Francisco. But in large measure Connelly's political activities, rather than his professional attainments, contributed most to his supreme court appointment by Governor Mon Wallgren in 1946.

The judge gained considerable partisan experience, beginning in 1932 when he served as Schwellenbach's eastern Washington campaign manager in his successful run for the U. S. Senate. When Franklin Roosevelt appointed Schwellenbach Secretary of Labor, Connelly became a key adviser on reorganization. He participated in state and local politics, serving as Democratic state committeeman and presiding over at least one state convention. In 1948 he managed Mon Wallgren's senatorial campaign and played a leading role in his gubernatorial race. But the political connections that brought him appointment failed him in his effort to remain on the supreme court.

Matthew Hill, former head of the University of Washington alumni association, noted public speaker, and unsuccessful candidate for U. S. Congress on the Republican ticket in 1938, filed against incumbent Justice Connelly in July 1946. Hill, well-known throughout the state, gained endorsement by the Republicans and several conservative groups. Connelly campaigned as a candidate of the liberal Commonwealth Federation, supported by the Democratic organization. Religion also played a role in the race. Hill was an active member of the Baptist Church and a high-degree Mason while Connelly was Catholic and a leader in the Knights of Columbus. Connelly, unable to turn back Hill's challenge, lost by over 60,000 votes in the November balloting.

Although he served less than a year on the court, Judge Connelly established a record with the bench and was regarded as a liberal on economic issues. With only a few decisions to his credit, he gave indications of being a fairly activist jurist, willing to intervene should he differ with the legislature, the governor, or their agents. Connelly's law clerk claimed the judge adopted an individual decisional style. He arrived at his conclusions largely on his own, rarely consulting with other judges, reluctant to lobby his colleagues. It was a style dictated by his freshman status and the fact that he was an appointee and one of only three Democrats on a bench dominated by Republican conservatives. The brevity of his tenure also worked against his becoming influential in persuasion, bargaining, or working compromise. As soon as he began to become part of collective deliberations, he entered a bitter campaign that eventually led to his defeat.

Although nearly all of his experience was at the trial level, Judge Connelly carefully and thoroughly undertook his appellate work. The judge's clerk described how he and Connelly went about their deliberations:

> Judge Connelly would give me the facts (usually orally)—his point of view—direct me to brief it—to write a preliminary paper—then we would discuss the final "firming up." [We could have had] more discussion and reasoning even though we were very close.

He remembered the judge as "outwardly friendly and giving to everyone," someone who made him feel like a "member of the family." "We walked and talked a lot about cases and 'everything.' " Their working habits sometimes involved midnight to 8:00 A. M. sessions, ending with breakfast together.

After leaving the bench in January 1947, Judge Connelly returned to his Spokane law practice. He died of heart failure in August of that year.

The judge, a member of the Elks, Spokane Early Birds, Press Club, and Athletic Roundtable, remained supportive of his alma mater, assisting the law school in gaining initial provisional accreditation with the American Bar Association.

Selected References

H. James Boswell, *American Blue Book: Western Washington* (1922), p. 93; and memorial services, *Washington Reports*, vol. 36, 2d (1950), pp. xx-xxiv.

Herman Denton Crow
January 19, 1905-October 22, 1915

Born: April 15, 1851
Delaware, Ohio
Ohio Wesleyan, A.B. (1871); M.A. (1887)
Congregational
Died: October 22, 1915
City Attorney (1876-1881)
State Senate (1898-1903)
Republican
Appointed

Herman Crow's father, Thomas Denton Crow, was a principal of the preparatory department and instructor in Latin and Greek at Ohio Wesleyan University; his mother was Henrietta (Downs) Crow of Delaware, Ohio. While still a youngster, Crow's family moved to Urbana, Ohio, where Thomas began a legal career. After graduating from Urbana High School, Herman entered Ohio Wesleyan, graduating in 1871 in the same class with future Vice President Charles W. Franklin and future Washington Governor Samuel G. Cosgrove. Returning to Urbana, Crow began studying law, being admitted to the Ohio bar in 1873. On the advice of his doctor, Crow spent a year in the drier climate of Texas, but returned to Urbana to practice law, enter politics, and raise a family. He served five years as city attorney, became active in Republican politics, and did graduate work at Ohio Wesleyan. In 1886 Crow moved to Winfield, Kansas, to continue law practice. He played a prominent role in Republican politics and served on the state executive committee of the Republican Clubs of Kansas. In 1890 he went to Spokane to represent a wealthy client, and remained there to join in partnership with Judge W. E. Richardson and, later, James A. Williams.

Crow gained appointment to the state senate in 1898 to finish an unexpired term, then was elected to the position, serving until 1903. Progressive in his politics, he supported railroad reform legislation, local option laws, the factory act — which regulated working conditions — and the eight-hour work day bill. He chaired the Senate Judiciary Committee during his last legislative session. Crow served as a Washington State College regent (1901-1905), and was a presidential elector in 1904.

The legislature authorized Republican Governor Albert E. Mead to expand membership of the supreme court to seven in 1905. Geography and politics played important roles in his selections. He appointed fellow Republicans Milo Root of Seattle and Herman Crow of Spokane, thereby achieving geographical balance. Crow's appointment was also politically strategic, since he had supported progressive legislation favored by the governor and, although a lifelong Republican, had the support of many eastern Washington Democrats. Most county bar associations also recommended his appointment. He won impressive electoral support in 1906, 1908, and 1914.

His progressive approach to the law, characteristic of his years in the legislature, typified his views while on the bench. For example, in *Scott v. Stark* he expressed approval of statutes providing assistance for widows and dependent children: "Such statutes are passed to prevent dependency. They are humane laws and voice a sound public policy." In October 1915, while still on the court, Judge Crow's health deteriorated rapidly and on the twenty-second he died, a cancer victim.

Judge Crow married Martha Florence Medenhall of Delaware, Ohio, in October, 1877. They were the parents of one son, Denton M. Crow, who became a lawyer, practicing in California and Spokane. In 1915 Chief Justice George E. Morris delivered a memorial to the state bar association in which he recalled the basic qualities of Herman Crow:

> He was a man of deep learning, bright intellect and, in recognition of this fact, three different institutions have conferred upon him the honorable degree of LL.D. To his friends, I take it, his most noticeable characteristic was his manliness and his amiability. He was a true gentleman, and never forgot it. His thought, speech and act was always kindly. He never spoke evil of anyone; his life was devoid of malice, more so I think than that of any man with whom I have ever come in contact.

Selected References

W. C. Wolfe, *Sketches of Washingtonians* (1906), p. 145; C. S. Reinhart, *History of the Supreme Court of the Territory and State of Washington* (n.d.), p. 78; and Washington State Bar Association *Proceedings* (1915-1916), pp. 179-181.

Carolyn Reaber Dimmick

January 2, 1981-January 15, 1985

Born: October 24, 1929
Seattle, Washington
University of Washington, B.A. (1951)
University of Washington, J.D. (1953)
Protestant
Assistant Attorney General (1953-1954)
King County Deputy Prosecutor (1955-1959;
    1960-1962)
District Court (1965-1975)
Superior Court (1976-1980)
U. S. District Court (1985-)
Republican
Appointed

Carolyn Reaber Dimmick was the daughter of Maurice C. Reaber, a master mariner for the Alaska Steamship Company, and Margaret T. (Taylor) Reaber, an author and college teacher. With her father often absent from home, her mother provided stability for Carolyn and her brother. Margaret Reaber earned a bachelor's degree from the University of Washington, taught school for a year, then returned to the University of Washington to complete a master's degree. Marriage prevented her from pursuing a teaching career, married women then being barred from full-time teaching. She remained at home to raise the family, and occasionally taught as a substitute. In later years she taught at Central Community College in Seattle, and wrote children's books after retirement. It seems apparent that her strong, independent mother provided a role model for Carolyn.

Carolyn Reaber, born in Seattle on October 24, 1929, grew up in that city, attending public schools and graduating from Lincoln High in 1947. She helped with family finances by working in the circulation department of the *Seattle Post-Intelligencer.*

In the fall of 1947 Dimmick enrolled at the University of Washington, not yet sure of her major. The study of law had not entered her mind: she divided her studies between classes in business and sociology. After completing her third year of undergraduate work, she "went through the [university] catalog and found that you didn't need a math prerequisite for a law major." Undergraduates then could enter law school after three years of work and receive a B.A. degree upon completion of the first year of law school. Enthused by a business law class earlier in her studies, she thought a year in law school would be a less painful way to a college degree. The University of Washington Law School accepted Dimmick.

She thrived on the law curriculum, and classmates elected her to law review. However, because of her work at the *Post-Intelligencer,* she had to decline. She graduated with an LL.B. in 1953, one of only a few women in the class.

Dimmick's first job, with the attorney general's office under Republican Don Eastvold, found her writing general opinions. Then she handled the legal concerns of the Department of Forestry. In 1954 she transferred to Seattle as an assistant attorney general attached to the Department of Labor and Industry. Later, when asked to return to Olympia for another assignment, Dimmick resigned in order to remain in the Seattle area.

Immediately after resigning, the King County Prosecutor's Office hired her for the domestic relations division as a divorce proctor, a job traditionally assigned to women. In that same year, 1955, she married Cyrus A. Dimmick, whom she met while both worked for the attorney general in Olympia. After a year in the domestic relations division, Dimmick transferred to the criminal division, handling morals cases brought to the district courts. In 1959 she left the criminal division to care for an infant son, Taylor, born in 1958.

Her leave did not last long. Several judges before whom she had handled cases persuaded Dimmick to supervise family and juvenile investigations for the courts. She returned full-time to the prosecutor's office in 1960, resigning two years later when daughter Dana was born. Soon she was again lawyering, but now in private practice out of her home.

In 1965 a vacancy on the northeast King County District Court occurred, and several local attorneys urged Dimmick to apply to the county commissioners for the appointment. Although the position is officially nonpartisan, politics usually dominate the selection process. Dimmick had not been politically active except during her tenure with the King County Prosecutor's Office, when she campaigned for her Republican boss. Still, the county commissioners, two Democrats and one Republican, impressed with her previous record, unanimously appointed her to the vacancy. At thirty-six she became only the third woman serving in the state judiciary at that time.

From the beginning, Judge Dimmick became extremely active in judicial organizations. A representative listing of her associations includes: American Judicature Society, Board of Governors of the American Judges Association and of the Washington State Magistrates Association, King County Public Defenders Advisory Committee, Judicial Ethics Committee of the Washington State Magistrates Association, Judicial Administration Division of the American Bar Association's National Conference of Special Court Judges, and Committee on Court Services for Children and Families of the Washington Council of the National Council on Crime and Delinquency.

At the end of 1975, Judge Ward Roney of the King County Superior Court retired. Governor Dan Evans, responsible for filling the vacancy and hoping to place more women and minorities on the Washington bench, appointed Judge

Dimmick to the post, although Dimmick knew the governor only slightly. On January 16, 1976, Dimmick joined thirty-six men and two women then serving on the King County trial bench.

In King County, Judge Dimmick treated first offenders and those involved in non-violent crimes leniently. She dealt with repeat offenders and those guilty of violence more severely. Indeed, Judge Dimmick developed a reputation for "toughness" regarding hardened criminals; a "law and order" judge is not an inappropriate description. She continued her activities in professional organizations, becoming a charter member of the National Association of Women Judges, serving on the American Judges Association, and participating in a number of Superior Court Judges' Association committees.

State Court of Appeals Judge Fred Dore won election to the state supreme court in late 1980, vacating his Division One court post. Judge Dimmick applied for the pending vacancy. In the meantime, Supreme Court Justice Charles T. Wright died, creating a vacancy on the high court. Governor Dixy Lee Ray interviewed Dimmick for what Dimmick thought was the court of appeals position. Judge Dimmick recalled the circumstances of her supreme court appointment in these words:

> I had applied for [the court of appeals] vacancy. The letters went down to Governor Ray with recommendations for the appellate court position. After I had applied...Justice Wright died and now there was a vacancy on the Supreme Court. I never applied for the vacancy on the Supreme Court. When I talked with Governor Ray I was talking about the appeals court in Seattle... She was talking about the Supreme Court. ...Had the only vacancy been the Supreme Court I would not have applied. I did not plan to move to Olympia... So, when you say I applied for it, it was there suddenly.

Justice Dimmick became the first woman to sit on the Washington Supreme Court and only the fourteenth woman on state courts of last resort in the United States. Justice James Dolliver sat next to the new justice on her first day on the high bench and passed her the following note: "Which do you prefer: 1) Mrs. Justice; 2) Ms. Justice; 3) O! Most Worshipful One; or 4) *El Maxima.*" Justice Dimmick quickly returned the note with this response: "All of the Above!"

During her four years on the state's high bench Justice Dimmick became perhaps the most conservative member regarding criminal matters. Her voting record in 1981 placed her somewhat right of center; she agreed most often with moderate Justice Floyd Hicks. By 1984 she had become more conservative, disagreeing most often with moderate-to-liberal Justices Robert Utter, James Dolliver, and Vernon Pearson. She often found herself in the minority, filing dissents. Her goal was not only to win over some justices, but "to keep the majority 'honest.' " She explained her motives:

> I would say, personally, when I write a dissent, I hope to get [enough votes to win the] case... I'll write a dissent where I'll hope to pick up that opinion with

a persuasive dissent... Sometimes I'll write a dissent because I'm outraged... I want to open their eyes."What are you doing here?" I'll use rather stark language. I want to get their attention but I don't want to be overbearing... If I don't get their attention... I would withdraw it before publication... I'm not reluctant to write a dissent.

No opponent filed against Justice Dimmick in the 1981 campaign, but in 1984 she faced token opposition. Alan Merson's primary challenge was, he admitted, a crusade. He felt the constraints placed on what could be said during judicial campaigns by Canon Seven of the *Code of Judicial Conduct* deprived the public of the information it needed for a considered vote. He found no fault with his opponent; neither did the state bar association, which supported Dimmick by 2,877 votes to 514. Voters returned Dimmick to the high court by nearly 300,000 votes in the September primary. Her name appeared on the general election ballot unopposed.

Even prior to Justice Dimmick's reelection in 1984 she had become the leading candidate for an appointment by President Ronald Reagan to the U. S. District Court in Seattle. She had the support of both Washington senators, as well as the state bar association and the American Bar Association. To assure that her friend and ideological companion, Court of Appeals Judge Barbara Durham, would be given serious consideration for the vacancy, Dimmick resigned from the supreme court immediately after having been sworn in on January 14, but before being confirmed to the federal post. Her resignation at that moment allowed outgoing Republican Governor John Spellman to fill her supreme court vacancy with Judge Durham before Democratic governor-elect Booth Gardner took office the next day. The gamble paid off when the president nominated her to the federal district court and the senate confirmed her. On April 17, 1985, she took the oath of office.

Selected References

Carolyn Dimmick's oral history interview is in the supreme court collection, Washington State Archives. Also see Susan Cook, "Carolyn Reaber Dimmick: A Biography," Dimmick file, same collection; *The Olympian*, 13 Jan. 1981 and 24 Jan. 1981; *Seattle Post-Intelligencer*, 28 Jan. 1980 and 8 Nov. 1984; and *Seattle Times*, 5 Dec. 1980.

James Morgan Dolliver
May 6, 1976-

Born: October 13, 1924
Fort Dodge, Iowa
Swarthmore, B.A. (1949)
University of Washington, J.D. (1952)
United Methodist
Administrative Assistant to Member of
  Congress (1954-1960)
Administrative Assistant to Governor
  (1964-1976)
Republican
Appointed

James Morgan Dolliver, when viewed from a narrow professional perspective, seemed an unlikely candidate for the supreme court. His experience as a practicing attorney barely totaled four years. From a political perspective, however, he was an ideal choice. He served nearly eighteen years as close adviser to elected officials, first a congressman and then a governor. His political responsibilities under Governor Daniel Evans acquainted him thoroughly with the judiciary. He advised on about 100 of the governor's judicial appointments, and remained an active member of the governor's policy team, confronting matters that occasionally appeared on court dockets. Further, Dolliver's involvement in numerous religious, educational, and civic affairs allowed him to sense what Justice Oliver Wendell Holmes, Jr. called the "felt necessities of the time," and to be what Governor Dan Evans meant by a "people's judge."

Dolliver was born on October 13, 1924, in Fort Dodge, Iowa. His father, a successful attorney, served six terms as a Republican congressman. His great uncle represented Iowa in the U. S. Senate. Not surprisingly, politics attracted James. The future judge grew up in Fort Dodge, attending public schools. The Methodist Church played an important role in both his youth and adult life. "There is no question being a religious person has an effect on you," he once stated. "Does your religious life impinge upon your public life? Yes. Does it dominate it? No."

Upon graduating from high school, Dolliver joined the navy as an aviation cadet, gained commission as an ensign, and flew air/sea rescue patrols for the U. S. Coast Guard. He returned from military service to continue his education at Swarthmore College in Pennsylvania, graduating with high honors in 1949.

Drawn to the Pacific Northwest by summer jobs in Olympic National Park, the future justice chose the University of Washington School of Law for his legal training, planning ultimately to practice law in Washington.

Dolliver continued his academic successes in law school. He was a contributing editor of the *Washington Law Review*, student body president, judge on the university's traffic court, and member of the Delta Theta Phi legal fraternity. Equally important, he attended classes with many future leaders of the Washington bench and bar.

Upon graduation, Dolliver served as law clerk for Washington Supreme Court Judge Frederick G. Hamley. Under the judge's guidance, Dolliver gained an appreciation of and respect for the court's policy-making powers.

In 1953, after his year as law clerk, Dolliver set up a law office in Port Angeles, lost a race for county prosecutor, and left after a year and a half to be Republican Congressman Jack Westland's administrative assistant. After six years in Washington, D. C., he returned to sole practice in Everett. He devoted considerable time and effort to local Republican politics. In 1962 he ran for Snohomish County Prosecutor, again losing, this time to future Congressman Lloyd Meeds. However, through his Republican activities, he met the majority leader of the state house of representatives, Daniel J. Evans, who lured Dolliver to Olympia as attorney for the Republican caucus. In 1963 Dolliver became a strategist for Evans's successful race for governor, and after the election he stayed on as chief of staff.

Dolliver and Evans formed a mutually reinforcing team in the day-to-day work of the governor's office and in long-range policy planning. They generally pursued mildly liberal policies. Anti-pollution laws and environmental issues concerned them both. Dolliver also served as the governor's liaison with the bar association, negotiating and screening judicial appointments. In this capacity, Dolliver and Evans formed a list of prerequisites for the bench: judicial temperament, non-partisan objectivity, electability, geographical diversity, endorsement by the state bar's selection committee, and Republican affiliation—although the candidate need not be avidly partisan. Most observers gave Evans high marks for his judicial appointments.

James Dolliver failed to fit the judicial mold that he and the governor had formed. But from another perspective he was an ideal choice for the high court. Evans believed the court's membership should reflect a wide variety of professional and political backgrounds. The resolution of policy issues finding their way to the supreme court would benefit from the collective wisdom of a court composed of former legislators, judges, prosecutors, and leaders in the bar. Seen in this light, James Dolliver's varied credentials qualified him for the bench. Perhaps the only attribute missing was the requisite number of years in private law practice. But several other members of the court could provide insights gained from years of lawyering. Indeed, someone with Dolliver's mixed experience would bring a unifying perspective to the court's deliberations.

In 1970, Evans urged the Washington State Bar Association to consider the qualifications of Dolliver for the vacancy of retiring Supreme Court Justice Matthew Hill. The bar's judicial selection committee found Dolliver qualified, but the association's board of governors, concerned that he lacked sufficient law practice experience, deleted his name from the approved list. The governor could have appointed Dolliver without the bar's endorsement, but it would be difficult to win election later without its support. Dolliver requested that his name be withdrawn from consideration.

For much the same reason, Evans also withdrew his recommendation of Dolliver for a federal district court appointment. The American Bar Association's standing committee on the federal judiciary withheld its approval because of Dolliver's lack of attorney experience, and the Senate Judiciary Committee would likely have balked at the appointment. So Evans removed his assistant's name from the list. With the governor nearing the end of his third term and expressing doubts about another run for the governorship, it appeared as if Dolliver's chances for a court appointment were fast disappearing.

The sudden death of Justice Robert C. Finley in March 1976 provided the governor with an unanticipated appointment to the supreme court. He made it clear that James Dolliver was his first choice. Evans thought his administrative assistant was "probably the best qualified person" he had ever "appointed to any position." He would be "a people's judge." He did not ask the Washington State Bar Association for its endorsement, nor did it attempt to intervene. On May 6, 1976, James Morgan Dolliver took his oath and donned the robes of judicial office. He liked his new position and, despite the doubts of some, proved to be a success. However, almost immediately, his spot on the court came under threat.

Walla Walla County Prosecutor Arthur Eggers, a Republican, and Fred Dore, Democrat, challenged Dolliver in his first election. Dore had the advantage of Democratic support and name familiarity, and he took the September primary handily. Dolliver barely edged Eggers for a chance to run against Dore in the general election. Campaigning intensified, with Dolliver winning the bar association's preferential poll, garnering the endorsement of the state employees' union, and gaining support from the governor and Republican party. Dolliver's campaign spent nearly twice as much money between September and November as it had for the primary. Most of the funds went for television ads during the last ten days of the contest. After trailing Dore in the primary by 100,000 votes, Dolliver won by a comfortable 41,000-vote margin in November.

Pragmatism characterizes his approach as a supreme court justice. He seems to follow his "instincts," according to one of his law clerks. The justice, keenly aware of the political, social, and economic trends in the state and nation, also has a strong sense of equity and justice, gained from his many civic, charitable, and religious activities. Dolliver, a voracious reader, brings to his decision-making considerable information quite apart from the legal authorities presented by attorneys and case books.

His role model on the bench—besides Judge Hamley—was Justice Charles Horowitz. Dolliver was drawn to Horowitz's views that the court makes policy and that judges have values upon which they often must rely in their deliberations. Of Horowitz he wrote:

> [He] taught me the importance of values for anyone who wanted to be a good judge. He helped me to understand not only the need for and necessity of values in decisionmaking, but also that a judge should not be ashamed of or try to hide the importance of values.

Dolliver assumes a stance between the liberals and conservatives on the court. Over the years he agreed most with Justices Vernon Pearson and Robert Brachtenbach and disagreed most with his 1976 election rival, Justice Fred Dore. On occasion, he leads the court in dissenting opinions. He tends to use dissent as a forum for lecturing the majority on what he perceives as the correct view of the law, rather than as a means of persuading members to join his view. He regards

> dissent [as] an entirely different way of writing. [In] the typical dissent you've got one issue. You can see it right there and you just press that one button and if it doesn't persuade them, well, ok.

Politics is the art of the possible. Those who successfully practice the art know when to stand firm and when to compromise. For most of Justice Dolliver's professional life he pursued the politics of others—congressman or governor—and struck agreements with others whose demands needed to be met. However, as a judge, he has the opportunity to reassert his own values, an opportunity never allowed him in the political world. A more moderate-to-conservative Dolliver emerges, a strong dissenter who often eschews the need for unanimity, and an energetic activist who lives as much in the world outside the Temple of Justice as in.

The justice's constant exposure to the world outside the cloistered walls of the temple of justice—the astonishing range of his affiliations in educational, civic, religious, and charitable organizations and his interest in politics and society—tests and renews his values.

However, Justice Dolliver has not supplied the bond that unified the often-divided court, as Governor Evans hoped. Rather than serving as the compromiser, Dolliver merely adds his viewpoint to the other eight, resulting in balanced but often tentative court decisions. Although his on-and-off bench relations with colleagues are cordial, Dolliver has tended to be a loner, the bulk of his time outside of court business consumed by his own service, professional, religious, and civic activities.

Dolliver met his wife, Barbara Babcock, while both were undergraduates at Swarthmore College. He majored in political science while she studied English. They married immediately after graduation. The family grew to six children. Of the three girls (Jennifer, Nancy, and Beth) and three boys (James, Peter, and

Keith), only Keith has followed his father into the law profession. Barbara taught English at Centralia Community College and South Puget Sound Community College, then returned to Centralia, from where she retired. She writes poetry and shares her husband's interest in history and historical preservation by printing many of her works on her own ancient, authentic, hand-set printing press.

Selected References

Dolliver's oral history interview is in the supreme court collection, Washington State Archives. Also see Kim Meyer, "Justice Dolliver: Keeper of Society," Dolliver file, same collection; and *Seattle Post-Intelligencer,* 23 Apr. 1976, 25 Oct. 1976, and 5 Oct. 1985.

Charles Tenney Donworth
September 12, 1949-December 31, 1967

Born: February 15, 1892
Seattle, Washington
Yale University, A.B. (1914)
University of Washington, LL.B. (1916)
Catholic
Died: June 10, 1976
Seattle Assistant Corporate Counsel
    (1920-1923)
President, Seattle Bar Association (1934)
Republican
Appointed

From the beginning, the law and judiciary played an integral role in Charles "Carl" Donworth's life. He was born on Seattle's Queen Anne Hill on February 15, 1892, the son of Judge George Donworth, the first federal district judge to preside in Tacoma, and Emma Laura (Tenney) Donworth. Carl's father came to Seattle from Maine in 1888, gained appointment to the federal bench in 1909, resigned in 1912, and formed one of the most successful law firms in the state: Donworth, Higgins, and Todd.

After West Queen Anne Elementary School, Carl attended Phillips Andover Academy and graduated from Yale University with an A.B. degree in 1914. He received his law degree from the University of Washington in 1916, winning the coveted Carkeek Prize for the best legal thesis in his class. That same year he gained admittance to the Washington bar and entered private practice with his father in Seattle.

At the outbreak of World War I, Donworth attended officers' training camp at the Presidio near San Francisco, earning commission as a second lieutenant in the infantry in 1917. After his promotion to first lieutenant, Donworth transferred to Fort Lewis, Washington, as assistant judge advocate. Upon release from the army he returned to Seattle and his father's law firm.

The future judge was appointed assistant corporate counsel for Seattle in 1920, serving until 1923. While with the corporate counsel's office, Donworth oversaw the complicated condemnation proceedings prior to acquiring land for the city light department's transmission lines from the Skagit River project. He also handled legal matters regarding a bond issue for financing the Seattle street railway system.

Donworth, active in professional affairs, served as vice president of the Washington State Bar Association (1923-1924) and president of the Seattle Bar Association (1934), and was a member of the American Bar Association and the American Law Institute. He sat on a number of state and county bar committees throughout his legal career. He also served on the boards of directors of several business enterprises, including Seattle Trust and Savings Bank, First Realty Corporation, and Maltby-Thurston Hotels, Inc.

Although not very active in Republican party affairs, Donworth's bar association endeavors, his respected family name, and his earlier work as attorney for Seattle brought him to Governor Arthur Langlie's attention. In August 1949, Langlie announced Donworth would replace retiring Supreme Court Justice William Steinert. His appointment surprised many. Langlie had appointed his old friend and another Seattle resident, Frederick Hamley, to the high court only a few days earlier and most observers thought his second appointment would come from the state's east side. But a special committee of the state bar had placed Donworth's name on its list of recommended candidates and the governor selected him from a number of qualified aspirants.

Some observers of gubernatorial politics saw the appointment of Donworth as atonement for Langlie's slight of the legal profession when he appointed Hamley without state bar approval. The Donworth appointment met with nearly universal approval from the profession.

No one filed against Donworth in his first election attempt a few months after his appointment. In 1956 and 1962 he faced only token opposition, easily defeating his rivals.

In his eighteen years on the bench, most people regarded Donworth as fairly conservative and restraintist. However, one of his former law clerks found it difficult to pinpoint the judge's particular judicial philosophy:

> I would have great difficulty in placing Judge Donworth in either... the Frankfurter (Restraintist) or Douglas (Activist) category. I could never imagine Judge Donworth citing as authority for his opinion the fact that "this offends my Anglo-Saxon concept of law"; however, I couldn't classify him as an activist even though his stand in protection of First Amendment Rights exceeds that of Justice Douglas.

The judge was not dogmatic. "Occasionally he would be assigned a case in which he appeared to be in the majority, only to change his mind on reflection and further research," stated his clerk. Then he would write a proposed majority opinion "different from what was voted and try to persuade others to switch also."

Donworth often wrote exceedingly long opinions, the length largely due to thoroughness rather than duplication and dicta. Scholarly and "scrupulously fair," one of his clerks recalled that "he took every case seriously — even cases that others might have quickly brushed aside." An excellent example of thoroughness and careful consideration of all issues argued came in the *Lemon v. Langlie* case of

1954. The central issue involved whether shifting a number of state executive offices to Seattle constituted moving the seat of government in violation of the state constitution. Donworth's opinion, voiding the move, covered a number of procedural issues as well as the seat of government question. The judge reviewed the history of the issue from territorial times to the present with a classical review of the constitutional framers' intent. The late Justice Charles Stafford, a Donworth admirer, described the impact of the case:

> In 1954 an entire state government was forced to return to the State Capitol, Olympia. Today, that move is history, but at the time... it was extremely unpopular with the powers that be in all major centers of population in this state. Nonetheless, [Donworth] wrote that opinion, with his usual courage, and with his deep respect for the need of a constitutional government to operate within the confines of the constitution.

Carl Donworth, courteous, proper, unassuming, and a gentleman of the "old school," rarely raised his voice in conference debates even though he might have held strong convictions on an issue. He wrote 493 majority opinions and only sixty-four dissents during his eighteen years on the state's high court. But he was proud of those few dissents.

Donworth's style involved working closely with his law clerk. The clerk would review an entire trial transcript, review all the briefs, hear the oral argument, and "prepare a complete opinion which was then delivered to the judge." According to one clerk, "We met in consultations several times a week. The most important meetings were those after he had read the first draft of an opinion I had [written]. He would tell me whether he agreed or disagreed and he would then tell me how the judges had voted in conference." The judge then worked on his own draft of the opinion.

Not only did Donworth view the judge-clerk relationship as a means of assuring a more thorough opinion product; it was also an opportunity for learning, an opportunity eagerly offered and seized. According to one of the justice's clerks:

> He wanted his opinions to be as perfect as he could make them, and certainly was never content to let the clerks do his job... Probably his greatest attribute as a teacher was the time he spent with his law clerks discussing their rough drafts of proposed opinions and pointing out things they may have overlooked.... I thought of him as my teacher—the best teacher in the field of law I ever had.

Another clerk recalled the teacher-student relationship between judge and clerk:

> Personally, I thought that one of the most valuable gifts Judge Donworth gave to his law clerks—or at least to me—was giving them a chance to learn how to think like a good judge must think, and making them analyze both the facts and the law in the record in an appealed lawsuit as a good judge should analyze the law, based on the facts established in the record.

According to the state constitution, "The judge having the shortest term to serve not holding his office by appointment or election to fill a vacancy, shall be the chief justice." This meant that Donworth, as the most senior elected judge, was to take his turn as chief in January 1957. He proved reluctant to assume the often burdensome administrative tasks that went along with the chief justiceship. He finished out the few months remaining in Frederick Hamley's term as chief in late 1956 but thereafter, apparently by mutual consent, declined when it was his turn.

Judge Donworth, forced to retire at the mandatory age of seventy-five in 1967, most reluctantly left the court and on occasion returned as *pro tempore* judge. His last visit to the bench came in the highly controversial *Yelle v. Kramer* case in 1974 when he joined eight other retired judges as a full *pro tempore* supreme court. All the sitting justices had disqualified themselves in an issue concerning whether the legislature or voters—through the initiative process—should set salaries of public officials, including judges. The court majority, including Donworth, accepted Initiative 282 as constitutional, permitting the initiative process to intervene in establishing salaries.

Although Donworth was in his eighties during the Yelle hearings, he accepted the temporary appointment with pleasure and with an eagerness consistent with his approach to the challenges of the law throughout his long and respected career.

Donworth married Evelyn Carey in 1918 and they became the parents of Charles Carey and Mary Evelyn. His first wife died in 1934 and Charles married Dorothy Lee Griffin in 1945. He was a member of the Catholic Church, Seattle Historical Society, Knights of Columbus, American Legion, Rainier Club, American Judicature Society, Order of Coif, and Phi Delta Phi legal fraternity. Donworth died in 1976.

Selected References

C. W. Taylor, *Eminent Judges and Lawyers of the Northwest* (1954), p. 58; Charles Sheldon and Frank Weaver, *Politicians, Judges and the People* (1980), pp. 68-76, 91, 98, 148; memorial services, *Washington Reports*, vol. 88, 2d (1977), pp. xxviii-xxxi; *Seattle Post-Intelligencer*, 11 Je. 1976.

Fred Hudson Dore
January 2, 1981-

Born: July 31, 1925
Seattle, Washington
Seattle University (1943-1945)
Georgetown University, B.A. (1946);
    LL.B. (1949)
Catholic
State Legislature (1952-1974)
Court of Appeals (1977-1980)
Democrat
Elected/Appointed

Justice Oliver Wendell Holmes's often quoted statement that the "life of the law has not been logic; it has been experience," indeed captures the essence of Fred H. Dore's high-court career. Dore's presence on the court represents a lasting marriage between politics and judging. As the court considers issues of public policy, politics and the law become inextricably mixed, requiring jurists to view questions of law through a political perspective. After more than two decades in the forefront of politics, Justice Dore is in a position of being able to balance the competing demands of the traditional view of judging as merely discovering the law, with the modern version that regards law as an extension of politics.

Fred Dore gained his interest in politics from his family, many of whom were active in the Republican party in the Seattle region. His time as a student at Georgetown in Washington, D. C., further piqued his curiosity. Finally, acquaintances and clients urged him to become politically involved. Despite his Republican heritage, Dore became drawn to the Democrats because theirs appeared to him to be the only party attempting to deal with social inequities. His victory in the 1952 race for the state house of representatives proved noteworthy in that he was the only non-incumbent Democrat to buck the Dwight Eisenhower landslide and win a seat in the lower house. At age twenty-seven, he also was among the youngest to serve in the legislature.

Dore regarded himself as a populist legislator. He chaired the Judiciary Committee, served on other key committees, and became assistant floor leader. In 1957 he sponsored the court administrator law, designed to maximize efficiency of the state's judiciary.

In 1959 King County commissioners appointed Dore to a senate vacancy in Seattle's Thirty-seventh District. While in the upper house he chaired the Public Utilities, Financial Institutions, and Appropriations committees, and served on the Commerce, and Constitution and Elections committees. He sponsored or co-sponsored bills dealing with education, aid to the needy, consolidation of the system of courts of limited jurisdiction, and aid to the handicapped. He successfully sponsored the first legislation in America funding research on Sudden Infant Death Syndrome (SIDS). The Dores had lost a daughter to the mysterious disease, and he maintained his interest in SIDS after leaving the legislature, helping to establish a national foundation for research. As chairman of the Joint Interim Committee on Facilities and Operations, Dore became involved in a long-range study of state legislatures with the goal of increasing the effectiveness of the Washington body. The committee's final report, published in 1965 and co-authored by Dore, recommended a number of innovations, most of which were subsequently adopted. At the national level, he served as a delegate to three Democratic conventions, in 1956, 1960, and 1964.

In 1968 Democrat Attorney General John J. O'Connell vacated his position as the state's chief legal officer to run for governor. Senator Fred Dore filed for attorney general on the Democratic ticket, running second out of five. A year later, Dore ran for mayor of Seattle, a position held by his uncle in the 1930s. Again, he narrowly lost. In 1972 Dore filed again for attorney general, winning the Democratic primary but losing to the Republican incumbent, Slade Gorton, in the November balloting.

Someone bombed Dore's Seattle home in 1970. He never discovered who was responsible or why they felt compelled to victimize him. Although it meant relinquishing his legislative seat, Dore moved his family to north Seattle because of fear of further violence. Nonetheless, he soon returned to his legislative desk. He challenged the Republican incumbent in his new district, the Forty-fifth, and won handily, becoming one of a handful of senators to be elected to represent two different legislative districts. However, a redistricting bill in 1974 gerrymandered Dore out of the Forty-fifth District and, forced to run in the Forty-fourth, he lost his reelection bid to Republican Lois North by some 300 votes. For the moment, Fred Dore was without a public office after more than two decades of service.

During his legislative days Dore had changed his solo practice into a partnership under the name of Dore, Cummings, and Dubuar. He handled criminal, personal injury, probate, and other general practice cases. He also served as general counsel for United Parcel Service and did regulatory work for Eastern Washington Natural Gas. His United Parcel case, successfully argued before the state supreme court, authorized UPS to enter the general freight business for small packages. United Parcel built upon that victory to become shippers of general freight throughout the United States and world. "In retrospect," Dore believed "this was probably the most important case" he handled as an attorney.

In another important legal victory, *Dore v. Kinnear* in 1971, he successfully represented, without a fee, 27,000 north Seattle taxpayers and secured a class action rollback of taxes and a six million dollar refund. He received the North Seattle Exchange Club's "Book of Golden Deeds" for his efforts. Grateful taxpayers also provided him with considerable support for his judicial campaigns. Throughout his legal career, Dore argued sixteen cases before the state's high court, winning fifteen. Although partisan politics had thus far captured his attention, after failing in his senate reelection bid, Dore's interest turned to the nonpartisan judiciary.

Governor Dan Evans, in the last few months of his administration, appointed his close adviser, James Dolliver, to the Washington Supreme Court. In the next election, both Dore and Walla Walla Prosecutor Arthur Eggers filed against Dolliver, resulting in, until then, the most expensive race for the court in state history. Although Dolliver outspent Dore by a two-to-one margin, Dore beat both of his adversaries in the primary. He and Dolliver vied for the post in the general election. Dore's campaign emphasized courtroom experience and his long and varied legal practice as compared to the incumbent's meager legal experience. Politics, however, not experience, dominated the election. Dolliver had advised Republican politicians and Dore was a lifelong Democrat. Governor Evans mobilized activists within the Republican party. Dore gained labor endorsement and assistance from many Democratic friends and clients. Of those attorneys responding to the state bar poll, seventy percent favored Dolliver. Television played a major role in deciding the outcome. Dolliver's supporters closed out the campaign with TV spots in the last ten days, which likely made the difference. He turned the race around, defeating Dore by 41,000 votes after having trailed him by nearly 100,000 in the primary.

Dore had known Democratic Governor Dixy Lee Ray from serving as trustee of the Pacific Science Center while Ray directed the center. He supported Ray in her gubernatorial race. In 1977, Governor Ray appointed him to division one of the court of appeals. A year later he won election to the post, and then again to a full term in 1979. But, the state supreme court remained his goal.

Dore correctly viewed the state's court of last resort as a policy-making and precedent-setting body. Also, if he timed it right, he could run for the high bench and still retain his court of appeals spot if unsuccessful.

Justice Charles Horowitz became seventy-five in January 1980 and had to step down at the end of the year under the mandatory retirement law. Judge Dore filed for the post against a fellow court of appeals justice from division two, Edward Reed. The campaign issues centered around the contestants' political and judicial experience. Reed had served on the state's judiciary for ten years, possessed modest Republican credentials, and was regarded as conservative. Dore gained the endorsement of the State Labor Council and the Seattle Police Officers' Guild, and was viewed as liberal. Of those who responded to the state bar poll, sixty-five percent preferred Reed. In a weakened condition from an illness, Dore nearly withdrew from the contest. But he remained and, through the last minute use of television, soundly trounced his opponent in the primary by more than 80,000 votes, moving to the November election unopposed. Although Dore won election to the supreme court, the record will show he was appointed. Governor Ray selected him to complete a few days of Horowitz's short term. Justice Fred H. Dore took his oath of office on January 2, 1981, ten days before he would have taken over as an elected judge.

Fred Dore came from a family of lawyers. His grandfather, John Fairfield Dore, a Boston attorney, moved his family to Seattle at the turn of the century. His two sons, Fred and John, became attorneys. John became mayor of Seattle in the 1930s, serving two terms, while Fred was elected justice of the peace. In 1922 Fred, Sr. married Ruby Kelly and they had four children. The father died in 1932, leaving Ruby to raise the family.

Fred, Jr. attended O'Dea Catholic Prep School in Seattle, graduating as salutatorian in 1942. A bad back kept him out of the service during World War II, and he enrolled in business and accounting courses at Seattle University, a Jesuit school with an atmosphere that reinforced his Catholic upbringing. As a freshman he won awards for public speaking. During a career-day presentation he heard an attorney from the Seattle law firm of Bogle and Gates speak about how law can make a contribution to society. He transferred to Georgetown University's School of Foreign Service to finish his undergraduate work, then enrolled in the university's law school.

As a first-year student, he was a finalist in the school's moot court competition, and won the competition the next year. He graduated twenty-fourth in his class in 1949. Upon returning to Seattle he joined the respected law firm of Padden and Moriarity, remaining with them until going on his own in 1952.

Dore feels his legislative experience provided him "a real advantage." Many issues the justices confront come from "across the street" at the legislature and his twenty-two years of legislative experience give him an understanding of the process, problems, and personalities involved in creating legislation. "Legislative intent," an important judicial criterion, is no mystery to him. The give and take of the legislative process trained Dore in advocacy skills, persuasion, and compromise. Learning these skills assisted him in serving on a court occupied by independent-minded and strong-willed lawyers who can sometimes be persuaded, rarely influenced, and never manipulated. Dore feels at ease with a collective approach to decision-making as a result of his legislative experience. In an effort to prove to others, his colleagues, and possibly himself that "politicians" can also be good judges, Dore works hard:

> Now that I am here I see in many ways the supreme court as more powerful than the governor and the legislature, because we say what they mean no matter what they say... That's why you should be well prepared... If you're consistently

reliable in what you say then others depend upon you. If you're wrong and half accurate, then people don't rely on you. That's what you want to develop among your colleagues – that you are reliable.

Justice Dore writes a considerable number of dissents. Between 1985 and 1988 he wrote 110 opinions, of which fifty-three were dissents or concurrences. Twenty-two of these were solo opinions. On occasion he succeeds in persuading his colleagues to join him, making his opinion that of the majority. The adoption of his dissent in *Donovick v. Seattle First* (1988) by the U. S. Court of Appeals in *Whitehead v. Derwinski* (1990) is illustrative of the effectiveness of his dissents. In the first five years of his tenure he had over a dozen dissents become majority opinions. Since taking his seat on the bench, he has also written his share of the court's majority opinions.

Initially, the justice tended to assume a hard-line toward criminal appeals, but has moderated somewhat. He clearly takes a liberal view regarding free speech, press, religion, and assembly issues.

Justice Dore's voting found him in agreement most of the time with the late Justice Hugh Rosellini and William Goodloe. On criminal appeals he tended to join Justices Carolyn Dimmick, Barbara Durham, or Rosellini, but again, in more recent years he joined the more moderate members of the bench.

Judge Dore has been on the state's court of last resort for ten years and future issues, different colleagues, and changing contexts may alter his behavior. However, his politics now are in a delicate balance with the law, a combination that, in the hands of the less skilled, could be ineffective. His competitive nature – reinforced by law school, legal practice, and courtroom advocacy, and refined in the legislative halls and on the campaign trail – lends itself to resolving many of the policy issues confronting the court. However, the collective demands of the high court's decisional process are not always met through a competitive approach.

In January 1991 Fred Dore became chief justice. His agenda as chief included working toward establishing superior courts on the east side of Lake Washington, extending the use of video tape records in judicial proceedings, and further articulating constitutional and human rights. The chief justice dedicated himself to "support the proposition that everyone in the state seeking legal consultation can secure it for a reasonable fee, from the thousands of lawyers who cry out for legal employment." His ability to urge his colleagues to join him in pursuit of these goals will largely determine his success.

Recently, Justice Dore has suffered from a blood condition which, on occasion, requires rest and supplemental oxygen from a portable unit. Both the justice's doctor and the judicial conduct commission have concluded that the malady does not hinder his judging. The commission dismissed the matter, finding no evidence of disability.

Fred Dore married Walla Walla's Mary Shuham in November 1956. They had six children: Margaret, Fred, Teresa, Christine who died of SIDS, Timothy, and Jane. The justice has actively participated in a number of professional and service groups, serving as a member of the Uniform Law Commission, Judicial Council, Washington Statute Law Committee, Washington State Arts Commission, American Bar Association, and as a trustee of the Pacific Science Center. His hobbies are "politics, hard work, supporting my family, getting my family educated, golf, and bridge."

Selected References

Dore's oral history interview is in the supreme court collection, Washington State Archives. Also see "Alumnus of the Year," *Seattle University News* (1989), pp. 1-2; *Seattle Post-Intelligencer,* 23 Mar. 1984; *Seattle Times/Post-Intelligencer,* 29 Nov. 1987; and *The Olympian,* 17 Jan. 1991.

Samuel Marion Driver
May 9, 1940-November 21, 1942;
December 1, 1945-April 22, 1946

Born: May 22, 1892
Wamic, Oregon
University of Washington, LL.B. (1916)
Georgetown University, LL.M. (1926)
Protestant
Died: September 12, 1958
Prosecuting Attorney (1922-1923; 1926; 1935-1937)
U. S. Attorney (1937-1940)
U. S. District Court (1946-1958)
Democrat
Appointed

Samuel Driver was born in the small fruit-growing community of Wamic in north-central Oregon near Mount Hood, the son of Frances Marion and Adelia (Lucas) Driver. Samuel attended grade school in Wamic and went to public high school in The Dalles, Oregon. He enrolled at the University of Washington, earned his LL.B. in 1916, and entered law practice shortly thereafter in Seattle. He then joined A. J. Hensel in a law office in Waterville, an eastern Washington farming community. During World War I, Driver served with the Ninety-first Division in France, being discharged in 1919 as a corporal.

Three years after returning to Waterville, voters elected Driver prosecuting attorney for Douglas County, but he resigned after a year to serve as secretary to Congressman Sam B. Hill. While in the nation's capital, Driver attended Georgetown University Law School and earned his advanced law degree in 1926. That summer he returned to Washington state as deputy prosecutor for Spokane County. Within a few months he moved to Wenatchee to engage in general practice with Jay A. Adams until he was elected prosecuting attorney for Chelan County, serving from 1935 to 1937. In 1937 Driver gained appointment as U. S. Attorney for eastern Washington, with offices in Spokane.

In 1940 Governor Clarence Martin selected Driver to fill the supreme court vacancy left by fellow Spokanite, James Geraghty. He was elected without opposition for the balance of Geraghty's term in 1940. Although his official tenure in office extended over six years, Driver served only three because of leaves during the Second World War, when he entered the U. S. Army's Judge Advocate General's Department as a major. Overseas for one year, he was discharged in 1946 as a colonel. After returning to the supreme court for a few months, President

Harry Truman appointed Driver federal district court judge for eastern Washington.

His output on the state bench totaled only ninety-six opinions, including one concurring and two dissents. Of these opinions Justice Matt Hill wrote:

> [W]e find lucidity and a clarity of thought and an ability to get quickly to what one of our law professors...was wont to call "the meat in the coconut." There is evident throughout all his legal writing a firm grounding in the common law; a thorough researching of any new or novel proposition; an appreciation that the law cannot be static, but must adapt itself to changing customs and conditions; and a deep concern for human rights.

Justice Driver's most cited—and longest—opinion started as a dissent in *Texas Company v. Cohn* in 1941. He convincingly argued for the constitutionality of an excise tax upon the distributors of fuel oil, ultimately carrying his colleagues with him.

Judge Driver was relatively liberal and activist in his decisions. He supported some governmental regulation of business, closely scrutinized legislation under constitutional attack, and generally did not hesitate to ignore precedent if necessary to achieve "correct" results.

While on the federal bench, the chief justice appointed Driver to serve on the U. S. Supreme Court's advisory committee reviewing federal rules of criminal procedure. During his time on the committee, 1947-1956, he continued to urge procedural revision and reform on both the federal and state benches. He served with distinction on the federal bench until his death; he was fatally injured while crossing a highway in California to inspect a field of grain.

Until his appointment to the state supreme court, Driver had been fairly active in Democratic politics. He continued his interest in the American Legion, Veterans of Foreign Wars, Athletic Roundtable, Phi Delta Phi legal fraternity, and the Early Birds. In 1922 he married Sue Glascock of Bridgeport, Washington. They were the parents of Janeil and Garth Edward.

Selected References

An oral history interview with Sue Driver, the justice's wife, is available in the supreme court collection, Washington State Archives. Also see the John Ripple interview, same collection; Samuel Driver papers, Manuscripts, Archives and Special Collections, Washington State University Library; *Wenatchee Daily Sun*, 31 Jan. 1935; and memorial services, *Washington Reports*, vol. 53, 2d (1959), pp. xvii-xxiii.

Ralph Oregon Dunbar
November 11, 1889-September 19, 1912

Born: April 26, 1845
Schuyler County, Illinois
Willamette University (1865-1867)
Congregational
Died: September 19, 1912
Clerk, U. S. District Court (1869-1871)
Territorial Legislature (1878-1887)
Prosecuting Attorney (1880-1882)
Goldendale City Attorney (1880-1886)
Washington Constitutional Convention
    (1889)
Republican
Appointed

Ralph Oregon Dunbar was born in Schuyler County, east-central Illinois, near the confluence of the Illinois and LaMoine rivers. His father, Rice Dunbar – of Scottish ancestry, born in Ohio – was a carpenter and builder. His mother, Jane Miller Brisbin, was a Pennsylvania native of Dutch background. Ralph was the ninth of twelve children.

In 1846 Rice Dunbar moved the family in an ox-drawn covered wagon across the plains to the Oregon Territory. He served as captain of the wagon company that included members of the Donner party, who took a cutoff to California and met with tragic events at what was subsequently named Donner Pass. Dunbar led the group through the Klamath country and turned north, arriving in the Waldo Hills, near Salem, Oregon, on New Year's Day, 1847. During the trek west Indians stole much of their livestock and the company abandoned many of their wagons for lack of draft animals. The Dunbar family, like others in the company, arrived lacking many of the necessities for their new life in the West. Jane Dunbar rode the one remaining horse, carrying the one-year old Ralph in her arms. Celebrating their arrival, Jane and Rice added "Oregon" to their son's name.

Initially, the Oregon country's opportunities evaded the Dunbars, as noted in the following account:

> When they arrived in Salem they were without money and provisions, and they lived that first winter almost entirely upon boiled peas... Added to this were many hardships and privations... The sacrifices they made and the hardships they endured were the means of opening up this region to the latter civilization, and to them is due the debt of gratitude that can never be repaid.

Rice Dunbar worked as a carpenter and builder of saw and grist mills until hard times drove him to the California gold fields in 1849, leaving his family behind. Dunbar returned to the homestead empty-handed and threw himself into developing his land. The future jurist's mother, a devout Methodist, died in 1858 at the age of forty-nine. In 1863 his father moved to nearby Salem, where he died in 1871 at the age of sixty-nine.

Ralph Dunbar attended Willamette University in Salem, where he taught for two years while pursuing his studies. In 1867 he moved to Olympia to study law under the supervision of Judge Elwood Evans. Two years later the Washington Territorial Supreme Court admitted Dunbar to practice. He had a 170-acre parcel of land in Olympia where he raised cattle and bred horses.

Chief Justice of the Territorial Court Orange Jacobs appointed Dunbar clerk of the United States District Court in 1869, where he served until 1871. He then moved to Yakima to practice law, remaining there until 1875 when he established an office in The Dalles, Oregon. Soon, however, he moved to Goldendale, Washington, where he formed a prosperous partnership with future Supreme Court Judge James B. Reavis and had a 280-acre wheat and horse ranch.

Dunbar, like his father, became active in Republican politics, and in 1878 was elected to the upper house of the territorial council, while also serving as probate judge for Klickitat County. In 1880 voters elected him prosecuting attorney for Klickitat, Kittitas, Yakima, Clark, and Skamania counties. He entered the lower house of the territorial legislature in 1885 and his fellow Republicans selected him speaker. From 1880 to 1886 Dunbar owned and edited the *Goldendale Sentinel,* a paper known for its unwavering support of Republican causes. He also served as city attorney for Goldendale for several terms during the 1880s.

The future jurist went to the Washington constitutional convention in 1889 in Olympia and became chairman of the Committee on Tide and Grant Lands, largely responsible for writing constitutional Article XVI on school lands. Following the convention, like Judges John Hoyt and Theodore Stiles, Dunbar played a leadership role at the party nominating convention that met in Walla Walla to draw up the list of Republican candidates for the fall ballot. This convention determined the course of Dunbar's future public career.

Dunbar actively sought nomination as Washington's first congressman. Unfortunately for Dunbar's aspirations, eastern Washington's delegates split their support between Dunbar and Mark Fullerton, who would later also sit on the supreme court. Consequently, John L. Wilson won the Republican nomination by three votes over Dunbar and went on to become Washington's first congressman. One delegate, a Mr. Ettinger, recalled his feelings at the Republican convention, which resulted in Dunbar's eventual nomination as a supreme court candidate:

> I felt a little uncomfortable about not supporting Dunbar [for Congress]. So I went to Fullerton and told him how I felt. I said there was no use getting mad

about this thing. It's politics. I'll tell you what we ought to do. Let me nominate him as one of the judges of the Supreme Court. He is a lawyer. You go see him. So Fullerton went to tell him. He came back and Dunbar was with him. Dunbar said, "I live down there in the sticks, and I have never tried but one or two pro- bate cases and contests in the land office... I can't qualify for that place." I said, "No one is qualified. We're all pioneers here. We'll take a chance with you. We know no law, no precedents here, we have only three volumes of reports."

Dunbar won the October election by nearly 10,000 votes over his closest Democratic rival. He also won four subsequent elections until his death immedi- ately following a successful primary race in September 1912.

Justice Dunbar was the first incumbent to remain continuously on the high bench until his death. He served nearly twenty-three years, wrote 1,248 opin- ions, and penned eighty-five dissents, beginning a tradition of accountability through the use of dissent.

Dunbar tended to take a moderate-to-conservative posture on those issues that presented the judges with questions about the role of government in the affairs of business and the regulation of property. He expressed the prevailing restraintist stance of the majority. For example, he once wrote in an opinion:

> Once it is conceded that this is a rightful subject for legislation...there is no limit to legislative authority and it is not the province of a court to speculate or theo- rize upon the practicality, practicability of the laws or the good or bad effects which may result from such laws.

According to one of the leaders of the early bar, Preston M. Troy, Dunbar's greatest attribute was a blend of humility with a respect for the law:

> [H]e had the warm-blooded human impulses of a red-blooded man, curiously blended with the calm equipoise of an analytical judicial mind which at once kept him closely in touch with the viewpoint of the average man and in accord with the growth and expansion of his time and, on the one hand, caused him to hold in proper check radicalism and iconoclasm to the end that he was a safe conserva- tor of society. His wealth of common sense was a never-ending resource which, couple[d] with his honesty, his industry, his fearlessness and his love of humanity made him an ideal judge.

Dunbar's style of decision-making involved considerable study and intuition. He prepared himself well, depending less upon brilliance than hard work. He approached each case with a particular resolve: "The only way to decide a case is to make it your own, dig into it, and then decide it." According to attorney John P. Harman, the judge

> was from all viewpoints probably the most satisfactory man we have had on the supreme bench. He was not prominent in technicalities, but he could dig into a record, find the salient points, determine the real equity and then in a language both plain and convincing, give the reasons for the conclusions reached.

Dunbar married Claire White in 1873. The Dunbars were members of the Congregational Church and had three children, two sons, Fred and John, and a daughter, Ruth. John served a term as Washington's attorney general.

Selected References

Fred Lockley *Conversations with Pioneer Women* (1981), pp. 230-234; Washington State Bar Association *Proceedings* (1913), p. 151; Julian Hawthorne, *History of Washington,* vol. 1 (1893), p. 557; "Judge Ralph Oregon Dunbar," in the Beardsley manuscript, Washington State Archives; and Charles Sheldon and Michael Stohr-Gillmore, "In the Beginning: The Washington Supreme Court a Century Ago," *University of Puget Sound Law Review,* vol. 12 (1989), pp. 247-284.

Barbara Durham
January 14, 1985-

Born: October 6, 1942
Anacortes, Washington
Gonzaga University (1961)
Georgetown University, B.A. (1964)
Stanford University, J.D. (1968)
Deputy Prosecutor (1968-1970)
District Court (1973-1976)
Superior Court (1977-1980)
Court of Appeals (1980-1984)
Republican
Appointed

In response to a reporter's question about necessary background for sitting on the supreme court, newly appointed Justice Barbara Durham stated: "I have a personal bias in favor of judges working their way up through the judicial system so that when one gets to the higher court, one is familiar with the system, bottom to top."

Coming up through the ranks is indeed what Judge Durham did. She accepted an appointment in 1973 to serve as part-time district court judge for Mercer Island. After three years on this court of limited jurisdiction, voters elected her to the King County Superior Court, where she served until 1980, when she became the first woman to sit on the Washington Court of Appeals. In 1985 Governor John Spellman appointed her to the state's supreme court, the second woman so honored. She took her oath of office on Spellman's last day as governor. Although only forty-two years old, she brought to the high court a rich judicial experience unmatched by her colleagues: she was the first person on the supreme court to have served in all four levels of the state's contemporary court structure.

There are a number of clues in Justice Durham's background that explain her drive to excel, but few hints as to the sources of her views on proper judicial role. She regards herself as a conservative in criminal law. Upon her appointment to the supreme court she said, "The court has been criticized for a rather sudden left turn philosophically. I think the new blood on the court will bring us back more to the middle. It's a real challenge." She had long been bothered by the high court concerning itself more with legal technicalities and rules than with "guilt-or-innocence, the ultimate right or wrong." In her view,

the trial is the one time when a person has the ability, the opportunity, to prove
guilt or innocence and you've got to give him the benefit of the doubt... But
once a person was convicted and that determination made... I... believe in stiff
sentencing.

When Governor Dixy Lee Ray interviewed her in 1980 for appointment to
the court of appeals, she and the governor agreed that judges should not legis-
late. The governor sought a judicial restraintist for the court of appeals and found
one in Judge Durham. Thus, five years later, Justice Durham began her tenure
on the high court with a reputation as a restraintist and avowed conservative
regarding criminal law.

Despite her aim to bring the court "back more to the middle," Justice Durham
has said that she is attentive to what the other judges say in conference and tries
to incorporate their views into her opinion:

[T]o the extent that I can be intellectually honest... I'll accommodate as much
as I can but if we have five votes and the change would weaken a principle that
I believe in, I would probably go ahead and write it in the way I believe.

Over the initial three years of her tenure, Justice Durham wrote her share
of the majority opinions and voted with the majority in eighty-five percent of
the cases. This placed her nearly at the court average. She does lobby her colleagues, admitting that "lobbying is part of the discourse" and a necessary part
of court dynamics. It is, of course, through lobbying or informal conferring that
agreements are reached.

Except for her views on crime and punishment and on the court substituting its view of public policy for that of the legislature, Durham regards herself
as a moderate jurist. In the first three years of her tenure, she ranked second
behind Justice James Dolliver in providing majority opinions with the deciding
or important "swing" vote. In other words, she often supplied the decisive vote
needed to achieve or solidify the majority. Her voting record and decisional habits
suggest that Justice Durham understands the need to be cognizant of her colleagues' concerns.

Durham takes both a collective and individual approach to her dissents. She
drafts dissents in crucial cases to persuade others to her view. She denies using
dissent simply to "blow off steam." But if too many concessions are necessary
to gain votes, she will write dissents without regard for her colleagues: "I want
to keep my record clean." From 1985 through the first half of 1988, Durham
dissented less than average for the nine justices, attesting to her persuasiveness
as well as her willingness to accommodate in most cases confronting the court.
Of course, this could also mean that she is on the winning team, the conservative-
restraintist judges having a majority on the court, making dissent often unnecessary.

Consistent with her restraintist views, Durham has, on occasion, criticized the court's exercise of judicial review. Many of her concerns about constitutional issues arise out of search and seizure cases and disputes over police and trial procedures. In her view, the constabulary ought not to be unduly hindered in its efforts to keep streets safe. However, she recognizes that the legislature does occasionally write unconstitutional acts necessitating court intervention. But her concern is that legislation should not be disapproved "merely because it offends the court's sense of social policy." She strongly disagrees "with the practice of second-guessing the elected representatives of the people."

Justice Durham was born in Anacortes, Washington, on October 6, 1942. Her father, who managed movie theaters, died when Barbara was eleven. With sole responsibility for supporting herself and two daughters, her mother returned to teaching. The family moved to Vashon Island, where Barbara attended high school. Although working summers and after school, Barbara found time for numerous extra-curricular activities, including cheer squad, student council, and debate. Debating was one of her favorite activities; this interest in turn attracted her to the law as a career. However, even as a little girl she always asked "Why?," wrote "contracts," and questioned her parents. Her father predicted she would make a good lawyer.

After high school, the future jurist attended Gonzaga University in Spokane on a scholarship. Her interest in debate led her to transfer the next year—1962—to Georgetown University in Washington, D. C., where, again, she had a scholarship and majored in finance. She became the first woman to compete for the prestigious Philodemic Debating Society. Upon graduation in 1964 Durham accepted a job with Merrill Lynch in New York City. After an unsatisfying year of analyzing financial statements for the firm, she applied to several law schools, accepting admission to Stanford.

While at Stanford she became attracted to the politics of Ronald Reagan and the Republican party. She thought she might have been the only Reaganite among her Stanford classmates. She continued to work at odd jobs during the school year. In the 1960s not many women studied law, and those who did were not always treated seriously by their male classmates or faculty. Being a part-time cocktail waitress and former cheerleader seemed not to fit the chauvinists' picture of a lawyer. However, Durham's debating talents and hard work soon, although begrudgingly, won respect.

After graduation she accepted a position with King County Prosecutor Charles O. Carroll and spent the first six months handling morals cases. Two years in the prosecutor's office conditioned her to take a hard line toward those convicted of crimes. The office also introduced her to Washington politics. Republican Carroll typically urged his deputies to become politically active, especially in his reelection campaigns. This was Durham's singular involvement in partisan politics. In 1970 she left the prosecutor's office to begin private practice in the partnership of Wacker and Durham; later she joined Kempton, Savage, and Gossard. She continued private practice after her appointment by the King County Council as a part-time district court judge on Mercer Island, which began Durham's judicial career.

Judge Durham's appointment to the supreme court was the product of precise timing. President Ronald Reagan had nominated Justice Carolyn Dimmick, the first woman to sit on the state high bench, for a federal district court position, but the senate had not yet confirmed her. Voters had recently reelected her to another six-year term on the state court. To permit outgoing Republican Governor John Spellman to fill Dimmick's position before Democrat Governor-elect Booth Gardner took over, Dimmick took a chance on senate confirmation, resigned, and allowed Spellman to appoint Durham as her replacement on his last day in office. Even without Dimmick's insistence that Durham replace her, it was likely that he would have appointed Durham: in missing out on an earlier appointment it was understood that the next court vacancy was hers. The state bar association had approved Durham and she had a fine reputation. With the only woman on the court leaving, Spellman also felt compelled to replace her with another woman. Few criticized the appointment and no questions arose over the last-minute resignations and appointments which, in fact, had been negotiated months earlier.

Justice Durham succeeds in part because she is a woman in a highly competitive system dominated by men. That competition has compelled her to excel. Her father's death left mother and daughters to fend for themselves. Durham's mother often reminded her daughters that they needed an education to make it on their own. In most of her undergraduate and law school classes, Durham was either the only woman or one among a few. As a member of the debate squad she invaded a man's world. She was one of but a few women hired in the King County Prosecutor's Office. As a private attorney she always defended clients before male judges, usually against male opponents. Her appointment to the district court came because of an effort by the county commissioners to place a woman on the bench. She ran against a man for the court of appeals position, where gender became an issue. Judge Durham was the first and, for a long time, only woman on the state's appellate bench.

Justice Durham is married to Dr. Charles Divelbiss; it is her second marriage. They have no children. Outside-the-court activities include entertaining friends in their Seattle home, gourmet cooking, boating, and promoting animal welfare. Her court workload, however, calls for many hours at her office desk at home, where she conducts research and drafts memos and opinions, maintaining contact with the Temple of Justice via a computer modem link-up.

Selected References

Durham's oral history interview is in the supreme court collection, Washington State Archives. Also see *Bellevue* (Fall 1987), pp. 1-3; *Spokane Spokesman-Review*, 1 Dec. 1984; *Everett News Tribune*, 14 Oct. 1987; and *Seattle-King County Bar Bulletin* (Oct. 1984), p. 5.

Overton Gentry Ellis
May 10, 1911-May 11, 1918

Born: October 26, 1860
Nodaway County, Missouri
University of Missouri, B.A. (1883)
University of Virginia Law School
    (1884-1885)
Died: November 9, 1940
Assistant Prosecuting Attorney (1886-1887)
Tacoma City Attorney (1904-1906)
Democrat
Appointed

Overton G. Ellis, the son of Dr. Thomas Cowie and Jane Harris (Gentry) Ellis, was born near the Nebraska and Iowa borders in northwestern Missouri. Ellis graduated as valedictorian from the University of Missouri in 1883 and attended the University of Virginia Law School from 1884 to 1885. He continued his law studies in the office of Edwards and Ellison in Maryville, and was admitted to the Missouri bar in 1886.

Ellis began his professional career in Maryville and soon became assistant prosecuting attorney for Nodaway County (1886-1887). He became title attorney for the Lombard Investment Company of Kansas City in 1887 and was the company's trial attorney between 1889 and 1892. Ellis resigned in 1892 and moved to Tacoma to continue his legal practice in what was then a village situated near the southern end of Puget Sound.

The future judge practiced alone until forming the law firm of Ellis and Fletcher in 1901, a partnership expanded to Ellis, Fletcher, and Evans in 1908. He served as Tacoma City Attorney for a two-year term beginning in 1904. Ellis served on the Tacoma Charter Commission that drafted the city's new charter in 1909.

In 1910 Judge Frank Rudkin resigned from the state supreme court to accept a federal appointment. Although Democrat Ellis was Republican Governor Marion E. Hay's second choice for the vacancy, most applauded the selection. With the exception of the short-term appointment of Stephen Chadwick, this was the first time a governor had crossed party lines to make a supreme court appointment. Hay remarked that he made his selection "wholly upon the recommendations from attorneys in whom I have absolute confidence, not from one but from many parts of the state."

Appointing a Democrat proved to be good politics. The Progressives had succeeded in discrediting the partisan election of judges after the 1910 election. The appointment of Ellis sat well with this influential segment of state politics. Further, Ellis had not been an active Democrat. Also, since Rudkin was from Seattle, an appointment from the state's west side was, by tradition, necessary. Ellis easily won the election in 1912 for a full six-year term but chose not to run for reelection, resigning seven years and a day after his initial appointment. He returned to Tacoma where he rejoined his old law partner, Robert H. Evans.

Ellis married Jennie Wilhite of Kansas City in August, 1894. He was active in several societies, including the Sons of the American Revolution (serving as president for two terms), Washington Historical Society, Tacoma Club, the Commercial Club, Washington State Bar Association, and American Bar Association.

Selected References

Washington State Bar Association *Proceedings* (1914), pp. 179-185; C. S. Reinhart, *History of the Supreme Court of the Territory and State of Washington* (n.d.), p. 77.

Robert Corpening Finley
January 8, 1951-March 23, 1976

Born: November 7, 1905
Marion, North Carolina
Duke University, B.A. (1930)
Duke University, LL.B. (1934)
Georgetown University, LL.M. (1936)
Methodist
Died: March 23, 1976
Federal Housing Administration (1934-1935)
Federal Alcohol Control Administration (1935-1937)
U. S. Department of Justice (1937-1940)
Office of Price Administration (1942-1945)
Democrat
Elected

Robert Corpening Finley was a man shaped by complex experiences. He once wrote, "Life is change—often lively and sometimes dramatic. It is not in complacency, but in the courage to grow, that we find the answers to the problems of life and living... And law is life, in all its kaleidoscopic multi-dimensional realities." Finley's life experiences shaped his view of the law.

Finley was born on November 7, 1905 in fairly secure circumstances in Marion, North Carolina. His parents, Robert Sylvester and Willie Grace (Corpening) Finley, owned a drug store in Asheville, a city in the Blue Ridge Mountains of eastern North Carolina, where Robert grew up. He attended public schools in Asheville, graduated from high school in 1923, and enrolled at Trinity College (now Duke University) in Durham, North Carolina. While there he participated in a number of undergraduate activities. He was leader of the college orchestra, played on the varsity football squad, and joined a fraternity. His academic interests were economics and English, but playing the saxophone and clarinet with an orchestra and student dance band gave him the most satisfaction.

Finley left Trinity before completing his studies to play with such big name dance bands as those led by Bunny Berrigan, Tom Truesdale, and Hal Kemp. Later he formed his own band. Although fairly successful, the hand-to-mouth existence of jazz musicians, the drudgery of one-night stands, and an injury to his hand convinced Finley that opportunities for a more satisfying and stable career lay elsewhere. He returned to Durham and Duke University to complete his undergraduate studies and, in 1932, enrolled in the university's law school.

It is not clear why law attracted him, but the future judge thrust himself into legal studies with enthusiasm. His peers recognized his leadership qualities and elected Finley president of the student bar association, where he made the study of professional ethics his particular interest. In 1934, in the depths of the Great Depression, he received his LL.B. and entered the job market. But, for talented and committed young attorneys, Washington, D. C. and President Franklin Roosevelt's New Deal provided an opportunity to participate in a great experiment. Finley's restless nature, already evidenced by years on the road with big bands, led him from one federal agency to another.

Finley first joined the Federal Housing Administration. In 1935 he became an examiner with the Federal Alcohol Administration. While working for the administration, he completed studies for his master of laws degree at Georgetown University. Attracted to the idea of working with those caught up in the criminal justice system because of economic circumstances, Finley left the nation's capital in 1937 to work as a probation officer with the federal Bureau of Prisons in North Carolina. After a short time he became discouraged; his efforts at rehabilitation seemed not to work. Within a year he returned to Washington, D. C., as an attorney with the claims division of the Department of Justice.

An article Finley wrote for the *Georgetown Law Review* impressed Washington's Attorney General Smith Troy, who invited the future judge to the state to work with him. Finley had married Olympia native Werdna Phillips in 1937 while working for the alcohol administration, and the idea of relocating in the West attracted them. He accepted Troy's offer. Finley's assistant attorney general's roles found him working with the highways, social security, and education departments in Seattle, and later with the state unit of the Office of Price Administration (OPA). In 1944 Finley returned to the nation's capital to serve with OPA's director of food enforcement. But with his wife Werdna and their two children, Pat and Randy, he returned to Seattle in 1945 to embark on a legal career in private practice. Their third child, Sparkle, was born in Seattle in 1947. That same year Robert opened a second office in Renton. But Finley became restless again and, encouraged by some of his clients – many from the labor movement – decided to run for the supreme court. Werdna remembered it as a major decision, but "he felt that the work of the supreme court was what he was most suited for."

The 1948 campaign proved unique and unfortunate for the relatively unknown Finley. The Seattle and Washington State Bar Associations, for the first time, conducted preferential polls on each of the court races. They intervened in the electoral process to prevent the reelection of Judges William Millard and Joseph Mallery, two of the three incumbents on the ballot. Finley's race against incumbent John S. Robinson was not part of the bars' concern and the lawyers apparently felt compelled to support at least one of the incumbents. Consequently, they recorded overwhelming support for Robinson. Had the Millard or Mallery races not drawn the bar associations into the campaigns, Finley might have fared much better. As it was, he survived the September primary, but lost to Robinson by more than 130,000 votes in the November election.

In 1950, Finley filed again for the court against incumbent George B. Simpson. Simpson's reputation as a conservative jurist led labor to support Finley. But again the bar favored the incumbent. Because only two filed for the position, the winner of the September primary would move to the general election unopposed. Finley had acquired name familiarity from his 1948 campaign, and his organization, with the support of labor and the Grange, remained intact. He campaigned on his extensive experience in the federal government and in general practice. His efforts paid when he won by some 30,000 votes, an unusual accomplishment against an incumbent. On January 8, 1951, Robert C. Finley took his oath of office and began a judicial career that, as Werdna Finley had correctly predicted, "most suited" him.

Judge Finley's opinions are found in fifty volumes of the *Washington Reports* spanning over twenty-five years. But it is perhaps not a distortion to suggest that his lasting impact on the court came as much from the manner in which he molded the law as from the content he gave it. His judicial style made him an exceptional judge.

Justice Benjamin Cardozo served as Finley's role model, and leaders in the realist school of jurisprudence provided him with his norms for decision. He often quoted from Cardozo's *The Nature of the Judicial Process* and largely accepted the master's sage advice:

> My analysis of the judicial process comes then to this, and to little more: logic, and history, and custom, and utility, and the accepted standards of right conduct, are the forces which singly or in combination shape the progress of the law. Which of these forces shall dominate in any case, must depend largely upon the comparative importance or value of the social interests that will be thereby promoted or impaired.

According to Cardozo, a judge who openly recognizes the policy implications and personal thrust of his or her decisions assumes a greater burden than those who delude themselves into thinking they are merely discovering the law and applying it. Finley argued that adopting the Cardozo "formula. . . implies or poses significantly the matter of individual responsibility. . . If judgment, discretion, or choice there is, then it follows there is responsibility for decision making." Not surprisingly, law clerks serving the court during Finley's tenure on the bench, along with appellate attorneys, viewed the judge as one of the most liberal-activist jurists. He was result-oriented and deeply concerned with the public's interest. Justice Robert Brachtenbach, who admired Finley greatly, recalled that he

> was more concerned about what the effect of a case would be on people rather than following what some book said from the past. Bob Finley refused to become entangled in the dry web of ancient rules.

Being result-oriented and activist did not absolve him of accountability. But it was accountability to the community and the public. Social interests provided the judge's frame of reference. This required that he be attuned to society and assumed that he could discern a single or overriding social interest.

The judge saw a distinct advantage in the collegial feature of appellate courts: "Several heads are (or should be) better than one." And he regarded it a necessity that there be a give-and-take between and among judges. One of his law clerks remembered that Finley persuasively sought signatures on his draft opinions: he inserted excerpts from opinions of other justices' prior decisions, hoping to convert them to his view. The judge wrote a considerable number of dissenting and concurring opinions. This practice coincided with his "responsibility" perspective. He expressed his view of dissents in one of his numerous articles on the judging process:

> [T]he filing of a dissent is more indicative and [a] more truthful and accurate reporting practice as to what a court decided; hence, more useful to lawyers when members of a court cannot agree unanimously. The filing of an opinion as though a decision is unanimous, when in fact it is not, is to my mind actually a questionable practice.

Finley's first written opinion, in 1951, was a dissent in *Senior Citizens' League v. Department of Social Security.* He dissented in part and concurred in part, agreeing with the majority that an answer should be provided to whether the law conflicted with the constitution, but disagreeing on how the majority answered. The court should always deal with "questions of large public importance," he claimed, and believed that the voice of the judges "might very well be of some considerable importance and perhaps of some assistance." But he "strongly disagree[d] with the majority view respecting the constitutionality of the delegation of legislative power." Thus, his concern for policy issues meshed with his idea of responsibility: when judges are compelled to answer issues of public interest they should confront them directly; and when they disagree they should record their reasons. To do otherwise is to avoid responsibility.

Two characteristics marked Finley's tenure on the supreme court: one, his keen interest in and commitment to the appellate process; the other, his restless nature. Finley, extremely concerned with the courts bogging down in excessive litigation, archaic practices, and unresponsive rules, became one of the first jurists to address the problems of judicial administration. He devoted considerable time and effort—through speeches, articles, seminars, and conferences—to streamlining court business procedures, and in the process developed a national reputation for judicial reform. This reputation encouraged him to pursue another elusive goal: appointment to the U. S. Supreme Court.

In 1963, after Finley had served on the bench for nearly a dozen years, rumors circulated that Justice William O. Douglas contemplated retirement after nearly twenty-five years on the nation's highest court. The supreme court traditionally had a Westerner, and replacing one Washingtonian with another made some political sense. A letter-writing campaign, directed at Attorney General Robert Kennedy and key members of the senate, urged Finley's consideration. But Justice Douglas remained, ultimately to serve more than a third of a century on the U. S. Supreme Court.

When Justice Tom Clark of Texas retired in 1967, Washington's congressional delegation, especially Senators Henry Jackson and Warren Magnuson, brought Finley's name to the president's attention as a possible replacement. Finley also called for support from his many admirers among other state courts and advocates for judicial reform. However, Finley apparently was never given serious consideration, and the appointment went to Thurgood Marshall.

One more opportunity for high-court appointment tempted Finley. Justice Abe Fortas, criticized for questionable financial and philanthropic associations, resigned from the supreme court in 1969. Republican President Richard Nixon was not likely to appoint a Democrat to the court. But White House Counsel John Ehrlichman knew Finley well and regarded him as highly qualified. The judge, realizing his chances were slim, thought it well worth the effort trying for the appointment:

> This is probably the last time around for me: however, by reason of some things that are cooking, I do feel that the chances are somewhat better this time for some attention and consideration at the White House.

The appointment never came, but Finley consoled himself by remarking that "just the fact of being recommended and supported... prompts a good feeling of well-being and gratitude on my part."

Despite his disappointment at being passed over for the U. S. Supreme Court, Finley could be proud of his and his colleagues' accomplishments. His concern for judicial administration helped encourage Washington to institute a Court Administrator's Office; pass a constitutional amendment allowing *pro tempore* judges to sit on the court to substitute for disqualified or absent justices; adopt guidelines to allow press and media coverage of trials without threatening fair process; institute an intermediate court of appeals system; and establish a court commissioner for the high bench.

Justice Finley's off-bench activities reflected his restless nature. Red Kelly's Tumwater Conservatory in Olympia, a popular food and drink establishment known for its sophisticated jazz, was his home away from home, where he frequently participated in jam sessions. In his later years he added pottery and painting to his already considerable carpentry skills. Fishing and calling square dances competed for the few moments remaining from court work, hobbies, and professional activities.

Finley also cherished family life. Werdna Finley recalled that their children Pat, Randy, and Sparkle were individuals right from the start. If they showed special interest in anything, we did everything we could to encourage it and to help them explore the subject. They were...terribly interesting people from the beginning.

Pat became a successful Broadway musical actress, television entertainer, and Seattle TV talk-show hostess. Randy was president of Seven Gables Theaters in Seattle. Sparkle became a New York director and producer.

On the morning of March 24, 1976, Tumwater police received a call from Finley's office: the justice had not arrived at work and could not be reached by phone; would they drop by his home? The police found him dead in bed. He had passed away quietly that night, at the age of seventy. With nearly 400 of his close friends and colleagues he had recently celebrated his twenty-five years on the state's high bench.

Justice Robert C. Finley believed judge-made law is "a reality of life." Judges are involved in "weighing of social values in light of human experiences." Justices have an obligation to "honestly and fully set forth for the public" their views on the law. Justice Finley's views of life and the law inextricably colored his judicial decisions.

Selected References

Seattle Times, 1 Aug. 1976; *Seattle Post-Intelligencer,* 25 Je. 1969 and 28 Jan. 1979; memorial services, *Washington Reports,* vol. 86, 2d (1976), pp. xxvi-xxxi; *The Olympian,* 15 Feb. 1976; C. W. Taylor, *Eminent Judges and Lawyers of the Northwest* (1954), p. 56; Melanie Males, "And Hopes He has done Justice: Robert C. Finley of the Washington Supreme Court," typescript, Finley file, supreme court collection, Washington State Archives; Finley papers, Manuscripts, Archives and Special Collections, Washington State University Library.

Harry Ellsworth Foster
July 8, 1956-December 5, 1962

Born: February 13, 1898
McConnellsville, Ohio
University of Washington, LL.B. (1921)
Society of Friends
Died: December 5, 1962
Assistant Attorney General (1928-1933)
Republican
Appointed

Justice Frank P. Weaver, who served on the supreme court with Harry Foster, remembered his colleague with fondness and respect:

> He was quite a student of the law. He was an Anglophile and a great admirer of the English opinions... He was the first, or almost, to use footnotes in Washington Supreme Court opinions. He was known as "Footnote Harry" in the Court and among many lawyers. He was an expert in Workman Compensation cases... I consulted frequently with him to straighten out my thinking.

It was a typical assessment of Judge Foster. He was an enviable source of advice on the law, and his personality attracted those seeking assistance. The judge's close acquaintances universally remarked on his industry and tireless energy. At his memorial service in 1963 his brother, Stanbery Foster, remembered:

> If the occasion required a re-evaluation of the law or the clarification of a rule, he would, with meticulous care, trace the steam engine back to the teakettle, marking, with usable description, each historical milestone of its evolution.

Judge Foster's dissent in *In re Borchert*, in which he traces the history of fee justices of the peace from Magna Carta to Glocca Morra, serves as a testament to his scholarship. Foster, an avid student of American history, also possessed an impressive knowledge of Washington state history. From all accounts, Judge Foster typified a "lawyer's judge" who had not lost sight of the place law plays in the course of history. And he enjoyed his work. As Judge Matt Hill put it, "Here was a man who thought he had the most wonderful job in the world... his work was a never-ending joy."

Foster, born in McConnellsville, a small town in southeastern Ohio fifty miles from the West Virginia border, was one of four sons of Howard Ellsworth and Cora (King) Foster. The elder Foster, an attorney, practiced the kind of law typical of small town America at the turn of the century. The family moved to Seattle in 1900, where Harry attended Horace Mann Elementary School and Broadway High School, graduating in 1916. In the meantime, his father established himself within the profession and the community, being elected twice to the Washington House of Representatives, serving from 1910-1914.

Harry grew up in a climate of law and politics, and committed himself to the law as his life's work. Unlike his father, he became only minimally involved in Republican politics. He enlisted in the navy during World War I and served one year, after which he returned to Seattle to attend the University of Washington, graduating from the law school in 1921.

Foster immediately began practicing law in Seattle, remaining until 1928; he then became an assistant attorney general in Olympia and served until 1933. From then until his appointment to the supreme court, he practiced in Olympia. Foster participated in bar association activities, serving two terms as president of the Thurston-Mason counties bar association. He was also on the Judicial Council (1950-1956), the Statute Law Commission responsible for codifying state law, and the state bar association's advisory committee on codification. Admitted to practice before the U. S. Supreme Court in 1928, Foster established a reputation when he won a ruling of insanity for his client, Guido Grassi, cheating the gallows of a condemned murderer. Foster earned no fee for his effort, but this victory and others garnered him respect from fellow attorneys.

In July 1956, Judge Frederick G. Hamley accepted an appointment to the Ninth Circuit Court of Appeals in San Francisco just before completing his six-year term on the supreme court, creating both a short-term and a full six-year vacancy. Harry Foster filed for the full term, stating his candidacy "was not self-inspired." He yielded to "widespread urging from leaders in the bar who not only were satisfied" with his qualifications but who also "felt the vacancy properly belonged to Southwest Washington." Five other aspirants filed for the open position including John F. Dore, a member of a well-known political family in Seattle and an active Democrat. On July 8, 1956, Republican Governor Arthur Langlie appointed Foster to the remaining few months of Hamley's short term, allowing him to campaign as the incumbent and giving him a distinct advantage over his opponents. One candidate accused Langlie of giving "Foster a campaign contribution from public funds [his pay as a judge], and the opportunity of having his picture taken wearing a judge's robes." But Langlie retorted he made the appointment without "giving any consideration to political considerations." When the vacancy occurred he proceeded "to fill it." Besides, "the court had considerable business to transact." Foster's campaign received a boost with the state bar association's endorsement. He and Dore won in the primary, and Foster turned back Dore's challenge in the November balloting by 413,097 to 354,529 votes. In 1962, Foster ran unopposed.

Foster established himself as a moderate, usually positioned between conservatives like Judges Charles Donworth and Matthew Hill and liberals such as Judges Robert Finley and Hugh Rosellini. He penned 172 majority opinions. But his scholarship was perhaps his unique contribution to the court's deliberations. As one of his law clerks remembered, "Judge Foster was not a provincial judge, he looked at the whole theory of the law, not just the state of Washington." According to another, the judge relied mostly on his own "knowledge of the law," "his own research," and, often, "his feeling for what was 'right.'" A random review of some of his opinions attests to his unique manner and thorough scholarship.

Dissenting in a workmen's compensation case in 1960, *Liljeblom v. Department of Labor and Industry,* Judge Foster quoted with relish an early opinion criticizing the majority's ruling which turned on technicalities to deny an award in a workmen's compensation case: "The new legislation was carved from the horror of lawyers and judicial trials." An extended footnote then traced the course of similar legislation in Britain, concluding that by "1946 Parliament lost patience altogether and decided that the only way to make the Acts work at all was to forbid lawyers to have anything to do with them." Typically, the study of the British experience came not from legal sources but rather from what lessons history provided. Again, in *Sauls v. Scheppler,* another 1960 case, Foster, in dissent, livened the opinion with a footnote from a psychology textbook. In another dissent he gave *The Saturday Evening Post* equal prominence with *The Journal of the American Judicature Society,* the *New York University Law Quarterly,* and the *Notre Dame Law Review.* Legal research for Judge Foster was "like panning for gold, and finding the nuggets he wanted–a never-ending thrill."

Sybil Lucy McMeekin and Harry Foster married in Olympia on October 28, 1925. They had two daughters, Marian and Joan, and one son, Harry S. The judge belonged to the Masonic Lodge and the American Judicature Society. In 1959 students at his alma mater honored him with membership in the Order of Coif. On December 5, 1962, shortly after his victory in the 1962 elections but before he began his second full term on the state's court of last resort, Judge Foster died of a heart attack.

Selected References

C. W. Taylor, *Eminent Judges and Lawyers of the Northwest* (1954), p. 459; *Seattle Times,* 31 Jy. 1956, 6 Sept. 1956, and 21 Je. 1965; memorial services, *Washington Reports,* vol. 62, 2d (1963), pp. xxiv-xxxi.

Walter Melville French
January 10, 1927-September 13, 1930

Born: January 30, 1874
Ray, Michigan
Hillsdale College, A.B. (1896)
University of Washington Law School, LL.B.
  (1901)
Episcopalian
Died: September 13, 1930
Superior Court (1912-1926)
Democrat
Elected

Walter French was born in southern Michigan, the eldest of Ezekiel and Mattie (Mitchell) French's six children. When Walter was a baby the family moved to Hillsdale, Michigan, where he later gained his education in the public schools. After high school he entered Hillsdale College, where he graduated in 1896. He then accepted a teaching position in Kansas. In 1897 French volunteered for the Spanish-American War, commissioned as a second lieutenant in the Twenty-second Kansas Volunteers. Immediately after his discharge that year he moved to Seattle.

French and another future supreme court judge, Walter Beals, began their legal studies in the first law class of the newly formed University of Washington Law Department in 1899. During his studies French worked as a clerk and delivery boy for Hemphill Brothers Groceries. He became the first University of Washington law graduate to be admitted to the bar in 1901, and immediately formed a law partnership known as Sweeny, French, and Steiner. After his marriage in 1904, French moved to Alaska as an attorney for mining and coal companies. The next year he returned to Seattle and formed a prosperous partnership with Judge Clay Allen. In 1912 voters elected French to the Kitsap County Superior Court. He was reelected without opposition four subsequent times.

Several vacancies occurred on the supreme court during Governor Ernest Lister's tenure, but the Republican chief executive refused to appoint the Democrat French. If he were to achieve a seat on the high bench, a personal goal, election appeared to be the only approach. In 1918 Warren Tolman defeated French for a two-year term on the bench. In his second try, in 1926, French unseated incumbent O. R. Holcomb for a full term. Between those elections

French had served as visiting superior court judge throughout the state, helping jurisdictions with crowded dockets. Lawyers and voters across Washington came to know him, enabling him to unseat Holcomb. French's service on the court was cut short by death on September 13, 1930 at the age of fifty-six.

Judge French had been relatively active in partisan affairs prior to his election as judge, serving as secretary for the state Democratic convention in 1910. He ran unsuccessfully for the state legislature from the Forty-sixth District and actively campaigned for William Jennings Bryan's presidential drive. He belonged to several fraternal and veterans' groups, including the Spanish-American War Veterans Organization, Masons, Elks, Shriners, and American Legion. He also belonged to the Arctic Club, Earlington Golf Club of Seattle, Tacoma Country Club, and Olympia Golf and Country Club.

In 1904 Judge French married Bessie Clark from Seattle. Her family came to Seattle in 1880, where her father became prominent in business and construction. They had no children.

Selected References

C. S. Reinhart, *History of the Supreme Court of the Territory and State of Washington* (n.d.), pp. 82-3; Lloyd Spencer and Lancaster Pollard, *A History of the State of Washington,* vol. 3 (1937), pp. 4-5; *Seattle Legal News,* 24 Jy. 1915.

Mark Araunah Fullerton
January 9, 1899-September 15, 1931

Born: November 13, 1858
Marion County, Oregon
Willamette University, B.S. (1878)
Protestant
Died: September 15, 1931
Prosecutor (1887-1889)
Republican
Elected

Mark A. Fullerton, born on his father's farm near Salem, Oregon, attended public schools in Marion County and entered Salem's Willamette University in 1875. Although he developed an interest in law at Willamette, he graduated in 1878 in engineering. The county employed him as a surveyor. He became Deputy U. S. Surveyor in 1882, responsible for platting an Indian reservation south of The Dalles, Oregon. Fullerton read the law in his spare time until Judge Stratton of The Dalles took him under his tutelage. The Oregon bar admitted him in 1883 and he practiced in Salem until 1885 when he and his boyhood friend, Stephen J. Chadwick, moved to Colfax, a small farming community in southeastern Washington Territory. The two opened a law office and remained partners until Fullerton won election to the state's highest bench in 1898. Chadwick, a Democrat, and Fullerton, a Republican, each became leaders in their respective political parties, and each served together on the supreme court.

Fullerton served one term (1887-1889) as Whitman County Prosecutor. In 1898 the Republican convention nominated him as its candidate to replace retiring Judge Elmon Scott on the state supreme court, and in November, Fullerton defeated his closest rival by nearly 8,000 votes. He then began the longest tenure on the supreme court—thirty two years—of all eighty-eight justices. He won an unprecedented six consecutive elections. In 1908 his law partner Chadwick joined him on the bench. When he died in 1931, only four other sitting state supreme court justices in the United States exceeded Fullerton's thirty-two years of service.

Because of his long tenure, overall judgments of Fullerton's positions are difficult. As membership on the court changed, Fullerton's position relative to other justices also changed. In the early 1900s the judge tended to be somewhat moderate-to-liberal in negligence and criminal cases, often siding with the underdog. He felt that everyone should have his or her day in the appeals court. For example, in *Brown v. Davis* in 1904 he insisted that:

> Courts should not be over zealous in searching for reasons for dismissal of appeals. The purpose of an appeal is to have a review of a cause upon its merits and the construction of the statutes should be with a view to accomplish this end, rather than to dispose of them without such review.

In these earlier sessions, Fullerton became the bench's leading dissenter. Later, when membership changed and the court shifted away from its conservative stance, Fullerton dissented less and tended to occupy a centrist position.

Justice Fullerton gained national recognition, especially for his opinion in a Workers' Compensation Act case. According to one reporter:

> It reversed a year-old New York Supreme Court decision which held the act unconstitutional.
>
> Theodore Roosevelt, former United States President and editor of *The Outlook*, commented favorably on the decision on which many states now base such legislation.
>
> Judge Fullerton's opinions were known throughout the nation for their clarity. One prominent judge once said: "I don't think much of Washington's courts but I enjoy reading Fullerton's opinions."

In 1887 Judge Fullerton married Ella Ione Rounds, a native of Michigan whose family had moved to Colfax. The Fullertons had three sons: Roscoe, a lawyer, Lynne, a physician, and Charles, a public official in the insurance commissioner's office. Fullerton belonged to the Masons, Elks, and United Workmen. He was an avid duck hunter, fisherman, and gardener. Judge Fullerton died of a stroke in Olympia at the age of seventy-three.

Selected References

William Prosser, *The History of the Puget Sound Country*, vol. 2 (1903), pp. 177-178; H. James Boswell, *American Blue Book: Western Washington* (1922), p. 56; W. C. Wolfe, *Sketches of Washingtonians* (1906), p. 169; Lloyd Spencer and Lancaster Pollard, *A History of the State of Washington*, vol. 3 (1937), pp. 385-386.

James Michael Geraghty
August 15, 1933-April 29, 1940

Born: February 2, 1870
County Mayo, Ireland
Georgetown University Law School (1898)
Catholic
Died: April 29, 1940
State Legislature (1897)
Spokane Corporate Counsel (1905-1907;
    1916-1932)
Director of Efficiency (1933)
Democrat
Appointed

James M. Geraghty was born in 1870 in County Mayo, Ireland. His parents, Patrick and Bridget (Haley) Geraghty, brought their family to America in 1880 and settled on a farm in Indiana. James went to public school in Rush County, Indiana, before moving to Spokane in 1892. First employed as a teamster, he decided to improve his lot by enrolling in business school. He then found employment as a stenographer in the legal department of the corporate counsel of the City of Spokane, and the experience convinced him to study law.

He began studying law in the office of city attorney W. H. Plummer while making $50 a month as Plummer's assistant. In 1896, running on the Fusion ticket (Democrats, Populists, and Free Silver Republicans), Geraghty became the youngest member of the Washington House of Representatives. While in Olympia he took the state bar exam and was admitted to practice in 1897. The 1897 legislature elected Judge George Turner of Spokane as United States Senator, and Turner took Geraghty to Washington, D. C. as his private secretary. While in the nation's capital, Geraghty attended class for one year at Georgetown University Law School. In 1900 Geraghty returned to Spokane to practice law with John P. Judson and later joined Judge Turner when the senator's term ended. In 1905 Geraghty gained appointment to a two-year term as Spokane Corporate Counsel under a Democratic administration. In 1916 a nonpartisan city administration called him back to that office and he served until his selection as a key member of Governor Clarence Martin's cabinet.

As Spokane's city attorney, Geraghty was in the center of city government. As he described his responsibilities: "I have become a sort of unofficial adviser in everything... They come to me on nearly everything, probably because I have been around the city hall so long." Geraghty also became a leading spokesman for Spokane city government throughout the state, and for Democrats generally during legislative sessions in Olympia. He attended several Democratic national conventions and headed the Washington delegation to the Chicago convention in 1928. Even so, he disliked the limelight. When advising others he chose his words carefully, and was little known outside of politics and government. But those within the corridors of power admired him and sought him out. When the Democrats swept into office in the 1932 landslide, new governor Clarence Martin, from eastern Washington, chose his old friend and advisor James Geraghty as his first cabinet appointee to head the Department of Efficiency. According to one newspaper account of Geraghty's appointment:

> As efficiency director Mr. Geraghty will have control of the vitally important offices of supervisor of banks and banking and supervisor of savings and loans. Governor Martin has said he expects Mr. Geraghty to thoroughly reorganize the banking department, his aim being to protect depositors against failures.

Geraghty also headed the Highway Patrol, assumed responsibility for the state Emergency Unemployment Relief Commission, and wrote the governor's budget. Immediately upon his appointment, job seekers, representatives of businesses, and politicians hounded him. A busy man, he was not easily found:

> Those who did find him saw a sparely built, erect man, with a lean Irish face, topped by a thatch of hair that has been black and is graying now.
> They found a man sparing with his words, and those words soft spoken, but with definite ideas of government gained in a lifetime of public affairs.
> Geraghty's economy of words and dislike for the limelight are proverbial. He has long been an important factor in Democratic state affairs.

Why would an active partisan, within a few months of assuming one of the state's most important administrative offices, accept appointment to the rather cloistered, apolitical supreme court? The answer lies in the issues then facing the bench. The governor's state budget was to be balanced on a proposed increase in the business and occupation taxes, while an income tax imposed on voters by means of the initiative process was to finance public schools. Both tax provisions were before the supreme court.

The court had split 4-4 on both issues with Judge Emmett Parker unable to hear the cases because of illness. He announced his retirement, giving Governor Martin an opportunity to determine the outcome of an important case by appointing Parker's replacement. He chose Jimmy Geraghty.

Despite the rather obvious political reason behind the governor's choice, Martin urged his close friend to "call them as you see them" and added that the appointment was "without any strings attached." Geraghty responded to the governor during his swearing-in ceremony: "I am glad you said that. If I didn't know you felt that way I wouldn't have accepted this appointment."

The court scheduled a new hearing for the cases, and three weeks after his appointment Geraghty broke the deadlock by validating the B & O tax. Unfortunately, from the perspective of the governor, Geraghty proved unable to carry a majority of his colleagues in the income tax case and wrote a dissent along with three other justices.

Geraghty's announcement to seek election to the Parker position in 1934 surprised many observers. They thought with the tax cases out of the way the judge would prefer to return to active politics. Geraghty explained his choice to seek election to a full six-year term:

> I have always been interested in politics, but have never been a politician. By that I mean that I have strived to regard and use politics as a necessary tool to promote the rights and interests of the community, not for any selfish objective. The ideal judge should be absolutely divorced from any personal prejudices or partisanship with the welfare of human beings his foremost objective and consideration, in keeping with the constitution and the law.

He survived the primary against three opponents by a margin of 111 votes over his closest rival and defeated his opponent in November by more than 40,000 votes.

Although Judge Geraghty adhered to moderate-liberal Democratic political attitudes, he proved reluctant to intervene judicially in issues he thought need not be resolved. In one of his last opinions he gave expression to this reluctance:

> The record is voluminous, and the briefs deal exhaustively with questions not now before us for decision. If we were to follow the arguments of counsel to a conclusion, the results would be to prejudgment of the issues in any action brought by the administrator to recover the stock. This, we should not do.
>
> A painstaking examination of the record satisfies us that the trial court did not abuse its discretion.... Having reached this conclusion, we do not wish to embarrass a further hearing on the merits by the expression of an opinion as to the ultimate facts.

John Rupp, one of the first law clerks with the Washington Supreme Court, recalled Judge Geraghty's characteristic personality and working habits:

> Judge Geraghty was an interesting man... Much of his adult life before he came on the Court in 1933 had been spent as Corporation Counsel of the City of Spokane. He used to tell me tales beginning with, "When I was running the City of Spokane..." I asked my father [Otto Rupp] about that, and Dad assured me that it was not mere rhetoric and that Judge Geraghty had indeed run the city. My father started practicing law in this State in 1903, and he knew "Jimmy Geraghty" very well. Dad also told me that it was not good form to remind Judge Geraghty that he had once driven a brewery wagon.
>
> Judge Geraghty was a well-read man. One day in conversation he learned that I had not read Albert J. Beveridge's "Life of John Marshall." He lectured me about that deficiency with such vehemence that I read it promptly...

Judge Geraghty used to roust me out of the library and take me to his chambers to discuss the cases on which he was working. He would sit me down and then pace around the room, talking all the while and punctuating his remarks with sweeping gestures with his cigar. At first I thought that I was supposed to contribute to the discussion, and, since I read all the briefs, I knew a little about each case. So I would chip in with helpful remarks. Soon, however, I realized that that was not my role at all. I was a sounding board. He had reached a point in the decisionmaking process where he needed to express his thoughts orally and aloud. I confined my remarks, then, to appreciative murmurs. After a while he would say, "Thank you very much, Mr. Rupp, you have been a great help to me." So I would thank him, in turn, and leave. I suppose that I was a help, at that, but not because of any ideas that I contributed.

Geraghty's mastery of municipal law manifested itself in his last opinion, filed three days before his death. The case resolved the issue of whether a particular Spokane ordinance was subject to a citizens' referendum. Spokane argued that either the ordinance was susceptible to a voters' repeal or it was null and void. Judge Geraghty agreed. Either let the voters decide or the ordinance was invalid. His brethren on the high bench showed their respect for his scholarship with a rare display of unanimity in the *en banc* case. The opinion ended with two simple words: "ALL CONCUR." Geraghty began his political career supporting the causes of the City of Spokane and ended his judicial career still in support of his city.

Judge Geraghty's judicial stance did not coincide with his political image. Although he served as Governor Martin's leading advisor in fashioning and implementing New Deal Democratic policies at the state level, and the governor appointed him largely because he hoped Geraghty would take a liberal approach, students of the court classified him as neutral on the activist-restraintist issue and moderate on legal matters.

A recurring kidney disease sidelined the judge in December 1939, and in the spring of 1940 he was hospitalized. On April 29, 1940, Judge Geraghty passed away, mourned by hundreds in the legal fraternity and political world.

In November 1908, Geraghty married Nora Toolen, a native of Indiana. They had nine children: Thomas, Nora, Helen, Anna, James, John, Patrick, Cecil, and Sheila. They belonged to the Catholic Church and the judge actively supported Catholic affairs both in Spokane and Olympia.

Selected References

Lloyd Spencer and Lancaster Pollard, *A History of the State of Washington*, vol. 4 (1937), p. 660; Charles Sheldon, *A Century of Judging: A Political History of the Washington Supreme Court* (1988), pp. 95-96, 110-111, 203, 237, 268-277; *Seattle Post-Intelligencer*, 16 Aug. 1922; *Spokane Spokesman-Review*, 15 Aug. 1933.

William Cassius Goodloe

January 14, 1985-July 17, 1988

Born: September 19, 1919
Lexington, Kentucky
University of Washington, B.S. (1945)
University of Washington, LL.B. (1948)
Christian Scientist
State Senate (1951-1959)
Superior Court (1972-1984)
Republican
Elected

William C. Goodloe ran for the supreme court in 1984 as an avowed conservative bent upon returning the court to a more restraintist approach to the law. During the campaign he repeatedly argued that "the trend of the supreme court in protecting the criminal defendant's rights as opposed to the victim's rights has been extremely out of balance." He intended to restore the balance. A review of Justice Goodloe's life and career suggests his political experience shaped his restraintist view of the role of courts, while his heritage dictated his conservative values.

The Goodloe name in Lexington, Kentucky, identified a prominent family. William's father, as Judge Goodloe later phrased it, "was born with a silver spoon in his mouth." William himself was born on September 19, 1919 in the family residence, the spacious Loudin mansion which the judge jokingly called his "log cabin." Today it is the city's art museum. Goodloe can trace his ancestry to those who arrived on the Mayflower and participated in the American Revolution. His family included Lincoln's ministers to Belgium and Russia, and two U. S. Senators, Henry Clay and John L. Wilson.

Despite his initial advantage in life, William's father, trained as an engineer, never established himself in several business ventures. In hopes of improving its economic position, the Goodloe family, including eight-month-old William, left Lexington in 1920 for California. They moved to Santa Barbara, then Los Angeles, and finally Pasadena, where William attended a military school in preparation for a navy career. When the naval academy rejected him because of color blindness, he enrolled at Pasadena Junior College. The family fortunes improved when William's mother inherited a modest sum of money from the estate of her father, Congressman and Senator John L. Wilson, a half owner of the *Seattle Post-Intelligencer* when the Hearst Corporation purchased it. These funds, together with money William's father earned working at construction projects, saw the family through the depression.

Goodloe's mother, born in Spokane, urged her son to venture to the Pacific Northwest. He packed his Model A Ford and headed for Seattle with but forty dollars in his pocket. Goodloe planned to enroll at the University of Washington, but could not afford out-of-state tuition. In order to earn tuition money and establish residency, he began working for the General Insurance Company. However, as a member of the reserves for nearly five years, the navy called him into active duty at the outset of World War II. He served in all theaters of the war, saw action on convoy duty in the Atlantic, and won a combat commission. While in the service he married a registered nurse, Phyllis Ruth Clarke, whom he had met while working for the insurance company. Upon discharge in 1945, Goodloe returned to Seattle, enrolled at the University of Washington, and completed requirements for a bachelor of science in law in 1945. He entered law school the next year, completing his law studies in 1948.

The new lawyer first attempted practice out of a room in his boarding house in the university district. As his family grew it became necessary for him to supplement his fees as an attorney by working night shift at the Boeing plant. After a year he moved to downtown Seattle in association with Ed Merges, and the next year formed an enduring partnership with a law classmate, Stuart W. Todd. They practiced together until Goodloe's election to the superior court.

Soon after establishing his downtown practice, politics, which had bestowed prominence on many of his forefathers, lured Goodloe to challenge the Seattle establishment in an unsuccessful 1950 city council race. The next year he won election to the state senate from the Thirty-second District, serving two terms. He rose to chairmanship of the Judiciary Committee and minority floor leader of the Republicans. He authored and co-sponsored legislation authorizing the Seattle World's Fair and proved instrumental in passing a bill establishing the King County Metro District. In the meantime, he mounted an unsuccessful 1955 campaign for mayor of Seattle. In 1958 he lost his bid for a third term in the senate when the right to work ballot initiative brought out labor votes and large numbers of Democrats, dooming most Republicans. In 1962 he narrowly lost a supreme court race against incumbent Orris Hamilton, and two years later lost his bid to become lieutenant governor. In 1970 incumbent supreme court Justice Charles Stafford defeated Goodloe in a second supreme court election attempt. However, two years later he won election to the King County Superior Court, where he served until his successful—and unique—1984 race for the high court.

Goodloe spent a little more than $17,000 in both the hotly contested primary and general elections during a time when expenditures for statewide supreme court positions could involve over $100,000. In the primary he ran against four opponents: an experienced, moderate-to-conservative appeals court judge, Dale Green, who overwhelmed Goodloe in the state bar poll by 1,411 to 928; a highly popular former president of the state bar association; and two fairly well-known attorneys. In the November election all major newspapers endorsed Green, and even some Republicans lent Green their support. Goodloe, sixty-two years old, had been out of partisan politics since his election to the King County Superior Court in 1972 and lacked name recognition in eastern Washington. Still, he won the November election by more than 85,000 votes.

Two aspects of Goodloe's campaign account for his victory: he was organized, and he was motivated by a spirit of adventure and optimism. He had begun planning his race two years earlier. Over the years, Goodloe had built a cadre of conservative supporters from those he worked with as Republican state chairman and had met subsequently while presenting slide lectures on "Great Americans" and giving patriotic talks at schools, churches, picnics, Masonic dinners, business luncheons, community groups, retirement homes, and private gatherings. He mailed an advertisement to more than 1,000 supporters, asking them to place it in their local newspapers. Later, the Public Disclosure Commission fined him, and the Judicial Qualifications Commission admonished him for the ad's content, how he financed it, and a delay in filing reports. Most thought it a trivial matter wholly unintended by him and his campaign manager.

He campaigned in a recreational vehicle with a large sign, "GOODLOE FOR SUPREME COURT," bolted on the side, and met with groups, editors, and potential voters. He visited every major city and many towns throughout the state, staying in parks and camping areas. He organized a committee of ham radio operators to spread the word of his campaign. With the help of family members, he printed all his campaign materials on his own printing and silk screen press at home. Although all of this cost very little, he had $100,000 in reserve from the sale of an orange grove in California to finance a television campaign. It was not needed. His law-and-order view of the legal system struck a responsive note with voters. Significantly, his opponent seemed uneasy soliciting votes while Goodloe enjoyed campaigning.

Justice Goodloe came to the high bench with some apprehension, an open mind regarding his colleagues, and a willingness to learn. In an interview after serving six months on the court he admitted his apprehension:

> I came down here with the objective of looking for the Cardozos. Truly and humbly cultivating them and picking their brains and seeing how I [could] benefit from them... I picked out two very early on whom I was going to listen to and emulate if possible. Now that I have been...here it has been a levelling process. I've been disappointed. What it has done is increase my personal esteem of myself and I have not yet found the giant... I've decided as of now that the best thing I can do now is to work hard, study the cases very carefully and just make my decisions the way my conscience tells me. There really is no one as of now I can look to for leadership.

When all the votes are counted in the 512 cases heard by the court during Goodloe's tenure, they show that he indeed remained independent. Despite his conservatism, he agreed mostly with Justices Fred Dore and James Dolliver, two of the bench's activist-liberals. He disagreed most, although not excessively, with James Andersen, a conservative, and Vernon Pearson, a liberal.

As a result of working within a multi-judge court, he changed his attitude regarding the role of dissent:

> I came down here with the attitude I would be the lowest in dissent. I've discovered that I can't. Certain things as a trial judge [bothered me]. I've discovered that this court needed a trial judge... My basic premise is that I think they are wrong and I am right and I'm going to say so. If I'm lucky they'll agree with me and I'll become the majority.

Goodloe wrote more than his share of dissenting opinions and cast more dissenting votes than his colleagues. After serving another year, Goodloe explained further his dissenting views:

> I picked this up from Bob Utter. He came in one day and said "Dang you Bill! You joined me in dissent. I'm so right about this that I wanted to be alone." I've come to feel that way about it. I dissent because I think they are wrong and frankly I don't care whether they join me or not.

However, Goodloe was not a loner. His legislative experience, and, as he described it, being a "political" man, convinced him he should cooperate. When asked if he consulted informally with colleagues, he quickly responded, "Yes!"

> Some of the justices call it lobbying and they think it improper. I love to be lobbied because I want to know what they say and what their views are. I don't say whatever you say is going to be it and my attitude is that if you have any problems or if you have anything to say, I want to hear you... I want to hear everything, every point of view and I'm going to listen. But it doesn't mean you're going to sell me a bill of goods and I'm going to buy it... Let's call it conferring.

Goodloe wrote slightly less than his share of majority opinions, but when he wrote for the court, his conferring and willingness to listen paid off. As the assignment judge, he made notes during conference regarding the other justices' views and attempted to integrate their perspectives into his majority opinions. This enabled him to garner slightly more than his share of his colleagues' votes.

Although Justice Goodloe remained within the mainstream of the court when writing for it, his dissenting behavior tended to isolate him. This would suggest that Goodloe was either not adjusting personally to some of the other members of the court, to their viewpoints regarding the law, or to the demands of appellate decision-making. For whatever reason, the lack of adjustment was confirmed on June 3, 1988, when he announced he would retire. The sixty-eight year old justice gave no cause for his resignation. However, earlier he hinted at two reasons, personal and legal:

I find it very difficult to come in here as a very idealistic candidate for the supreme court. . . having some very idealistic ideas on how it works. I find two problems. . . There was one [law and order] issue before the court that was a very prominent issue in our campaign. Four of us [campaigned on that issue]. . . I wrote a concurring opinion [instead of sticking with the other three]. . . What has happened is that they are madder than hell. I'm accused of being a traitor to the campaign.

The personal affront hurt him deeply. He was bothered by the politics permeating the court's deliberations. Decisions on the court were not "purely law as I thought. . . I'm disillusioned. This is awful strong language." Also, he felt that some members of the bench failed to appreciate his efforts on behalf of the court's celebration of the bicentennial of the U. S. Constitution. As the court's representative, he had delivered nearly fifty addresses, some outside the state. Perhaps the final straw came when his colleagues discouraged him from participating in the Sixth International Conference of the Association for the Unity of Latin America. Goodloe approved the association's efforts and its goal of a united Latin America. He wrote the first three drafts of a constitution for the United States of Latin America and wanted to attend the 1988 conference in Santa Domingo. But his colleagues claimed attendance conflicted with the court's hearing schedule. Thus, for a variety of reasons, his disillusionment reached sufficient proportions by spring 1988, and he resigned.

After announcing he would leave the court, the press made much of Goodloe's recommendation to the governor that he appoint a minority justice from eastern Washington to replace him. The media quickly, but incorrectly, pointed out that as a retiring justice, his recommendation was unprecedented. Although not common, other retiring and retired judges had endorsed candidates. Nonetheless, the governor heeded Goodloe's timely advice: if the justice delayed his retirement a few months, his position would be filled by election, depriving the chief executive the appointment. Governor Booth Gardner's appointment of Charles Z. Smith, a respected African American lawyer, former judge, and law professor from Seattle, to some extent followed Goodloe's recommendation.

Although he claimed it had no bearing on his decision to leave the court, a week after retirement Goodloe announced he would file against former Senator Slade Gorton for the Republican nomination to the U. S. Senate. He believed Gorton to be too moderate for many Republicans. "I guess the word frustration is about the best way to describe what I'm getting from the grassroots," he said. "They think that Slade Gorton is on the liberal side of center." His late start, narrow conservative base, lack of campaign funds, and Gorton's popularity led to Goodloe's resounding defeat in the Republican primary. He ran third, attracting only 26,224 votes of over 600,000 cast.

Justice Goodloe does not hide his pride in heritage and country. He often speaks about the greatness of early American leaders, has served as state governor for the Society of Mayflower Descendants, and belongs to the Society of

Cincinnati — descendants of officers who fought with George Washington at Valley Forge. The Daughters of the American Revolution awarded him the National Medal of Honor in 1976. He also received the Good Citizenship Medal from the Sons of the American Revolution in 1973, and an honor certificate from the Freedoms Foundation in 1977. Pride in country, reflected by these memberships and awards, accounts for Justice Goodloe's commitment to public service. It can, in part, explain why he often contested elections, the winning of which appeared impossible. He believes that one should act upon deeply held views even against overwhelming odds of succeeding.

William and Phyllis Goodloe have seven children and eighteen grandchildren. After retirement, the justice continued his involvement with the Association for the Unity of Latin America, and served on the board of the National Center for Constitutional Studies. The Association awarded him the Grand Cross of the Badge of Gold in 1988 for his draft constitution. He also served as *pro tem* judge in Seattle, assuming special assignments, and was the Washington director for the American Freedom Coalition, a conservative political action committee that organizes at the grassroots level and lobbies the state legislature. His conservative observations of state, national, and international politics are published in his weekly *The Goodloe Report*.

Although Goodloe called his abortive 1988 senate race his "last hurrah" in partisan politics, he has considered a race for the U. S. Senate as an independent under the banner of the American Party and remains active in promoting the party in the state. He organized the Judicial Forum, a citizens' watchdog group committed to replacing activist judges on the state benches with conservative restraintists. Politics is a driving force in Goodloe's life and remains so even in his so-called retirement.

Selected References

Goodloe's oral history interview is in the supreme court collection, Washington State Archives, as are the Goodloe papers. Also helpful is the Stuart Todd oral history interview in the same collection, and Goodloe's monthly newsletter, *The Goodloe Report*.

Merritt J. Gordon
January 14, 1895-June 1, 1900

Born: March 17, 1857
Sherbrooke, Quebec
Protestant
Died: June 5, 1925
South Dakota Constitutional Convention
(1886; 1889)
South Dakota Legislature (1889-1890)
Superior Court (1892-1894)
Republican
Elected

Merritt J. Gordon, born in Sherbrooke, Canada, a small city approximately fifty miles north of Vermont, received his early education in public schools in Huntington County, Quebec, and in nearby Clinton County, New York. In 1874 he moved to Lanesboro, Minnesota, where he worked as a bank teller. He studied law under the supervision of an attorney and was admitted to the Minnesota bar in June 1878. In 1879 he moved to Dakota Territory, in what was later South Dakota, and opened a law office. There he met and married Jennie Thompson, and they became parents to a son and daughter.

The future judge was elected a member of the Dakota constitutional conventions of 1886 and 1889. He served as district attorney for Brown County in northeastern South Dakota from 1884 to 1888, presided over the Dakota Fifth Judicial District Bar Association from 1885 to 1889, and was Aberdeen City Attorney for two terms. Active in Republican circles, he unsuccessfully sought the party's nomination as territorial delegate to Congress in 1886. When South Dakota achieved statehood in 1889, voters elected Gordon to the first state legislature where he chaired the House Judiciary Committee. In the spring of 1890 he moved to Olympia and became associated with Colonel T. V. Eddy in the practice of law.

Gordon, elected to the Thurston-Mason County Superior Court in 1892, served two years before winning election to the supreme court on the Republican ticket in 1894, defeating the closest Democrat by nearly 20,000 votes. He resigned in June 1900 to accept the position of counsel for the Great Northern Railway Company in Spokane. Later, in 1909, Gordon moved to Tacoma to return to private practice in the partnership of Gordon and Nolte.

Although returning to law practice, Gordon remained active in the legal and political concerns of the high bench. According to one newspaper account:

> After Gordon left the state's high bench in 1900 he continued in active politics, evincing from time to time especial interest and activity in the selection of members of the supreme court, which activity continued up to and including the campaign of 1908 when he was active in raising a fund for use in advocating the candidacy of ex-Judge Milo Root.

It was this relationship with Judge Root that proved to be Root's undoing and the beginning of Gordon's fall from grace.

Rumors persisted in 1908 that Gordon had been short in his accounts with the Great Northern Company and that some of this money had been used to influence supreme court decisions. Specifically, some critics accused Supreme Court Judge Root of showing Gordon a draft of a denial of rehearing in *Harris v. Great Northern Railway Company,* and claimed Gordon rewrote parts of it so that it narrowed the opportunities to bring future cases against the railway company.

Judge Root chose to resign from the high bench, but Gordon's troubles continued. When he left his position with Great Northern, it was not clear whether he resigned willingly or under pressure from the company. In January 1909 Gordon was arrested for embezzling $9,200 from the Great Northern Company. Later, in May 1909, a grand jury indicted him, handing down additional charges.

During the grand jury investigation, Great Northern had promised full cooperation. But when the trial began, the company failed to produce subpoenaed materials, including vouchers, records of transactions, and other matters handled by Gordon. Railroad witnesses failed to appear and the Great Northern accounts in the Spokane Old National Bank were ruled inadmissible. Spokane County Prosecutor Fred Pugh was frustrated at every turn by the obstinacy of Great Northern and the brilliant tactics of defense attorneys Frank Graves, N. E. Nusum, and Potter Charles Sullivan.

At the end of Gordon's trial in March 1910, Superior Court Judge H. L. Kennan made the following ruling:

> It appears to me that there is no evidence to show that this defendant appropriated this money to his own use... The state in a case of this sort must show that the money was used for his own purposes and not diverted for other legitimate use, and I can not find this has been done. In the absence of representatives of the railway company to claim irregularities against him, the state can not make out the case. I therefore grant the motion of the defense and will instruct the jury [to rule] for the defendant.

How could a respected member of the legal profession, who had served with distinction nearly six years on the state's highest bench, two as chief justice, be so careless with a company's funds? One acquaintance of Gordon suggested an answer:

Gordon is one of the most remarkable men I have ever seen. He could stay up all night, hire an automobile in the morning, go into the country with a party of friends, sing a few songs, drink some booze, and return to town apparently refreshed and ready for the legal business in which he was interested. On these trips he usually insisted on paying all expenses. He is a very good story teller, a good listener, and one of the best entertainers I ever knew. Apparently he has no sense of the value of money, and I often wondered what would be the finish at the clip at which he was going.

Although found not guilty in 1910, Judge Gordon did not regain the prominence he enjoyed before the publicity surrounding the trial. He returned to Tacoma to practice law, only to be the victim of another tragedy. On June 5, 1925, a runaway automobile struck down and killed him as he attempted to cross one of the steep bayside streets in downtown Tacoma.

Selected References

Arthur Beardsley, "Root-Gordon Scandal," chapter 41 of Beardsley manuscript, Washington State Archives; C. S. Reinhart, *The History of the Supreme Court of the Territory and State of Washington* (n.d.), pp. 85-86; H. James Boswell, *American Blue Book: Western Washington* (1922), p. 182; W. C. Wolfe, *Sketches of Washingtonians* (1906), p. 176; Charles Sheldon, *A Century of Judging: A Political History of the Washington Supreme Court* (1988), pp. 44, 46.

Mack F. Gose
February 12, 1909-January 11, 1915

Born: July 8, 1859
Sullivan County, Missouri
Whitman College
Episcopalian
Died: January 31, 1942
Pomeroy City Attorney
Pomeroy Mayor and Member of City Council
(1898-1904)
President, Washington State Bar Association
(1915)
Republican
Appointed

John M. and Hannah J. (McQuown) Gose, Mack F. Gose's parents, left Missouri for the West, first stopping at Boise, Idaho, then moving on to Walla Walla in Washington Territory. They arrived but a few days after their son's sixth birthday. Mack was one of four children, all of whom achieved prominence in professional and public life. Their father, trained as a physician, became a farmer and successful orchardist. Mack attended Walla Walla public schools and then enrolled in Whitman Seminary, later known as Whitman College. He studied law with John B. Allen and B. J. Crowley, both legal and political leaders of their time. The Washington bar admitted him in 1883, and he immediately associated with the firm of Allen, Crowley, and Gose. He soon moved to the southeastern farming community of Pomeroy, where he joined E. V. Kuykendall in the practice of law.

Gose became active in Republican politics, was elected mayor of Pomeroy in 1898, served as a member of the city council for several terms, and also as acting city attorney. He also was vice president of the First National Bank of Pomeroy.

According to Ewart M. Baldwin's history of Garfield County,

> The first and most absolute political boss of Garfield County was Samuel Goodlove Cosgrove who was later elected governor. Cosgrove was a man of strong opinions given to political maneuvering and who had never learned the art of compromise. He was soon joined in 1896 by an ex-Democrat named M. F. (Mack) Gose. With Cosgrove's death in 1909, Gose inherited the mantle as political boss, which he exercised with more finesse until his death. While Cosgrove was alive, he was the one who called the tune. He was combative and heavy handed. He

demanded loyalty and could be vindictive. Gose was much smoother. He may not have been much less determined than Cosgrove, but he worked his will with wit and a generally unruffled exterior. Although he may not have been Irish, he had kissed the Blarney stone and was a gallant with the ladies, very much at home in southeastern Washington society and later in Olympia.

When Cosgrove won his election as governor in 1908 he was unable to take office because of ill health. His one official act was to urge Governor Albert E. Mead to appoint his old friend Mack Gose to the vacancy created by Judge Milo Root's refusal to serve his elected position in 1909. In 1910 Gose easily defeated two opponents for the remaining four years of Root's term. He lost in the 1914 primary and was forced to retire from the high bench. According to a close observer of elections during that year, Gose "had spent nearly all of his time in the little town of Pomeroy, had very little acquaintance in the large cities and was not boosted by any political or semi-political organization or special interest." The Republican party label had assured Gose's election in 1910, but the new nonpartisan election system in 1914 made him vulnerable.

During his term on the court Judge Gose tended to view the law from a slightly broader perspective than many of his contemporaries. Although not an extremist, he willingly considered the nature of the society in which the law played such an important role. For example, in *State v. Somerville*, he asserted a sociological perspective:

> Courts in passing upon the reasonableness or unreasonableness of a statute, and deciding whether the legislature has exceeded its authority power to such an extent as to render the act invalid, must look at the terms of the act itself, and bring to their assistance such scientific, economic, physical, and other pertinent facts as are common knowledge and of which they can take judicial notice.

However, Gose cautiously exercised judicial review: "Courts are not concerned with questions of the propriety, advisability or wisdom of any statute." Actually, the judge expressed the views of progressives of the period. He would have them scrutinize law cautiously, although from a broad social perspective.

Gose had been active in professional affairs, and almost immediately upon his retirement from the supreme court the Washington State Bar Association elected him president. After his term as president he continued to take part in important state bar matters.

During World War I Gose chaired the Coal Miners Price Control Board appointed by the federal fuel administrator. He also served as chairman of Liberty Loan committees and helped other volunteer organizations, such as the Red Cross. He chaired the board of overseers of Whitman College for many years and actively participated in Kiwanis Clubs in Pomeroy and Olympia, the Masons, and Knights of Pythias. Judge Gose married Lelah B. Seeley of Illinois and they had one daughter, Lelah.

In his 1915 presidential address to the Washington State Bar Association, Judge Gose reflected upon his times and, thereby, provided clues about his thinking on important public matters:

There are those who spend much time in deploring the tendency of the times in the direction of a purer democracy and who decry every measure which tends to a breaking away from the old order of things. . . . There are those who believe that all initiatives, the referendum and the recall. . . are the panaceas for all our political and economic ills. The practical worth or lack of worth of the more democratic remedies must be tried under modern conditions in the scales of experience. . . All of these changes speak a desire for growth, for the attainment of better things. I have great faith in the integrity and common sense of our people. An informed electorate is, generally speaking, a trustworthy one. The growth and development of our country along political, judicial, industrial and educational lines abundantly attests the truth of this statement. The man who wrote the lines: "Just bristle up and grit your teeth and keep on keepin' on," was a sane and wholesome counselor. We as lawyers may profit by his words if we will put the thought into action. Let us not be content in reflecting upon the great names in our profession in the past, and the service they rendered to our country and to humanity, but rather let us adopt the slogan "Keep on keepin' on."

Selected References

Julian Hawthorne, *History of Washington,* vol. 1 (1893), p. 585; Lloyd Spencer and Lancaster Pollard, *A History of the State of Washington,* vol. 3 (1937), p. 217; Washington State Bar Association *Proceedings* (1915-1916), pp. 120-130.

Thomas Eugene Grady
November 25, 1942-November 30, 1945 (temporary);
January 10, 1949-January 10, 1955

Born: November 19, 1880
Chippewa Falls, Wisconsin
St. Paul College of Law (1901-1902)
University of Minnesota, LL.B. (1904)
Presbyterian
Died: April 5, 1974
Deputy Prosecuting Attorney (1905-1906)
Superior Court (1911-1917)
Yakima City Attorney (1917-1923)
President, Washington State Bar Association
(1939-1940)
Republican
Appointed/Elected

Thomas Eugene Grady was born November 19, 1880, in Chippewa Falls, Wisconsin, to Thomas Paul and Eliza Jane (Fisk) Grady, who worked a small farm. His parents wanted something better for their four children. His father had always "admired the prosperous bookkeepers...and professional and semi-professional people who lived in the nice homes in Chippewa Falls," and he advised young Tom: "Instead of working as hard as I've had to, I want you to 'sling ink.' "

After learning typing and shorthand, Tom secured employment as a clerk with the Great Northern Railroad in St. Paul. His experiences with the railroad and admiration for a local lawyer convinced him to study law. In 1901 Grady enrolled at the St. Paul College of Law and, after one year, transferred to the University of Minnesota School of Law to enter its four-year night program. At first, law study came hard, but when Grady came under the tutelage of Professor James Page his studies improved substantially. He received his LL.B. in 1904. Immediately upon graduation Grady headed west to pursue his legal career.

His first winter, in Whitefish, Montana, convinced him this was not the place to begin practice. Looking to Seattle as his ultimate destination, Grady traveled to Yakima to visit an uncle. The weather seemed attractively mild after the harshness of Wisconsin and Montana, and Grady decided to stay. Employment as a court reporter helped pay bills until the Washington bar admitted him in 1905. With the assistance of his uncle, Grady became deputy prosecuting attorney for Yakima County. He sent for his parents to join him and in June 1908 married his Wisconsin sweetheart, Alice Mildred Beane. Her family had moved to Spokane about the time Grady arrived in Yakima. They reared four children, Thomas Eugene, James Edward, Howard Martin, and Alice Winifred.

After two years with the prosecutor's office Grady went into private practice. In 1911 Governor Marion Hay appointed him, as a compromise candidate, to a newly created superior court judgeship for Yakima County. In those days, court-watching entertained local townspeople, and Judge Tom Grady's courtroom became a favorite. Young William O. Douglas used to drop in to watch the court dramas when Grady presided. Later, on a visit to Yakima in the middle of his own career, Justice Douglas referred to Judge Tom Grady as "the salt of the earth." However, Grady's courtroom popularity did not transfer to the polls. He lost a bitter reelection campaign in 1917 and returned to private practice in successive partnerships. He also served as Yakima City Attorney.

Although not deeply involved in Republican politics, Grady actively participated in bar association affairs. He served as president of the Yakima Bar Association in 1922 and the Washington State Bar Association in 1939-1940. He worked on the Judicial Council and a number of state bar committees including the board of examiners. He also served a term on the board of governors. His activities in the profession and popularity among his colleagues played an important role in his initial appointment to the supreme court in 1942, and his election in 1948.

Governor Arthur Langlie, following a state bar recommendation, appointed Grady temporarily to the state supreme court in 1942 to fill in for Judge Sam Driver, who had received a leave to accept a commission in the U. S. Army. Driver rejoined the high bench in December 1945, and Grady reentered private practice in Yakima with William B. Clark and his son, Thomas E. Grady, Jr. However, he hoped to sit again on the state's high court. When Bruce Blake indicated his intention to retire in 1946, Grady announced his candidacy for the vacancy:

> I enjoyed the work on the bench and my association with the other judges. I found my experience of many years as a trial lawyer very helpful in working out the problems presented to the court. If my judicial work has been satisfactory to the members of the bench and bar of the state I would like to be chosen to serve an elective term as member of the court.

Unfortunately, Edgar W. Schwellenbach also filed and, with his wider name familiarity and vigorous campaigning, defeated Grady in the September 1946 primary by nearly 82,000 votes. Two years later Grady returned to the judicial campaign trail and this time succeeded in winning a seat on the state's high bench.

Because of his behavior on and off the bench and personal financial problems, Judge William Millard had incurred the wrath of the organized bar, whose members eagerly sought to remove him from the court. They selected Grady as their candidate. He welcomed the opportunity to return to the state's court of last resort and to challenge an incumbent he believed had brought disgrace upon the court. Actually Grady and Millard had a falling-out of sorts during the former's temporary court tenure. In one campaign announcement Grady charged that "our courts, in order to command the respect of the public should be presided over by judges whose personal and judicial conduct are above reproach." He obviously spoke about Millard. The "conduct and judicial attitude of one member" had created "deplorable conditions" within the court.

The Seattle Bar Association supported Grady in the September primary in its first preferential poll for the supreme court by a 440 to 195 vote. He also prevailed in the poll of the profession in Pierce, Yakima, and a number of other county bar associations. Both Millard and Grady survived the primary and faced each other in the final November balloting. Again the Seattle bar endorsed Grady over Millard by a vote of 761 to 198. Voters followed the bar's advice and Grady defeated the incumbent by slightly less than 26,000 votes.

During his interrupted nine years on the supreme court, Grady wrote 147 opinions, thirty-eight dissents, and nine concurrences. Justice Matthew Hill recalled that:

> Almost invariably when a case was assigned to him there would be an opinion in circulation within a relatively short period of time, frequently within three or four days. I mention this merely as an indication of his "let's get the job done" approach to the problem [of backlogged cases].
>
> His conference views frequently found their way to opinions written by other members of the Court. His comments on the passing sheet . . . many times resulted in changes which improved opinions. What I remember best was a little personal note, which read: "Re 2nd paragraph on page 6, I agree with what you are saying, but does it really need to be said?" and it really didn't.

Judge Grady had an individualistic opinion-writing style. When the cases were assigned to him,

> He would write his own in his own way in long hand. . . He would write them short. He felt that you shouldn't make a monument out of a case. . .[y]ou should decide the case on its merits and then quit. . . [H]e'd been practicing law long enough [to know] that you ought to use cases as tools. It's hard to plow through a case that rambles on and gives a lot of dictum. . .and tries to become a textbook by consulting a whole lot of citations. [He wrote] short, concise opinions and to the point. Lawyers liked them.

His dissents were sometimes longer than when he wrote majority opinions for the court. His tenure on the superior court bench in Yakima made him sensitive to pressures on trial judges and what especially irritated him was the supreme court's second-guessing a trial judge and appearing to retry the case. For example, in *Donner v. Donner,* a 1954 case, he wrote:

> This is another of the many cases to be found in our reports in which we have made reference to the rule to be applied when a court considers the sufficiency of evidence, a motion for non-suit, or a motion for a directed verdict, and then have proceeded to become a trier of fact or have approved the action of a trial court becoming such, and by such process have defeated the case of the plaintiff.

Law clerks who served on the supreme court and lawyers who regularly appeared before the high bench regarded Grady as a reluctant intervener in the political and social process. In his view, the court should limit itself strictly to narrow legal issues and exercise restraint. Judge Grady was a moderate, eschewing extreme liberal or conservative solutions to policy issues brought to the court.

At the end of his elected term Grady chose not to run for reelection because he would reach the mandatory retirement age of seventy-five before the term expired. Instead he went into semi-retirement, practicing law on a part-time basis and consulting with other attorneys. He remained active in professional and civic affairs, including the Masons, Elks, and Boy Scouts. In 1958 he headed a lawyer's group supporting a right to work initiative measure that generated heated debate throughout the state.

Judge Thomas Grady, Jr., remembered with fondness his father and the era he represented:

> He was of the Gay Nineties. He was mid-Victorian. His family was mid-Victorian. The sisters were school teachers and later trained nurses and registered nurses. But they were the stiff-necked kind... Dad wore pants that came down—cuffless—and tapered a little bit and he never did work in anything but those. That's what he was used to and to hell with it... When the tailor died and he couldn't get them anymore, he didn't know what he was going to do. He'd have to wear pants with cuffs on them that were the same size all the way down. [He said] "they'd whip you to death if you got out in the wind." He couldn't understand some of the attitudes that were beginning to develop... He was from that day and age, the gaslight era.

Selected References

The oral history interview of Thomas Grady, Jr. is in the supreme court collection, Washington State Archives. Also see memorial services, *Washington Reports,* vol. 83, 2d (1974), pp. xxiv-xxxi; *Seattle Times,* 17 Mar. 1946 and 1 Aug. 1948; C. W. Taylor, *Eminent Judges and Lawyers of the Northwest* (1954), p. 51; and *Washington State Bar News* (Jan. 1988), p. 10.

Richard Post Guy
November 1, 1989-

Born: October 24, 1932
Coeur d'Alene, Idaho
Gonzaga University (1957)
Gonzaga Law School, J.D. (1959)
Catholic
Law Clerk (1957-1959)
Assistant Attorney General (1959-1961)
Attorney for Washington Speaker of House
    of Representatives (1963)
Deputy Prosecutor (1961-1964)
Superior Court (1977-1981; 1985)
Democrat
Appointed

In July 1989, rumors circulated that Justice Vernon Pearson contemplated retirement from the state's high bench. Democratic Governor Booth Gardner might again have an opportunity to make a court appointment. Pearson confirmed the rumors by announcing in August he would leave the bench on October 31. As weeks passed, Gardner showed little haste in filling the vacancy. Pressures mounted for the governor to select someone from eastern Washington, since only Justice Robert Brachtenbach, originally from Yakima, came from east of the Cascades. After four months of thorough evaluation and behind-the-scenes campaigning, Governor Gardner, the day before Pearson left, finally announced Spokanite Richard P. Guy as his choice.

At least eight highly competent candidates vied for the appointment. However, in the fifty-seven-year-old former superior court jurist, Gardner found a person who would bring "a variety of experience to the court" and hopefully provide "balance which will serve all the citizens of the state." Although Guy was apparently surprised, he had nearly gained an earlier appointment to the high bench when Gardner chose Charles Smith. Since that time he had often reminded the governor of his availability.

Guy's Democratic credentials, although not extensive, were unblemished. Never a candidate for partisan office, he had served as Democratic Governor Dixy Lee Ray's Spokane County campaign manager in the 1970s and had worked in Wes Ullman's gubernatorial campaigns. The Washington State Bar Association had placed him on its approved list. Numerous business and political leaders from both parties also urged the governor to bring geographical balance to the bench. Finally, the new appointee had wide experience in nearly all aspects of the state's legal system. Many observers anticipated that the new justice would be a centrist on the bench, enhancing his hoped-for conciliatory role.

A product of Spokane's public schools, Guy graduated from Gonzaga University's law school in 1959. While in law school he had clerked for family court Judge Kathleen Taft. His first job after graduation was as assistant attorney general, representing the Department of Social and Health Services and the Department of Labor and Industries. Guy moved to the Spokane County Prosecutor's Office in 1961, serving as the chief criminal deputy. He also served a stint in the civil division. In 1963 he took a short leave to serve as attorney for the speaker of the house of representatives in Olympia. A close friend of speaker William Day, Guy had acted as the family's attorney on several occasions. That same year Richard Guy and Lynn Kaiser, a career counselor, married. They have three daughters: Vicky, Heidi, and Emily.

Guthrie Industries of Spokane lured the future judge away from public agency work, appointing him corporate counsel for the firm from 1964 to 1966. For three years Guy was area director of a U. S. Agency for International Development consulting firm. This work took him to West Africa and Ethiopia to pursue business opportunities for client investment banks. Upon his return from Africa in 1969, Guy gained appointment as executive vice president and corporate counsel for Pacific Securities Companies. Corporate reorganizations, loan agreements, collections, personnel matters, proxy statements, and Securities Exchange Commission filings constituted his new responsibilities.

In 1977 Governor Ray appointed Guy to a superior court vacancy in Spokane. After four years he resigned from the bench. With his low judicial pay he felt he could not provide college educations for his three daughters. However, he returned to the superior bench in 1985 in a temporary capacity until the governor chose a permanent jurist.

Guy joined the thirty-two member Spokane law firm of Winston and Cashatt, becoming a partner in 1982, and remained there until his appointment to the state's high bench. He practiced largely in the business area, with frequent court appearances.

With such a wide legal experience both in and out of the courtroom, Governor Gardner expected—and Justice Guy anticipated—he would provide a unifying ingredient to an often-divided high bench. Senator Phil Talmadge, a keen observer of the state's court of last resort, predicted Guy would "bring a solid perspective to the issues and will help build consensus among the justices." Another attorney speculated Guy was "going to be able to heal some of those wounds, that he can bridge all the gaps, at least for a while." His approach to the law seemed favorable to the role. In the words of one friend: "He is fiscally conservative, but definitely compassionate to those with true human needs."

By remaining professional, not choosing sides, and maintaining long-standing friendships with the other members of the bench, Guy also believed he could play a unifying role. He viewed dissent in the court's deliberations as something to be minimized:

> You have a visualization of what you are going to do. I saw myself coming here and really wanting majority opinions [with] wide majorities so that the lawyers and judges could understand that this was a strong opinion of the court and expressed the view not of just the five member majority... I think that is important. I can see coming down on the side of the majority—even having some reservations—because I wanted to deliver [that message] to the bar.

However, he soon admitted that making compromises to achieve a strong majority could be a strain: "The truth of the matter is that you have to be what you are, you have to believe in what [you decide]. You may very well have to dissent and it may be five-four."

His first few months on the bench indicated that his concern for bringing the court together remained strong: he had not yet yielded to a sense of independence. Guy participated in thirty-two of the court's opinions between his appointment and August 24, 1990, dissenting three times, concurring once, and voting with the majority the remaining times. The court unanimously agreed in twenty-four of the thirty-two decisions. If the pattern continued, and if it could be attributed to the new justice, the prediction that Guy could play a conciliatory role was near the mark.

Guy's dissenting vote in *Johnson v. Labor and Industries* seemed to confirm the observation of some that he would be a compassionate justice. He agreed with Justice Fred Dore that the "majority's erroneous interpretation of [the law] unfairly and illegally deprives injured workers, without spouses or children, of vested property rights."

His one written dissent, in *State v. Fjermestad,* suggested that in the area of criminal law—the area most often dividing the bench—Guy maintained a balanced view. Although voting to uphold a conviction, he wrote:

> Deterrence of illegal and improper police conduct should be of paramount concern to this court in protecting and preserving the rights of individuals. Whenever such unlawful behavior occurs, the evidence derived from such conduct is inadmissible. However, the effect in doing so should not be so all encompassing that the police cannot perform their function of protecting the public.

Similarly, writing for a unanimous bench in *State v. Nixon,* Guy recognized the need to balance the rights of the accused with the needs of society:

> Our holding today is not intended to expand the scope of prosecutorial discretion, nor is it intended to suggest that a loss of juvenile jurisdiction could never result in a due process violation. We merely hold that absent a showing of deliberate or negligent delay on the part of the State which results in a loss of juvenile court jurisdiction, a juvenile's right to due process is not violated.

In June 1990, after Justice Guy had completed his seventh month on the state's court of last resort, former Governor John Spellman announced an interest in running for a supreme court seat. Since a new appointee is normally vulnerable, having not yet established a record and lacking name familiarity, a challenge to Guy, who would be campaigning for the remaining four years of Pearson's term, seemed most likely, even though three other justices sought reelection.

On July 25, 1990, Republican Spellman officially announced he would challenge Guy in the September primary. The former governor emphasized his administrative experience and public service as attributes qualifying him for the supreme court. For his part, Guy cited his judicial and legal experience. He also maintained that it was important eastern Washington be represented on the high bench. The media saw the contest as a race between east and west, and professional vs. political backgrounds. Guy enjoyed the backing of thirty-seven of the thirty-nine county prosecutors, an overwhelming positive rating from the Seattle-King County Bar Association, endorsement from the state's leading newspapers, and labor backing. Governor Gardner lent his support, as did leaders in both political parties. Nonetheless, Spellman's name familiarity and his west-side connections made him a formidable candidate.

Justice Guy's vigorous campaigning, Spellman's apparent complacency — relying almost exclusively on his reputation — and the media's ample campaign coverage gave Guy the primary victory. By gathering over 58 percent of the vote, Guy's name appeared alone on the November general election ballot.

With the security of the remaining four years in Pearson's term, Justice Guy might well succeed in bringing some unanimity to the state's high bench. On the other hand, this security might tempt the justice to chart an independent course. Justice Richard Guy's role on the high bench remains to be defined.

Selected References

Guy's oral history interview is in the supreme court collection, Washington State Archives. Also see *Spokane Spokesman-Review,* 31 Oct. 1989; *Seattle Times/Post-Intelligencer,* 5 Nov. 1989; *Tacoma Morning News Tribune,* 2 Oct. 1990; *The Olympian,* 31 Oct. 1989.

Hiram Elwood Hadley

March 20, 1901-October 7, 1902;
January 13, 1903-January 11, 1909

Born: January 16, 1854
Sylvania, Indiana
Earlham College (1872-1874)
Union College of Law, B.L. (1877)
Presbyterian
Died: January 13, 1929
Bellingham City Attorney (1891-1896)
Superior Court (1896-1900)
President, Seattle Bar Association (1915)
Republican
Appointed/Elected

Judge Hiram Hadley's ancestors were devout Quakers of Scottish and English descent. His parents, Jonathan and Martha (McCoy) Hadley, lived on a homestead inherited from Jonathan's father in west-central Indiana. Hiram, the eldest of three sons, was born in the homestead farm's log cabin. He received his early education in Rush Creek School near his home and later attended Bloomingdale Academy and Earlham College, both affiliated with the Society of Friends. He taught school to finance his college education. The future jurist enrolled in the Union College of Law in Chicago—later Northwestern University School of Law—graduating in 1877. He began practice in Bloomington, Illinois, where he remained until 1881. While in Illinois, Hadley took an interest in politics, gaining election as president of the Young Men's Garfield Club. He returned to Rockville, Indiana, to practice law in his native county, remaining until 1889. At the urging of a friend who wrote glowing accounts of the Pacific Northwest, Hadley gave up a promising legal and political career in Indiana to resettle in Sehome (Bellingham), in the new State of Washington.

Two years after arriving in Washington, Hadley formed a law partnership with Thomas Slade and his brother Lindley Hadley, who later was elected to Congress. He started a new partnership a few years later with Charles Dorr, Lindley, and the third Hadley brother, Alonzo. In 1891 Hiram won election as city attorney for Bellingham, then called New Whatcom. As city attorney he was instrumental in consolidating the four rival communities surrounding Bellingham Bay into the new City of Bellingham.

Hadley became one of the few Republicans to survive the Populist-Democratic sweep in the county and state in 1896 when voters elected him to the Whatcom

County Superior Court. Endorsed by all three parties for a second term on the trial bench, he ran unopposed. People often cited the bipartisan support Hadley enjoyed as an example of the way judges should be endorsed, and it provided a forerunner for the nonpartisan ballot instituted a few years later. A later newspaper account explained Hadley's broad appeal:

> In 1900, before the days of a non-partisan judiciary, he had as high an honor paid him as any man could receive. A committee of three lawyers, a Democrat, a Populist and a Republican, went before each of the three party conventions in Whatcom County and asked that no one be nominated to succeed Judge Hadley. This was granted and Judge Hadley was elected to succeed himself by unanimous vote.

In 1901 the legislature temporarily expanded the supreme court from five to seven justices to attack a large case backlog. Under provisions of the statute, Governor John R. Rogers would appoint one judge from each of the two major parties. He chose Hadley for the Republican slot. Hadley's bipartisan support made him an acceptable Republican for the Democratic governor. Upon completing the temporary appointment, Hadley returned to private practice long enough to organize a campaign to return to a regular term on the high bench. His popularity convinced the Republican slate-makers to name him their candidate for the court. Indeed, his name at the top of the ballot enhanced the entire Republican ticket, as the *Seattle Post-Intelligencer* noted:

> The changes are all in favor of Judge Hiram E. Hadley heading the ticket. It is believed he will have a larger majority than any of the congressional candidates, owing to the fact that there is a general feeling of confidence in him and that factional fights, local differences and political prejudices do not affect his vote.

He successfully challenged James Reavis in 1902, earning a full six-year term.

Judge Hadley assumed a position of leadership on the court after only a short time. He dissented from his colleagues infrequently and wrote more than his share of the court's opinions. His moderate views of the law and of the role of courts in the state's political system placed him in the "swing" position between liberals and conservatives.

Hadley left the bench at the end of his term in 1909 and formed a law partnership in Seattle with his son Clyde and the son of his former partner in Bellingham, John Dorr. Later the firm became Hadley and Hadley and then Hadley, Hay, and Hadley in association with Edward Hay, the son of former Governor Marion E. Hay. The retired judge served on several state bar committees, and the Seattle Bar Association elected him president in 1915.

Judge Hadley married Mattie Musgrave in 1879. They became the parents of five children—three sons and two daughters. He was active in the Seattle Chamber of Commerce and prominent in Republican circles. He directed Will E. Humphrey's campaign for reelection to Congress, and chaired the Seattle mayor's special mediation committee that settled a serious Teamster's strike. He belonged to the Presbyterian Church, serving as trustee and elder, was a high Mason, and a Knight Templar. Besides achieving considerable success in his law practice, Hadley made several profitable real estate investments throughout the state. Judge Hadley died of cancer in January 1929 after a long battle with the disease.

Selected References

W. C. Wolfe, *Sketches of Washingtonians* (1906), pp. 184-185, 194; C. S. Reinhart, *History of the Supreme Court of the Territory and State of Washington* (n.d.), pp. 117-118; William Prosser, *History of the Puget Sound Country,* vol. 2 (1903), pp. 555-556.

Frank Hale
January 14, 1963-January 13, 1975

Born: August 5, 1911
Tacoma, Washington
University of Washington
Deputy Prosecutor (1938-1939)
Assistant U. S. Attorney (1939-1940)
Municipal Court (1946-1953)
Superior Court (1953-1963)
Democrat
Appointed

If anyone could be regarded as a product of the Great Depression, it was Frank Hale: the social and economic lessons of the 1930s shaped his political thinking. Forced to withdraw from the University of Washington for financial reasons, he later earned enough money from selling ice cream at Point Defiance and working in sawmills to allow him to return intermittently. After accumulating two years of academic credits, Hale quit for good and began to study law with a Tacoma attorney, Charles T. Peterson. He had earlier wanted to become a doctor, but lacked the funds for such prolonged training. Law study seemed an acceptable alternative. Later, he recalled that, "This was the old fashioned, Abe Lincoln type of clerkship. There was a course exam and quizzes at the end of each month. I had to buy the books for each course."

Frank would also "hang around the law school." Friends suggested interesting lectures to attend and, on occasion, put him up for the night. His description of these excursions into law school: "I guess you might call it 'auditing.' "

Hale's father had impressed the need for hard work on Frank and his two brothers early in their lives. His father came to Tacoma from Steubenville, Ohio, and worked at a number of jobs to support his family. Frank attended public schools in the Tacoma area, including a one room school in Hylebos, before his short-lived enrollment at the university.

After studying the requisite four years and passing the prescribed number of exams under the close supervision of Charlie Peterson, Frank signed up for the state bar exam, passed, and entered his chosen profession in 1937. He immediately opened his own law office, but soon joined the Pierce County Prosecutor's Office under Harry Johnston, remaining until 1939. With the assurance of a steady job, Frank felt he could support a family, and he married his long-time sweetheart, Mary Oliver, in 1938. While he worked in the prosecutor's office she completed study for a registered nurse's license at Tacoma General Hospital.

Hale avidly supported Franklin D. Roosevelt, viewing him as the savior who pulled the country out of the deep depression with such programs as federal deposit insurance, unemployment compensation, and social security. Being part of the New Deal crusade excited the young attorney and he enthusiastically threw himself into local Democratic politics. He served as president of the Pierce County Young Democrats for a time and in 1939 was rewarded for his partisan activities with an appointment as Assistant U. S. Attorney.

At the outset of World War II Hale enlisted as a private in the airborne infantry. He rose to the rank of captain while serving in several major battles in the European Theater, and was wounded during the Battle of the Bulge. As he described it:

> The Germans captured our mortars and turned them on us. They were firing from behind our lines. I got a million dollar wound that knocked me right into the white sheets. If you could get into the hospital without getting too badly mutilated, it was called a million dollar wound.

Honorably discharged in 1945, Hale returned to the U. S. Attorney's office.

In July 1946 Hale filed for Pierce County Prosecutor under the Democratic ticket but lost in the primary to fellow Democrat Hugh J. Rosellini, who later became a close friend and supreme court colleague.

In October 1946, Tacoma Police Court Judge Billy Richmond resigned to run for superior court. The county commissioners immediately selected Frank Hale to fill the vacancy. Hale talked about the appointment with his usual candor:

> I was in the U.S. Attorney's office at the time the county Democratic chairman called and said that the county commissioners would appoint me. You see the commissioners were Democrats. The mayor ran on a non-partisan ticket, but he was a Republican and everybody knew it. Evidently, the commissioners and the mayor couldn't agree on anyone else... When I told... my boss, the U.S. Attorney, that I couldn't afford to take the job, he reminded me it was a stepping-stone to the superior court. He said, "I think it's time for you to fish or cut bait." He conned me into it.

Because his appointment came shortly before the November general election, it was too late for the official ballot to carry his name, necessitating a write-in campaign. Hale received a write-in vote of 1,034, easily outdistancing his two rivals.

In 1951 Pierce County gained two more superior court judgeships, one to be filled by appointment and the other by election. Hale filed for the elective position and in the September 1952 primary election garnered over fifty percent of the total vote, defeating two other candidates. His name appeared on the November ballot unopposed.

Hale's family had by now grown. He and Mary were parents of four children: Dennis, Gretchen, and twins Alice and Allen. The judge walked every day to his office in the county-city building, no matter what the weather. He belonged to the Tacoma Elks, Veterans of Foreign Wars, Eagles, Kiwanis, and the American Legion, as well as the Superior Court Judges' Association. He enjoyed being a judge and described serving on the superior court bench:

> In Superior Court there are enough cases during the year to make it interesting. Trial work does have its monotonous moments. You might get a string of divorce cases; or you get a case where the contractors built a house on which the owner refuses to pay, claiming faulty workmanship involving only a small amount, and numerous experts testifying on the number of nails driven and other minute details; or a small accident case involving injury to vehicles but no personal injury to the parties. On the other hand, the trial judge doesn't have to take work home over the weekend.

In 1962 Governor Albert Rosellini offered Hale a position on the state supreme court. He turned it down for two reasons. First, he had not yet served the requisite ten years on the superior court to be eligible for a pension plan. Experiences with the Great Depression still haunted him. Should he be defeated in the election to retain his seat, he and his family would be financially strapped. Also, he would have to mount an election campaign in less than a year's time. However, another longer-term vacancy occurred on the court shortly thereafter and, quite to everyone's surprise, including Judge Hale's, Governor Rosellini offered it to him again. This time he accepted. The governor wrote later about the appointment:

> [H]is name had appeared on a Washington State Bar Association list. I knew him personally as a good lawyer, a good judge and a man of high integrity, common sense and good judgment. These factors coupled with recommendations from many members of the Bar who had observed his judicial behavior were quite significant in my selection.

By the time it would be necessary to run for election, Hale would have accumulated enough tenure on the state courts to qualify for a pension. So, on January 14, 1963, Justice Hale became a member of the state's court of last resort. In his one election bid in 1964 the justice ran unopposed.

Justice Hale's votes and opinions are hard to characterize. One of his former law clerks felt that it was "difficult to classify J. Hale along these [liberal-conservative] lines as his attitude and approach varied with the issues... I would use the term 'populist' to describe him in that he tended to think in terms of what was good for the common man." However, in many matters, the justice deferred to the legislature—a restraintist trait. For example, in *State v. Williams* Hale wrote in dissent:

> A good restraint among many to be practiced by the judiciary is to curb its tendency to act as a mini-parliament... the separation of powers of government into

three separate branches probably represents the highest achievement of constitutional theory. A basic tenet of the separation of powers proposition is that legislators shall enact laws and judges shall interpret, apply and enforce them.

On law and order issues he supported the prosecution. In government regulation and taxation issues he was, as his early New Deal commitment would suggest, on the side of the government. Labor most often received his support in business-labor issues and he leaned toward the individual in business vs. individual kinds of legal disputes, again a reflection of his New Deal liberalism. However, he often viewed civil rights issues from a conservative perspective, being especially critical of decisions favoring Indian treaty rights.

People who know Justice Hale almost always comment on his independence. One of his former clerks observed that the justice "was not afraid to differ from the views and research of the others . . . [He] felt the people had elected him for his own judgment in all matters."

Hale did his own writing, jealously guarding this most crucial stage in the decisional process. Law clerks were researchers, "sounding boards," and critics, but not drafters of opinions, especially not dissenting opinions. During his last few years on the court, he dissented from his brethren more often than any other justice. A Hale dissent could be expected in nearly one out of five cases. He explained his attitude toward dissents in his typically independent and confident manner:

> It's much easier to sign another's opinion and there's a temptation to be lazy. I guess the best statement I heard on that is 'when your indignation overcomes your inertia' you'll write a dissent. It's hard work and unrewarding, but it's a hallmark of laziness not to write a dissent. You're not playing fair with the public. You owe the court and the profession a delineation of your reasons. It's a question of morals. I consider a judge a lightweight who simply writes "I dissent."

An old friend, Gerald Schuklin, said of Hale at his induction as chief justice: "In his years on the bench, Frank Hale has shown a rugged pioneer honesty, a wise understanding of human nature, and a deep respect for his country and its institutions." A few selections from Hale's opinions reflect these traits and also display his sense of humor and joy in the use of words:

> Probably no greater bastion of free speech can be found in the country than in the nation's pool halls.

> Most accidents are caused; a few simply happen.

> Forever is a long time, even in the forested regions of the Pacific Northwest.

> Shall the happy picture of tugboats and barges, log booms and rafts, and ships of the sea—towing and being towed in bustling harmony upon the broad waters of the mighty Columbia— suffer the discordant intrusion of the business and occupation tax?

There is a saying that what one does not know does not hurt him, but, when it comes to surgical operations, this old bromide has turned out to be no more than a half truth.

Some individuals cannot stand sudden prosperity. Defendant made a conspicuous but unlikely display of affluence, and it caused his undoing when a jury found him guilty of burglary.

Despite scientific advances in animal husbandry, there has not yet been born a black angus steer that is temperamentally inclined to observe the motor vehicle code.

Glaziers should glaze and lawyers should scriven, and neither ought to do the other; for, when glaziers write and lawyers glaze, they are apt to make porous contracts and drafty windows.

On January 13, 1975, after twenty-nine years of judging, Chief Justice Frank Hale retired from the state's highest bench at age sixty-four. He and Mary retired to their Johnson Point home on Puget Sound a few miles north of Olympia. Fishing, gardening, reading, travel, and grandchildren all compete for their attention.

Selected References

Hale's oral history interview is in the supreme court collection, Washington State Archives. Also see Kerry Radcliffe, "Cases, Courtrooms, and Conviction," Hale file, same collection; *Seattle Post-Intelligencer,* 22 Mar. 1984; *Tacoma News Tribune,* 28 Sept. 1952, 10 Je. 1974, and 12 Jan. 1975; *Seattle Times,* 11 Je. 1974; Charles Sheldon, "An Interpretation of the Judicial Process: The Washington Supreme Court as a Small Group," *Gonzaga Law Review,* vol. 13 (1977), pp. 97-139; and Sheldon and Frank Weaver, *Politicians, Judges and the People* (1980), pp. 61-69.

Orris Lee Hamilton
January 22, 1962-January 8, 1979

Born: November 10, 1914
Prosser, Washington
American University, LL.B. (1940)
Presbyterian
Assistant Attorney General (1940-1941)
Prosecuting Attorney (1946-1948)
Superior Court (1948-1961)
Democrat
Appointed/Elected

Richard W. Gay, publisher of the Prosser *Record-Bulletin* and longtime friend of Orris Hamilton, remembered the judge during his days in Prosser:

> He was known as an extremely hard worker. It was common to see lights on [in] his corner office on the top floor of the darkened courthouse late at night. He was there boning up on the law regarding cases before him. I don't think many people felt he started his career with an over-abundance of talent. But he grew in knowledge and ability and ultimately became highly respected. When [Governor] Al Rosellini appointed him, the Republicans scoffed and I heard one Democrat (who wanted the job) say the appointment was a joke. His hometown is very proud of him.

After a review of his public life, this impression prevails: Orris worked hard at meeting if not surpassing the demands of the particular office he held.

The future judge was born on November 10, 1914 in Prosser, where the family had been prominent in Democratic politics. His father, Garrison Wire Hamilton, served as Washington Attorney General from 1933 to 1940. The elder Hamilton's marriage to Nellie J. Lundquist was his second, and Orris was the only child from that union, although he had one step-brother and two step-sisters. Orris attended public schools in Prosser, graduating from high school there in 1934 after one year in Olympia.

Hamilton's interest in law began when he clerked for his father in Olympia in 1933. The combination of talking politics and law with his father and the political environment in Olympia convinced him to attend law school. An opportunity to work in Washington, D. C., with the Department of Fisheries beckoned. Hamilton welcomed the exciting opportunity to observe New Deal politics firsthand while gaining a legal education. He worked full-time with fisheries (and later with the Bureau of the Census and the Securities and Exchange Commission) during the day and attended night classes at American University's Washington College of Law. Graduating with an LL.B. in 1940, he promptly gained admittance to the District of Columbia and Washington bars. Upon the death of his father, Orris returned to Olympia to work as an assistant attorney general with his father's successor, Smith Troy. In 1942 he became associated with the Seattle law firm of Falknor, Emory, and Howe.

After a few months with the Seattle firm, Hamilton joined the army during World War II and attended officer candidates' school, successfully completing the rigorous ninety-day program. After further infantry training the army shipped him to Europe, assigning him to the Forty-fourth Infantry Division where he soon engaged in fighting. Lieutenant Hamilton received a Bronze Star for bravery in one of his many encounters with the enemy. In France, German bunker fire pinned down his unit. Without regard for personal safety, he moved to an exposed observation post and directed artillery fire on the German position. The bunker was taken and the area secured. The military honorably discharged him as an infantry captain in 1946.

Upon his return to Prosser, Hamilton first set up his own office and then formed a law partnership with Maloy Sensney. He became active in a number of community groups and in Democratic politics, winning election as Benton County Prosecutor in 1946. When a vacancy occurred on the superior court bench for Benton, Adams, and Franklin counties in 1948, Governor Mon C. Wallgren appointed Hamilton, making him, at age thirty-four, the youngest judge then serving in Washington. The appointment followed a rather bizarre set of circumstances, and to Hamilton, it "came rather surprisingly." With Wallgren out of the state, Lieutenant Governor Vic Meyers, temporarily assuming the reins of state government, appointed someone from the west side to the new post. But Secretary of State Earl Coe refused to certify the appointment. The governor hurried back, persuaded the appointee to withdraw, and then turned to Hamilton. Although he had been number three on the bar's list, he was the only Democrat, which, of course, made the difference.

As a trial judge, Hamilton proved to be a "stickler" on the rights of the accused even before the U. S. Supreme Court forced such protections upon states. He was especially concerned with guilty pleas. If "he had doubts about" a plea, "he would not accept" it. The judge was always ready for trial. According to his former assistant prosecutor and law partner, Maloy Sensney:

> He was an extremely hard worker. He briefed every case himself before the trial began. This was very unusual for [a] judge. . . [O]ften times Orris knew more about the case law relevant in a particular case than either of the lawyers involved. He worked long hours to stay abreast of the work load he forced upon himself. . . He was obsessed with the idea that he had to be prepared for each case.

Often he met with Sensney after both had worked late into the night to share light conversation over a cup of coffee at Ford's Grill. Then the judge would return to "his office and maybe work until two or three in the morning," even though a hearing might be scheduled for nine the next morning.

In 1957 Justice Edgar Schwellenbach, originally from eastern Washington, passed away, allowing Democratic Governor Albert Rosellini to make his first high bench appointment. Hamilton was a serious contender and actively sought the post, but the governor selected Judge Robert Hunter of Ephrata. In 1962, when Justice Joseph Mallery of Tacoma retired, Hamilton expected the appointment to go to someone from the west side of the state. Nevertheless, Hamilton wrote a letter to the governor expressing his interest, checked with the state bar office to make sure his name remained on their approved list, and then went about his business. The governor acted as expected and offered the appointment to Judge Frank Hale of Tacoma. Hale turned down the offer, although he accepted a subsequent appointment, and Rosellini promptly called Orris Hamilton, who quickly accepted. On January 22, 1962 Hamilton became the fifty-eighth judge of the Washington Supreme Court.

In his first electoral defense, Hamilton faced a serious challenge from former Republican State Chairman William C. Goodloe, who would be elected to the court in 1984. With support from Governor Rosellini, Democrats, and the bar, Hamilton defeated Goodloe in the September primary by fewer than 20,000. Nonetheless, his name appeared on the November 1966 general election ballot unopposed, and he won a six-year term. In the 1972 primary he turned back the challenge of Seattle attorney George Faler by more than 200,000 votes.

Throughout his seventeen-year court tenure, most observers regarded Hamilton as a moderate judge, restraintist in the exercise of judicial power. He became slightly more conservative after his first few years on the bench. For example, in his first five years he held with the defendant in criminal cases 56 percent of the time. But in his last five years he supported the appeal of the defendants only 26 percent of the time. In such matters as tax cases, however, he remained consistent throughout his tenure, holding for the government about two-thirds of the time.

Hamilton demanded proper procedures. For example, in *Mempa v. Rhay* in 1966, the judge dissented from his brethren because they failed to grant the same procedural protections to a parolee as to others. The U. S. Supreme Court later adopted his dissent. In *State v. Green* in 1979, Hamilton, writing for the court, struck down the state's death penalty initiative as violating the cruel and unusual punishment provisions of the Bill of Rights as applied to the states through the Fourteenth Amendment. After serving as a trial judge for over a dozen years he also understood and appreciated the pressures on the trial bench and consistently supported the discretion exercised by trial judges. The supreme court ought not to "substitute [its] findings . . . for those of the trial court," he wrote in a 1962 case.

Hamilton had an individualistic decisional style. He tended to keep his own counsel, write his own opinions, and, although concerned with consensus, he rarely lobbied for his position. According to one of his law clerks:

> When assigned to write the majority opinion my judge almost always tried to get the results dictated by the conference vote in the simplest, most direct and least controversial way.

As in his early days in Prosser, the judge worked alone, long, and hard to polish his decisions. Another clerk referred to this deliberative process:

> When assigned to write an opinion, my judge would tell me the result of the conference vote and discuss very generally how he thought the result should be reached. I was to draft an opinion consistent with that result. When the draft was given to him, he did not ask for nor did he want any further discussion between us or any additional effort on my part on that case. He tended to regard his law clerk's product as but one minor item to be considered in reaching his own conclusions. He independently researched the issues he felt were involved and never asked me to check or verify his research.

Law clerks rarely served as "sounding boards," and most input they provided took the form of an exchange of draft opinions, memos, or written research papers. Hamilton maintained a somewhat distant relationship with his clerks, largely as a result of his personality and style. He appeared to his law clerks as shy, remote, and somewhat ill-at-ease with them.

On occasion the judge lagged in completing his writing assignments, largely because of his desire to be confident of his arguments. This left little time for writing dissents or concurrences. A former law clerk recalled that the judge "rarely wrote or joined in a dissent or a separate concurring opinion." If he wrote a dissent, it was "usually very short."

Hamilton felt compelled to vote or write a dissenting opinion in only about four percent of all cases, about half the court average. Winning more votes and possibly laying a groundwork for future cases prompted the few dissents he penned.

Judge Hamilton availed himself of several general sources for deciding cases. His ranking of these reflected a restraintist and traditional perspective regarding judicial decision-making. First in importance came constitutions; these were followed, in order, by statutes, common sense, precedents, justice, and public interest. During his years on the bench he tended to side with the more restraintist and conservative members, such as Justices Frank Weaver and Charles Wright.

In late February 1978, Justice Hamilton became ill during a court session, requiring a short hospitalization. Although only sixty-three years old, and with apparently unassailable support in any subsequent election drive, he announced retirement. His motives were simple:

> The conclusion of my present term as a Justice of the Supreme Court will mark 30 years of direct association with the judicial system of the State of

Washington – 13 years as a superior court judge and 17 years as a Supreme Court justice. . . . While it may not be so for others, to me 30 years in the judicial branch of government marks a milestone which I do not deem desirable to bypass. Accordingly, I have decided to step down at the conclusion of my current term to make room for new blood, so to speak.

In June 1947 Hamilton and Shirley I. Rosenberg of Lewiston, Idaho, had married. They had three children: Deea, Christopher, and Denise. After retiring, Shirley and Orris traveled in their motor home and tended their garden at their Olympia home. He also enjoyed hunting. Since 1979 he has, on several occasions, returned to the high court bench as a *pro tempore* justice.

Throughout Justice Hamilton's long career he was involved in a number of professional, social, and civic groups. He served as vice president and president of the Superior Court Judges' Association, was a member of the Institute of Judicial Administration, the National Institute of Crime and Delinquency, and the American Judicature Society, and attended the National Conference of State Trial Judges. He actively participated in Sigma Delta Kappa, Free Masons, Elks, Veterans of Foreign Wars, American Legion, and Shriners. He helped organize the Benton-Franklin Counties' Youth Center, went to the Little White House Conference on Children and Youth, and served on the state Child Welfare Advisory Committee.

Selected References

Hamilton's oral history interview is in the supreme court collection, Washington State Archives. See also John Pierce, "Background as Determinant of Judicial Policies and Decisions: Orris Hamilton," Hamilton file, same collection; Hamilton papers, Manuscripts, Archives and Special Collections, Washington State University Library; and *The Olympian,* 22 Je. 1979.

Frederick George Hamley

October 6, 1949-July 6, 1956

Born: October 27, 1903
Seattle, Washington
University of Washington, LL.B. (1932)
Unitarian
Died: May 5, 1975
Seattle City Council (1935-1938)
Superintendent, Seattle Water Department
 (1938)
Assistant Counsel, Bureau of Reclamation
 (1938-1940)
Director, State Department of Public Ser-
 vice (1941-1943)
U. S. Ninth Circuit Court of Appeals
 (1956-1975)
Republican
Appointed

The old adage that "a judge is simply a politician who knew the governor" might describe the case of Frederick George Hamley. Despite the political nature of Hamley's appointment, his service on the supreme court and subsequent tenure on the U. S. Circuit Court of Appeals proved noteworthy.

Hamley, born in Seattle on October 27, 1903, was the third supreme court judge to have been a native Washingtonian. He had a spotty attendance record in Seattle area public schools because of a need to interrupt studies to pay his share of family expenses. However, he determined to complete his education. He graduated from high school at age twenty-three. With his brother Charles he lived on a ten-acre farm in Bellevue owned by his maternal grandfather. Between 1922 and 1927 they formed the Hamley Brothers Florist Company and sold produce, cut flowers, bulbs, and seeds at the Seattle Pike Street Public Market. Through their efforts, Frederick and his brother accumulated enough money to pay tuition and expenses at the University of Washington School of Law. Frederick graduated first in his class in 1932, was on the debate team, served as editor of the law review, and belonged to Phi Beta Kappa and Order of the Coif. Upon completing his law studies, he married Marjorie E. Wood of Seattle. They had two daughters, June and Arlene. The Washington bar admitted him in 1932 and he began law practice under his own name in Seattle.

In the late 1920s and early 1930s a political machine that tolerated—even encouraged—corruption and graft controlled Seattle. Some young, dedicated city residents, including Fred Hamley, formed a group called the New Order of Cincinnatus, hoping to rid Seattle of corruption. By 1935 three of its members or supporters, including Hamley and Arthur B. Langlie, had gained seats on the city council. A friendship developed between these two young reformers that would influence the public careers of both. In 1938 the New Order of Cincinnatus assisted in electing Langlie mayor. One of his first appointments was to make Fred Hamley superintendent of the Seattle Water Department. Hamley also served on the Board of Public Works and the Committee of Standardization, and advised the mayor.

After three months in the city administration, Hamley resigned in August 1938 to accept appointment as assistant district counsel for the federal Bureau of Reclamation. Assigned to the Grand Coulee Dam project, he had responsibility for all litigation relating to construction. After two and a half years with the bureau, Langlie, recently elected governor, called Hamley to Olympia as special assistant state attorney general. In April 1941 the governor appointed him state director of public works.

The lure of law again beckoned and Hamley left Langlie's administration in May 1943 to become assistant general solicitor (later general solicitor) for the National Association of Railroad and Utilities Commissioners, headquartered in Washington, D. C. The organization represented state public service commissions and Hamley handled litigation concerning regulations for public utilities and common carriers. He remained with the association until September 1949 when Langlie appointed him to the state supreme court to fill the vacancy created by Clyde Jeffers's resignation.

Not all elements of the legal community supported the appointment. Hamley had been out of the state for nearly six years, although Seattle remained his voting residence. Langlie had previously agreed not to appoint any judges not approved by the state bar association. When the association initially submitted a list of possible appointees for the vacancy, Hamley's name was missing. The governor returned the list, asking the bar to consider his old friend and advisor. The association gave its approval and Hamley received the appointment to the remainder of Jeffers's term. In July 1950, Hamley filed for both the short term of the two months left in Jeffers's term and for the new, full six-year term. He remained unopposed for the short term but Hugh Rosellini, William J. Millard, Jr., and Lyle Iverson entered the race for the six-year position. Rosellini outpolled Hamley in the September primary by nearly 30,000 votes. After a bitter campaign Hamley turned back the challenge, defeating Rosellini by 10,000 votes in November.

Once on the court Judge Hamley soon dispelled any doubts detractors may have held about his ability. He proved to be a competent and valued member of the court. Judge Matt Hill described his opinion-writing style:

> A Hamley opinion is meticulously accurate in its statement of the facts necessary to an understanding of what is to be decided; it is studiously thorough in its discussion of the principles of law involved, and crystal clear in the conclusions reached and why. Each is a gem in its own particular setting—no wasted words, no sterile platitudes, and a joy to one who is searching to find out what the law is and why.

The judge involved his law clerks intimately in deliberations. The clerks would read the briefs and trial record and research the law on those cases assigned them, writing a summary for the judge. The summary included jurisdictional information, facts of the case, a recommended disposition, and a discussion of any apparently conflicting law or evidence and the reasons for their inapplicability. From this summary the judge would write his opinion. The clerk would review the finished product, catalog all citations and, when appropriate, add materials.

Judge Hamley, "highly intelligent and capable," often would finish his opinion assignments "a month early and then take cases of judges who were behind." He had an individual decisional style involving little post-conference discussion with colleagues. Although not an outgoing person, Hamley provided a degree of leadership to the bench simply through his reasoning powers. As one law clerk noted, he "was articulate and unafraid to express his views. His monumental intellect and unshakable honesty made it easy for him to persuade others to his point of view."

Pierce v. Yakima Valley Memorial Hospital Association was one of those opinions described by Judge Hill that persuaded others to join in the majority despite the fact that it overruled nearly sixty years of precedent. Hamley opened the opinion with a concise statement of the issue: "This appeal presents a single question, namely: Where a paying patient of a charitable, non-profit hospital sustains injuries by reason of the negligence of a nurse, may such patient recover damages from the hospital?" After a complete review of Washington precedents and a thorough coverage of other jurisdictions, Hamley concluded:

> The factors upon which any public policy is based – the relevant factual situation and the thinking of the times – are not static. They change as conditions change, and as ways of looking at things change...
>
> We therefore believe it to be appropriate after this lapse of time...to reexamine the public policy there announced, in light of present conditions and present day thinking...
>
> It is our opinion that a charitable, non-profit hospital should no longer be held immune from liability for injuries to paying patients caused by negligence of employees... Our previous decisions holding to the contrary are hereby overruled.

Despite the liberal-activist results in *Pierce,* clerks and attorneys regarded Hamley as a political and legal moderate and a judge tending to balance activism and restraint.

In 1956, Homer T. Bone, longtime Washington political figure and judge, vacated his seat on the U. S. Court of Appeals, Ninth Circuit. With the acquiescence of Washington's Democratic senators Warren Magnuson and Henry Jackson and the insistence of Republican Governor Langlie, President Dwight Eisenhower nominated Judge Hamley as Bone's replacement. Although no one voiced objections to the appointment in hearings before the Senate Judiciary Committee, a Seattle lawyer had filed a complaint against the judge, delaying approval. Senator William Langer, ranking Republican on the committee, felt compelled to delay the confirmation in order to investigate the complaint, which proved to be frivolous. Langer concluded that "Judge Hamley apparently is as fine a man who ever wore the leather. I said 'apparently' because I have not met the judge. I am sure he will be confirmed immediately after my report." On June 28, 1956, the full senate did unanimously confirm Hamley on a voice vote.

While on the federal bench from 1956 to 1971, Hamley continued his interest in appellate reform by participating on the faculties of judicial seminars, writing articles, and delivering speeches. As a result of his own experience, Hamley became concerned with the lack of opportunity for new appellate judges to prepare themselves for their work, and for experienced judges to keep abreast of the changing technicalities of appellate decision-making. Largely through his efforts, the New York University School of Law established a permanent and popular series of judicial seminars.

In 1971 he chose to go on senior status at the age of sixty-seven. He continued to sit on the bench and to participate in circuit business, but at a more leisurely pace, until his death in May, 1975.

The judge was active in the Washington State and American Bar Associations, serving on important committees. His specialty was public utilities law, although after nearly a quarter of a century on the appellate bench he had become a generalist. When time permitted, Hamley partook in community affairs. He served as director of the Olympia Young Men's Christian Association for four years and was president of the Olympia Community Fund. The judge served as a member of the citizens' advisory committee on high school education and chairman of the governor's state-wide committee on educational television.

Judge Robert Finley, who served with Hamley on the state's high court, recalled his friend with affection:

> Fred Hamley was a sort of shy and retiring person. You had to know him quite well to really appreciate his fine person[al] qualities. While shy and retiring, he could be and was, of course, very, very firm and not the least bit reticent in expressing his views on cases heard by the court. He also was very, very firm and dedicated in pushing for those things, professionally and otherwise, in his life in which he was convinced he should and could assist in accomplishing.

Selected References

Hamley papers, manuscripts collections, University of Washington Library; C. W. Taylor, *Eminent Judges and Lawyers of the Northwest* (1954), p. 57; *Seattle Post-Intelligencer*, 6 May 1975; memorial services, *Washington Reports*, vol. 85, 2d (1975), pp. xxviii-xxxiv; memorial proceedings, U. S. Court of Appeals, Ninth Circuit, *Federal Reports*, vol. 528 (1975), pp. 1-22.

Henry Edson Todd Herman
September 23, 1931-December 1, 1932

Born: January 21, 1891
Highland, Illinois
Washington University, LL.B. (1912)
Died: January 21, 1950
Deputy Prosecutor (1917)
Republican
Appointed

Henry E. T. Herman was born in Highland, Illinois, about fifty miles east of St. Louis, Missouri, to Henry and Nettie (Todd) Herman. Herman received his early education at Smith Academy in St. Louis. After earning his bachelor of law degree from St. Louis's Washington University in 1912, he moved to Spokane to pursue his profession. By 1917 the future judge had been appointed deputy prosecuting attorney of Spokane County. At the outbreak of the First World War, Herman enlisted, achieving the rank of first sergeant of the infantry as well as first sergeant of field artillery. Coincidentally, he served under the command of Captain Charles T. Donworth, who later would also have a seat on the state's high bench. Upon returning to civilian life in 1918 Herman began an active private practice in partnership with Edward B. Powell.

In later years an old friend remembered Herman in these words: he "was about 5′3″ and about as wide...was an excellent lawyer but still a character." He was fairly active in county and state bar affairs and Republican politics. According to one newspaper account:

> For a number of years, since before the first election of Governor [Roland] Hartley in 1924, Herman has been an outstanding supporter of the executive. He is classed by friends as a "wet", having been credited with being a leader in the movement which gained an antiprohibition expression at the Republican state convention.

When Judge Mark Fullerton died, Herman seemed a logical choice to fill the vacancy: his partisan credentials were impeccable, loyalty to the governor proven, legal ability unquestioned, and eastern Washington residence helpful, since Fullerton had also been from east of the Cascades. On September 23, 1931,

Governor Hartley appointed Herman to the supreme court to complete the remaining year of Fullerton's term. Judge Charles Donworth recalled Herman's style:

> His opinions reflect Judge Herman's keen, analytical legal mind, and their brevity belie the labor with which they were prepared. The accurate and succinct statement of the legal problems involved in these cases and their sound solution should serve as models of judicial expression.
>
> Judge Herman's most notable opinion was in *Baxter v. Ford Motor Co.* It was a landmark case which has been referred to with approval by many courts of last resort. In this case, a manufacturer of an automobile was held responsible to the purchaser, who had bought the car from a dealer, because of a misrepresentation in the manufacturer's advertising. This was the first decision in this country in which the rule was adopted.

While on the high bench Herman wrote sixty opinions for the court and five dissents.

On September 13, 1932, just a few days short of having served a year, Judge Herman faced a primary election challenge from fellow Spokanite Bruce Blake. Blake defeated Herman by more than 50,000 votes, largely because of the name familiarity Blake had developed over the years by appearing on the ballot in 1924 and in 1926.

Herman returned to Spokane and immediately regained prominence in the profession. His former partner, Richard S. Munter, recalled:

> By reason of his exceptional ability, practically all of Judge Herman's time during the last decade and a half of his life was used by members of the Spokane Bar associating him in the trials and appeals of difficult cases. In such work he was very happy.

Because of his mastery of epigrammatical expression and possession of a keen sense of humor, Judge Herman was in great demand at social events and as a banquet speaker. Always the gentleman, Governor Hartley once remarked that "Judge Herman knows more of what is in the Book of Etiquette than anyone I know." One of the judge's friends added: "and follows it less." Although he expressed an interest in returning to the supreme court, he never again received appointment, and he actively practiced law until his death in 1950.

Judge Herman married Gladys Downing in August 1926 and they had two daughters, Nettie and Jane. The judge was a member of the Washington Athletic Club, Elks, Moose, Eagles, and Order of Redmen.

Selected References

Seattle Post-Intelligencer, 23 Sept. 1931; *Seattle Times,* 23 Sept. 1931; memorial services, *Washington Reports,* vol. 36, 2d (1950), pp. xxxii-xxxvi.

Floyd Verne Hicks

January 10, 1977-January 17, 1982

Born: May 29, 1915
Prosser, Washington
Central Washington College, B.A. (1938)
Washington State College, (1940-1942)
University of Washington, LL.B. (1948)
Protestant
Superior Court (1961-1963; 1982-1985)
U. S. Congress (1965-1977)
Democrat
Elected

Floyd V. Hicks began his public career as a superior court judge, served in Congress, was elected to the supreme court and, coming full circle, returned to his old position as superior court judge. Of course, much transpired in the interim.

Hicks was born and grew up in Prosser in eastern Washington, graduating from high school there in 1932. He matriculated to Central Washington College of Education in Ellensburg, completing an education degree in 1938. He taught and coached basketball at Wapato, Lacey, St. Johns, and Snohomish high schools while taking advanced work in education at Washington State College. In 1942, he enlisted as a private in the U. S. Army Air Corps, being discharged with the rank of captain in 1946. With the help of the G. I. Bill, he entered the University of Washington School of Law in 1946, graduating with an LL.B. two years later.

Hicks practiced law in Tacoma for thirteen years, first with Don Eastvold, who later became Washington Attorney General, and then with William Goodwin, later appointed to the federal bench. He accepted appointment to the Pierce County Superior Court in 1961, returning to private practice two years later. Elected to the U. S. House of Representatives in 1965, he served until 1977, the same year he won election to the state supreme court. He resigned from the high bench in 1982 to accept an appointment to the superior court bench, from which he retired in 1985.

What appears to be a rapid succession of career changes was often dictated by serendipitous factors. For example, Governor Albert Rosellini and Senator Henry Jackson persuaded him to run for Congress from the Sixth Congressional District in order to fill out the Democratic ticket. Hicks, assuming he stood little chance of winning against long-time incumbent Thor Tollefson, saw the campaign as a way to establish his Democratic credentials for possible appointment to the state or federal benches. He also felt an obligation to the party and to the governor for his earlier superior court appointment. "I knew it wasn't going to be easy to find anyone else to be the sacrificial lamb," he later said. To everyone's surprise, he won the 1964 election and reluctantly moved to Washington, D. C. In his words, "I was running to fill the ticket and lightning struck." Governor Rosellini remembered that Hicks "ran an easy-going campaign and he won. Nobody was more surprised than he was, unless it was me. Another case of the politics of reluctance."

Congressman Hicks developed a reputation for party loyalty, support for moderately liberal causes, and hard work. The six foot, two inch white-haired Westerner became a favorite of reporters covering Congress because of his candid, often blunt responses to questions. He was a strong player on the Henry Jackson-Warren Magnuson Democratic team. Before he left Congress he became a member of the Armed Services Committee and chaired the subcommittee on manpower and housing of the Government Operations Committee. His voting record earned him a favorable rating with the liberal Americans for Democratic Action and a poor score with the conservative Americans for Constitutional Action. Praised by environmental groups and labor organizations, he still never felt quite at home in the nation's capital. Congressman Hicks hinted several times he would not seek reelection, and on June 26, 1975, announced he would not run again.

When Justice Robert Hunter resigned from the state supreme court in 1976, Hicks decided to run for the post. He faced court of appeals judge Keith Callow. Hicks had not fully recovered from a nervous disorder that caused dizziness and left him unable to walk without assistance. He had lost several pounds and admitted he looked like "death warmed over." He made only one trip to the state, speaking to a teachers' group, believing it wiser to conduct his campaign from Washington, D. C. He relied on support from fellow congressmen, name familiarity, and television commercials. Although the state bar overwhelmingly supported Callow, Hicks gained important assistance from the Democratic party and labor organizations, and had ample funds. Without much effort, he defeated Callow in the September primary.

Many observers anticipated the new justice would continue to follow his liberal congressional voting behavior. But Hicks developed a reputation as a middle-of-the-road judge with slightly activist leanings. Concerned that the court had become too lenient in considering criminal appeals, he also believed the justices should continue to protect if not expand civil rights, and go slow regarding changes in tort precedents. Because of his moderate views and abilities at persuasion, Justice Hicks had a decisive impact on court deliberations.

He dissented only in about ten percent of cases, below the court average. He felt dissents had two purposes: to "be on record on [particular] viewpoints" and to attempt to pick up another vote. He agreed most often with his eastern Washington counterpart, moderate Justice William Williams. Between them, they had a moderating influence on a court split fairly evenly between liberals and conservatives.

Although he felt a considerable need to "catch up" with the law and "judging," Justice Hicks was pleased to be back on the bench:

> I feel so much more comfortable than I did in Congress. I never felt that I ever had completely learned what I ought to know as things went on down there. You were dependent on someone else's advice on how you were going to vote on this or that. Of course, when I was in law practice and when you had a case you were going to [appeal], you felt you knew everything there was to know about the thing, and you were comfortable with it. Now its back to that same situation... I find that I'm having to work longer than I care to, [but]...I'm enjoying [it] really immensely. I have a great sense of satisfaction so far... I'm really pleased to be on the court.

Two problems, however, confronted the outspoken but easy-going justice. First, the heavy reading requirements in reviewing case briefs, trial records, and draft opinions became a burden. He had developed cataracts in both eyes and an operation only partially corrected one. Also, while commuting from Tacoma to Olympia he had been in two fatal accidents on the crowded I-5 freeway, neither caused by his negligence. He considered resigning from the court.

Judge Robert A. Jacques of the Pierce County Superior Court announced his retirement late in 1982, prompting Justice Hicks to contact Republican Governor John Spellman about possible appointment to the trial bench. "I liked the work [at the supreme court] very much," he recalled, "but it was in my best interest [to seek the superior court appointment]. I wanted to keep on working. It will be better for me and for my family." The governor agreed, and on November 20, 1982, at the age of sixty-six, Hicks returned to the same bench from which he had launched his political career twenty years earlier. Spellman, responding to criticism that he had appointed a Democrat, said, "Here is a man who was elected to Congress in that district, well regarded by his colleagues...and who says he would like to give up commuting and serve on the superior court." Besides, the move would allow the governor to appoint someone of his own choice and political affiliation to the state supreme court. Judge Hicks carried his full load of cases on the Pierce County bench and retired from public life in 1985.

Hicks and Norma Jeanne Zintheo of Olympia married in 1942 and had two daughters, Tracie and Betsie. The judge held membership in the Kiwanis and served as president of the Parkland, Washington, group. He was also president of the Parkland Parent Teacher Association and was a member of the Parkland Sewer Commission.

Selected References

See the Hicks oral history interview in the supreme court collection, Washington State Archives. Also see *Prosser Record Bulletin*, 1 Sept. 1977; *Seattle Post-Intelligencer*, 29 Nov. 1981; *Tacoma News Tribune*, 21 Nov. 1981; and Charles Sheldon, *A Century of Judging: A Political History of the Washington Supreme Court* (1988), pp. 305-334.

Matthew William Hill

January 13, 1947-December 31, 1969

Born: June 26, 1894
Bozeman, Montana
University of Washington (prelaw)
University of Washington, LL.B. (1917)
Baptist
Died: February 28, 1989
Assistant U. S. Attorney (1923)
Temporary Superior Court Judge (1944)
Republican
Elected

Matthew W. Hill was born in Bozeman, Montana, the only child of Saxton D. and Mary Elma (Noe) Hill. Matthew's father, an employee of the Northern Pacific Railroad, quit the railroad in 1901 to work a 160-acre farm in Illinois left to the family by his wife's father. Having little inclination for, or success with, farming, Saxton Hill returned to railroading after three years. He left Matt and his mother to manage the farm until he could relocate the family in Lester, Washington, where the Northern Pacific employed him as roadmaster. In January 1906, Matt and his mother moved to their new home in Lester. His mother started a Baptist Sunday School. Matt met his future wife, Irma Verne Young, in a youth group in that same church, where her father served as minister. They married in 1924 and were the parents of Lane Irma, Mary Bea, and Matthew Hale. Irma Hill died in 1981.

Matt attended public schools in Illinois, then went to seventh through ninth grades in Lester's small one-room school. He completed grades ten through twelve at Stadium High School in Tacoma. In 1912 Hill enrolled at the University of Washington in a combined liberal arts-law degree program, graduating with a law degree and *cum laude* honors in 1917. While at the university he was a varsity debater, vice president of the student body, and member of several honorary fraternities and social clubs.

After college, Hill taught social studies for one year at Fairhaven High School in Bellingham. He served with the coast artillery during World War I and, upon discharge, joined the Washington Title Insurance Company as a title examiner, remaining until 1921. From 1921-1923 Hill practiced law in Seattle. In 1923 he accepted an appointment as Assistant U. S. Attorney, serving in that capacity for eight months. In 1924 the University of Washington Alumni Association selected Hill executive secretary after he had served as that organization's president in 1921. He "enjoyed [the work] very thoroughly," but his success in the job led indirectly to his resignation.

Largely through Hill's efforts, the 1928 session of the legislature approved a generous budget for the university, which Governor Roland Hartley vetoed. Hill and other representatives of higher education succeeded in persuading the legislature to override the governor's veto. In retaliation, Hartley fired all members of the University of Washington Board of Regents, replacing them with his own loyalists. The president of the university resigned, and Matt Hill felt compelled to follow suit. He later admitted that "if it had not been for Governor Hartley I probably would have spent the rest of my life working with the University of Washington in one capacity or another." However, in 1929 he returned to private practice, first on his own, then with Allen, Foude, and Hilen (1923-1941), and finally as a partner with Lee Newman, which later became the law firm of Hill, Newman, and Cook.

In 1932 Hill ran for the state legislature from the Thirty-second District, in which the university is located, hoping to carry on his fight for the university and against the governor. He survived the primary but lost in the Democratic landslide in November.

Hill tried partisan politics again in 1938 when he ran against Warren G. Magnuson for the First District seat in the U. S. House of Representatives. His campaign centered on the failures of the New Deal, on the argument that business should be given the same rights as labor, and on the charge that Magnuson had ignored the state's concerns. Hill, described by a Seattle newspaper as a "tireless worker in civic, church and charitable affairs, and a public speaker of wide repute," nonetheless lost. This proved to be Hill's last foray in partisan politics, but not his last campaign for elective office.

Hill always wanted to be a judge. When Adam Beeler vacated the superior court to accept appointment to the state's highest bench in the fall of 1930, Hill and fourteen other candidates vied for the King County Superior Court vacancy in the November write-in campaign. Hill placed a distant fourth. Another opportunity presented itself during World War II. Two members of the King County Superior Court took leaves of absence beginning in 1941 to serve in the armed forces. Governor Arthur Langlie thought King County had a sufficient number of judges and initially refused to fill the vacancies. However, in 1944 Langlie lost his reelection bid to Democrat Mon Wallgren who, before taking office, said he would fill the vacancies. To prevent the Democrat that opportunity, Langlie, in the last few weeks of his term, appointed Matt Hill to serve until the elected incumbent returned from military service.

When the superior court incumbent returned, Hill resigned after eighteen months on the trial bench. He gained great satisfaction from the close personal nature of the trial bench: "I never did anything in my life I enjoyed more than the trial court... I had no ambitions to go to the Supreme Court."

Ed Connelly's appointment to the supreme court in 1946 had not been popular with some segments of the bar and public. With the encouragement of many members of the supreme court, the bar, and west-side community leaders, Hill successfully challenged the Spokane resident in 1946. In the July primary, Hill outpolled Connelly and another candidate, then swamped the incumbent in November. This was the last time Judge Hill would face opposition in his campaigns. He attributed his success to the fact that he was well known throughout the state as a visiting judge and to his reputation as a public speaker in demand at community and church events, commencements, Fourth of July picnics, and fraternal gatherings. He maintained his public speaking activities throughout his twenty-three years on the state's high court.

He threw himself into the work of the high court with the same enthusiasm and energy that characterized his efforts as alumni secretary, lawyer, and judge. He was the first to arrive at his chambers in the morning, usually around six after walking from home. In the evening he would leave after six with a briefcase filled with court records or briefs to review that night. He really did not mind the long hours, and usually had his opinions in circulation within a few days.

> In writing the majority opinion in a close case, I'd write it the way it ought to be written, then I would begin to go over it and wonder where a change could be made here and there to appeal to so and so if I thought I had a chance of persuasion... To get a couple of votes you'd add a paragraph here or delete a paragraph there. There is a limit to what you can do. You've got to be intellectually honest. You can't impinge on the verities. But sometimes you can say a thing differently that takes the curse off of it.

Hill liked informal persuasion. He would often drop in on a colleague for a chat on a variety of subjects, then bring up a particular case or a phrase in an opinion in order to reach agreement before the opinion finally circulated. One of his former colleagues, Judge Frank Weaver, remembered Matt Hill's energy with these words:

> Matt really had only two hobbies—work and making speeches all over the state... Matt is unique. He could subsist on five hours of sleep. He would never walk if he could trot. He always ran upstairs. It was not unusual for him to be in his office at six a.m., work eight or nine hours, then be driven a hundred miles or so, give a speech, and then be driven back to Olympia...
> When Matt was driven any place he always rode in the back seat. He was usually asleep before the driver shifted into high gear. . . . I never went any place in the state that someone would not say, "You probably know my good friend, Matt Hill."

Hill's flair for writing, his skill for forging agreement among his colleagues, and his courage all came to public display in a 1951 decision, *Power Inc. v. Huntley.*

Hill filed a dissent concerning the constitutionality of a four percent corporate income tax passed by the recent legislature to balance the state budget. His dissent picked up the needed votes to become the majority opinion. Hill wrote:

> Finally, it is urged upon us that to declare the appropriation act unconstitutional would throw the fiscal affairs of the state in chaos...
>
> The West Virginia court used a quotation from Shakespeare...to answer the argument of subsequent financial chaos, saying that if it were to avoid its clear duty because of a claim of expediency
>
> 'Twill be recorded for a precedent,
> And many an error by the same example
> Will rush into the State: it cannot be.'
>
> It is our view that Chapter 10 of the Laws of 1951...contains two unrelated subjects in the Title and in the act and is unconstitutional and void in its entirety.

Because of Judge Hill's opinion, the governor called a special session of the legislature to deal with the "fiscal chaos."

According to experienced appellate lawyers and law clerks, Judge Hill was fairly conservative and restraintist, characteristics he readily recognized. However, he thought himself less conservative after twenty-three years on the bench than when he first donned the robes of judicial office.

After his retirement he confided that, from a judicial viewpoint, "The world is changing and what was the proper thing ten years ago may not be the proper thing today." Judges have "to be aware of changing social conditions and changing attitudes."

Judge Hill's dissent in *Pierce v. Yakima Valley Memorial Hospital Association* in 1953 illustrates his restraint. The majority opinion had withdrawn certain types of immunity from nonprofit hospitals:

> I shall not take issue with the very thorough and able majority opinion as to the desirability of the results achieved. I do insist that a change in a doctrine which has become fixed as a matter of public policy should be sought from the legislature, regardless of the reason upon which the rule is made to rest...
>
> The views expressed by the majority if unanswerable upon the merits, should be presented to the legislature by the interested parties. There is, in my opinion, no justification for a change by the court in a doctrine which has become fixed as a matter of public policy.

On December 31, 1969, Judge Hill had to retire from the state's high bench because of Washington's statutory seventy-five year age limit. In his twenty-three years on the court he authored 685 majority opinions, 110 dissents, and sixty-nine concurring opinions, having participated in nearly 4,200 cases. Only five other supreme court judges had served longer.

The judge continued his frenzied pace after he left the bench, speaking throughout the state, participating in nonpartisan campaigns, and remaining active in fraternal and service organizations. His activities while on and off the bench were so numerous that only a partial listing is possible: Linfield College trustee; Baptist Church lay minister; board member of the Family Society of Seattle, Young Men's Christian Association, American Red Cross, Washington Temperance Association, Olympia Community Chest, and Berkeley Baptist Divinity School; grand master of Masonic Order; first vice president of General Council of the Baptist Convention; member of the Boy Scouts, Washington and Northern Idaho Council of Churches, National Conference of Christians and Jews, Washington Historical Society, Young Men's Republican Club, American Legion, Eagles, Kiwanis, Knights of the Round Table, and the National Committee for the Prevention of Alcoholism.

In June 1970, Hill accepted an appointment to hear appeals from the Water Pollution Control Commission, which soon gave way to membership on the pollution control hearing board of the Department of Ecology. His fellow board members elected him chairman, and he gained reappointment to the board for a six-year term in 1972. Also in 1972 he served as a member of the shorelines hearing board and a special citizens' committee to resolve an Aberdeen school board-teacher dispute. He also participated in a number of initiative measure campaigns. Judge Hill's "retirement" remained a busy time. After a lengthy illness, he passed away on February 28, 1989 at the age of ninety-four.

Judge Hill was a unique person gifted with a decisive intellect, a Christian commitment, and a store of inexhaustible energy. His Baptist upbringing made him an excellent example of the Protestant ethic at work. His study of the law gave him the content for his life's work, while his parents provided him with the desire to excel.

Selected References

See Hill's oral history interview in the supreme court collection, Washington State Archives; C. W. Taylor, *Eminent Judges and Lawyers of the Northwest* (1954), p. 54; *The Olympian,* 2 Mar. 1989 and 31 May 1990; *Seattle Post-Intelligencer,* 2 Mar. 1989; and memorial services, *Washington Reports,* vol. 113, 2d (1989), p. xliii-lvii.

Oscar Raymond Holcomb

January 11, 1915-January 10, 1927;
April 22, 1927-January 9, 1939

Born: December 31, 1867
Haubstadt, Indiana
Southwestern Indiana Normal School (1888)
Chicago College of Law, LL.B. (1892)
Episcopalian
Died: September 13, 1948
Prosecuting Attorney (1895-1898)
State Commissioner of Arid Lands
  (1898-1901)
Ritzville Mayor and City Councilman
  (1899-1908)
Superior Court (1909-1915)
Democrat
Elected/Appointed

Oscar R. Holcomb, born December 31, 1867 in Haubstadt, Indiana, was the son
of Silas Mercer and Mary Ann (Hopkins) Holcomb, both members of Indiana
pioneer families. His father, a lawyer, fought in the Civil War as an officer with
the Sixty-third Indiana Volunteer Infantry and was wounded several times. Following the war he returned home to Gibson County and resumed law practice.

Oscar received his early education in the county public schools, graduating
from high school in Fort Branch, Indiana. While working on his father's farm
he attended Southwestern Indiana Normal School for two years, after which he
taught for three years. He studied law with his father during vacations and then
at the Chicago College of Law, where he graduated in 1892. He practiced law
in Evansville with Clinton Staser, later to become his father-in-law. In 1893 he
became attorney for the St. Paul office of the Northern Pacific Railroad. The
Staser family moved to Tacoma, Washington, and Holcomb, eager to remain near
his future wife, asked his superiors for an assignment in the West. Late in 1893
the company sent him to Ritzville, Washington, to settle land claims against the
railroad. Taken by the area and its opportunities, he resigned his position with
the railroad and set up a law office in Ritzville. He and Eva Staser married in
1894. Their family eventually grew with the addition of three boys—Silas,
Maurice, and Leland—and three girls—Marjorie, Mariam, and Mary.

In 1895 Holcomb gained appointment as prosecuting attorney for Adams
County and was elected to that position the next year. He successfully prosecuted
the county's first murder case. He resigned as prosecutor in 1898 to accept Governor J. R. Rogers's appointment as State Commissioner of Arid Lands. Because

several large companies opposed government involvement in developing irrigation, Holcomb was unsuccessful in his efforts to promote irrigation in eastern Washington. In 1899 the legislature abolished the office and Holcomb returned to private practice in Ritzville.

After serving six terms as city councilman, voters elected Holcomb mayor, and he served from 1905 to 1908. A school board member for several years and an active member of the Episcopal Church, Holcomb participated in virtually every community undertaking that moved Ritzville from a makeshift village to a modern town.

The future judge became a leading figure in Democratic politics in eastern Washington. Nominated to be Commissioner of Public Lands on the Democratic and Free Silver Republican "Fusionist" ticket in 1900, he failed to win the general election. Two years later he ran, again unsuccessfully, for Congress as a Democrat. However, his political destiny lay in the judiciary. In 1908, upon the urging of local progressive leaders in the Ritzville community, Holcomb agreed, as he put it, to attempt to "rid the people of an unjust, malicious, tyrannical and drunken judge." Voters rewarded his efforts, and he donned the robes of judge of the superior court responsible for a vast three-county jurisdiction in southeastern Washington.

Some people urged him to submit his name for nomination to the high bench at the 1910 Democratic convention, the last year of partisan contests for the supreme court. He refused because of his belief in nonpartisanship for judges and his commitment to supreme court candidates nominated by the nonpartisan convention intent on challenging nominees of the two major parties. Some had considered Holcomb a serious candidate for appointment to a vacancy on the state's high bench on several occasions, but his liberal and independent attitudes failed to impress the state's chief executive. In 1914, before he finished his second term on the trial bench, he mounted a successful campaign for the supreme court, pushing aside incumbent Mack F. Gose by nearly 6,000 votes in the September primary, which assured him victory in the November election.

In 1926, after Holcomb had served two full terms on the state's high bench, Walter French, superior court judge of Kitsap County, defeated him during a reelection bid. In an unprecedented move, Holcomb was then reappointed to the supreme court in April 1927 to fill the vacancy left when J. B. Bridges died. Republican Governor Roland Hartley's choice of the Democratic Holcomb raised a few eyebrows among Republican stalwarts, but the appointment made political and practical sense. Holcomb was from eastern Washington, although he had been practicing law in Seattle since he left the bench in January. Only two other Easterners then served on the bench and the appointment would redress the geographical imbalance. Also, since Hartley had received some support from Democrats in his political battles, the appointment of the old-time Democrat Holcomb clearly expressed the governor's appreciation. Hartley, in the midst of reorganizing his administration, wanted to avoid a prolonged battle over a court appointment. Finally, Bridges had been ill during his last few months and a back-log of cases developed. A quick appointment of the conscientious and experienced Holcomb would enable the court to move again with a full complement of judges.

A year after his appointment, Judge Holcomb narrowly turned back the challenge of Bruce Blake in the November balloting. Challenged again in 1932, he easily prevailed to win a full six-year term on the high bench. His expertise in the legal and political aspects of irrigation rights and farming issues provided the court with leadership. However, his liberalism often found him isolated from most of his colleagues on other issues. He did not hesitate to dissent from his brethren on a number of economic and social issues. For example, in *Langill's Estate* in 1920 he angrily chastised his fellow judges:

> By the majority decision the disintegration of the probate code of 1917 is begun... Their reasoning is wholly inconsistent and illogical... It is positively legislating and creating disqualifications which the statutes did not create... The majority opinion is manifestly wrong.

Fellow Judge Thomas E. Grady noted Holcomb's liberal approach to supreme court litigation in these terms:

> Judge Holcomb believed that the members of the court were to a high degree conservative in their approach to the judicial problems of the time, and had advocated a more liberal attitude, particularly with reference to matters of pleading and practice and the interpretation and application of remedial and social legislation.

In July 1938 Holcomb announced he would take advantage of the recent law allowing judges to retire on half pay and not seek another term. His salary was then $7,500. Hip trouble and a slight paralysis of the throat further prompted the retirement. After nearly twenty-four years, Justice Holcomb left the bench on January 9, 1939. He died at the age of eighty on September 13, 1948.

Selected References

D. W. Durham, *History of Spokane and the Inland Empire*, vol. 2 (1912), pp. 696-697; *Seattle Times*, 4 Nov. 1928; memorial services, *Washington Reports*, vol. 36, 2d (1950), pp. xxv-xxxi.

Charles Horowitz

January 13, 1975-December 31, 1980

Born: Brooklyn, New York
January 5, 1905
University of Washington, B.A. (1925)
University of Washington, LL.B. (1927)
Oxford University, B.A. (1929); M.A. (1952)
Jewish
Died: March 25, 1989
Court of Appeals (1969-1974)
Democrat
Elected

Few persons have brought more impressive credentials to the supreme court than Charles Horowitz. His outstanding educational, professional, civic, and scholarly accomplishments proved instrumental in his selection as a judge and contributed to his effectiveness on the bench. He was born on January 5, 1905 in Brooklyn, New York, eldest of five children of Harry and Fanny Horowitz. The elder Horowitz arrived in America the year before from Tsarist Russia and worked as a cloth cutter in New York's garment district. He later became a tailor. Charles Horowitz spent his earliest childhood in the tenement district of lower east side Manhattan. The family moved to Seattle in 1913 when Charles was eight years old.

Horowitz attended public schools in Seattle, selling papers and delivering magazines after class to help with family expenses. In the evening he sold candy at a Seattle movie theater. During the summer he worked at fruit and vegetable stands, mowed lawns, and helped a roofing contractor. His earnings also assisted with his college education after Horowitz entered the University of Washington at the age of seventeen. He earned Phi Beta Kappa honors and graduated *magna cum laude* in 1925.

Hoping to make law his career, Horowitz went immediately to the University of Washington School of Law, graduating in 1927 with *summa cum laude* honors. He served as editor-in-chief of the *Washington Law Review* and wrote several of the *Review's* first law notes. His law school record and general scholarly accomplishments led to a coveted three-year Rhodes Scholarship at Oxford University where he completed his studies in two years, earning a B.A. degree in jurisprudence with first-class honors in 1929. In 1952 he returned to earn a master's degree from the prestigious English institution.

Horowitz's professional career, spanning nearly a half century, was equally impressive. Horowitz passed the Washington bar in 1927 and upon returning from England joined the law firm of Preston, Thorgrimson, and Turner where he became a full partner in 1933. He lectured frequently at the University of Washington and served on the Washington Uniform Legislation Commission for a number of years, assuming the chairmanship in 1964. Horowitz also chaired the joint editorial board of the uniform probate code, which had the responsibility for periodically updating the code. Earlier, as co-chairman of the special national probate committee, he had prime responsibility for writing the code. A member of the American Law Institute, he also served as president of the Seattle Bar Association in 1957-1958. He chaired the citizens' advisory committee to the Joint Interim Committee on Facilities and Operations of the Washington state legislature which studied legislative reform. He later became a trustee of the American Bar Foundation and belonged to the American Judicature Society. In recognition of his professional activities, his colleagues in the state bar honored him with their Award of Merit in 1962.

Although a life-long Democrat, Charles Horowitz was not especially active in partisan politics. However, a continuing interest in public issues extended back to childhood days and the experiences of his father in the early years of labor strife in the garment industry. Although Horowitz strongly advocated labor unions, in his law practice he handled mostly civil matters and on occasion acted as a court-appointed attorney for criminal defendants. He developed a special interest in probate and estate planning.

In 1968 the Washington legislature proposed, and the voters ratified, a constitutional amendment providing an intermediate court of appeals responsible for much of the appellate work then burdening the supreme court. According to an agreement with the legislature, Republican Governor Dan Evans would appoint twelve judges, at least four being Democrats. He selected Horowitz as one.

Evans based his choice largely on Horowitz's professional reputation, labor support, and bar activities. Subsequently, Horowitz won election to the appeals bench in 1970 and reelection in 1972, both times unopposed.

Judge Horowitz had seriously contended for an appointment to the state's high bench only a year after assuming court of appeals' responsibilities. In October 1971, Justice Morell Sharp was nominated to the federal district court bench and Horowitz was among the final two or three considered for the pending supreme court vacancy. In November, however, Horowitz wrote a controversial decision upholding the right to protest the Viet Nam war by affixing a peace symbol on the American flag and hanging it upside down from an apartment window. Whether his opinion became a factor remains unclear, but his Democratic background did not make him an altogether attractive appointee for Republican Governor Evans. In any event, on December 20, Evans appointed Judge Robert Utter, Horowitz's court of appeals colleague and close friend.

In June 1974, Chief Justice Frank Hale announced his retirement from the high court upon completion of his six-year term in January, 1975. The first open seat in two decades attracted five election contenders: Superior Court Judge Francis Holman, Court of Appeals Judge Harold J. Petrie, Tacoma attorney Robert Comfort, former Seattle councilman Liem Tuai, and Charles Horowitz. The latter announced his candidacy in early July after several people urged him to run, including Arnie Weinmeister, head of the state Teamsters Union. In 1954 Horowitz had successfully represented Weinmeister, a former All-American football player at the University of Washington and all-pro tackle with the New York Giants, in a pro football contract.

Horowitz's age became a campaign issue. He would have to retire shortly before completing his full six-year term under the state's mandatory retirement statute. He avoided direct comment on the matter, continually emphasizing his broad experience. "The real issue," he said, "is who is best qualified for service."

Horowitz received the top rating in the state bar's preferential poll and had strong backing from Weinmeister's Teamsters. He survived the September balloting, leading his nearest rival, Liem Tuai by more than 12,000 votes. Both moved to the final November election.

Again, Horowitz stuck to his credentials theme and again won an overwhelming majority in the state bar poll, but that hardly assured victory. Before the campaign ended, Horowitz and his supporters spent $72,853, constituting the largest amount invested to that date in a state judicial race. His efforts succeeded; he turned back Tuai's challenge in November, 498,917 to 377,445 votes. On January 13, 1975, Charles Horowitz took his oath of office as justice of the Washington Supreme Court.

Justice Horowitz quickly assumed a moderating role on the court. Although generally a liberal on economic and individual rights issues, he often eschewed liberalism to provide a restraining influence on his colleagues. He willingly recognized the policy role of the court and the importance of personal values in a judge's decision, frequent hallmarks of liberal judges. But he also accepted the Holmes/Brandeis/Frankfurter restraintist tradition. In an article written shortly before his retirement, the justice gave shape to this view:

> [U]nstated premises and assumptions are ordinarily not thought of as sources of law. Yet, within the area of his permitted discretion, a judge's scheme of values, notions of duty, devotion to logic, personal background and experiences, overall philosophy, and notions of public policy, morality and ethics all have a bearing upon the choices he makes in adopting one mode of reasoning rather than another to justify his decision.

In espousing the ideology adopted nearly a century earlier by Oliver Wendell Holmes, Jr., Horowitz restated the approach of the legal realists of the 1920s and the judicial behavioralists of more modern times, recognizing that personal values and non-legal factors often entered into a judge's decisions, compelling him to act with care.

Horowitz's view of judges' roles reflected his behavior on the bench. For example, he reluctantly dissented. He saw little value in dissenting unless he believed it an important principle or unless he could win the majority to his side. Failing this, he acquiesced to the majority or simply voted with another dissenter's opinion.

Still, his first recorded opinion was a dissent in which he chastised the majority for not adhering "to its own admonitions that the court is not a super-legislature; that [it] is not at liberty to substitute its own wisdom for that of the legislature." A law clerk described how Horowitz reached his decisions:

> He would first make up his mind on what he felt would be the correct result, which on hard cases would sometimes take quite a while. The Judge was open to suggestions and discussion during this time. After he made up his mind on the correct result, his whole energy was devoted to making his point of view as persuasive as possible, through gathering authority to back his point, formulating arguments and marshalling evidence in the case... The goal was to win a majority, whether 9-0 or 5-4.

The justice could, on the one hand, become irritated at his colleagues for misreading the intent of legislators; yet on the other hand he could quickly and decisively strike down a state action that threatened individual rights. During his first year on the bench he wrote the important opinion giving "teeth" to the state's Equal Rights Amendment. Indeed, the enactment he upheld, Article 31 of the state constitution, even more thoroughly protected women's rights than the Fourteenth Amendment to the U. S. Constitution.

To summarize the 270 opinions Justice Horowitz wrote during the six years he served on the high bench would be formidable, but two characteristics are evident. First, Horowitz's desire to research the law meant that no relevant authority would go uninvestigated. He consulted law review articles, encyclopedia, treatises, histories, and sometimes ancient authorities. Reading the justice's footnotes often is as educational as his text. Second, the justice believed history to be important. Much like Justice Hugo Black of the nation's high court, Horowitz provided attorneys, other judges, and students of the law with a thorough review of the history of a particular legal issue or constitutional doctrine.

Perhaps the major impact of Justice Horowitz on the court and his colleagues came from his scholarship and frank recognition of the responsibilities of judging. Justice James M. Dolliver, who sat with the judge for five of his six years, described these lasting legacies:

> A report on a case by Charlie Horowitz was a magisterial performance. What preparation! While I have always tried to be prepared on my own cases and those of other judges, when I compare my degree and quality of preparation to that of Charlie's I am as a grasshopper to the ant. Notebooks bulging with information: the full text of cases, observations of textbook and law review writers, an ominous stack of reports and a step-by-step analysis of the matter before us.

Accompanying the scholarship was a recognition of the role of values. In the words of Justice Dolliver, "He helped me to understand not only the need for and necessity of values in decisionmaking, but also that a judge should not be ashamed of or try to hide the importance of values." This recognition teaches judges humility. Awareness of the court's policy role as well as one's personal values prevents a judge from exercising power without responsibility. In this area, Justice Charles Horowitz "set a standard for the court that will serve it well."

On March 23, 1930, Charles married Diana Glickman and they had two children, Caroline Ann and Elinor Louise. On December 31, 1980 Justice Horowitz stepped down from the state's court of last resort. At age seventy-five he returned to his old law firm in Seattle and began again the practice of law. On March 25, 1989 the eighty-four year old justice passed away.

Selected References

"Dedication to the Honorable Charles Horowitz," *Washington Law Review,* vol. 56 (1981), pp. 162-178; C. W. Taylor, *Eminent Judges and Lawyers of the Northwest* (1954), p. 97; *Seattle Post-Intelligencer,* 19 Sept. 1974 and 27 Mar. 1989; Jenifer A. Lewis, "Profile: Justice Charles Horowitz," *Seattle-King County Bar Bulletin* (Nov. 1987), pp. 5, 32.

Chester Ralph Hovey
October 4, 1921-January 8, 1923

Born: January 21, 1872
Holyoke, Massachusetts
Protestant
Died: November 9, 1953
City Attorney (1902-1908)
Prosecuting Attorney (1899-1901; 1910-1912)
President, Washington State Bar Association
  (1921)
Republican
Appointed

Chester Hovey, the son of George A. and Jennie (Dyer) Hovey, was born in Holyoke, Massachusetts. He graduated from public high school in Durand, Wisconsin, in 1888 and that same year moved to Ellensburg. Hovey worked odd jobs and in a grocery store, studying law at night with Judge Ralph Kauffman, longtime superior court judge of Kittitas County. At age twenty-one, the Washington bar admitted Hovey and he began practicing law in Ellensburg.

In 1899 Hovey won election as prosecuting attorney for Kittitas County, serving until 1901. He returned to that office from 1910 to 1912. In the intervening years he acted as Ellensburg City Attorney. Although a Republican by inclination, Hovey was not active in party affairs. But he was a leader in the local bar and achieved statewide recognition with his election as president of the Washington State Bar Association in 1921. He developed a reputation as an expert on water rights and irrigation law. His presidency of the state bar, expertise in irrigation law, party affiliation, and eastern Washington residency led Governor Louis Hart to appoint Hovey to the supreme court bench in 1921 to fill the vacancy created by Judge Wallace Mount's death.

Otto Rupp, former president of the Washington State Bar Association, recalled one particular case handled by Hovey that displayed his courage and brought him to Governor Hart's attention:

> The federal government proposed to build in the Kittitas Valley a very large irrigation project, a project eagerly desired by the people of that county. A few land owners...affected by the construction...and Hovey thought...that such construction, due to the charges to be made for water, would not be of any advantage to them but would practically amount to the confiscation of their property. They

asked Judge Hovey to represent them. He was reluctant to do so, as he knew that such action would be regarded by most of the residents of the county, his clients and friends with pronounced disfavor. Nevertheless, as he told me, he believed it was his duty to represent these land owners, and he did so, to his very considerable financial detriment. Time, however, has not only healing in its wings, but also sometimes brings compensation in addition to the inner satisfaction arising from a duty performed. It was the knowledge of this courageous action on Judge Hovey's part which in large part led Governor Hart to tender Hovey an appointment to this Court.

Judge Hovey lost in his only attempt to hold his seat by election. In 1923 William Pemberton put together a coalition of Democrats, labor, and the Grange to retire Hovey from the bench. Rather than returning to Ellensburg, Hovey moved to Seattle where he set up practice and again became active in professional affairs, winning election as president of the Seattle Bar Association in 1929.

Judge Matthew Hill remembered Judge Hovey's brief tenure on the bench with these words:

Judge Hovey ranks as one who clarified, not one who confused. With a brevity which was remarkable. . . he expressed himself in firm and unequivocal language. In him there was no flash of shallowness or resort to words or phrases to cover an uncertainty of mind. He was direct and forceful. Again and again, one marvels at his ability to go to the core of a complex and confusing problem and lay bare the decisive fact upon which the whole case turns. A little impatient at times with doctrinaire advocacy of extreme positions, his opinions indicate a firm belief in the right of a man to be let alone. But he knew too, that there can be no true liberty except as supported by law.

In those days, a by-law of the State Bar Association made it a duty of the president in his annual address to comment upon the important decisions of the Supreme Court rendered during the year. Two of the five decisions discussed by President Joseph McCarthy at the meeting in Tacoma in August 1922 had been written by Judge Hovey.

Judge Hovey married Grace J. Painter of Ellensburg in 1895 and the couple had two children, Joseph and Ann. The judge was a member of the Elks Club and was active in the Ellensburg Chamber of Commerce.

Selected References

H. James Boswell, *American Blue Book: Western Washington* (1922), p. 41; memorial services, *Washington Reports,* vol. 46, 2d (1955), pp. xviii-xxv.

John Philo Hoyt
November 11, 1889-January 11, 1897

Born: October 6, 1841
Austinburg, Ohio
Ohio State (1866)
Union Law School, LL.B. (1867)
Died: August 25, 1926
Prosecuting Attorney (1869-1870)
Michigan Legislator (1871-1876)
Arizona Territorial Secretary and
    Governor (1876-1918)
Washington Territorial Supreme Court
    (1879-1887)
Republican
Elected

John P. Hoyt, one of the five original judges of the Washington Supreme Court, was the son of David and Susannah (Fancher) Hoyt, born on a farm near Austinburg, Ohio. He received the rudiments of an education while working on the farm and then attended public school and the Grand River Institute in Austinburg. He taught school until he volunteered for the Union Army during the Civil War, serving four years with the Eighty-fifth and Eighty-seventh Ohio Infantry and the Second Ohio Artillery. Upon his release in 1866, Hoyt enrolled at Ohio State and then Union Law School in Cleveland, Ohio, graduating in 1867.

Hoyt began to practice law in Michigan where he became interested in Republican politics. He was elected prosecuting attorney for Tuscola County in 1869 and again in 1870. He married on December 17, 1869 and had two sons and one daughter.

Voters elected him to the Michigan House of Representatives in 1871 and reelected him for a second term. He served as speaker from 1874 to 1876. President Ulysses Grant appointed him secretary of the Arizona Territory in 1876 and governor a year later. Named governor of Idaho Territory in 1878, Hoyt did not accept the commission because he felt the man he was to replace had been unjustly removed. Hoyt persuaded President Rutherford Hayes to reinstate the person. He achieved his goal of becoming a judge when he gained appointment as justice of the supreme court of the Washington Territory. He served on that bench from 1879 to 1887.

At one of the early meetings of the state bar, Judge Hoyt shared some of his territorial experiences, revealing something about the practice of law then:

I reached the State, then Territory, of Washington in February, 1879. The first term of court which I was called upon to hold was at Vancouver, and to one whose practice at the bar had been confined to a common law state the motions to strike out and strike in (make more definite and certain), founded upon reasons conceivable and inconceivable. . . which were fired at the court by guns, as to the caliber of which it then had little knowledge, was most bewildering, if not absolutely alarming.

Congress amended the National Bank Act in 1886 to allow certain new types of banks to incorporate. Seattle banking pioneer Dexter Horton took advantage of the act and formed a corporation with Hoyt, Arthur Denny, Joseph R. Lewis, and William S. Ladd as major stockholders. Eventually the organization became known as Seattle First National Bank. Upon completion of his term on the territorial supreme court in 1887, Hoyt became active in the bank as manager while remaining one of its major stockholders. He also joined with Denny in several real estate ventures.

The politics of statehood, however, drew Hoyt back into public life. King County voters elected him to the constitutional convention in Olympia where he presided over that important gathering. With statehood, Hoyt played a leading role at the Republican nominating convention and the party selected him to run for the state supreme court after he withdrew his name from consideration for a U. S. Senate seat.

During the campaign Hoyt drew criticism for favoring the Northern Pacific Railroad while a territorial judge. He also allegedly denied the Seattle anti-Chinese rioters of 1886 the right of appeal. The *Seattle Post-Intelligencer* discounted the accusations and, with some delight, pointed out that every attorney in Judge Hoyt's twelve county district had signed a petition for his reappointment as territorial judge. The allegations failed to make any significant inroads with voters, who confirmed the entire Republican judicial slate in the October 1889 election. Hoyt drew the seven-year term on the five-member court. In 1896 he became the first incumbent judge to be defeated in a reelection bid when James Reavis and the Fusionist Party swept to victory throughout the state.

Hoyt took a moderate stance on the high court regarding constitutional issues, often joining Judge Thomas Anders to provide balance between the activists and restraintists. He wrote more than his share of majority opinions. For example, between 1890 and 1895 he penned 312 of the court's opinions, twenty-three percent of the total. However, he was also the leading dissenter, writing sixty-five dissenting opinions, voting sixty-nine times with other dissenters, and concurring fifty-two times. Of the 1,186 cases the court heard over its first five years, Hoyt was out of harmony with a majority of his colleagues fourteen percent of the time.

Because of his frequent dissents and apparent dislike for much of the compromise necessary for unanimity on an appellate court, Judge Hoyt provided little leadership to the early bench. With his vast experience in politics, the law, and judging, combined with his considerable prestige, one would think he might have taken a more practical approach to issues confronting the supreme court. However, it may well be that this diverse and rich background convinced the judge of the correctness of his views. Nevertheless, Hoyt was not a maverick outside the mainstream of politics and law. He simply proved to be less effective than might have been expected.

Following his defeat, Judge Hoyt returned to his business concerns, continued as regent of the University of Washington, serving from 1889 to 1902, and taught at the university's law school from 1902 to 1909. From the early 1900s to 1912 he served as United States referee in bankruptcy for the northwest.

Judge Hoyt belonged to the Grand Army of the Republic and the Association of Washington Pioneers, serving as its vice president in 1925. He resided in Mercer Island until his death in 1926 at age eighty-five.

Selected References

Seattle Times, 26 Sept. 1889; *Seattle Post-Intelligencer,* 28 Sept. 1889 and 17 Je. 1919; Charles K. Wiggins, "John P. Hoyt and Women's Suffrage," *Washington State Bar News* (Jan. 1889), pp. 17-20; Julian Hawthorne, *History of Washington,* vol. 1 (1893), p. 615; Charles Sheldon and Michael Stohr-Gillmore, "In the Beginning: The Washington Supreme Court a Century Ago," *University of Puget Sound Law Review,* vol. 17 (Winter, 1989), pp. 247-284; C. S. Reinhart, *History of the Supreme Court of the Territory and State of Washington* (n.d.), pp. 58-65, 104-105.

Robert Thomas Hunter
October 11, 1957-January 10, 1977

Born: September 29, 1907
Lawton, Oklahoma
University of Washington (1926-1931)
University of Washington, LL.B. (1934)
Presbyterian
Justice of the Peace (1937-1946)
City Attorney (1936-1946)
Superior Court (1946-1957)
Democrat
Appointed

Robert Hunter always wanted to be a lawyer, following the example of his father, Alfred Lewis Hunter, a pioneer attorney, Democratic political activist, and Oklahoma state legislator. A star debater and orator at Lawton High School, Bob's teams won regional contests and placed fourth in the state finals in his senior year, 1925. Upon completion of high school he and several friends packed their belongings in the back of a Model T pick-up and headed west to seek such fortunes as the land provided. Bob hoped to continue his education at Stanford University. In the meantime he accepted employment with his uncle, Captain Jack Vickers, in a Kennewick, Washington, apple orchard, starting as a picker and handyman, earning fifty cents a day plus room and board. With the apple season completed, his uncle and cousin convinced Hunter to enroll at the University of Washington in preparation for law school. Following their advice, he moved to Seattle and found a job washing dishes at a boarding house to help pay schooling costs.

Expenses outran earnings in the spring of 1927, prompting Hunter to answer a newspaper ad seeking salesmen for subscriptions to *The Pictorial Review*, a popular magazine of the time. He had considerable selling talent and that summer not only earned a respectable commission but also a $150 scholarship. That, along with earnings from working again for his uncle, allowed Hunter to return to the University of Washington in the winter quarter to continue his studies. The next summer he again excelled at selling the popular magazine. For each of the next several years Hunter alternated between going to school two quarters and selling magazine subscriptions and working odd jobs the remaining six months.

Finally, in 1934 the future judge graduated from the University of Washington School of Law. In February 1935 he passed the bar exam, but again sold magazines in Alaska to earn enough to open his own office. He joined an old classmate, Clifford Moe, in the practice of law in Grand Coulee, a boom town witnessing construction of the nation's largest concrete dam. Hunter lived in a tent during part of the first difficult winter, but his practice began to prosper. He made a name for himself by winning awards for workers injured on the construction site. One appeal, known as the "Lunch Hour Case," established a principle in labor law allowing workers to sue contracting companies if injured during lunch breaks.

Whenever state and national political figures visited the construction project, Bob Hunter hosted them, showing them around and introducing them to local Democrats. He became known as "Mr. Democrat" in Grant and Douglas counties, actively working in the congressional, senatorial, and gubernatorial campaigns of Mon C. Wallgren. He served as Grand Coulee City Attorney for 10 years, justice of the peace for Grant County for nine years, and city attorney for several surrounding incorporated areas. While city attorney, Hunter proved instrumental in convincing the state legislature to provide funds to pave Grand Coulee's streets and to assist the city with a modern water system.

In 1946, after Governor Wallgren appointed Superior Court Judge Ed Schwellenbach to the state supreme court, he offered Hunter the vacant superior court position. Hunter had not sought a career on the bench, but accepted the Wallgren offer, thinking a short stint on the bench would be a "nice experience." He remained "tremendously enthusiastic about practicing law," and so certain that he would soon return to private practice that he failed to sell his law practice or close his Grand Coulee office. "I'll be going back," he asserted. "This is just a little experience." The "little experience" lasted for 30 years.

Governor Albert Rosellini, Hunter's classmate in law school, had worked with the judge frequently in Democratic politics. When Schwellenbach died in December 1957, Hunter became a prime candidate to fill the state's high bench vacancy. Politics also assisted Hunter. The seat had traditionally gone to an eastern Washington resident. Having served throughout the state as visiting judge during eleven years on the superior court, he was well known to the legal profession. He had also served as secretary and president of the Superior Court Judges' Association and had been the judges' representative on the judicial council for seven years. His name appeared on the bar association's approved list. Governor Rosellini selected his old friend and classmate and on October 11, 1957, Judge Hunter began his supreme court career.

Judge Hunter either ran unopposed or faced only token opposition in his campaigns. Even if confident of reelection, Hunter felt it necessary to campaign. Here is how he described his efforts in 1958:

Filings opened on July 1st of 1958, and I anxiously waited, hoping that I might be...lucky. As the thirty-day filing period transpired I grew more apprehensive. On the final day I thought I had it made, but just five minutes before the deadline, a prominent lawyer from Seattle came into the office of the Secretary of State and filed for my position. What a let-down. Now I would have to campaign in all 39 counties of the State...

I visited almost every county during the summer recess, and my campaign tactics fell into a pattern. First, I would go to the local paper with my picture and news story. I made a point to chat with the editor.

To keep my campaign non-partisan, but to touch base with political leaders, I called on both County Chairmen of the Democratic and Republican parties.

In the larger cities, I arranged a short interview in the television stations, to be run during the news hour. My loyal court reporter in Ephrata, Marion Shutt, had mailed out to over 150 weekly newspapers in the state a short news story on the occasion of my initial appointment. During the election campaign, many of them reprinted the picture and details from my background.

In both of his contested elections—1958 and 1970—he received overwhelming support from the Seattle and state bar associations and, through his "old fashioned" campaigning, easily turned back his opposition in the primaries. Despite the costs of campaigning and time lost from court business, Judge Hunter regarded the popular election of judges as desirable. It "keeps judges close to the public," he noted. "They have no tendency of becoming tyrannical or demagogic in any way. They are considerate of everyone's rights and they are not just dealing with their conscience."

Judge Hunter had a moderate bench philosophy and was a neutral on an activist-restraintist scale. Although he generally observed and protected individual rights in criminal cases, he also recognized society's needs. For example, in 1968 he stated:

I think the pendulum has swung as far as it will go and more likely will go in the other direction. I think [the justices] have gone as far as necessary in the protection of the rights of individuals. As far as I'm concerned I feel the decisions written by this court should not in any way extend the rights of the accused that have been established by the United States Supreme Court.

The judge's decisional style involved working closely with his law clerk. According to one:

It was typically our procedure to sit down after the original briefing had been completed, and argue the case between ourselves. Each of us would take one of the two positions. At the conclusion, we would switch sides and re-argue the matter. Justice Hunter would then make a decision, as to his position on the case. Subsequent to oral argument and conference, the judge would inform me as to those areas he wished to discuss in his opinion. I would write a rough draft and then proceed to discuss it sentence by sentence with him. It was [his] belief that this close relationship...produced a better finished product.

Judge Hunter sought a collective judgment on each of the cases assigned him. He utilized conference notes extensively throughout the drafting process in order to take into account his colleagues' concerns. Rarely did he pen a dissent.

Writing opinions never came easy. He envied such fellow judges as Frank Hale and Joseph Mallery who seemed to write effortlessly and often appeared to enjoy the task. He exercised great care in drafting opinions: "It was an eerie feeling to know that what you write today is the precedent for the law of tomorrow." The judge aimed for brief opinions that would settle the issue but not discuss more factors than absolutely necessary. He admitted on occasion he would write a lengthy opinion in order to convince a recalcitrant colleague to stay with or join the majority.

Justice Hunter was particularly proud of his efforts as chief justice to gain approval for establishing the court of appeals. Within a few months of the governor's signature on the bill authorizing the new court, he and his colleagues had written rules, provided support personnel, and obtained facilities for the new judges. A news release from the chief justice in 1970 described the efforts: "It was the highlight of my judicial career that, as Chief Justice, I had the privilege of inducting into office the twelve new members of this first Court of Appeals of our state."

He was also proud to be a part of the reform effort establishing the bench-bar-press guidelines mutually agreed upon by the legal profession, newspaper editors, and judges developing rules to prevent a confrontation between the right to a fair trial and freedom of the press.

Justice Hunter, an unassuming person, often appeared out of place in the sometimes "stuffy" social circles of Olympia. After nineteen years in Olympia, he and his wife Maureen returned to their quiet home in Ephrata, a small city just over the mountains from Seattle. Fishing, hunting, gardening, and socializing with neighbors and friends from Grand Coulee days appealed more to the Hunters than the bustle of Olympia.

Justice Hunter is a member of Lions International, Washington State Grange, Elks, Eagles, and Moose, and is past grand master of Odd Fellows. He is also a member of Alpha Sigma Phi college fraternity and Phi Alpha Delta law fraternity.

Bob and Maureen Neary married on Christmas Day, 1938. They are the parents of three daughters and one son.

Selected References

See Hunter's oral history interview in the supreme court collection, Washington State Archives, and the Hunter scrapbook, same collection. Also see Hunter, "The Practice of Law in the Early Days of Grand Coulee, 1935-1946," *Pacific Northwest Forum* (Fall 1988), pp. 3-17; Hunter, "The Practice of Judging with the Superior and Supreme Courts of Washington," *Pacific Northwest Forum* (Winter 1989), pp. 2-23; *Moses Lake Herald,* 11 Nov. 1988; *Seattle Times,* 22 Dec. 1968; *Wenatchee Daily World,* 10 Oct. 1957; and *The Star* (Grand Coulee), 6 Feb. 1969.

Clyde Garfield Jeffers
January 9, 1939-September 6, 1949

Born: July 2, 1881
Hampton, Iowa
University of Iowa, LL.B. (1905)
Presbyterian
Died: February 15, 1956
Prosecuting Attorney (1913-1917; 1920-1921)
Assistant Attorney General (1922-1923)
Superior Court (1923-1939)
Republican
Elected

Clyde Garfield Jeffers was born on a farm near Hampton, a small community in north-central Iowa. His mother died when Clyde was twelve years old and he lived with his grandmother while finishing Hampton High School. His brother, Lyle, attended the University of Iowa and paid Clyde's tuition to study law there. Clyde maintained high scholastic standards, belonged to Sigma Alpha Epsilon fraternity, and was an outstanding two-miler for the university track team. In 1905 he graduated with an LL.B., gaining admittance to the Iowa bar the same year.

Jeffers practiced law for a short time in Iowa. Failing health prompted his move to Santa Monica, California, in 1907 and then to Arizona, where he remained until 1908. That year he moved to Spokane to practice with Judge Warren W. Tolman. In 1910 Jeffers moved to Wilson Creek, Washington, and shared an office with attorney C. J. Lambert until being elected prosecuting attorney for Grant County. He served two terms, 1913-1917, then resumed private practice in Ephrata. He was again elected prosecuting attorney in 1920, a post he held for a year before resigning to serve as assistant attorney general at the state capital. Governor Louis F. Hart appointed him to the superior court of Grant-Douglas counties in 1923 and he won election the next year and reelection four subsequent terms until he moved to the supreme court in 1939.

Both as an attorney and visiting superior court judge, Jeffers practiced or presided over trials throughout the state. He also served as president of the Superior Court Judges' Association. Although he came from a sparsely populated area, his statewide reputation permitted him to survive a close contest for the supreme court involving five candidates in the 1938 primary. He received the endorsement of retiring Judge O. R. Holcomb as well as substantial support from the legal profession. In the November balloting he defeated Ernest M. Card by nearly 60,000 votes. In 1944 he ran unopposed for another term on the high bench.

Judge Jeffers was a careful and detailed student of the law. His lengthy opinions went beyond simple explanation of the law in a particular case to record the evolution of that law. In cases involving constitutional questions he would often describe the dilemma confronting the court. For example, in *Livingston v. Ayer* he reported on the difficulties of exercising judicial review:

> In approaching this question, we are mindful of the rule as to the presumption of constitutionality of legislative acts, and we are also mindful that it is not within the province of a court to question the wisdom of a legislative act. But we also have in mind the fact that when it becomes the duty of this court to pass upon the constitutionality of an act of the legislature, we must determine whether or not such act does in fact violate some provision of the constitution;...if the court performs its full duty, it will not shut its eyes to obvious facts which would compel a conclusion that the act is unconstitutional...[rather than declare] the act...constitutional upon the mere presumption of constitutionality, or upon the rule that we cannot question the wisdom of the legislature in passing the act, or upon some declared policy or purpose contained in the act, which policy or purpose cannot be substantiated.

Judge Jeffers tended to determine that challenged laws normally did not violate some provision of the constitution. He was indeed a judicial restraintist. In his view a judge should not question legislative motives. Neither should he allow public policy considerations to color his decisions. Law clerks and experienced appellate attorneys viewed Jeffers as leaning decisively to the right in those cases lending themselves to either a liberal or conservative judicial response.

Judge Jeffers's fragile health always threatened to limit his judicial activities, but he served ten years on the state's high court. After suffering several heart attacks, he announced his retirement in July 1949.

Jeffers served as president of the Ephrata Chamber of Commerce, grand master of his Masonic Lodge, and belonged to the Elks. A deeply religious person, Judge Jeffers also served as an elder of the Presbyterian Church in Ephrata. In 1908 he married his childhood sweetheart, Ruth Nye of Spokane, who passed away in 1930. They had three daughters, Elizabeth, Jean, and Josephine, and two sons, Richard and Donald. The judge married Garnette Robinson of Chehalis in 1935. They remained in Olympia after his retirement in 1949. Jeffers died in 1956.

Selected References

Memorial services, *Washington Reports,* vol. 50, 2d (1957), pp. xxx-xxxv; *Seattle Times,* 7 Aug. 1949; Lloyd Spencer and Lancaster Pollard, *A History of the State of Washington,* vol. 3 (1937), p. 47; C. W. Taylor, *Eminent Judges and Lawyers of the Northwest* (1954), p. 382.

Charles William Johnson
January 14, 1991-

Born: March 16, 1951
Tacoma, Washington
University of Washington, B.A. (1973)
University of Puget Sound, J.D. (1976)
Elected
Democrat

Charles W. Johnson's arrival at the Temple of Justice was indeed a product of unusual circumstances, not altogether unanticipated or unplanned by him. Near the end of the filing period for the September 1990 primary elections, Johnson entered the race for the seat held by Chief Justice Keith M. Callow. Johnson paid his $893 filing fee with hope, which he alone held, of victory. Incumbents are rarely challenged, attorneys from sole practice who serve the needs of ordinary clients almost never file for the supreme court, and chief justices almost never lose reelection bids. The last time a chief justice lost came in 1896 when James Reavis replaced Chief Justice John P. Hoyt on the state's high bench.

Although filing for the office appeared to many to be a spur-of-the-moment decision, Johnson had contemplated the move for more than a year. Convinced that standard campaigns, employing lawn signs, mailings, and newspaper ads, were too expensive and ineffective, he also guessed correctly that the public generally ignores newspaper endorsements. The voters, unfamiliar with judicial candidates, would vote for the one whose name appeared most familiar. Johnson also believed Callow did not have a solid backing from lawyers, even though the Seattle-King County Bar Association gave him its highest rating.

With more than twenty years of judicial experience, Callow was completing a two-year term as chief justice. He had been and was still active in a number of court reform projects at the state and national levels. Many observers assumed Callow would win with little expenditure of money, time, or effort. However, Johnson defeated Callow by 50,000 votes in the primary. An obscure, thirty-nine year old attorney had become the eightieth justice of the state's high bench. As Johnson remarked later on his victory: "The timing was impeccable...and my opponent did exactly what he had to do for me to win — exactly nothing."

Callow, confident of victory, did not mount a campaign. Johnson never intended to campaign to any great extent. He declined to participate in the Seattle-King County candidate screening process, spent little money, and continued his business without interruption.

The news media concentrated on the more "exciting" race of incumbent Justice Richard Guy against former Governor John Spellman, and neglected to draw out either Johnson or Callow in interviews or pre-election reports. The leading newspapers endorsed Callow and believed his victory a foregone conclusion.

Almost no voter attention focused on the race. At least twenty-five percent of the voters neglected to cast their ballots for the office. Those who did apparently relied on name recognition. Some voters might have thought the candidate was Charles V. Johnson, a respected superior court judge in King County. Another Charles Johnson co-anchored the popular KSTW "Ten O'Clock News," the only west-side television news program available throughout the state. Finally, it became apparent that Callow's support was not as strong as many had assumed. All of these factors seemed to lead to Charles Johnson's victory.

Johnson gave more credit to his image than to the above factors. He felt his "down-to-earth" qualities attracted voters:

> I'm 39 years old and in private, sole practice and I'm coming from some place that Supreme justices traditionally don't come from... I'm in court representing clients; I'm an "in the trenches" kind of guy... People are sick of judges, attorneys and the justice system. It's clogged. It's slow and it's expensive... I've said more than once that lawyers are right up there with root canal. I'd be foolish to think that voter backlash wasn't part of my election.

Although most people knew little about Johnson, one close friend predicted the justice would serve honorably:

> What we can expect to find is a young man who will serve the Supreme Court with distinction. He has represented a lot of little people on all sorts of cases... He is a very people-oriented person. Over time he is really going to be an impact-type of individual. This state will be well served.

Even those confounded by Johnson's victory admitted that there was no evidence to suggest Charles Johnson would not valuably aid the state's high court.

Johnson was born in Tacoma on March 16, 1951. His father, a Tacoma attorney, was in sole practice from 1915 until his death in 1978. His work, like his son's, involved small legal matters for neighbors and friends, and brought in enough fees to keep the family somewhat secure but not without some financial worries. Charles Johnson's parents loved to garden; he recalled that their two-acre lot outside of Tacoma looked like a formal garden. His father took charge of the flowers, becoming an expert on rhododendrons, having propagated several special varieties. His mother cared for the vegetable garden. The family always had fresh or canned vegetables on the dinner table.

With his father as a model, Charles wrote essays on becoming a lawyer as early as grade school. After graduation from Curtis High, Johnson attended the University of Washington. He initially majored in pre-med, but after a frustrating experience with advanced math, switched to economics, graduating in 1973. During law school at the University of Puget Sound, Johnson successfully balanced work on the swing shift at a lumber mill with the demands of legal studies. He gained his J.D. degree in 1976, a member of Puget Sound's third law class.

Accurate predictions about newly selected justices are, of course, difficult. Johnson appeared to have given little thought to his task should he don the robes of judicial office. What few clues exist suggest that Johnson will be less restraintist and conservative than the justice he replaced. He has hesitantly indicated that the death penalty may be acceptable in some cases, is pro-choice concerning abortion, and worries about the environment. He favors close public scrutiny of the Commission on Judicial Conduct. He hopes the high court will pay more attention to solving the problem of clogged trial courts and encourage greater coordination among county courts. He views the "new federalism" emphasis of the high bench favorably.

Johnson's judicial style likely will be informal and open. He welcomes opportunities to share ideas with his colleagues and worries about the court's atomistic tendencies: instead of nine separate individual jurists, he would like to see all the justices working together as a court.

Johnson's first written opinion was a lone dissent in 1991 in *Hadley v. Department of Labor and Industries,* in which he took the majority to task for granting the department a "windfall recovery at the expense of an injured worker." Johnson's first majority opinion came in 1991's *State v. McCormack.* All the justices agreed with his analysis and ruling in the case which involved important issues of federalism and Indian treaty rights.

Justice Johnson has assumed a fairly independent role on the high bench. Perhaps he feels compelled to show the public that indeed he represents a segment of the state heretofore absent from the court, the "shirt-sleeves" lawyer. Or maybe he is working to show his colleagues that his election was not a mistake and he is up to the demands of the office. For example, in his 1991 dissent in *State v. Allert* he wrote, "The majority's reasoning in analyzing this issue is flawed. . . . [I]t ignores this court's unanimous holding in *State v. Bernhard.* In addition, the majority cites two Minnesota cases. . . Neither of these cases supports this proposition." For whatever reason, in the eighteen opinions he had signed through September 6, 1991, he dissented four times, concurred separately twice, and joined the majority in the remaining twelve.

Johnson is an avid sportsman, being both fan and participant. At six feet, four inches tall, he is still a formidable opponent on the basketball court and an enthusiastic downhill skier. Johnson's wife, Dana, is a medical receptionist for a Tacoma general practitioner. They have no children.

Selected References

Johnson's oral history interview is in the supreme court collection, Washington State Archives. Also see *Mason County Journal,* 25 Jy. 1991; *American Bar Association Journal* (Dec. 1990), pp. 26-27; *Puget Sound Lawyer* (Fall 1990), pp. 12-13; *New York Times,* 28 Sept. 1990; *Seattle Times,* 21 Sept. 1990 and 27 Sept. 1990; and *Peninsula Gateway,* 10 Apr. 1991.

Kenneth Mackintosh
March 30, 1918-April 15, 1928

Born: October 25, 1875
Seattle, Washington
University of Washington (1891)
Stanford College, B.A. (1895)
Columbia Law School, LL.B. (1900)
Methodist
Died: July 14, 1957
Prosecuting Attorney (1905-1909)
Superior Court (1912-1918)
President's Commission on Law Observance
    and Enforcement (1929-1931)
Republican
Appointed

Kenneth Mackintosh was the first member of the Washington Supreme Court born in the state. His parents were western Washington pioneers. His mother, Elizabeth Peebles, came from New York in 1865 to teach school in the little settlement of Claquato, Lewis County. She was the first woman to hold an official position in the territorial legislature and was a delegate to several Republican territorial conventions. Judge Mackintosh's father came early to Seattle and developed interests in lumber, saw mills, real estate, and mining. The judge learned politics from his mother and business acumen from his father.

Mackintosh attended common schools in Seattle and, at the age of sixteen, enrolled at the University of Washington. After a year there he transferred to the newly opened Stanford College, where he graduated with a B.A. in 1895. While at Stanford, Mackintosh became a close friend of classmate Herbert Hoover. Because of the "financial panic" of the early 1890s, Mackintosh had to seek employment before completing his education. He started as a hard rock miner, sorting ore from large dumps of excavated rock. Within two years he became superintendent of the Triumph Mine in Mariposa County, California. In 1897 Mackintosh quit the mine and enrolled in Columbia Law School in New York. He excelled in his studies, won a scholarship for his second year, and served a charter membership on the *Columbia Law Review* in his senior year. Upon graduation in 1900 Mackintosh stayed in New York long enough to be admitted to the bar, and then promptly returned to Seattle to join the law firm of Burke, Shepard, and McGilvra. In 1902 he left the firm and practiced alone for two years.

Mackintosh's public career began at the age of twenty-nine with his election as prosecuting attorney for King County. He served two terms, 1905-1909. His administration became known for the seriousness of its indictments – he won more than ninety percent of all cases brought to trial – and for hiring a group of bright young deputies who subsequently went on to outstanding public and professional careers. They included George F. Vanderveer, John F. Miller, John H. Perry, and the county's first woman deputy, who later became the first woman in the state to serve as justice of the peace, Reah M. Whitehead.

Mackintosh returned to private practice upon completing his second term as prosecutor in 1909. Elected to the Seattle Municipal Commission, charged with planning Seattle's growth, he later served as its president.

In 1912 Governor Marion E. Hay appointed John F. Main to fill the short term remaining in Judge Ralph Dunbar's supreme court position. This left Main's superior court position vacant, and Hay appointed Mackintosh. Mackintosh won affirmation at the ballot box the next year and reelection in 1916. While on the King County trial bench he helped introduce the presiding judge system to deal with crowded dockets more effectively. On April 15, 1918, Governor Ernest Lister, a Democrat, appointed Mackintosh, a Republican, to fill the vacancy left on the supreme court by the death of Judge George Morris. By appointing Mackintosh to the supreme court, Lister was able to select a long-time political ally to the superior court vacancy.

Mackintosh won election to the high court in 1918, running unopposed. In 1922 he led the judicial ticket with more than 138,000 votes. While on the supreme court Mackintosh helped create the judicial council and, as chief justice, organized the court to dispose of all cases before a new term began. Judge Mackintosh joined the conservative wing of the high bench, which tended to favor business, property rights, and the prosecution in criminal cases.

On April 16, 1928, ten years after his court appointment, the judge resigned to seek the Republican nomination as U. S. Senator. He easily won the party's nomination and faced incumbent C. C. Dill in November. Presidential candidate and old friend Herbert Hoover endorsed the judge, but to no avail. The incumbent Dill edged Mackintosh. Although prominently mentioned as a candidate for other partisan positions, the senate contest proved to be Mackintosh's last political race. He joined the firm of W. V. Tanner and John P. Garvin in Seattle late in 1928.

President Hoover did not forget his Stanford classmate. In May 1929 he appointed Mackintosh to the President's National Commission on Law Observance and Enforcement, known as the Wickersham Commission. The commission's prime responsibility was to recommend the proper enforcement of prohibition. Upon learning of his appointment, Judge Mackintosh indicated he would take a broad view of the tasks facing the commission:

> The main problem before the country is law enforcement, to remove conditions that allow murder and serious crime to go unpunished and to make life and property safer. Prohibition is not the main question. It is only incidental.

In January 1931, the Wickersham Commission recommended enforcing the existing law, but also suggested that if the results were not satisfactory, revision of the Eighteenth Amendment might be necessary. Mackintosh, however, believed that enforcement of the amendment as envisioned by its framers was impossible.

While the commission conducted its study, rumors circulated that Hoover was considering Mackintosh for appointment to the Ninth Circuit Court of Appeals to fill Frank Rudkin's position. Although very interested in the appointment, Mackintosh felt compelled to maintain a low profile until the commission issued its report. Despite objections from organized labor, President Hoover nominated Mackintosh to the court of appeals on January 8, 1932. In March, a subcommittee of the Senate Judiciary Committee, chaired by Senator John J. Blaine, began hearings on the nomination. A representative of the American Federation of Labor testified against the judge. Labor worried "because of opinions written by Mackintosh when a member of the Supreme Court of Washington State. . . It is feared that as a federal judge he would hold that picketing is unlawful." Other issues attracted public attention. Mackintosh had written a lawyer friend in Centralia praising him and the citizens of the area for the stand they took in the Industrial Workers of the World riots in which several "wobblies" were killed in 1919. Mackintosh claimed he merely lauded those who stood for enforcement of the law.

Some of the judge's critics also brought up the case of a twelve-year-old boy given a life sentence for murder. Mackintosh reportedly said the boy should be hanged. Mackintosh responded that he had been misunderstood: "All I intended to convey was that hanging would be the ultimate fate of the boy if he received a life sentence. I was entirely misunderstood. I never had any idea that in the immediate case the boy should be hanged."

Others testifying and sending letters to Congress raised minor concerns, but labor presented the most serious challenge. As the *Seattle Times* reported: "It appears that the only objection likely to receive serious consideration by the committee is that of labor."

The subcommittee failed to make its recommendation to the full senate before adjournment. In the November 1932 elections, Hoover and the Republicans lost, assuring the defeat of any lame duck Hoover appointments. Although the president renewed his nomination of Mackintosh before leaving office, the senate failed to act, saving appointments for the new Democratic administration.

After his failure to gain confirmation to the federal bench, Mackintosh returned to Seattle and private practice. He expanded his large real estate holdings in the city and remained active in civic affairs.

Judge Mackintosh was a Shriner, a Mason, and a member of the Elks, Eagles, and Moose lodges as well as of the Ancient Order of United Workmen and the Madrona Council of the Royal Arcanum. He founded the Native Sons of

Washington and belonged to the Rainier Club, College Club, Seattle Golf Club, and the Scandinavian Fraternity of America.

Francisca Arques, also a Stanford graduate, married Mackintosh in San Jose, California, in 1908. They had one son, Angus. The judge died in Seattle on July 14, 1957 at the age of eighty-one.

Selected References

Memorial services, *Washington Reports*, vol. 52, 2d (1958), pp. xvii-xxv; Lloyd Spencer and Lancaster Pollard, *A History of the State of Washington*, vol. 3 (1937), p. 165; H. James Boswell, *American Blue Book: Western Washington* (1922), p. 20; C. W. Taylor, *Eminent Judges and Lawyers of the Northwest* (1954), p. 177; *Seattle Times*, 31 Mar. 1918.

John Fleming Main
December 27, 1912-October 13, 1942

Born: September 10, 1864
Seaton, Illinois
Princeton, A.B. (1891)
University of Michigan Law School
  (1895-1897)
Presbyterian
Died: October 13, 1942
Law Professor (1904-1909)
Superior Court (1909-1912)
Republican
Appointed

John F. Main was the son of William R. and Sarah M. (Fleming) Main, born on a farm near Seaton in northwestern Illinois on the Iowa border. He grew up there, did preparatory schooling and some college work at Monmouth College, and transferred to Princeton in his junior year, completing his liberal arts studies in 1891. John wanted to be a lawyer, but the pursuit of his Princeton degree left him without funds to continue his education. He returned to Mercer County to teach school, advancing to principal and superintendent in four years. By 1895 he had saved enough money to leave his teaching position and enroll at the University of Michigan law department. Again, for financial reasons, he had to leave Michigan before he earned his law degree. Nonetheless, he won admittance to the Illinois bar in 1897. He practiced law in Aledo, Illinois, until 1900, when he moved to Seattle.

Main worked in a Seattle law office from 1900 to 1904 when he became a professor at the University of Washington School of Law. He resigned in 1909 to accept acting Governor Marion E. Hay's offer of an appointment to the King County Superior Court. Reelected to the bench in 1912, he resigned to accept appointment to the supreme court. The special nature of his appointment and subsequent election merit some attention.

In the September 1912 primaries Ralph Dunbar, O. G. Ellis, and Wallace Mount ran unopposed. Dunbar led all three in the vote, and all three incumbents were assured of winning. On September 29 Dunbar died, leaving two vacancies on the court—the final few weeks of his existing term and all of the new full six-year term he had won in the September balloting. In that same primary, King County voters had overwhelmingly endorsed Judge Main for another term on the superior court bench. Governor Hay appointed the popular Main to the remaining few weeks in Dunbar's short term and the judge's supporters immediately mounted a successful write-in, or "sticker," election campaign for Dunbar's full term. Main's victory, by nearly 12,000 votes over his closest contender, was the first successful statewide write-in campaign in Washington's history.

Only Mark Fullerton's thirty-one years on the high bench exceeded Judge Main's twenty-nine years. Observers of Main's long career regarded him as a slightly conservative jurist. But over the years the judge appeared to veer across the jurisprudential continuum. For example, in 1923 and 1924, Main tended to agree more often with the court's moderate members. However, he was then serving as chief justice and rarely dissented from the opinions of his brethren. He also wrote fewer than his share of the court's opinions. The explanation lies with the role he had then assigned himself. According to one account:

> As chief he was the presiding officer at departments, en banc proceedings, and conference deliberations. He determined the panel membership and assigned the court opinions in the more contentious cases. Thus, he had the prime responsibility for coordination, compromise, and communication. Apparently he viewed his role as working toward a court that was effective, cohesive, and authoritative. As such, he was compelled to seek compromise and to avoid disagreement as much as possible, and his own behavior reflected that compulsion.

Fifteen years later and shortly before he left the court, Justice Main, no longer chief, dissented from his colleagues quite frequently and wrote more than his share of the court's majority opinions. Now he joined with liberal Bruce Blake on contentious cases. However, the explanation for the apparent change was not that Main had somehow converted to the liberal cause after all the years, but, rather, a majority of the 1940s bench was now more conservative than Main, making it appear he had shifted to the left.

A few days before the September 8, 1942 primary election, Judge Main suddenly fell ill. Although he had won the primary, he announced he would decline the nomination because of his weakened condition. Judge Main passed away a few weeks later. After a court challenge, Main's seat on the court went to Joe Mallery, whose name appeared unchallenged on the November ballot.

Judge Main belonged to the Masons, Nile Temple of the Ancient Arabic Order, Nobles of the Mystic Shrine, Elks, Eagles, and Phi Delta Phi college fraternity, as well as the Tacoma Golf and Country Club, University Club, Seattle Golf Club, and Olympia Golf and Country Club. He married Mary G. Crouch of Illinois in June 1892, and they had one daughter, Margaret.

Selected References

H. James Boswell, *American Blue Book: Western Washington* (1922), p. 27; C. S. Reinhart, *History of the Supreme Court of the Territory and State of Washington* (n.d.), p. 77; Lloyd Spencer and Lancaster Pollard, *A History of the State of Washington,* vol. 3 (1937), pp. 34-5; Ewing v. Reeves, *Washington Reports,* vol. 15, 2d (1942), p. 75.

Joseph Arthur Mallery
November 9, 1942-January 15, 1962

Born: April 27, 1896
Winlock, Washington
Reed College (1916-1917)
University of Washington, LL.B. (1926)
Methodist
Died: March 2, 1982
Prosecuting Attorney (1926-1928)
Assistant U. S. Attorney (1928-1934)
Municipal Court (1934-1940)
Superior Court (1940-1942)
Republican
Appointed/Elected

Judge Mallery's father, Joseph H., a veteran of the Civil War, brought his wife Maria (Murch) Mallery and their four children west to Winlock, Washington, in Lewis County, after a grasshopper infestation destroyed crops on his homestead farm in Kansas. Joe was born on the "stump ranch" in Winlock where his father raised chickens and worked in a grocery store. Joe was three months old when they moved to Castle Rock, Washington, to be close to his father's newest venture, Mallery's Cash Store. As the son remembered, "the word 'cash' was a misstatement of fact. Few paid any attention to it except my father. He was soon back raising chickens." His father's politics proved important to the future judge: "Father was a rebel, honest and outspoken. He had a constitutional aversion to the majority. It was his idea that if too many people accepted a notion it must be wrong." His father, a populist follower of William Jennings Bryan, also admired Eugene Debs and Robert LaFollette.

Young Joe attended grammar school in Sandy Bend after his father had moved from town to a forty-acre homestead four miles south of Castle Rock. At Castle Rock High School, Mallery starred on the track team, anchored its debate squad, and played fiddle at local dances "for four bucks a night." After graduation he passed the teachers' exam and taught school, serving as principal and janitor for $630 a year at Scantygrease Grade School. He saved enough money to attend Reed College and marry high school classmate Mildred McClane, daughter of the editor of the *Cowlitz County Advocate*. They had two children, Joe, Jr. and Frances. Mildred died in 1933 and two years later Mallery married Lovella Wrigglesworth, who died in May 1962 following his retirement.

Mallery, drafted into the army, served the last six months of World War I at Port Angeles and Vancouver, gaining discharge as a buck private. For the next five years he taught school at Silver Lake and served as principal at Cathlamet.

From the beginning of Joe's adult life he aspired to public office, especially the U. S. Senate. Since "lawyers predominated in Congress and I wanted to be a U. S. Senator," he saved his teaching money, added it to a state veterans' bonus, and attended the University of Washington. He graduated with an LL.B. in 1926, fifth in his class.

Mallery opened a law office in Castle Rock and, after a few months with very little business, filed for election as Cowlitz County Prosecutor. Much to his and others' surprise, he won. He attributed his victory to the simple fact that he was "widely known and widely liked." The young lawyer gained a reputation as a vigorous and successful prosecutor of bootleggers during prohibition. Senator Wesley Jones, an avid "dry," heard of Mallery's efforts and recommended him to the U. S. Attorney. In 1928 the future judge moved to Tacoma as Assistant U. S. Attorney, largely responsible for trial work.

After an unsuccessful run as commissioner of finance for Tacoma, he became convinced that nonpartisan elections were the only route to public office during the Democrat-dominated 1930s for a former activist in the Republican Party and past president of the Pierce County Young Republicans. He successfully campaigned for the nonpartisan position of Tacoma Justice of the Peace in 1934 and gained assignment as Tacoma Police Judge four years later. In 1940 voters elected him Pierce County Superior Court Judge, and he served until his high court appointment in 1942.

Unusual circumstances surrounded Mallery's election and appointment to the supreme court. He had the audacity to challenge longtime incumbent Judge John F. Main, who had been on the bench since 1912. Main edged Mallery by only 685 votes in the primary and both advanced to the November balloting. For reasons of health, Main withdrew, unwilling or unable to face the rigors of further campaigning, leaving Mallery's name alone on the general election ballot. The third-place candidate in the primary challenged Mallery's sole placement on the November general election ticket, necessitating a supreme court interpretation. The court ruled that the law required only the candidate receiving the "next greatest" number of votes behind Main be advanced to the November ballot. In October Judge Main died, leaving three months in his unfinished six-year term. Governor Arthur Langlie appointed Mallery to the short term because he would assume responsibilities following the election anyway.

Mallery later described how he conducted that 1942 campaign, a carbon copy of his successful campaign for county prosecutor years earlier:

> We got in the car and we'd go to a town; we'd hit this town and I had the car full of leaflets: name, offices . . . bragging on myself. I'd head for the lawyer's offices and speak with them . . . and give them my cards. I had met some of them and

some I hadn't. Joe [son] and Frances [daughter] would walk up and down the business streets and pass out these cards everywhere... My wife did something, too... We made personal contacts. We didn't wait for making speeches. We just went out and hit the public personally.

In 1944 Mallery filed his candidacy for the U. S. Senate. Later admitting that he "had not learned his lesson," he lost soundly in the Republican primary.

Understanding Mallery's decision-making over the nearly twenty years he served on the supreme court bench is difficult. His legal insights were exceptional when an issue piqued his interest. One former colleague remembered that on many occasions "Joe would take off his shoes," sometimes put his feet on the table and start: "I don't have much to say about this case," and then launch into a thorough analysis of the issues and a complete review of relevant precedents, announcing an outcome upon which all would have to agree. His charming personality, colorful language, and unassuming manner stamped Mallery as a judge of the people.

However, personal conflicts on the high court came to the surface in the late 1940s in a public versus private power case. The Skagit County Public Utility District proposed to buy all the assets of the private Puget Sound Power and Light Company for $135,000,000 but needed court approval to consummate the deal. Mallery wrote an opinion endorsing the sale which, after the vote in conference, was to be the majority opinion. Judge Matthew Hill, a committed advocate of private power, wrote a strong dissent and, with a change in court personnel, a four-four split resulted. Chief Justice William Millard asked for a rehearing. When Mallery became chief in January 1947, he vacated the rehearing, letting the four-four split stand, which would have resulted in upholding the lower court's approval of the sale. However, his brethren overruled him and scheduled a rehearing.

By March 1947, all the judges but Millard had signed either Mallery's "majority" opinion or Hill's "dissent." Three months later Millard still had not affixed his signature to either. Under pressure from the state Grange and amid rumors that led to a rush on Puget Power stock, five of the justices, including Mallery, made public a memo to Millard, chastising him for failing to act. Millard immediately joined Hill's opinion and voted to void the sale. He then turned on his colleagues:

The action of Judge Mallery and his four associates in making an issue out of the manner in which the members of this court conscientiously attempted to perform their duty is without precedent in the history of the court. I do not see how anyone can arrive at any... conclusion other than that it is the opening gun in Chief Justice Mallery's campaign for reelection.

Mallery responded sharply:

Judge Millard's resentment over the explanation of delay, due to his holding up of the case, shows a reliance on secrecy that speaks for itself... The throwing of light on public affairs is in the public interest.

In the 1948 election, largely because of the publicity surrounding the Skagit PUD case, Mallery faced a challenge from a candidate with the bar's overwhelming endorsement. However, he turned back his opposition in the primary largely due to his incumbency, support from labor and the Grange, and his own campaign efforts.

In January 1962, after only one year into another six-year term, Joe Mallery announced his retirement from the bench. His wife, Lovella, seriously ill with cancer, required constant care. The state had recently increased retirement pay, and Mallery had become isolated from his bench colleagues. The Skagit PUD case still haunted him and a continuing debate with the National Association for the Advancement of Colored People had soured him on public office. Retirement seemed a welcome alternative.

The career of this self-made, outspoken, and colorful judge featured many outstanding moments and some setbacks. Not one to avoid controversy, at times he should have. Perhaps he took too seriously his own comment that "I might be wrong, but I'm never in doubt." He would have been better suited for the open and freewheeling U. S. Senate to which he aspired from the beginning of his public life.

Mallery, active in the Grange since age fourteen, was state president of the Eagles, a member of the Elks, Masons, Moose Lodge, and the American Legion. An accomplished violin player, he often joined with Judges Robert C. Finley (clarinet) and Richard B. Ott (drums) to provide entertainment for social events in and around Olympia. Travel throughout the world, and residency in Mexico and San Diego occupied Judge Mallery's retirement years. He died on March 2, 1982.

Selected References

Mallery's oral history interview is in the supreme court collection, Washington State Archives. Also see the Mallery papers, same collection; *Longview Daily News,* 30 Aug. 1960; *Seattle Post-Intelligencer,* 6 Mar. 1982; "Just Call Me Joe," *The Eagle Magazine* (Sept. 1945), pp. 12-14; C. W. Taylor, *Eminent Judges and Lawyers of the Northwest* (1954), p. 52; and memorial services, *Washington Reports,* vol. 97, 2d (1982), pp. xliv-xlvii.

Walter T. McGovern
January 8, 1968-May 13, 1971

Born: May 24, 1922
Seattle, Washington
University of Santa Clara (1941)
Gonzaga University (1942)
University of Washington, B.A. (1948);
  LL.B. (1950)
Catholic
Municipal Court (1959-1964)
Superior Court (1965-1967)
Federal District Court (1971-1987)
Republican
Appointed

In December 1963, Walter T. McGovern confronted a decision that would set the course for the remainder of his professional life. Several prominent Republicans and Seattle civic leaders had urged the young judge to resign from the municipal bench and run for mayor of Seattle. The suggestion obviously tempted McGovern:

> I've thought about running for mayor considerably, but I compare it with being away from home and the family and I just cannot do it. My family comes first. As mayor you're required to represent everybody in the city. You have got to be at the job all the time. Also I would have to leave the legal profession. I enjoy the judiciary. I'm not ready to leave it . . . I expect to run for higher judicial office.

At age forty-one, he decided to pursue a judicial career. It proved a fortunate choice.

McGovern was born in Seattle on May 24, 1922, the youngest son of Arthur and Ann Marie (Thies) McGovern. His father and uncle were partners in a salmon brokerage firm. The family moved to San Francisco when Walter was young and he became attached to another uncle, a successful attorney active in California politics after whom he was named and after whom he and one of his brothers modeled their careers. Walter's parents urged their sons to follow in the uncle's footsteps. The family returned to Seattle where Walter attended Seattle Prep, a private Catholic high school, graduating in 1940.

During World War II, McGovern, a University of Santa Clara student, enlisted in the officers' training program for the navy and received his instruction at Gonzaga University in Spokane. While at Gonzaga he captained the varsity basketball team and was student body president. After receiving his commission he served in the Pacific theater from 1944 to 1946, achieving the rank of lieutenant junior grade and serving on a landing ship tank. The judge remained in the navy reserve and retired as captain. After the war, McGovern returned to Seattle and to the University of Washington, earning a B.A. degree in English and his law degree from the university's law school in 1950.

At his first law job, with Kerr, McCord, Greenleaf, and Moen in Seattle, he became proficient at handling corporate and civil matters for the firm's banking and insurance clients. The young attorney, active in political and professional affairs, served as Republican precinct committeeman, and president of the Young Republicans of King County and the Evergreen Republican Club. He attended nearly all Seattle-King County bar meetings and all state bar conventions, being named to numerous committees. In August 1956, when only thirty-four, Mayor Gordon Clinton appointed him *pro tem* judge of the Seattle traffic court. Two years later, after he had combined court sessions with an active private practice, members of the bar asked McGovern to seek a full-time position on the Seattle bench. At first he was reluctant to give up private practice:

> Three members of the local bar association came and asked me if I would run for municipal court judgeship...and I said "no," I was not interested. They came about two weeks later and again asked me to file against the incumbent and I said "no." Another two weeks passed and they came and asked me and I said I would think it over and let them know on Monday. That weekend I told my wife what I was going to do and she was somewhat distraught. She knew how I enjoyed private practice. But when I told her of my decision she said, "let's go."

A committee of forty-four prominent attorneys, who regarded the incumbent as unsuitable, lent their support to McGovern's effort to unseat the veteran. Endorsed by the Seattle-King County Bar Association by a vote of 604 to 424, he easily defeated the incumbent and a third candidate. Having garnered more than fifty percent of the vote in the primary, he and his supporters celebrated apparent victory. However, the state legislature, in authorizing municipal judgeships, had neglected to exempt from the general election primary winners who attracted more than half the votes. McGovern had to establish his campaign organization for another race in the general election, where he again defeated the incumbent by a substantial margin. It was the first time in a Seattle judicial election that a challenger had unseated an incumbent. McGovern easily won reelection to the municipal post in 1963. He served his tenure on the city bench in the criminal division.

While a municipal judge, many people touted McGovern as a mayoral aspirant. But in December 1963, he decided to stay in the judiciary. In July 1964, he announced his candidacy for the superior court and again challenged a veteran incumbent. With the backing of the bar association and the endorsement of a number of labor organizations, he overwhelmed his opponent in the

September primary election and this time claimed victory without needing a run-off election.

In January 1967, Supreme Court Judge Charles Donworth reached the mandatory retirement age of seventy-five and would have to step down at the end of the year. Republican Governor Dan Evans, who a few months earlier had named Marshall Neill to the court, now had another opportunity to appoint a justice to the state's court of last resort. He called Judge McGovern on the afternoon of December 4, 1967, to offer him the job, and McGovern readily accepted. McGovern had worked with the governor when Evans represented the Forty-third District in the state house of representatives. McGovern had strong Republican credentials, a proven judicial record, and the state bar association's approval. No one opposed his appointment.

McGovern found judging at the appellate level significantly different from his municipal and superior court experiences. The municipal bench was "a court of human emotion." Problems "between husbands and wives and among neighbors" dominated the docket. On the lower courts a judge had to be more "mediator than a penalizer." On the superior court the

> continuing responsibility of the judge is. . . to assure all of the parties that their rights are safeguarded. [The judge] does this by strictly following the law. In the trial court he is not making law, but rather deciding the facts in a case in which he has heard the evidence and applying the law to those factual findings. In a jury trial, he advises the jury of the law which is applicable to the case at hand.

But the supreme court was different:

> [It] basically is a court of review, that deals entirely on points of law. We aren't concerned with establishing facts. . . A good supreme court judge thinks continuously, works hard, acts independently and impartially, and is dedicated to cutting through the extraneous matters, and getting to the heart of the legal issue. It's an arduous but rewarding task.

On the high bench, "everything has to be down in black and white," while at the trial level you "think out loud as you speak."

During McGovern's three-and-a-half years on the state's high bench he became known as a moderate, middle-of-the-road judge. One of his law clerks remembered with pleasure his short tenure with McGovern:

> The most important reason I enjoyed my clerkship was the "teaching" and gracious personality of Justice McGovern. In addition to being very personable, McGovern shared opinion writing duties with me, sought my counsel on decisions which he authored individually and allowed a great deal of flexibility in terms of work hours and tasks. . . Even though it was sometimes difficult to recognize my contribution to the opinion, it is my belief that the Justice gave careful consideration to whatever view point I might have expressed.

Justice McGovern's decisional style might best be described as "individual." He relied most heavily upon his own knowledge of the law and upon clues provided by precedent. However, his "feeling for what is right" was blended into the decisional equation. These individual factors were more important as sources for decision than what McGovern learned from his discussions with the other justices, what the lawyers noted in their oral presentations and briefs, and what research his law clerks conducted.

The justice penned sixty-nine opinions for the court during his short tenure and filed seven dissents. Not committed to an excessive use of the dissent, he chose instead to discuss disagreement informally with his colleagues and include their concerns when drafting opinions. His former clerks stated that he would usually dissent when he felt strongly on an issue and had a chance to persuade some of his brethren to join him. His view of the role of dissent was "to win over the majority or to win more votes," and to "lay the groundwork for the future" whereby in several years the court might accept his version. McGovern enjoyed drafting opinions but frowned upon a "law review" style of writing. An opinion should confront only those issues absolutely necessary to decide the case.

In 1971 President Richard Nixon sought Governor Daniel Evans's counsel to fill the federal district court vacancy of retiring judge William Lindberg. Evans, along with Washington's Republican Attorney General Slade Gorton, recommended Justice McGovern. John D. Ehrlichman, then an assistant to the president, also urged the president to nominate McGovern. The American Bar Association's standing committee of the federal judiciary gave its tentative approval. On March 26 President Nixon sent McGovern's name to the senate for confirmation. The Senate Judiciary Committee voted unanimously in favor of the appointment, and on April 21 the full senate—with Washington's two Democratic senators fully approving—confirmed McGovern. On May 14, 1971, he became a federal district judge for the western district of Washington.

Judge McGovern was back on the trial bench which, admittedly, he enjoyed more than the cloistered and contemplative supreme court. Almost immediately his court became embroiled in important and controversial disputes. In July he presided over an important sex discrimination case. Within a few months he decided issues involving redistricting, conscientious objectors, oil spills, and price fixing. Conflicts over Indian fishing rights, super tankers in Puget Sound, water pollution disputes, Indian rights to sell fireworks and liquor on reservations, and war protestors at the Trident submarine base near Bremerton filled his court's calendar. In 1979 McGovern assumed the post of chief judge for the district, and in 1987 took senior status. He still heard cases, but could adjust his case load.

McGovern married Rita Marie Olson, whom he had known since seventh grade, in June 1946, and had three children: Trina, Shawn, and Renee. His hobbies, which he shares with his family, are gardening and tennis. He has served as director of several investment companies, and devoted time to charitable work with the Medina Children's Service, Traveler's Aid Society, Seattle Committee on Alcoholism, and the Women's Studio Club rehabilitation center. He is a member of the Knights of Columbus and the Seattle Tennis Club.

Selected References

McGovern's oral history interview is in the supreme court collection, Washington State Archives. Also see *Seattle-King County Bar Bulletin* (Dec. 1987), p. 4, and (Je. 1988), p. 5; *Spokane Spokesman-Review,* 10 Sept. 1985; and *Seattle Post-Intelligencer,* 15 Nov. 1987.

William James Millard
December 1, 1928-January 9, 1949;
December 6, 1956-January 12, 1957

Born: January 30, 1883
Bismark, Missouri
Georgetown University Law School, LL.B.
  (1910)
Episcopalian
Died: December 12, 1970
Law Librarian (1917-1928)
Republican
Appointed/Elected

William Millard's father, Benjamin, emigrated from England and worked his entire adult life for railroads in America. His mother, Mary (Toler) Millard, was a native of Missouri. William attended public schools in Missouri and Texas, graduating from Houston High School. After high school he worked at various times as an engine wiper, timekeeper, postal clerk, machinist apprentice, and yardmaster's clerk for the Southern Pacific Railroad, belonging to the Brotherhood of Locomotive Engineers. His interest in the law started when he worked as a stenographer-secretary in the railroad's right-of-way legal department. In later life Millard pointed with pride to his working class and union background.

After passing a civil service exam, Millard went to Washington, D. C., to serve as a clerk in the U. S. War Department. He enrolled in Georgetown Law School's evening program, graduating in 1910 with a bachelor of laws degree. During school he served as a reporter for the U. S. House of Representatives, worked for a company that prepared the *Indiana Law Reports,* and clerked for the Multigraph Company. After admission to the Washington, D. C., bar in 1910, he practiced law there until 1914 when he moved to Seattle to establish himself as an attorney. In 1917 Millard became the supreme court law librarian, moving from Seattle to Olympia. On November 23, 1928, Governor Roland Hartley announced Millard's appointment to the soon-to-be-vacated position held by Judge William Askren.

As a justice of the state supreme court Millard established himself as a liberal activist, often opposing the court's conservative majority. He expressed his view of the role of a supreme court judge in his election campaign of 1936:

I don't consider cases as much as a judge as like a human being. The law should be used to further progress, not to block it. As long as I'm on the bench I'll continue to give my decisions along the lines that I think will be for the betterment and the greater happiness of the people of Washington.

Judge Millard gained national prominence with his opinion in *Westcoast Hotel v. Parrish,* which the U. S. Supreme Court upheld in 1937. It became known as the case that brought the "switch in time that saved nine," since the U. S. Supreme Court had been under serious attack for its anti-New Deal stance. In the *Parrish* case the nation's high court upheld Millard and the Washington minimum wage law for women. The publicity surrounding the case led to speculation that Millard might be in line for appointment to the federal circuit court of appeals, but the appointment never materialized.

Although a Republican, Millard seriously considered filing as a Democrat in the race against U. S. Senator Homer T. Bone in 1938. But he apparently thought better of leaving the relative security of the state's high bench for a tough and risky political campaign. He did accept a temporary presidential appointment to the National Railroad Adjustment Board in November, 1939.

During World War II, Millard made a contribution to the domestic war effort and, in the process, gained considerable publicity assisting him in his reelection victories. During the summer court recess of 1943 he worked as a carpenter's helper for the Puget Sound Shipbuilding Company and remained on the swing shift a few months after the court's new term began in September. Later, in 1945, the judge worked the night shift as a railroad freight yard clerk, and during harvest season labored in filbert orchards.

The relationship between Millard and his brethren became strained during the 1940s. In dissent the judge occasionally needled his colleagues for what he believed to be their misguided viewpoints. The conflict came to a head in the summer of 1947. Five members of the high bench publicly criticized Millard for delaying a decision asking approval of a multi-million dollar sale of the Puget Sound Power and Light Company to the Skagit County Public Utility District. The delay allowed further speculative buying of Puget Power stock on the New York market and brought the actions of the court into question. In a letter to the state Grange leadership, Chief Justice Joseph Mallery and four other justices warned Millard in the following blunt terms:

> The standing of this court will be affected if it should be established that stock-market manipulation can be directly attributable to the manner in which this court functions or fails to function. . .
>
> You owe it to this court to do your duty and function on this case immediately.

Millard cast his vote against the sale, turning on his colleagues. He correctly reminded his brethren that to divulge the record of a conference vote and the breakdown of majority and minority opinions before official announcement of a decision breached judicial ethics. Millard accused Chief Justice Mallery of raising the issue in order to gain reelection in the 1948 balloting when both he and Mallery would face the electorate.

The serious rift on the high court, coupled with rumors of attempted bribes, prompted the Thurston County Prosecutor's Office to investigate the incidents surrounding the PUD decision. The *Seattle Post-Intelligencer* conducted its own investigation, followed by state attorney general's office and Washington State Bar Association inquiries. By February 1948 Attorney General Smith Troy reported his findings.

> In summation it is our finding that Judge Millard did issue at least one check under conditions which, if the check were issued with fraudulent intent, would constitute a crime; that he borrowed money from pinball operators and a club official during the pendency of a decision in which they had a pecuniary interest; but without any evidence of offering or giving any judicial consideration as a condition of the loans; and without evidence that he permitted himself to be improperly influenced in arriving at a judicial opinion in the Skagit County P.U.D. litigation.
>
> The elimination of criminal action and intent from consideration does not, however, relieve Judge Millard from all public accountability for his actions nor does it foreclose all the public processes which may be brought to bear on this situation.
>
> [The] high honors and privileges [of judicial office] carry with them the compensating elements of high moral character, rigid self-discipline, and absolute integrity in private as well as public life. It is not sufficient within the code of judicial ethics for a judge to avoid evil; he must avoid even the appearance of evil.

The legislature failed to consider seriously any impeachment proceedings and the Washington State Bar Association, after studying Troy's report, concluded that "the final disposition of such matters must rest, with the electorate, acting either at the polls or through the legislature." It was at the polls that people made their judgment. With the Seattle Bar Association leading the attack, followed by most of the other county bars and the state Grange, Tom Grady defeated Millard by a substantial majority in the November balloting.

Millard continued to practice law in Olympia after his 1948 defeat, but people heard little from or about him for some time. In 1954 he gained admittance to the federal bar in Seattle. In July 1956, both Millard and his attorney son filed for positions on the supreme court, the son for a full six-year term and the father for a short thirty-eight day unexpired term. The obvious motivation for the elder Millard was to enhance his state pension from the then $291.55 rate to the new rate of $500 per month. The judge did not campaign for the position except to send a personal letter to old acquaintances. The letter read in part:

> I filed for the Supreme Court short term. . . to secure my pension and to enable me to pay my debts. . .
>
> I have not the funds with which to finance an extensive campaign, therefore I am writing to you and to other friends requesting that they pass the word in my behalf to their friends and acquaintances, especially to those who subscribe to the same principles which you and the undersigned are committed.

Millard succeeded, although his son did not. Because the court was in recess, he heard no cases, attended no conferences, and wrote no opinions, but he became only the fourth judge to return to the supreme court bench for a second interrupted term.

Encouraged by his temporary return to the political limelight and now in partial control of his financial situation, Judge Millard spoke out on public issues and twice attempted to return to politics. Upon completing his short term on the bench, he sent a fifty-three page report to governor-elect Albert Rosellini in which he argued against the establishment of an appellate court and the practice of paying legislators for living expenses. He also recommended that capital punishment be mandatory for certain crimes.

In February 1958, Millard announced his candidacy on the Democratic ticket for Congress. He explained the switch from his old Republican loyalties to the Democratic party in characteristic manner: "It is the only party that does anything for the poor man, and God knows I'm poor." However, his campaign failed to gain backing and he withdrew from the race in July. Millard continued to actively participate in public affairs, however. In October 1958 he became vice-chairman of the Western and Eastern Washington Committee of Business and Industry Against Initiative 202, a right to work measure designed to eliminate closed shop arrangements. Two years later Millard won nomination as a candidate for lieutenant governor on the Republican ticket. If elected, he said he would seek legislation to abolish the office as being unnecessary. He lost to incumbent John Cherberg. After this defeat, Judge Millard remained in retirement in Olympia, and died on December 12, 1970.

Millard married Gertrude E. Neuhauser in Annapolis in 1908 and they had four children: Gertrude, William, Jr., Alice, and Jean. They divorced and then remarried in 1924. In 1946 the couple again divorced. The alimony and child-support costs, along with the judge's penchant for gambling, caused many of Millard's financial problems. The judge had been active in fraternal affairs, being a member of the Masonic Order, Shrine, Odd Fellows, and Phi Delta Phi legal fraternity. He received honorary degrees from Georgetown University and the College of Puget Sound, where he served on the board of trustees. Millard was one of the leaders of the Washington State Bar Association, serving as secretary-treasurer for nearly ten years in the 1920s.

Selected References

Wenatchee Daily World, 28 Aug. 1947; *Washington State Bar News* (Aug. 1947), pp. 20, 23, and (Oct. 1947), pp. 29, 31; Lloyd Spencer and Lancaster Pollard, *A History of the State of Washington,* vol. 3 (1937), p. 1; memorial services, *Washington Reports,* vol. 79, 2d (1971), pp. xxvii-xxxv; C. S. Reinhart, *A History of the Supreme Court of the Territory and State of Washington* (n.d.), p. 120; and Charles Sheldon, *A Century of Judging: A Political History of the Washington Supreme Court* (1988), pp. 117-123.

John Richard Mitchell
May 11, 1918-January 11, 1937

Born: January 31, 1861
Republican Grove, Virginia
University of Virginia
Baptist
Died: March 24, 1939
Prosecuting Attorney (1897-1899)
Superior Court (1908-1918)
Democrat
Appointed

John R. Mitchell was born in rural Virginia. His father, John A. Mitchell, fought for the Confederacy during the Civil War. His mother, Mary F. Pringle, was a native Virginian. After attending public schools, Mitchell studied law with an attorney and then attended the University of Virginia for several terms. In 1888 he moved to Washington and passed the bar the next year. Between 1889 and 1893 Mitchell practiced law in partnership with Milo Root of Olympia.

Mitchell served as Thurston County Prosecuting Attorney between 1897 and 1899. Shortly after leaving the prosecutor's office he formed a law partnership with Thomas M. Vance which lasted until 1908 when Mitchell won election as superior court judge for Thurston County. He was reelected to the state trial bench for two additional terms without opposition.

In May 1918, Democratic Governor Ernest Lister appointed the Democrat Mitchell to fill a vacancy on the supreme court. Mitchell had been a serious contender for virtually all of the court vacancies during Lister's term of office, but the governor thought the Thurston County bench needed the judge. In that position Mitchell heard all the important state cases coming from Olympia. But by 1918 the governor, having found an acceptable successor for the superior court, elevated Mitchell to the state's high bench. Mitchell led all judicial candidates in the September and November 1918 balloting, a practice he repeated in 1924 and 1930.

In an address to members of the state Prosecuting Attorneys' Association in 1921, Judge Mitchell provided a glimpse at the supreme court's decisional process:

In the orderly dispatch of our business each of us, in a department or *en banc* as the case may be, examines all the briefs at hand in all the cases to be argued on any day, not later than the night before the cases are to be heard... After our discussions in the consultation room the Chief Justice makes assignments of the cases for further study and the writing of opinions. In the very nature of things it is manifest that when we first commence to read the briefs, we at that time, commence to form some opinion of the case. Now, remembering that judges are human and therefore find it is harder to unlearn than to learn, you can readily see the importance, for the sake of your cause and for our protection, of having your briefs in our hands at the very commencement of our reading the briefs...

[We] are often asked if oral arguments are useful. The matter is not even debatable – the emphatic answer is affirmative. Personally I make this confession; I have never listened to a lawyer's argument on the facts or law of his case without learning something helpful to a proper solution of the problems involved. I know other judges desire oral arguments. The wisdom of the course is suggested by the long established rules which provide for it... [O]ral discussion – [gives] the human touch and invest[s] the whole controversy with your faith in your contention, pressing home what you consider the most dominant features as to the facts and law of the case. In oral argument you are the teachers, we the pupils. You are advising us of something that you have thoroughly and recently studied, and we are engaged in learning of it from you.

Judge Mitchell tended to assume a moderate-to-conservative position on the court, often aligning with judges Jessie Bridges and John Main. He rarely dissented.

Because of ill health, Mitchell retired in 1937 and died two years later. He married Hallie Price of Clarksville, Tennessee, in 1891 and they were parents of one son, Richard Sharp, who became a prominent physician and surgeon. Mitchell helped form the Olympia Young Men's Christian Association, serving as its first secretary-treasurer. He was a member of the Baptist Church, Masons, Knights of Pythias, and Woodmen of the World.

Selected References

Washington State Bar Association *Proceedings* (1921), pp. 172-176; H. James Boswell, *American Blue Book: Western Washington* (1922), p. 34; C. S. Reinhart, *A History of the Supreme Court of the Territory and State of Washington* (n.d.), p. 122.

George Edward Morris
February 26, 1909-March 6, 1918

Born: July 17, 1862
Utica, New York
Genesee Wesleyan, B.A. (1880)
Albany Law School, LL.B. (1885)
Methodist
Died: March 6, 1918
Assistant City Attorney (1891-1892)
Superior Court (1902-1909)
Republican
Appointed

George E. Morris was the son of Reverend Edward E. Morris, a Methodist minister, and Eliza (McClements) Morris. Except for a few years in public schools, most of George's education came in church-affiliated institutions. After common school in Utica he attended Cazenovia Seminary and then went to Pennsylvania to work as a farm hand and clerk in a general store to earn tuition for Susquehanna Collegiate Institute at Towanda, Pennsylvania. In 1879 Morris entered Genesee Wesleyan Seminary, graduating in 1880. Morris became superintendent of his father's Sunday school and taught school in Elmira, New York, while studying law. In 1884 he entered Union University (Albany Law School), graduating with an LL.B. in 1885.

He practiced law in Interlaken, New York, between 1885 and 1887. The lure of the West took him to Kearney, Nebraska, for two years before an old classmate, Joe Lyon, invited Morris to Seattle to help him with his duties as Seattle City Attorney. Morris arrived in 1890 and won appointment as assistant city attorney in 1891, serving for over a year. He then went into private practice, first with Judge Richard Winsor and later alone until elected superior court judge for King County in 1902. Morris was one of the most popular judges in King County, being reelected to the superior court twice by overwhelming majorities. This popularity encouraged acting Governor Marion E. Hay to appoint Morris to one of the two newly created positions on the state's high bench in 1909. Only Judge Frank Rudkin represented the state's west side on the bench, prompting Hay to select Emmett Parker of Tacoma and Morris of Seattle. Morris led the Republican ticket when running for election a year later, garnering over 80,000 votes. In 1916, without the assistance of a party label in the nonpartisan balloting,

Morris still collected 120,000 votes. While still on the high bench, a serious stomach ailment ended his career and he died after an operation on March 6, 1918.

Judge Morris, a Thirty-second Degree Mason, served as venerable master of the Lodge of Perfection of Olympia. He also belonged to the Mystic Shrine, Elks, Woodmen of the World, Royal Arcanum, Improved Order of Redman, Olympia Golf Club, and Seattle Athletic Club. Judge Morris married Maude E. Myrole in Kent, Washington, on January 29, 1899 and the couple had one son, Theodore.

"He was accustomed to sit with calm mien and half closed eyes intently listening to the views of his associates, sometimes expressed with much force and vehemence," observed Judge Overton G. Ellis, who sat on the supreme court with Morris. "When his turn came he expressed himself with...vigor... This faculty of sifting to the determinative essentials [of] complicated questions...made Judge Morris invaluable to the deliberations of the Court."

Upon his death the *Seattle Post-Intelligencer* wrote the following about the judge:

> A person of rare charm, Judge Morris was held in high esteem, not only by members of his profession, but by the people throughout the state...
>
> A prodigious worker on the bench, his nature was too big and fine to permit him to limit himself to being sociable only with his professional associates. He had the kindly word and pleasant smile for everybody, and old neighbors and friends in Seattle all attest the fact that the judge never lost the "common touch." He was a splendid story teller, becoming the life of any party he joined, and his social nature inspired him to seek kindred spirits when his time was not devoted to the duties of his profession.
>
> As judge of the superior court...he presided at many notable trials during the nearly seven years he served on the bench of that court, and the number of decisions written by him since he became a member of the supreme court not only marks him as an industrious, but a painstaking judge.
>
> He had himself to thank for his rise in his profession, for whatever came to him he tried to do his best, and as chief justice . . . he earned not only the commendation of his associates, but of the superior court judges of the other counties and the bar generally for the manner in which he directed the work of its two departments.

Selected References

Seattle Post-Intelligencer, 7 Mar. 1918; Washington State Bar Association *Proceedings* (1918), p. 77; W. C. Wolfe, *Sketches of Washingtonians* (1906), p. 248.

Wallace Mount
January 14, 1901-September 4, 1921

Born: January 16, 1859
Oregon City, Oregon
University of Oregon, B.S. (1883)
Presbyterian
Died: September 4, 1921
Sprague City Council (1887)
Prosecuting Attorney (1888)
Superior Court (1889-1896)
State House of Representatives (1898-1900)
Republican
Elected

Wallace Mount was the oldest of fourteen children of Henry D. and Rebecca (Stevens) Mount. His father braved the dangers of a plains crossing to the far west at age eighteen and settled in the Willamette Valley near Oregon City. Judge Mount was born and grew up on his parents' farm, attended public schools in Silverton, Oregon, and graduated from the University of Oregon in 1883. After graduation he read law in the offices of George Williams, H. Y. Thompson, and George H. Durham of Portland, and gained admittance to the Oregon bar in 1885.

The future jurist practiced law in Portland for one year, then moved to Sprague, Washington Territory, to open a law office. He soon became prominent in Republican politics, being elected as a Sprague city councilman in 1887, prosecuting attorney for the Third Judicial District including Lincoln, Adams, and Douglas counties in 1888 and, upon statehood in 1889, superior court judge for Lincoln, Adams, Douglas, and Okanogan counties. He won again in 1892, but suffered defeat in his bid for a third superior court term in the Populist landslide of 1896.

Mount moved to Spokane to form the law partnership of Mount and Merritt. Turning his attention to the state legislature in 1898 he won election to the lower house from Spokane County. In the 1899 legislative session he chaired the house Committee on Counties and Boundaries and served on the Judiciary Committee. In 1900 Mount ran as a Republican for the supreme court and led the judicial ballot, defeating his nearest Democratic rival by more than 12,000 votes. Six years later he again led the judicial ticket, overwhelming the Democrats by nearly 40,000 votes. Reelected in two subsequent contests, he served a total of twenty years on the high court.

Judge Mount married Carrie Walker of Eugene, Oregon, in 1887. They became the parents of two sons, Frank and William. In 1896 Carrie passed away and three years later the judge married Ida (Hasler) Maloney, who had two daughters from a previous marriage, Hazel and Mira. The family attended the Presbyterian Church, and the judge was active in the Independent Order of Odd Fellows, Kiwanis, and Knights of Pythias.

Judge Mount gained recognition for his 1917 landmark decision that restricted certain forms of labor picketing. He gained a reputation for independence and courage from this and other decisions. During his last few months on the bench, failing health prevented the justice from carrying a full share of the court's business. In September 1921, Judge Mount's heart failed. He was sixty-two years old.

Stephen J. Chadwick eulogized the judge at the memorial services:

It was forty-three years ago that I first knew Wallace Mount. His outstanding characteristics were his great good nature, the evenness of his temper, his loveable qualities and his fairness in all his relations with others. He was a gentleman always and everywhere. He was possessed even in youth of those qualities that marked him and made him strong in his manhood...

His early public work was marked by an integrity of purpose which attracted the notice of those who knew the needs of the state, and he was called to the highest dignity that the state can offer, when he entered into a career that was to last for more than twenty years, and to be ended only by death...

He possessed a solid learning in the law. In him there was no flash of shallowness, or resort to words or phrases, to cover an uncertainty of mind. He was direct and forceful. Whether right or wrong as measured by the aggregate of opinion, he always believed himself to be right and was ever ready and able to defend his opinions against the ablest of his fellow judges.

He was strong in mind and strong in body. He met his duty, and accomplished the onerous demands of his office, with an ease and resolution that sometimes stirred the envy of those who finished the tasks assigned them by more laborious processes...

He believed inherently in law, in constituted authority; he believed that this was indeed a government of law and not of men; that the constitutions of our state and of our country were fixed anchors designed to withstand the storms of passion that must from time to time sweep the sea of public sentiment, and that they should not be dragged out of their fast moorings but sustained in reason until unrestrained emotion had wasted its energy and reason had again asserted its sway...

In all the years that it was my privilege to be associated with Judge Mount, I never heard him speak ill of any man.

Selected References

W. C. Wolfe, *Sketches of Washingtonians* (1906), p. 248; William Prosser, *History of the Puget Sound Country*, vol. 2 (1903), pp. 178-179; Julian Hawthorne, *History of Washington*, vol. 1 (1893), p. 666; Washington State Bar Association *Proceedings* (1921), pp. 177-180.

Marshall Allen Neill
April 24, 1967-November 16, 1972

Born: August 23, 1914
Pullman, Washington
Washington State University, B.A. (1936)
University of Idaho, LL.B. (1938)
Episcopalian
Died: October 6, 1979
Assistant Attorney General (1945-1967)
State House of Representatives (1949-1956)
State Senate (1957-1967)
Federal District Court (1972-1979)
Republican
Appointed

Marshall A. Neill's public life combined the qualities of lawyering, politicking, and judging into a delicately balanced whole. For twenty-nine years, "Marsh" practiced law in Pullman, Washington, in his own small law firm while serving as assistant attorney general for Washington State University and attorney for the City of Pullman. From 1949 to 1956 he represented Whitman County in the Washington House of Representatives and then moved to the senate, serving until his appointment to the supreme court in 1967. After five years on the state's high court, he gained appointment to the U. S. District Court for eastern Washington, where he remained until struck down by cancer at the age of sixty-five. As Judge Neill moved through positions of public responsibility, he consistently brought the same moderate values to his tasks and, according to all accounts, maintained the highest integrity and commitment.

Marshall Neill was born August 23, 1914, in Pullman, the second child of Roy A. and Maude (Cameron) Neill. His parents operated a florist shop in Pullman. Marsh's grandfather, Thomas Neill, practiced law in Colfax and Pullman and later served on the superior court bench. He founded the *Pullman Herald* newspaper and proved influential in having the small village selected as the location of the state agriculture college in 1890. Young Marsh attended public schools in Pullman, graduating from Pullman High School in 1932, and from Washington State University in 1936 with a B.A. degree in political science. He chose political science to gain access to law school rather than to further any interest in politics. Fortunately, the demands for entry in those days were few; Neill's undergraduate record was far from outstanding.

For as long as he could remember he had wanted to be a lawyer. As he explained:

> My grandfather was an Irish immigrant. He came to this country uneducated and read law in Indiana and in the Dakota Territories. He came out to the Territory of Washington and established a law office in 1887, which I have had the fortune to continue.

Following graduation, Neill commuted ten miles down the road to the University of Idaho Law School. There he excelled, graduating second in his class in 1938. After gaining admission to the Washington bar the same year, the future judge set up practice in his grandfather's office in Pullman and, with Hugh Aitken, formed a law partnership. Neill's son, Howard, later practiced out of the same downtown office.

Marshall's initiation into political and public service came inadvertently. While pleading the cause of one of his friends the "accident" happened:

> I was picked by the county commissioners because I went over and shot off my mouth about how they were treating a good personal friend of mine... They called my bluff. "Listen, if we appoint [the friend] to the Senate will you take over his opening in the House?" I could hardly say "no." That's how I got into politics.

Until that point Neill had not even claimed a political party. But his appointment as a Republican proved fortunate. He successfully defended his house seat in subsequent elections when Democrats, recognizing the futility of running against Neill, often refused to file for the office. He served until 1956, when elected to the senate. The soft-spoken, easy-going Neill gained respect from both sides of the aisle with a reputation for achieving compromise and consensus on divisive issues. Justice Robert Brachtenbach, who served with Neill in the legislature, remembered his friend's political talents:

> We worked on significant legislation, and I learned that you don't have political enemies, you have political friends... We worked together within our own political party, and I've seen many conventions when the wisdom of Marsh Neill prevented those disasters that sometimes happen within political parties.

In 1955 his Republican colleagues elected him house minority leader. In 1962 he was selected as the senate Republican caucus chairman. Neill also assumed positions of leadership within the state party structure. His work as a leader among Republican legislators brought him into close contact with Governor Daniel J. Evans, with whom he had also served in the house.

Neill adopted his grandfather as his professional role model. Judge Tom Neill inspired his choice of law as a career and his interest in a judgeship. When Judge Richard B. Ott announced his retirement in April 1967, Marshall Neill was in the "right place at the right time" to fulfill his career objective:

[I was] upstairs in the Senate as [Evans's] Senate leader and carrying the ball for his program. [I would go] down daily [to his office] and pound the table, disagreeing a lot of the time. But I followed him, he was my party leader. So when the word came that Judge Ott was going to retire I knew there was going to be an opening. I just went downstairs and said that is what I want.

The fact that Neill came from eastern Washington, the same section as Ott, and that the bar selection committee approved him, simply reinforced his case for appointment. The old adage that a "judge is simply a politician who knows the governor" holds true for Neill. But Governor Evans had ample opportunity to appraise the talents of his former Republican colleague. He knew whom he was appointing. The support of fellow legislators—Republican and Democrat—had much to do with his initial appointment and assured him strong backing throughout the state in subsequent election efforts. Actually, in both of his high court elections, no one filed against Neill; people viewed such a challenge as futile since the justice had well-organized supporters on both sides of the Cascades.

While on the court, Justice Neill authored 113 majority opinions, twenty-three concurrences, and twenty-eight dissents. His opinion-drafting process always considered the preferences of other judges when possible, often reinforced by informal discussions with or memos to his colleagues. He shared the actual drafting of opinions with his law clerk. According to one of his former personal assistants:

I usually met with the Judge on the morning of oral argument to discuss the cases. If one of us spotted an interesting case, we might discuss it earlier. Afterwards, we would thoroughly discuss any opinions the Judge was assigned. I wrote drafts of many (but not all) of these opinions. The Judge tended to keep concurring opinions and dissents. The Judge would occasionally ask for research on another judge's opinion which was bothering him—this might lead to a memo... I thought he...work[ed] more closely with [me] than any of the other judges [did with their clerks].

Justice Neill's decisions reflected a moderate approach to the law, although he viewed himself as a fiscal conservative and restraintist:

I have a strong feeling toward the legislative branch. I still feel it is the policy making body. I have always resisted...the activism of the courts. I don't think we are equipped nor trained for that... I fought with my colleagues many many times over this philosophy.

His many years as a politician had shown him that compromise, persuasion, and consensus achieved desired objectives. As a judge he often softened his views in order to achieve compromise. If he failed to convince a majority of his brethren, he would acquiesce. He wrote his few dissents more to "keep the majority 'honest' " and to "point out the impact of the majority's opinion on society," than to "win over the majority or to win more votes."

The time, effort, pressures, and costs of campaigning bore heavily on Neill. He felt that he did not have the independence necessary for ruling in many cases. For example, he "drew two or three cases just before he would have had to run for reelection which were political dynamite" and could have led to his defeat. He wrote a dissent in a teachers' pension case that could have caused the Washington Education Association to work against him. Taxpayers might well have protested after his dissent in the *North King County Taxpayers'* case. And he was convinced his opinion in the *DeFunis* case would be extremely unpopular. The security and independence of the federal bench appeared attractive.

In 1971 Neill contended unsuccessfully for the seat on the federal bench being vacated by Judge George Boldt. A year later another federal trial bench position opened up in Spokane. With support from Congressman Tom Pelly, Governor Evans, and Al Schweppe, a prominent Washington attorney, President Richard Nixon sent Neill's name to the senate for confirmation. It was most favorably received. At the hearing before the Senate Judiciary Committee, Senator Roman Hruska asked Neill about his law practice. "I'm a country lawyer and I do the best I can with whatever comes in the door that morning," responded Neill, to which Hruska replied, "Glad to see some of us left." The senate confirmed his nomination on a voice vote. After finishing his opinion assignments, including the reverse discrimination *DeFunis* case, Justice Neill resigned from the supreme court on November 16, 1972, and assumed his federal judicial office the next day.

Judge Neill's court suffered from one of the heaviest case loads in the federal circuit. Even working evenings at home and on Saturdays, and obtaining assistance from visiting judges, the onerous workload remained. Despite the heavy case load, Neill found the trial bench exciting. The close give-and-take with attorneys and juries pleased him and he found the day-to-day problems brought to the court challenging. But the burdens of sentencing always weighed heavily. On Sunday nights preceding Monday sentencing days, the judge rarely rested well.

Judge Neill married Marion Hackedorn of Pullman in 1938. They had three children: Marjorie, Martha, and Howard. The judge saw action with the navy in World War II during the campaigns for Okinawa and the Philippines. He belonged to and served as president of a number of business, professional, civic, and social groups, including the Pullman Chamber of Commerce, Kiwanis, Veterans of Foreign Wars, American Legion, Masons, Shriners, Whitman County Bar Association, and Washington State University Alumni Association. The judge received Washington State University's Alumni Achievement Award in 1971, and in 1976 the university's highest honor, its Distinguished Alumnus Award.

After taking leave from the court in April 1979 for cancer surgery, Judge Neill returned to his daily routine knowing the disease had progressed beyond hope. He died a few months later.

Selected References

Neill's oral history interview is in the supreme court collection, Washington State Archives. Also see Danielle Darcy, "Biography of Judge Marshall A. Neill," Neill file, same collection; and memorial services, *Washington Reports,* vol. 93, 2d (1980), pp. xxxv-xli.

Ralph Oliver Olson
September 10, 1952-January 15, 1955

Born: March 26, 1902
Alden, Minnesota
Carleton College
University of Minnesota, LL.B. (1924)
Presbyterian
Died: January 15, 1955
Justice of the Peace and Police Judge
    (1926-1936)
Superior Court (1936-1951)
Republican
Appointed

Ralph Oliver Olson was born in Alden, Minnesota, on March 26, 1902, the son of Ralph O. and Genevieve (Larson) Olson. The elder Olson, a prominent banker, lost everything in the crash of 1929 and spent the remainder of his life repaying those who had money in his bank when it failed. After graduation at age sixteen from St. Cloud High School, the younger Olson did undergraduate work at Carleton College and then went to law school at the University of Minnesota, earning his LL.B. with honors in 1924. He also won recognition at Minnesota as a second-team All-American football player. Immediately after graduating from the school of law, Olson, having tired of Minnesota's severe winters, traveled the length of the west coast seeking an ideal location to live and work. He chose Bellingham, a town with few lawyers and abundant recreational opportunities.

Olson married Clara Louise Moore of St. Cloud in 1924 and she accompanied her husband to Washington. They had three children: Phyllis Anne, Charles Ralph, and Dan Ralph. Their sons excelled in athletics at the University of Washington and both graduated from its school of law.

Olson passed the Washington bar exam in 1924. Two years later he won election as a part-time municipal judge, serving until 1936 when he was elected to the superior court for Whatcom and Island counties. Judge Olson became especially interested in the problems of young people in his community. He helped organize summer youth programs and originated a scholarship fund with the University Club of Bellingham.

A Republican, Olson participated only minimally in politics, although he did run unsuccessfully for mayor of Bellingham. Olson gained his reputation from work on the bench rather than political activities or his private law practice. Judging fit his talents well. He served as president of the Superior Court Judges' Association in 1947 and judges and lawyers throughout the state knew him because of Washington's visiting judges' system. When Judge Walter Beals resigned from the supreme court, Governor Arthur Langlie appointed Olson to fill the vacancy. He was forty-nine years old.

Two factors favored Olson's selection. First, some had criticized Langlie because none of his recent appointees came from the judicial ranks. Olson, on the other hand, had served on the bench for a quarter of a century. In an effort to add geographical balance to the court, the governor needed to choose someone from outside King and Spokane counties. As an established member of the Bellingham community, Olson qualified here, too. A member of the bar selection committee that recommended Olson recalled: "I do not think there were any political considerations as such given to his appointment and feel it probably was more a geographical recommendation of a highly considered person."

Olson, a tall man with a friendly demeanor and without any pretentiousness, ran unopposed for election in 1952. Judge Edgar Schwellenbach, who served with Olson, recalled the judge's working habits:

> He was one of the hardest working members of the court. He had a set pattern for the review of each case assigned to him. He read the record. He became familiar with the facts. He studied the briefs and appreciated the issues involved. He read every decision, text and periodical on the particular subject. In each case he asked himself two questions: What are the facts? What is the law? Not what should the law be, but what actually is the law? Having answered those two questions, he proceeded to apply the law to the facts.

Olson was moderate in his legal and political philosophy and a restraintist in his jurisprudence. Schwellenbach continued:

> Experience had convinced him that [justice] could best be accomplished by relying on precedent, upon the decisions of other judges who had previously been confronted with the same or similar problems, rather than by attempting to do justice in each individual case. He realized that the latter procedure, no matter how well intentioned, would create a chaotic condition in the law with the result that attorneys could not advise their clients, and trial judges would have difficulty in conducting their trials.

Judge Olson's use of law clerks reflected his long history of working with young adults and his relationship with his own children. First it was a student-teacher relationship. As the clerk gained knowledge and confidence, the relationship became more a partnership. According to one of his law clerks:

> Judge Olson had a different style of working with his clerk than the other judges on the court. After reading the briefs and transcripts and hearing the oral arguments, he and I would work together on the numerous drafts of an opinion before it was signed and circulated. We customarily did the research together and had many spirited discussions regarding the applicable law.

Olsen's clerks served as sounding boards, listening, commenting, suggesting, and criticizing—but not creating. The clerk researched and wrote notes in preparation for give-and-take sessions with the judge. According to a former clerk, Olson had "very definite views on each case assigned to him. He would take great pains to keep his opinions short and directly to the issue."

Judge Olson infrequently dissented, choosing to persuade through informal discussions and well-researched opinions. For example, in the 1952-1953 terms, Olson led his colleagues in writing for the court. He averaged thirty-five opinions per year, above the court average of twenty-seven. From his moderate perspective, he tended to provide the swing vote in divided cases. He and Judge Frank Weaver held the middle-of-the-road positions on the 1950s bench, agreeing with each other most of the time and disagreeing most frequently with liberal Judge Robert Finley and conservative Judge Thomas Grady.

Olson belonged to the Order of Coif, Phi Delta Phi, Beta Theta Pi, and the Bellingham University Club. An avid angler, he tied his own trout and steelhead flies and, when each proved its worth, retired it to a display case with a record of date, location, length, and weight of fish caught. Many people remarked on his ability to "read" a river for the best steelhead spots.

Without warning, Judge Olson collapsed at his Olympia home of a brain aneurysm and passed away on January 15, 1955. He was fifty-two years old.

Selected References

See the Charles and Dan Olson oral history interviews in the supreme court collection, Washington State Archives; memorial services, *Washington Reports,* vol. 46, 2d (1955), pp. xxx-xxxiv; C. W. Taylor, *Eminent Judges and Lawyers of the Northwest* (1954), p. 59; and Charles Sheldon, "The Washington Supreme Court: What it was Like Fifty Years Ago," *Gonzaga Law Review,* vol. 19 (1983-1984), pp. 231-263.

Richard B. Ott

January 24, 1955-March 31, 1967

Born: March 19, 1897
Ritzville, Washington
University of Idaho
University of Idaho School of Law, LL.B.
　(1919)
Episcopalian
Died: April 30, 1987
Prosecuting Attorney (1923-1931)
City Attorney (1925-1931)
Ritzville Mayor (1931-1933)
State House of Representatives (1933-1935)
Superior Court (1949-1955)
Republican
Appointed

Richard B. Ott, born in room one of the Ritzville Hotel on March 18, 1897, was the son of Sebastian and Christina (Hege) Ott. His father operated a vineyard in Germany before coming to America in 1893. With his brother, he built and managed the Ritzville Hotel and constructed and operated the Ritzville Flouring Mill. Richard attended local public schools while working in the mill after school and during summers. His high school debating experience and his brother John's encouragement convinced Ott to become a lawyer. He enrolled at the University of Idaho, but interrupted his studies to volunteer for the infantry during World War I. After officers' training, the army discharged him following the armistice as a second lieutenant and he reentered the University of Idaho School of Law, graduating with an LL.B. in 1919. Ott first practiced in Oakley, Idaho, but after a year returned to his home town, passing the Washington bar and opening an office across the street from the Ritzville Hotel.

Although his father had not been active in political affairs—and incidentally, distrusted lawyers—the younger Ott became a considerable force in Ritzville Republican politics. In 1923 he won election as Adams County Prosecuting Attorney, serving four terms. In 1931 he returned to private practice, forming a partnership with Edward G. Cross. During this period Ott served as Ritzville's mayor and city attorney. In 1933 he entered the state house of representatives and in the 1935 session served as speaker *pro tem.* His legislative experience served him well later as the legislative liaison for the Washington State Bar Association.

The future judge again entered the army in November 1942, serving as litigation officer with the Judge Advocate General Department. Discharged with the rank of major in 1946, Ott resumed his Ritzville law practice. When Adams

County gained a new superior court position in 1949, Governor Arthur Langlie appointed Ott to the post. Voters elected him to the position in 1950 and returned him to a full term in 1952. Two years later Judge Ott filed for the supreme court, although Hugh Rosellini soundly defeated him. Ott had the state bar association's endorsement, but Rosellini possessed name familiarity, had the support of labor, and had in place a network of support from his narrow defeat at the hands of Frederick Hamley in 1950.

Judge Ott believed he lost because he started his campaign too late. He recalled:

> Tom Grady was stepping down as...judge. It was then believed since eastern Washington had one-third of the state's population it should have three of the nine judges. I wouldn't run against Tom but he didn't announce his intention not to run until very late, which did not give me much time to make a statewide campaign.

Ott only reluctantly filed, with the election so near. But a few leaders in the bar convinced him to make the run. Many members of the Seattle bar came to know him through his military litigation in Seattle courts during World War II. He also presided over King County cases as visiting judge a number of times. Some segments of the bar sought a viable candidate to oppose Hugh Rosellini and chose Ott:

> In order to give me hope, there was this meeting at the College Club... There [were] at least 20 or 30 lawyers. Some of them were real prominent lawyers and they urged me to run. I don't know what they had against Hugh Rosellini. They never told me. They wanted me to run for it... They raised about $1,500.

Ott spent about $30,000 during his abortive run. A few months later Judge Ralph Olson died from a brain aneurysm. Within a week, Governor Arthur Langlie selected Richard Ott to the vacancy. The judge recalled the appointment: "[the governor] called me up and said you'd spent a lot of money to get on the supreme court, how would you like to have it for free? [The appointment is yours] if you can be over here by Monday...to take some *en banc* cases. We have to have nine judges." Ott responded, "If you say so I can make it!"

The appointment made sense. Ott had a solid reputation throughout the state as a result of presiding over trials in twenty-five of Washington's thirty-nine counties. He had strongly supported Governor Langlie, his "good friend." Finally, with eastern Washington underrepresented on the court, Ott proved a logical choice.

In four subsequent reelections Ott used state bar endorsement and eastern Washington support to overcome opponents almost always backed by organized labor.

Judge Ott had a cautious, conservative, and individualistic decisional style. Not reluctant to disagree with his brethren, the judge's record shows that on forty-four occasions his dissents gained enough signatures to become majority opinions, always a source of pride for Ott. One of his clerks recalled that the judge "felt very strongly about his convictions, and would seldom, if ever, compromise his position." He rarely lobbied for his point of view but "always hoped his opinion would sell itself."

His working relationship with his clerks was one of persuasion, compromise, and cooperation. According to one former clerk:

> [Ott] worked independently on research and would arrive at fairly independent conclusions. We would then get together and resolve our differences (usually the judge prevailed—but not always)... My judge was a man absolutely devoted to the judicial process. Although personally quite conservative where I was quite liberal our relationship was excellent. He was always willing to listen to and sometimes accept a contrary point of view. He enjoyed debate and believed it necessary to arrive at the truth.

While serving as chief justice, Ott was influential in negotiating the bench-bar-press guidelines that ultimately became the voluntary rules accepted by attorneys, judges, journalists, and police to establish a balance between the freedom of the press and fair-trial demands of the U. S. Constitution. He served as the first chairman of the bench-bar-press commission appointed in 1963.

Judge Ott retired from the supreme court in March 1967 to travel, golf, and continue his interest in photography. Before giving up judging entirely, he again practiced law and thus became eligible to sit as a *pro tempore* judge at the trial level. He announced his availability and fulfilled his longtime ambition of being the first judge in the state's history to sit over trials in all of the state's counties.

Judge Ott married Allene L. Mills of Sprague, Washington, in July 1926. They were parents of one daughter, Patricia. The judge belonged to the American Legion, serving as national vice-commander for a term. He was also a member of the Lions, Odd Fellows, Shriners, Masons, Patron of Eastern Star, and the Ritzville Chamber of Commerce. He served a term on the city's library board. During retirement the Otts traveled between a winter home in Yuma, Arizona, and Olympia. After a prolonged illness, Judge Ott died on April 30, 1987.

Selected References

Ott's oral history interview is in the supreme court collection, Washington State Archives. Also see M. A. Ratcliffe, "Justice Ott's Dissent Success: A Reflection on Dissent Behavior," Ott file, in the same collection; C. W. Taylor, *Eminent Judges and Lawyers of the Northwest* (1954), p. 178; *Seattle Times,* 17 Oct. 1973 and 10 Jan. 1977; and memorial services, *Washington Reports,* vol. 108, 2d (1987), pp. xxxvii-xliv.

Emmett Newton Parker
February 26, 1909-August 15, 1933

Born: May 12, 1859
York, Pennsylvania
Whittier College
Cincinnati Law School, LL.B. (1882)
Quaker
Died: December 8, 1939
Probate Judge (1882-1887)
Municipal Court (1890-1892)
Superior Court (1893-1897)
Tacoma City Attorney (1900-1901)
Republican
Appointed

Emmett N. Parker was born in York, Pennsylvania. His father, a miller, entered the Union Army and died shortly after the battle of Antietam, when Emmett was three. In 1863 his mother moved her family to Henry County, Iowa, to live with her brother. Emmett grew up on his uncle's farm. The family belonged to the Society of Friends. After public schools in the county, Emmett attended Whittier College in Salem, Iowa, for two years. Leaving Whittier, he clerked in dry goods stores in Burlington and Iowa City for three years. In 1879 he went to Cincinnati to study law in the offices of U. S. Attorney Warren M. Bateman. He also attended lectures at the University of Cincinnati Law School, graduating in 1882. Admitted to practice in Ohio the same year, within a few months he moved to Kidder County in Dakota Territory (North Dakota) to practice law. In Dakota, Parker served five years as probate judge and one term as Steele City Attorney.

Opportunities in the Pacific Northwest drew Parker to Tacoma in 1888. Within a year he became attorney for the Association of Wholesale Merchants and then Tacoma's first municipal (police) judge in 1890, serving until 1892. In 1893 he became superior court judge for Pierce County. After serving a four-year term, the mayor of Tacoma appointed Parker assistant city attorney and shortly thereafter, in 1901, voters elected him city attorney. He served until 1901.

Parker had been a serious candidate for appointment to one of the two new positions on the supreme court created by the legislature in 1905. In 1908 he ran a credible but unsuccessful primary race for the high court, garnering more than 34,000 votes. In 1909 geography aided him in his quest for a court seat. Seattle's Frank Rudkin was the court's only west-sider. Acting Governor Marion

E. Hay appointed Parker and George Morris to two newly created positions on the supreme court. In 1910 voters overwhelmingly affirmed Parker after Republicans nominated him in the last partisan convention to name judicial candidates for the supreme court. In 1916, 1922, and 1928 voters reelected Parker. In none of these elections did he have to campaign beyond the primary.

On the bench Parker tended to adopt moderate-to-liberal stances regarding, especially, government regulation and taxation. If measures threatening private property were in the public interest, they should stand. In *Reclamation Board v. Clausen,* for example, he wrote that a particular tax measure ought to be judged on the basis of its policy implications rather than on pure legal logic:

> That such a question...has proven so vexatious is...because of its inherent nature in that, in its last analysis, it is not one of exclusive legal logic, but is one more or less of policy and wisdom, properly determinable in light of the public welfare, present and future, in a broad sense; and hence is not a pure judicial law question.

A heart ailment kept Parker from full participation on the bench during the 1933 session and he missed two important decisions dealing with the constitutionality of income and business and occupation taxes. He resigned from the bench in August of that year.

Judge Parker was a charter member of, and one of the leading forces behind, the American Law Institute. The institute's objective was to codify the principal fields of judge-made common law into useful "restatements." Under the institute's auspices, Judge Parker traveled often to Washington, D. C., to consult with national leaders of the bar and became friends with U. S. Supreme Court justices and prominent attorneys. A life member, he served on the institute's executive committee for ten years.

Parker also participated actively in the Washington State Bar Association, serving on many of its committees. He was a delegate to the American Bar Association national convention in 1895 and served on the ABA's general council in 1923.

In 1884 Parker married Emma Garretson in Iowa City. They had four children: Anna, Theodore, Helen, and Evangeline. Judge Parker was a Thirty-second Degree Mason, an active Shriner, and a member of the Tacoma Commercial Club. Regarded as a scholar, he wrote extensively on legal subjects.

Selected References

C. S. Reinhart, *The History of the Supreme Court of the Washington Territory and State* (n.d.), pp. 79-80; *Seattle Times,* 8 Dec. 1939; H. James Boswell, *American Blue Book: Western Washington* (1922), p. 12.

Vernon R. Pearson
January 18, 1982-October 31, 1989

Born: September 17, 1923
Bantry, North Dakota
Jamestown College, B.A. (1947)
University of Michigan, LL.B. (1950)
Law Associate (1950-1951)
Office of Price Stabilization (1951-1952)
Court of Appeals (1969-1982)
Republican
Appointed

Initial impressions are clearly incomplete. When one meets Justice Vernon R. Pearson, he appears unassuming, soft-spoken, hesitantly thoughtful, gregarious yet shy. These traits do reflect the man, but what is often missed is a sharp, decisive, competitive, but open legal mind. All these characteristics reflect the justice's background.

Vernon was the second son of Reverend Claude M. and Golda Mae Pearson. Claude, his older brother, became a lawyer; Richard, born three years after Vernon, a chemist. A younger sister died at age six. The life of a Methodist minister and his family in rural North Dakota was not easy. Later, Justice Pearson recalled these early years:

> We lived a simpler life when I was a child. I grew up in North Dakota during the Great Depression. My father was a Methodist minister who served many small rural churches in the North Dakota conference. We moved frequently. Conditions at times were bleak when the crop failures caused by soil erosion were at their worst in the 1930s. Our clothes came from missionary boxes and our food from handouts. It was truly the worst of times and yet I have nothing but happy memories about it because there was always love and hope – optimism in our home.

The family knew poverty but also love and hope, and Vernon's parents instilled a respect for freedom and Christianity in their children.

Vernon attended a number of public schools, graduating in 1941 from Cando High School in North Dakota where he competed in football, basketball, and track while participating in debate, drama, and choir. Following graduation he enrolled at Jamestown College on an academic scholarship. The scholarship covered only tuition and books, so he worked evenings and weekends at the local

J. C. Penney store to cover other expenses. He participated in drama productions and competed on the debate team. After his sophomore year, World War II interrupted Vernon's schooling. He enlisted in the navy.

The navy assigned the future judge to a naval officers' training program at Minot State Teachers College, then transferred him to midshipmen's school at Cornell University. From there he went to Ft. Pierce in Florida to complete officer training. Reassigned to Providence, Rhode Island, to train as a commander of landing ships, Pearson became boat division officer on the *U. S. S. Sylvania.* On his first combat mission he picked up an engineering battalion in Marseille, France, and took it through the Panama Canal to join in the landing on Luzon in the retaking of the Philippines. He later became a navigator responsible for landing troops in Japan as part of the occupation. Pearson, ordered to participate in the atomic bomb testing project on Bikini Island, had his military enlistment extended for six months. Part of a team responsible for charting the island's waters in preparation for the test, Pearson took one of the last planes out of the island before the atomic bomb went off. Honorably discharged in 1946, he left the navy with the rank of lieutenant, junior grade.

A non-combat assignment while in the service convinced Pearson to choose law as his profession. The military tried people accused of serious disciplinary infractions before an officer hearing board, where lawyer and non-lawyer officers defended them. Pearson served as prosecuting "counsel" for a number of these hearings. The give-and-take of the adversarial process stimulated his interest.

The newly discharged veteran returned to Jamestown College, doubling up on courses in order to graduate with a degree in political science and social studies within a year. Graduating in 1947, he and Jean Robertson, whom he had met at college, were married. A registered nurse, she planned to work to help support Vernon during law school.

Pearson applied to a number of law schools and chose the University of Michigan. Jean and Vernon had a son, Robert, after Vernon's first year in law school. Jean, who had worked as a nurse at the University of Michigan hospital, resigned to care for their new son while Vernon took a half-time job at the law library. Because he had no spare time from his studies and work, the future judge declined an offer to join the prestigious law review staff. As a research assistant in his third year, he assisted a law professor, John Dawson, in writing a book on restitution and remedies. The dean of the University of Washington School of Law asked Dawson, an old classmate, to recommend a graduating law student to design and teach a new course in legal writing and research at Washington. Dawson chose Pearson, and within a few weeks the dean made an offer. Although Jean wanted to stay in the Midwest, the new opportunity and glowing reports of the region from Vernon's brother Claude, who practiced law in Tacoma, convinced the Pearsons to move to the Northwest in 1950.

After a year, Pearson realized he needed practical experience to effectively teach. He resigned from the university and began working as regional attorney for the Office of Price Stabilization in Seattle under the supervision of former state supreme court judge, William Steinert. His brother's law firm in Tacoma then offered him a position late in 1952 and Pearson joined, remaining in general practice with his brother for seventeen years. While practicing law, he became involved in 1968 in the Pierce County struggle between the conservative and moderate wings of the Republican party, helping to turn back conservatives from leadership positions. This excursion into party politics constituted Pearson's major, if not sole, partisan experience, but it established his Republican credentials.

A vacancy occurred on the Pierce County Superior Court in 1967. Pearson applied, and Governor Daniel Evans interviewed him for the position. The appointment went to someone else. The writing, research, and broad social issues involved in appellate work prompted Pearson, in 1969, to apply for a spot on the newly established court of appeals. This time Governor Evans selected him for one of the three judgeships in division two, located in Tacoma.

Pearson served twelve years on the intermediate appeals bench, and was twice chief judge of division two and presiding judge of the entire court of appeals in 1979. As presiding judge he helped establish better communication among the three divisions and instituted settlement conferences to help eliminate the growing backlog of cases. Several of his opinions subsequently came to be included in law school casebooks.

Pearson's appointment to the supreme court came as a result of being in the right place at the right time. Justice Floyd Hicks of Tacoma had been on the court for five years but, with eyes weakened by cataracts, began finding it difficult to read the voluminous briefs and opinions and conduct legal research. When a vacancy on the Pierce County Superior Court appeared, he asked Republican Governor John Spellman to appoint him to that trial bench, with its less rigorous reading requirements. Hearing of the pending switch in assignments, Judge Pearson wrote the governor indicating his interest in Hicks's position:

> I had something geographically in common with [Hicks]. I also pointed out to him that none of the appointments to the supreme court had ever come from Division Two of the court of appeals... I kind of indicated...that [Division One in Seattle] didn't have a corner on the talent. I sent a copy of my letter also to the state bar screening committee.

Spellman interviewed several candidates, including Pearson, who came strongly endorsed by the state bar committee. Spellman offered the position and Pearson accepted, taking the oath of office on January 18, 1982. He ran unopposed in the September 1982 primary elections and, again, in 1988.

Justice Pearson's record on the high bench was that of a moderate-to-liberal judge supportive of the state's Declaration of Rights, especially as applied to privacy issues.

Between 1982 and 1984 he often provided the swing vote between the more conservative and liberal justices in a number of cases. From his position between the two wings of the court, Pearson quickly assumed a leadership position on the bench. Between 1982 and 1984 he wrote only fifty-six opinions, but on average, garnered more votes for those opinions than any of his colleagues. When he wrote an opinion he received an average of seventy-nine percent agreement from colleagues. Between 1984 and 1989, with the election and appointment of conservative justices, Pearson was found more often among the remaining liberals of the bench.

An explanation for Justice Pearson's effectiveness can be found in his use of dissents. He had the lowest dissent rate of all members of the bench and when he dissented he had good reasons:

> If you are careless with dissents, they don't mean anything. I don't write a dissent just to get something out... I write a dissent to persuade a majority of the court. Unless it's a basic philosophical disagreement I won't write a dissent... Dissent to me should be saved for those things that matter and those things in which you have a real stake and have a chance to change.

Pearson did not vigorously consult or lobby the other justices, although he admitted listening to suggestions others submitted. He tended to agree with Justice William Williams more often than with his other colleagues, and disagreed most with Justice Fred Dore. However, those disagreements never went beyond the conference room. Remarks at the time of his ascendency to the chief justice's chair in 1987 indicated his concern for congeniality and compromise on the bench, which enhanced his position of leadership.

Justice Barbara Durham, with whom Pearson often disagreed, anticipated his conciliatory role. She believed he would "be a great healer on the court. He's the perfect chief because he'll bring us all together. He's got that kind of good spirit about him." The chief's approach was indeed calculated to create the "good spirit." According to Pearson, "If you want to be effective on the Court you have to be collegial. You have to be able to work with people."

During his tenure as chief, Pearson found himself and the court in a unique situation. The temple of justice had to be vacated in order to work on it to help protect it from possible earthquake damage. Justice James Dolliver had suggested a "visiting court" system before, and the new chief justice implemented the plan. Although the highway and licenses building provided temporary quarters, the court traveled about the state, holding hearings at law schools, colleges and universities, high schools, and various courtrooms. Given Pearson's concern that justices keep in touch with people, the visiting court experience fit well into his goals as chief. He cites his successes with increasing judicial salaries, securing a new pension system for judges, automating court records, and better coordination among the state courts as some of his accomplishments as chief.

The Pearsons have four children: Robert, Katherine, Stephen, and David. The justice has served on the Tacoma School Board, State Board of Education, and Mt. Rainier Council of the Boy Scouts, and has presided over the Northwest Tacoma Kiwanis Club and Tacoma Little Theatre.

As judge, Pearson also served as adjunct professor at the University of Puget Sound Law School, teaching one course a year on professional ethics. He chaired the Washington Judicial Council and the American Bar Association's task force on the reduction of litigation cost and delay.

In his last few months as chief justice, Pearson urged reforms in the selection process for state judges. As a result of a controversy surrounding the Judicial Conduct Commission's investigation of a superior court judge in Seattle, Pearson received a unanimous vote from the state Board of Judicial Administration to form a Commission on Washington Courts to determine how to "maintain and attract a quality judiciary."

In February 1989 the American Judicature Society honored Vernon Pearson with its coveted Herbert Harley Award in recognition of the improvements he made to the Washington judicial system as chief justice. In May, Gonzaga University bestowed its Law Medal award on the justice in recognition of his contributions to the field of law.

But the traditional roles of holding the court together, supervising its many programs, and acting as its spokesperson, coupled with the various court reform activities, and the controversy surrounding the Judicial Conduct Commission, took their toll. In July 1989, Pearson announced his resignation from the high bench:

> I . . . felt burnout after two years as chief justice. Had I had a three month sabbatical, I might not have done this. But I need to get away for a while. When it stops being fun and a challenge, you need to depart. It has gotten harder and harder to spend those weekends reading briefs and doing the work that needs to be done to be effective. And I don't want to serve on the court just for the prestige of the position.

Retirement for the sixty-six year old jurist has not meant giving up his concern for the administration of justice. He continues to hold two national chairmanships: the ABA task force on reduction of litigation cost and delay, and a Council of Chief Justice's coordinating committee on jurisdictional disputes between state courts and Indian tribes. He was instrumental in organizing a national conference of state supreme court justices and court officials from around the United States and representatives of some of the nation's 150 tribal courts. Mutual problems, understanding differences, and emphasizing Native American sovereignty were the subjects of discussion at the landmark conference. Despite an active retirement, Justice Pearson found more time for family, golf, and travel.

Selected References

Pearson's oral history interview is in the supreme court collection, Washington State Archives. Also see *Daily Journal of Commerce,* 24 Feb. 1989; *Seattle Post-Intelligencer,* 23 Dec. 1981, 30 Aug. 1988, and 27 Jy. 1989; *Spokane Spokesman-Review,* 12 Jan. 1987; *Washington State Bar News,* 17 Apr. 1971, pp. 11-12, 29; *Seattle Times/Post-Intelligencer,* 11 Jan. 1987; *Seattle-King County Bar Bulletin* (May 1988) and (Apr. 1989); *Bellevue Journal American,* 22 Oct. 1988; and *Aberdeen Daily World,* 19 Jan. 1991.

William Harrison Pemberton
January 8, 1923-January 25, 1925

Born: May 12, 1872
West Milton, Ohio
Earlham College (1892-1895; 1897)
University of Tennessee (1898)
Methodist
Died: August 3, 1938
Superior Court (1912-1921)
Assistant Attorney General (1933)
Supervisor of State Inheritance Tax Division
   (1933-1938)
Democrat
Elected

William Harrison Pemberton was born in the village of West Milton on the Still-water River in west-central Ohio on May 12, 1872, the youngest of five children of Joseph and Sydnia (Pearson) Pemberton. His father, a Quaker minister, raised the children in a strict but loving Quaker atmosphere. "Will" attended Earlham College, a small Quaker institution in Earlham, Indiana, where he excelled in debate, played varsity football, and displayed the independence of thought that characterized his later life. He also attended the University of Tennessee for a short time, permitting him to be admitted to the Tennessee bar in 1898.

Pemberton married Loie Thomas on March 14, 1897; their children were Joseph, Mary, Katherine, and William. Loie Pemberton, a state officer in the Women's Christian Temperance Union (WCTU) after they moved to Washington, had charge of the Loyal Temperance Legion in Whatcom and Thurston counties. Although the judge did not believe strongly in organized religion, he and Loie participated in the local Methodist Church where he often conducted Bible classes.

After moving to Bellingham, the Washington bar admitted him in 1902 by virtue of his Tennessee license. Pemberton began practicing law as a partner in the firm of Neterer, Pemberton, and Sather, and later with Robinson and Pemberton, serving mostly workers seeking redress from employers. Respect and support for working people came easy to this son of a Quaker who had known hard times and manual labor. He developed a reputation for persistence and stubbornness.

Pemberton was initially loyal to the Republican party but, after an abortive run for mayor of Bellingham, he permanently switched to the Democrats and supported William Jennings Bryan.

Pemberton, elected Whatcom County Superior Court judge in 1912, won reelection in 1916 with strong labor support. While serving on the superior court bench, Pemberton made his first run for the supreme court in 1914, losing the general election to Stephen Chadwick. Pemberton based his campaign on three promises: first, "protecting the people in their constitutional rights"; second, "the trial of law suits on the merits instead of upon technicalities"; and third, "absolute and unbiased justice between the people and their interests."

In 1915 Governor Ernest Lister seriously considered him for appointment to the vacancy created by Judge Frederick Bausman's resignation. Lister received a number of endorsements for Pemberton from newspaper editors, church groups, the Women's Good Government League, the WCTU, and Northwestern National Bank, but selected J. Stanley Webster. In 1918 Pemberton again campaigned for the high bench, made it to the final ballot, but lost in November by nearly 24,000 votes. With wide support from labor, church organizations, and the Grange, he finally won in 1922, defeating the appointed Judge Chester Hovey for the two years remaining in Wallace Mount's term.

Pemberton's short tenure on the court was characterized by many dissents and a liberal stance regarding labor issues. His personality as much as his legal views tended to isolate him from his brethren. Alan Gallagher's study of Pemberton places the judge's views in context:

> Such a judge of liberal and democratic sympathies in a conservative and Republican period, a supporter of regulation of business in an age which worshipped business, a supporter of labor and the working men in an age which hated and feared them, a supporter of juries in the face of replacement of their decisions by judges elected or selected by 'interests' was clearly not going to be acceptable to the business community and organized bar.

Pemberton's liberal stance in a number of key cases, and fear that if he remained the court might turn to the left, forced a coalition of establishment members to work for his defeat in 1924. The Seattle and state bar associations, businesses, and public power opponents backed popular Tacoma Superior Court Judge William Askren, who swamped the incumbent by more than 70,000 votes. Two years later Pemberton attempted to return to the high court, but a similar coalition succeeded in defeating him.

In 1932 the judge ran for the Democratic nomination for governor, losing to the eventual winner, Clarence Martin. In 1933 he served as a special assistant to the state attorney general in charge of prosecuting price-fixing among oil companies. Governor Martin then selected him as Washington state supervisor of the inheritance tax division, a post he retained until 1938. Remaining active in Democratic politics, Pemberton made an abortive attempt to gain his party's nomination for the U. S. Senate in 1934 but withdrew at the last moment.

While on a fishing trip in the summer of 1938 Pemberton, an avid outdoorsman, contracted pneumonia. Released from the hospital after a short stay, he visited his son in Bellingham but suffered a sudden relapse and died on August 3. Alan Gallagher summarized the judge's career:

> He proved a witness and standard-bearer for principles and interests which would not come into combination and power until the 1930s... Given his Quaker background, progressive beliefs, love of battle, respect for plain sense and language and the working man, he was a witness to values for which the times were not yet ready.

Selected References

Alan L. Gallagher, "William Pemberton, A Biography," Pemberton file, supreme court collection, Washington State Archives; Gallagher, "The Fighting Judge," *Washington State Bar News,* vol. 43 (1989), pp. 15-20; C. W. Taylor, *Eminent Judges and Lawyers of the Northwest* (1954), p. 373; *Seattle Times,* 3 Aug. 1938.

James Bradley Reavis
January 11, 1897-January 13, 1903

Born: May 27, 1848
Boone County, Missouri
University of Kentucky (1870-1872)
Christian Church
Died: April 29, 1912
Washington Territorial Council (1884)
Regent, University of Washington
    (1888-1889)
Democrat
Elected

James B. Reavis was the third child of six born to John Newton and Elizabeth (Preston) Reavis of Boone County, Missouri. His father was of Scottish ancestry and his mother came from a prominent Missouri pioneering family. Judge Reavis grew up on his father's stock-breeding farm in fairly comfortable circumstances, raised as a devout member of the Christian Church. James attended public schools and a private academy, then enrolled in the University of Kentucky at Lexington for three years, leaving before graduation because of illness. Reavis went to Hannibal to study law, and the Missouri bar admitted him in 1874. He earned a living as a journalist for a short time.

Reavis practiced law in Hannibal for nearly two years before moving to Chico, California. After five years he moved to Goldendale, Washington Territory, in 1880. The Democrat Reavis formed a partnership with Republican Ralph O. Dunbar, and both prospered with offices in Yakima and Goldendale. Like his partner, Reavis won election to the Territorial Council in 1884, representing six eastern Washington counties. He was instrumental in changing a law concerning the taxing of railroads and in gaining authorization to establish a school for "defective" children in Vancouver, Washington. In 1886 he was nominated for territorial governor, but the appointment went to Watson C. Squire. The future jurist, always interested in education, served as a regent of the University of Washington for two years and was on the Yakima school board, where he had moved.

The Democrats nominated Reavis as one of their candidates for the supreme court in 1889, a year the Republican slate swept to victory. Reavis received 24,539 votes, well behind the 32,686 votes given his closest Republican rival, Theodore

Stiles. In 1896 the Fusionists—a coalition of Democrats, Free Silver Republicans, and the Peoples' Party—nominated Reavis, and this time he won the election by 12,000 votes over Republican incumbent John P. Hoyt.

In 1902 the political tide turned, and Republican Hiram E. Hadley defeated Reavis by a substantial majority following a strenuous campaign. After he left the bench, Reavis's mental capacities declined. He occasionally acted quite violently. By 1909 his health had deteriorated to such a degree that he needed close supervision and was committed to the state mental hospital in Steilacoom, where he remained until his death three years later.

Several people have speculated on Reavis's health problems. Some believed they began when he lost his reelection bid. The physical strains of the campaign exhausted him and the defeat lowered his self esteem. But in 1903 his mental capacities remained high, as witnessed by his written analyses of important court cases. Others said that when he moved from Olympia to Tacoma and then to Seattle to start a new practice, financial difficulties weighed heavily. According to an acquaintance:

> In a business way Judge Reavis committed the mistake of not returning to his old home town of North Yakima, where he could immediately have resumed a large practice, for he stood well with all the people of central Washington. At his age he attempted to build up a business in communities where he was virtually a stranger; and the comparative failure of his effort produced a species of melancholy, which affected him during the last three years of his life.

Judge Reavis married Minnie Freeman of Nashville, Tennessee, in 1891. They had two children, a daughter and a son. The judge was active in the Odd Fellows, a charter member of the Washington State Bar Association, and an officer in the Christian Church. He also chaired the Yakima Chamber of Commerce before winning election to the supreme court.

Selected References

William Prosser, *History of the Puget Sound Country,* vol. 2 (1903), pp. 73-74; W. C. Wolfe, *Sketches of Washingtonians* (1906), p. 265; Washington State Bar Association *Proceedings* (1903), pp. 121-125, and (1912), pp. 188-189; C. S. Reinhart, *The History of the Supreme Court of the Territory and State of Washington* (n.d.), pp. 86-87.

John Sherman Robinson
January 11, 1937-May 21, 1951

Born: December 17, 1880
Mansfield, Ohio
University of Michigan, A.B. (1903)
Columbia Law School, LL.B. (1910)
Congregational
Died: October 9, 1951
Superior Court (1933)
President, Seattle Bar Association (1936)
Republican
Elected

John Sherman Robinson was born on a farm near Mansfield, Ohio. His father, Samuel, came to America from England at the age of four. His mother, Caroline Mattayaw, was a native of Baltimore, Maryland. His father went to the California gold fields in 1856, returning to Ohio to farm after eleven unproductive years searching for that fortune that eluded so many. John attended public schools in Mansfield and enrolled as an undergraduate at the University of Michigan where he received his A.B. degree in 1903. A star athlete in track and field, he excelled in the hurdles and, after an injury that plagued him throughout his life, switched successfully to the shot put. A student member of the athletic council, he captained the track team in his senior year.

Robinson became an instructor at the Michigan Military Academy in 1903. From 1904 to 1906 he served as principal of the Bessemer (Michigan) high school and superintended Bessemer schools in 1906-1907. In the fall of 1907 Robinson enrolled in Columbia Law School, graduating with an LL.B. in 1910, serving as associate editor of the *Columbia Law Review* in his third year. Immediately after graduation the future judge located in Seattle to begin his professional career. Within three years he formed a partnership with Ira Bronson; H. B. Jones joined a year later. In 1928 he became a member of the firm of Harroun, Robinson, Malloy, and Shidler. Robinson specialized in admiralty law, and served as counsel for the United States Emergency Fleet Corporation, Port of Seattle, and Puget Sound Pilots' Association.

Apparently, Robinson had been a serious contender for an anticipated new position on the federal bench for the State of Washington in 1930. However, Congress never authorized the position. Still seeking a place on the bench,

Robinson challenged King County Superior Court incumbent Otis Brinker. The Seattle bar backed Robinson, and he gave Brinker a close race, losing by only 223 votes. In 1933 Governor Clarence Martin appointed Robinson to one of four newly created superior court positions for King County. Salaries of the new judges were to be paid from court case fees, but the supreme court invalidated that fee system. Consequently, the state voided the four new positions and Robinson, along with his three colleagues, served only six weeks. Again, Robinson was frustrated in his attempt to sit on the bench.

With Democrats in power, it appeared unlikely that even an inactive Republican could gain a court appointment, so Robinson filed for the supreme court upon hearing of John R. Mitchell's intention to retire. Robinson's presidency of the Seattle Bar Association in 1936 and active participation in state bar affairs assured him the profession's support. Robinson led the field among the six candidates in the September primary. In the November election he defeated William R. Bell by nearly 80,000 votes. Coincidentally, Robinson handily defeated each of his subsequent opponents—Don Abel and Robert Finley—in 1942 and 1948, although both later became members of the supreme court. In 1948 Robinson had the distinction of being the only incumbent supported by the bar.

Judge Robinson was clearly of the "old school" of jurisprudence. His dissent in the 1938 decision of *Murphy's Estate* has been described as "typical of. . . Robinson's preference for just and fair results, and his refusal to be bound by legalistic principles which, too strictly applied, lead to harmful results." Indeed, Robinson held doubts about how modern judges went about their business:

> Mr. Murphy was a very able lawyer of the old school, accustomed to arrive at decisions by the studious application of sound legal principles to the matter at hand. We of the current vintage employ a semi-mechanical method. Trained under the case system, we have set up long, long rows of compartments and labelled pigeon holes and, when a given situation is presented, we run along these pigeon holes until we find one in which cases that appear similar have formerly been filed, and, having found it, straightway thrust the instant matter in, and thus our decision is made. This, I think, is what occurred in this case.

A number of law reviews favorably cited the dissent.

Judge Robinson had difficulty later in his tenure in completing his assigned opinions. The legislature had mandated that salaries be withheld from judges more than six months behind in their assigned opinions. In 1949 the state held back Judge Robinson's April salary for a few weeks while he completed his opinions. Robinson's problem developed from his thoroughness rather than from any lack of energy. A 1943 case illustrated his concern for completeness:

> In the hope of finding a more exact measure, we have made a comprehensive survey of the authorities. The encyclopedias, textbooks in tort and damages, the legal periodicals, and the case law of England and our own sister states have all been thoroughly examined.

John Rupp, one of the first law clerks hired in 1937, recalled "Robbie's" personality and decisional habits:

> I never knew anyone who disliked Judge Robinson – he was always fair minded and very wise and witty. I learned a lot from him and always had a good time learning it.
>
> Judge Robinson's sin, if one can call it that, was that he did not organize his workload well. My father told me that had been true of him as a practicing lawyer. "Robbie," said Dad, "will work eighteen hours a day on a matter that interests him and he will do a brilliant job of it. But while he's doing that, the ordinary routine work piles up until he gets a backlog that just weighs him down. And a lot of it never gets done." He had the same trouble on the bench. A case would intrigue him, and he would work on nothing else for two weeks. Or he would devote a whole week of constant work in preparing a dissenting opinion, while the cases in which he was to write the majority opinion would remain unattended. He wrote excellent opinions, but he was always chronically behind in his work.

Judge Robinson, relatively conservative regarding economic issues and criminal appeals, was also consistently restraintist in those cases which brought the court into a confrontation with the legislature or which dealt with controversial political issues.

At age seventy, after fourteen years on the supreme court, Judge Robinson announced his retirement effective May 21, 1951. He and his wife remained in Olympia. A little more than four months after his retirement, Judge Robinson suffered a heart attack and died on October 9, 1951.

On June 22, 1916, Robinson married Edith J. Lind of Tacoma, stepdaughter of superior court Judge W. O. Chapman. Edith graduated from Ellensburg Normal School and taught in Olympia. Active in a number of charitable and civic organizations, she was an authority on early American glass. The couple had three sons: John Jr., Sam, and Irving.

Robinson belonged to the Seattle College Club, Seattle and Broadmoor Golf Clubs, Rainier Club, and Phi Delta Phi and Alpha Delta Phi fraternities. His hobbies were golf and gardening.

Selected References

See the John Robinson, Jr. oral history interview in supreme court collection, Washington State Archives; H. James Boswell, *American Blue Book: Western Washington* (1922), p. 129; memorial services, *Washington Reports*, vol. 45, 2d (1952), pp. xxi-xxv; Lloyd Spencer and Lancaster Pollard, *A History of the State of Washington*, vol. 3 (1937), pp. 364-365; and C. H. Hanford, *Seattle and Environs*, vol. 3 (1924), pp. 252-253.

Milo Adelbert Root
January 19, 1905-December 2, 1908

Born: January 22, 1863
Wyanet, Illinois
Albany Law School, LL.B. (1883)
Congregational
Died: January 10, 1917
Probate Judge (1887-1890)
Prosecuting Attorney (1893-1897)
Republican
Appointed

Milo Root was born in a small town in north-central Illinois to William H. and Sarah Cordelia (Holroyd) Root. When Milo was thirteen the family moved to Albion, New York, where he attended high school. The future judge enrolled in Albany Law School and, graduating at age twenty in 1883, immediately headed west to Olympia. Root worked as a lumber camp laborer and taught school in Elma for a term while waiting to reach age twenty-one and become eligible for admission to the bar. Upon admittance in 1884, Root opened a law office in Olympia and in 1888 formed a partnership with future supreme court jurist John R. Mitchell.

Root served two terms as Thurston County Probate Judge (1887-1890) and twice won election as Thurston County Prosecuting Attorney (1893-1897). He participated in commercial and civic affairs while in Olympia, serving on the Olympia board of trade and as first vice president of the Olympia Young Men's Christian Association. In 1897 he moved to Seattle to open an office in partnership with former supreme court Justice John P. Hoyt. Later he became the senior partner in Root, Palmer, and Brown.

While in Seattle, Root involved himself minimally in Republican politics but devoted considerable time to civic affairs. He became the first president of the Seattle Civic Union, president of the Washington Society of Charities and Corrections, and a member of the Sons of the American Revolution and the Masons. He was also a member of "several secret societies" and a "trustee in several charity and benevolent organizations."

Judge Root married Anna Evelyn Lansdale in 1890 and they had five daughters and one son. The Roots belonged to the Congregational Church.

When the legislature expanded the supreme court membership from five to seven in 1905, Root notified Governor Albert E. Mead of his availability:

> I am informed that there is likelihood of a law being enacted increasing the membership of the Supreme Court... The matter of my being a candidate for one of the appointments has been kindly suggested. But until about ten days ago I did not decide to ask for one of the appointments. Thus I told Mr. Palmer and Mr. Brown, my partners, that I would like the appointment... if it could be had without a scramble or unseemly effort on my part. So I now repeat the same statement to you.

Root had considerable support. Various endorsements described him as "a man among men," a "conscientious, public-spirited man," "above reproach," "an advocate of clean politics." Walter Beals, who later sat on the supreme court, wrote that "Judge Root is particularly the friend of the young lawyer, freely placing his large knowledge and experience at the service of the younger members of the bar here." Governor Mead, himself an attorney, knew of Root's abilities. Geographical considerations weighed heavily with the governor when he selected Root from Seattle for one position and Herman D. Crow from Spokane for the other.

Judge Root's promising career took an abrupt turn downward in 1908 with a legal dispute involving the Great Northern Railway Company. Root, along with a majority of the court, sided with the claimant in a suit against the railroad. The court denied a petition for rehearing, but in a brief, unsigned *per curiam* decision Judge Root modified some aspects of the original ruling, apparently upon the request of M. J. Gordon, attorney for the railroad. This allowed the railroad to avoid similar liability claims in the future. To some observers something seemed amiss when a denial of a petition for a rehearing resulted in a modification favorable to the railroad. Judge Root requested that Chief Justice Hiram Hadley appoint an investigating committee to clarify the situation and stifle the many rumors circulating in the legal community. The state bar association agreed to review the matter. However, before it appointed a committee, Judge Root submitted his resignation to Governor Mead, effective immediately. Only two months earlier Root had won nomination for another six-year term and on November 3 voters had reelected him.

Although Root's resignation came before the bar's committee reported, the judge gave his version of the situation in his letter of resignation:

> At different periods I have held the offices of probate judge, prosecuting attorney and judge of the supreme court. In each of these positions I have been attacked and have resisted attack successfully. My record has been finally approved by the people of this state by election to the high office with which I am now honored.
> But human nature has its limits of endurance. The final linking of my name with a scandal attached to a former justice of the supreme court who for years

has been a warm and, as I believed, a devoted friend of mine, is the culmination of a series of calamities.

My relations with Judge [Merritt] Gordon will bear the closest investigation and will reflect no more upon me than indiscretions of friendship. Yet I realize that for a justice of the supreme court there should exist not even an indiscretion; especially as I realize that any reflections upon any member casts a cloud upon the entire court; and I do not wish to be the means of casting any such cloud even in the slightest degree.

On January 7, 1909 the state bar association's special committee made its report:

We are constrained to conclude that the conduct of Judge Root...was a gross breach of judicial and professional propriety. Such conduct would be intolerable in practice and would lead to abuses almost as serious as would corruption itself. It has been characterized by Judge Root himself as an imprudence, but in our opinion it deserves much more severe characterization and shows such want to appreciation of duties of a judge of the supreme court as to unfit him from occupying that position.

On January 12, Milo Root again wrote the governor, laying out his response to the committee:

As I stated to the committee I now repeat, that my actions in that matter were solely on the view that the court should decide correctly a point of law. This was done, and the opinion in the case rendered which I believe then, and believe now, as sound law, and in this I believe I am supported by other judges and most of the lawyers in the state. I did not act from evil motive or for the purpose of giving one litigant an undue advantage over another. The case was decided against the railroad company both times...

Touching these matters, and all others criticized by the report, I desire to say emphatically that any mistake I made was one of the head and not of the heart. As a member of the court I always worked hard and endeavored to be fair and just to all parties, and I never rendered or assisted to render a decision that I did not honestly believe to be the law.

At its annual meeting the state bar association accepted the report of the investigating committee and passed a resolution referring the report to the grievance committee to "cause disbarment proceedings to be instituted against Milo A. Root, if in the judgment of said committee such proceedings can be successfully maintained." The grievance committee did not institute proceedings and the entire matter appeared to have been resolved and forgotten.

In the fall of 1916, Judge Root announced his intention to run for the King County Superior Court. Since leaving the high court, Root had devoted himself to legal and civic affairs in Seattle. He sat often as special judge on the trial bench, served as president of the Beacon Hill Improvement Club, was a trustee of the Washington Children's Home Society, and involved himself in the city's social life. Some elements of the legal profession threatened to bring out the 1908 affair again if Root filed for the superior court position. He refused to withdraw and the Seattle Bar Association voted to publish condemnation of his candidacy. The profession felt that the 1908 incident would "seriously impair his fitness as judge of the Superior Court of this county and would tend to bring the bench into disrepute." Root countered, claiming his resignation from the supreme court "was a mistake." The Seattle bar requested "the press of King County to publish the 1908 report," which it did. Judge Root lost the election.

In defense of Root, *The Seattle Legal News* claimed that corporate lawyers did not want to see Root return to the bench, for he had made powerful enemies:

> The opinion of Judge Root [against the railroads in *Smith v. St. Paul, Milwaukee and Minnesota Railway Company*] together with his decision upholding the eight hour law [*Normile v. Thompson*] and his decision holding that keeping a place for selling pools on horse races was prohibited by the gambling statutes [*State v. Shanklin*] and his decision against letting technicalities defeat substantial justice [*Douglas v. Badger St.*] and other similar decisions, may explain why certain "interests" did not want Judge Root to remain on the bench... Action[s] speak louder than words.

Whatever the motives of those who wanted Root removed from the judiciary and whatever his motives in dealing with M. J. Gordon, Root appeared to be a tragic figure caught up in affairs not of his making. In January 1917 shortly after his censure by the Seattle Bar Association, Judge Root passed away in Seattle from pleurisy and pneumonia.

Selected References

W. C. Wolfe, *Sketches of Washingtonians* (1906), p. 272; Washington State Bar Association *Proceedings* (1909), pp. 121-130; *Seattle Times*, 12 Jan. 1916 and 2 Nov. 1916; Charles Sheldon, *A Century of Judging: A Political History of the Washington Supreme Court* (1988), pp. 40, 44, 54-56, 217.

Hugh J. Rosellini
January 10, 1955-November 26, 1984

Born: June 16, 1909
Tacoma, Washington
College of Puget Sound (1927-1929)
University of Washington, LL.B. (1933)
Lutheran
Died: November 26, 1984
State House of Representatives (1939-1945)
Superior Court (1948-1954)
Democrat
Elected

Hugh J. Rosellini's father and mother were both born in Florence, Italy, although their families had lived for generations in the small agricultural village of Lucca in the Tuscany region. Hugh's father, Primo, arrived in America in 1898 at age fourteen and passed through Ellis Island to begin life in the new land. He obtained a job with the Northern Pacific Railroad in Chicago. Judge Rosellini recalled how his father worked up to a position of responsibility with the railroad: "They were building the railroad west. My dad could talk Italian and English so he eventually was taking care of payroll records for 400 Italians working on the railroad... He started with the railroad in Chicago, then progressed to the West Coast, ending up in Tacoma."

Rosellini's father quit the railroad when he arrived in Tacoma and went into what Hugh called the "saloon" business, owning St. Helen's Wine and Groceries. Primo Rosellini supplied all of the familiar Italian foods – in bulk – to the many Italians working on the railroad, in the mills, and in lumber camps. The saloon and store soon became the center of Italian social and political activities in Tacoma.

Hugh's mother, Cesarini Marchetti, emigrated from Italy with her family. Her father and brothers also found work with the railroad. Primo, who had not known Cesarini in Lucca, met her in Lakehead, a small train stop near Tacoma. Primo was nineteen and Cesarini sixteen when they married. Hugh was born June 9, 1909, in Tacoma, the eldest child in a family which later included a son, Primo Jr., and a daughter, Doris. As was the tradition – and to ease burdens on the young Cesarini – Hugh's grandparents raised him. He admitted they were not strict and tended to spoil him. However, both his parents and grandparents insisted that he become educated:

> My grandparents came from Italy... It's a place where you could escape your peasant status only by education. That and the ethic of working were drilled into me. You can't achieve anything unless you work hard for it. Education was of the highest priority. The old Italians had high ethics and values. You respected older people. You believed in a Supreme Being.

The grandparents spoke only Italian in the house, which caused some difficulties for Hugh when he began school. Not proficient in English, his predominantly Norwegian and Swedish classmates soon singled him out for taunts and teasing. On a number of occasions the future judge got into fights on the playfield during and after school. But under the tutelage of a devoted third grade teacher, Hugh learned his fractions, read advanced books, and was quickly promoted, skipping the fourth grade entirely. In 1922 he enrolled in St. Martin's High School in Lacey, near Olympia, where he learned, under the Benedictines, the discipline which became important in later college and law studies. An average student, he played on the school football and basketball teams. In the summers he worked in an Eatonville sawmill.

Orman Vertrees summed up Rosellini's formative years:

> A fighting pride in his Italian heritage coupled with a ferocious devotion to hard work, both manual and intellectual, characterized Hugh Rosellini's early years... [T]aunts of "Wop" and "Dago"... instilled a strong sympathy for the underdog and an aversion to invidious discrimination... His working class background further prepared him to accept New Deal Democratic politics and economic policies with open arms.

Young Rosellini enrolled at the College of Puget Sound, a Methodist institution in Tacoma, still unsure of his career goals. One particular incident, however, brought them into focus. Hugh was involved in an auto accident while driving his father's car, causing $400 in damages. A jury trial settled the issue of who was at fault, finding both drivers to be so. But the other driver had no money so Hugh's father paid all. Hugh, fascinated by the trial procedures and the lawyers' antics, decided to become a lawyer, and transferred to the University of Washington as a junior in 1929 at the onset of the depression.

During summers of those university years Hugh continued to work in the Eatonville mill; during the school months he lived with his grandparents. He took classes from Charles Horowitz, who later sat with Rosellini on the state supreme court. A classmate and old high school chum, Albert Rosellini, later became the governor of Washington. Although Al and Hugh were unrelated, they became fast friends, studied together, and talked politics. In 1933 Hugh graduated with his LL.B.

Passing the Washington bar exam proved easy compared to securing gainful employment during the winter of 1934 when the depression paralyzed business.

Interviews with law firms proved fruitless so he opened his own law office. Hugh gradually developed a general practice making ends meet with court-appointed clients. He subsequently rented office space in Tacoma from Harry Arnold Patterson at $25 a month, with Patterson providing secretarial assistance free of charge. Partisan politics soon occupied much of Rosellini's spare time.

Unemployment, the dislocations and deprivations of the Great Depression, and especially the anti-labor reactions of business and state government, thrust the future judge enthusiastically into Franklin Roosevelt's New Deal politics. He became active in the Young Democrats, joined the politically active Parkland Grange, the pro-labor Eagles, and campaigned for Democrats such as Homer Bone and Clarence Martin. In 1938 Hugh ran for the state house of representatives from Tacoma's Twenty-eighth District. With assistance from his wife, a skilled campaigner, as well as Democratic clubs, the Grange, and ethnic groups, Rosellini, campaigning door-to-door, defeated the incumbent by a few hundred votes. He used his own money and small contributions to fund the campaign, which totaled but a few hundred dollars. Although railroad workers endorsed him, labor generally ignored Rosellini. This later changed when virtually all labor groups supported the young legislator.

Rosellini quickly established himself as a supporter of programs promoted by the Grange, labor, Eagles, Old Age Pension Union, and the liberal Washington Commonwealth Federation. Throughout Rosellini's six-year legislative career he supported traditional liberal causes: adequate welfare programs for the truly needy, public housing and slum clearance, sufficient tax revenue to support public assistance programs begun in the depression, pro-labor legislation, public ownership of electric power, conservation measures, regulation of business, and civil rights. Vertrees summarized Rosellini's legislative experience:

> At the end of his seven-year legislative career in 1945, [Rosellini] could be described as a pro-labor, pro-environment, pro-education, pro-civil liberties liberal Democrat who at the same time could handle himself well in the muddy trenches of political warfare.

Rosellini, recognized for his leadership abilities, won a place on the powerful House Rules Committee. From that position he met on a regular basis with Governor Mon C. Wallgren and they became close political and personal friends.

Because the burdens of legislative affairs cut into his law practice, Rosellini did not file for another term after the 1945 session. Instead, he ran unsuccessfully for Pierce County Prosecutor. Thereafter, he settled into a sole law practice. However, when Judge Edward Hodge of the Pierce County Superior Court died early in 1948, Rosellini's friends urged Governor Wallgren to appoint the thirty-seven year old to the vacancy. On January 5, the governor did so and Rosellini began a judicial career that spanned thirty-six years.

Although a successful trial jurist, Rosellini decided to run for the state supreme court in 1950. Unknown in much of the state, he seemed to be embarking on an impossible task by filing against incumbent appointee Frederick Hamley. Rosellini said he had made the choice "because when you're young, anything seems possible." Governor Arthur Langlie's powerful Republican organization backed Hamley and, after Rosellini led in the primary, west-side newspapers and religious, Republican, and legal establishments rallied around the incumbent, turning the results of the September primary around. Judge Hamley defeated Rosellini in the statewide race by fewer than 10,000 votes. Judge Rosellini remembered that campaign for its bitterness and what he regarded as unfair and unethical tactics. Responding to allegations of his own unethical behavior, Rosellini wrote:

> In some campaigns malicious rumors are spread to discredit one candidate and this ensures the election of another... A Judge should be above such conduct. He should be just and fair even in the heat of a political race with his future at stake. It is my considered belief that a Judge should remain courteous in the face of political clamor and indifferent to partisan influences... "With Malice Toward None", I seek your vote.

Rosellini never forgot that campaign. In 1954 he tried again for a spot on the state's high bench. Chief Justice Thomas Grady, then seventy-four years old, withdrew from a reelection bid as only one year remained before the mandatory retirement law would force him to leave. Superior Court Judge Richard Ott from Adams County ran for the vacancy, facing Rosellini. Since only two candidates filed, the September primary would determine the winner. Labor and the Grange backed Rosellini and the legal establishment supported Ott. Relying on the name familiarity gained in 1950, Rosellini swamped Ott, 217,660 to 185,607. Rosellini would run unopposed in two of his remaining four supreme court reelection bids, and face only token opposition in the others.

Even before Rosellini wrote his first opinion, the media and the legal profession correctly regarded him as a liberal jurist. However, this did not isolate him from his conservative brethren. Until near the end of his long career on the state's high bench, the judge received more than his share of supporting votes when he wrote majority, concurring, or dissenting opinions. However, in the last ten years of his long tenure he tended to be less liberal and to dissent more often from the opinions of the majority. This shift was partly due to Rosellini's less liberal stand on some law and order issues – particularly search and seizure – and to the more liberal stance of the court itself.

With perhaps one exception, Rosellini remained a strong supporter of individual civil rights and a staunch backer of the state constitution's Declaration of Rights. That exception concerned Indian treaty rights affecting fishing, hunting, and taxation. Rosellini, an avid hunter and fisherman, disagreed with Judge George Boldt's decision declaring that Indians should receive at least one-half of the fishing harvest from traditional fishing grounds. Rosellini generally supported labor in labor-management issues; favored the government in government regulation and taxation cases; sided often with the underdog in housing, welfare, and workmen's compensation; and agreed with the plaintiff in tort cases.

Despite disagreements with the bench's more conservative members, Judge Rosellini provided stability and leadership. Judge Frank Hale, who served with Rosellini, recognized these traits in his colleague:

> [In conference] Hugh was always very pleasant. He liked to go to the blackboard and draw away. He'd lecture like a law professor. He'd draw boxes for the plaintiff and defendant and then draw big slashes when he'd come to a conclusion... He did this more than anyone else. Hugh would be a peacemaker if the judges did show personality splits. He would try to erase any acrimony.

Given Rosellini's years in public office, his easy-going manner, soft, unassuming voice, and polite old-world manners, it is not surprising that he played such a reconciling role.

Oral arguments, supplemented by queries from the judges, proved important to Justice Rosellini's deliberations. Along with the written briefs filed by the attorneys, oral arguments influenced his decisions more than the pre-hearing memos written by law clerks, conference discussions, or the circulation of draft opinions. When Rosellini dissented, as he did in nearly one-fourth of the cases during his later years on the bench, he saw his actions as vehicles to win more votes from his colleagues, to lay groundwork for future cases, and to improve the court's opinion.

While chief justice from 1965-1967, Rosellini served as chairman of the nationally recognized state bench-bar-press committee established to reconcile conflict between free press and fair trial rights. He also influenced the legislature to propose and the public to approve a court of appeals for the state. He served as a member of the judging panel for the Roscoe Pound hearing of the moot court honors program at UCLA in 1968 and mediated between the judiciary and the Alaska Bar Association during the writing of Alaska's *Code of Ethics*. He belonged to the American Judicature Society, served on the board of directors of the Tacoma Boy's Club, and in 1981 won the Pierce Chapter of the National Conference of Christians and Jews "Outstanding Citizen" award. He also belonged to the Elks, Moose, Eagles, and Grange. But perhaps most of all, Justice Rosellini loved fishing and hunting with old friends:

> [He worked] hard, but he played with the same enthusiasm he devoted to his work. His leisure hours were spent in pursuit of salmon and steelhead in Western Washington waters. He was an avid fly-fisherman, a duck and pheasant hunter, and he also enjoyed moose hunting in Canada. Justice Rosellini was a connoisseur of fine dogs, fine fish, fine game, and good cooking. He loved nothing more than freezing with his friends Bob Hunter and Jim Bates while they wet their lines and made sure many a big salmon or steelhead never got away.

The justice earned an intense loyalty from those who worked with him. His law clerk, Joanne Bailey Wilson, served as his assistant for twenty-six years. Rose Gittings was his administrative assistant for twenty-nine years.

Hugh married Yvonne Crissy, a ballet dancer and teacher, in 1938. They became parents of a son, Tracy, and two daughters, Gayle and Lynne. Yvonne died in September 1982 at the age of sixty-seven. A few weeks later the justice had triple bypass heart surgery. In October 1984 he submitted to more open-heart surgery, and died the next month, a few weeks from the end of his last term on the bench. He had served on the supreme court nearly thirty years, a term exceeded by only two other justices. The record of his judicial career is found in over 800 of his opinions published in fifty-seven volumes of the *Washington Reports*.

Selected References

Rosellini's oral history interview is in the supreme court collection, Washington State Archives. Also see Orman Vertrees, "Mr. Justice Hugh J. Rosellini: A Study of His Reference Groups and His Supreme Court Voting Behavior" (unpublished Ph.D. dissertation, Washington State University, 1986); *Seattle Times*, 29 Oct. 1978; *Seattle Post-Intelligencer*, 17 Jy. 1977; *Washington State Bar News* (Jan. 1984), p. 26; and memorial services, *Washington Reports*, vol. 103, 2d (1985), pp. xxviii-xlviii.

Frank H. Rudkin
January 10, 1905-February 14, 1911

Born: April 23, 1864
Vernon, Ohio
Washington and Lee University, B.L. (1886)
Catholic
Died: April 3, 1931
Superior Court (1901-1905)
U. S. District Court (1911-1923)
U. S. Court of Appeals (1923-1931)
Republican
Elected

Frank H. Rudkin was born in Trumbull County, Ohio, on the Pennsylvania border a few miles north of Youngstown. His parents, Bernard and Winnifred (Leonard) Rudkin, both natives of Ireland, had five sons and one daughter. Frank attended public schools in Trumbull County, then Washington and Lee University in Lexington, Kentucky, where he received a bachelor of law degree in 1886. The following year he moved to Washington and set up practice in Ellensburg and North Yakima. Rudkin developed an expertise in irrigation law, a specialty in considerable demand in that area. The Rudkin "golden rule" to which he adhered in his practice and in which he advised young attorneys was simple and direct: "Now you stay with your law and your evidence, and to hell with friends and foes."

Rudkin had been a Democrat all of his adult life until he split with the party in 1896 over the gold and free silver issue. Although not active in partisan politics, he steadfastly adhered to the tenets of the Republican party after that. He started his judicial career as a justice of the peace in Ellensburg. In 1900 he won election to the superior court bench as a Republican, with jurisdiction over Kittitas, Yakima, and Franklin counties. Again running on the Republican ticket, Rudkin won election to the supreme court in 1904, overwhelming his closest Democratic rival by nearly 48,000 votes. He was reelected in 1910.

While on the state supreme court Rudkin developed a reputation for bluntness, devotion to his profession, and conscientiousness. He was "systematic, and methodical in habit, sober and discreet in judgment, calm in temper [and] diligent in research."

Rudkin was the first Washington Supreme Court jurist appointed to the federal bench. Upon the recommendation of Senator Wesley Jones, President William Taft selected him to fill the 1911 vacancy on the United States District Court caused by the death of Edward Whitson. Again at the behest of Senator Jones, President Warren Harding elevated Rudkin to the Ninth Circuit Court of Appeals in 1923. A year later Rudkin was seriously considered for a vacancy on the United States Supreme Court created by the retirement of Justice Joseph McKenna. The *Seattle Times* speculated on the appointment:

> Repeated reports that Associate Judge Joseph McKenna plans soon to retire from the United States Supreme Court are now coupled with the prediction that Judge Frank H. Rudkin of Washington State will be promoted from the Ninth Circuit . . . to succeed him. Judge Rudkin is said to be highly regarded by his associates on the bench and by members of the bar, who would approve his selection for the highest court as a reward of merit.
>
> The President is not obligated to select a successor to Justice McKenna from the Pacific Coast or the Ninth Circuit, but it is generally believed that this section will be first considered. Justice McKenna was appointed from California.

Not only were McKenna and Rudkin from the West, both were also Irish Catholics. Nonetheless, President Calvin Coolidge turned to his attorney general, Harlan Fiske Stone, to replace McKenna. Rudkin became the presiding judge of the Ninth Circuit in 1931.

Judge Rudkin married Pearl A. Morford of North Yakima on October 3, 1903. After she died the judge married Ellen Rose Dotty in Spokane in 1921. Rudkin had one daughter, Monie. Upon his death in San Francisco in 1931, the *Seattle Daily Times* reported:

> Judge Rudkin was recognized by members of the bench [and] of [the] bar not only in the Northwest but throughout the nation as one of its leading jurists, and was frequently mentioned as a possible member of the United States Supreme Court. He was considered one of the most democratic members of the Federal Court, tolerant in his views and a keen student of the law.

Selected References

Washington State Bar Association *Proceedings* (1906), pp. 170-173; N. W. Durham, *History of Spokane and the Inland Empire*, vol. 2 (1912), pp. 267-268; C. W. Wolfe, *Sketches of Washingtonians* (1906), p. 273; C. S. Reinhart, *History of the Supreme Court of the Territory and State of Washington* (n.d.), p. 78.

Edgar Ward Schwellenbach
September 3, 1946-September 22, 1957

Born: March 16, 1887
Frederick, South Dakota
University of Wisconsin, LL.B. (1924)
Episcopalian
Died: September 22, 1957
City Attorney (1927-1935)
Prosecuting Attorney (1931-1939)
Superior Court (1939-1946)
Democrat
Elected/Appointed

Edward Ward Schwellenbach was born on March 16, 1887, in Frederick, a small farming community of 100 inhabitants in northeastern South Dakota, the son of Frank W. and Martha (Baxter) Schwellenbach. Edgar grew up in Wisconsin, served in the First World War, and lived a fairly complete and productive life before turning to the law as a profession. At the age of thirty-seven he graduated from the University of Wisconsin Law School. He immediately gained admittance to the Wisconsin bar, but moved to Seattle and passed the Washington bar in 1925. In 1926 he moved to Ephrata, beginning a long attachment to eastern Washington and the Columbia Basin.

"Ed" Schwellenbach's public career began in 1927 when he became Ephrata City Attorney. In 1930 voters elected him prosecuting attorney for Grant County and he won reelection in 1934. During his first term he distinguished himself as a thorough and vigorous prosecutor and competent trial lawyer. During his second term he assumed a leading role in promoting the development of Grand Coulee Dam and securing continued appropriations. He appeared twice before the U. S. Supreme Court and won a legal battle to require Grand Coulee Dam contractors to pay personal property taxes on their equipment to hard-pressed Grant County. His brother, Louis B. Schwellenbach—senator, Secretary of Labor, and federal judge—shared with him these exciting times both for Democrats and the Columbia Basin.

When Judge Clyde Jeffers won election to the state supreme court, Governor Clarence Martin appointed Schwellenbach to fill Jeffers's vacancy on the superior court. He served as a trial judge for seven years, from 1939 to 1946, surprising many critics who had not expected someone with Schwellenbach's background as a prosecutor and partisan politician to remain objective once on the bench.

Early in the summer of 1946 Judge Bruce Blake announced his intention to leave the high bench in September, enticing Schwellenbach and Tom Grady to file for the vacancy. Schwellenbach turned back Grady's challenge by 188,296 to 106,187 votes in the primary, leaving him unopposed in the general election. Because of his Democratic party credentials, Governor Mon Wallgren selected Schwellenbach to begin his official supreme court duties early in September upon Blake's retirement.

While a member of the supreme court, Schwellenbach wrote 279 opinions. Judge Charles Donworth, citing two of the Schwellenbach's landmark decisions— *Adkisson v. Seattle* and *Owens v. Scott Publishing Company*—noted that these opinions showed the judge:

> possessed to a marked degree the ability to view the legal problems involved in a case with the utmost objectivity. He had the inherent sense of justice springing from a high sense of moral integrity. His adherence to the applicable rules of law as he interpreted them was unwavering, yet he was always tolerant of the views of those who disagreed with him.

Justice Schwellenbach's decisional style included a vigorous give-and-take with his law clerk. He wanted an independent clerk not reluctant to express disagreement. The justice once told a clerk he was being "paid to disagree." One former clerk described his close decisional relationship with the judge:

> My judge treated me as a junior partner. Although the ultimate form of the opinion was his responsibility, nevertheless, he relied heavily on my assistance and utilized my abilities to the utmost.
>
> The judge would read the trial court record while I briefed the law. Then he wrote a rough draft which I would redraft. Then we would argue back and forth... We swore and sweated and argued and swore some more, but in the end we were both proud of his opinions.

Schwellenbach headed the court during the critical years between 1948 and 1952. The court had been split by several acrimonious elements, and its image had suffered substantially with the public and members of the profession. As chief justice, Schwellenbach restored a sense of common purpose to the court. He conducted an unprecedented statewide "tour" for its members and their wives, meeting with the public and contacting attorneys. Judge Charles Donworth also recognized the social role that Schwellenbach assumed on the court: "He was always ready to interrupt his own work to discuss with other members of the Court their judicial problems. His suggestions were most helpful, because they were frank and forthright expressions of his own views."

As might be anticipated, Judge Schwellenbach retained his New Deal views while on the court. He was relatively liberal in decisions concerning criminal law, government regulation, and civil rights. However, he did not aggressively pursue a liberal solution to legal issues. He was, generally, neutral in his attitude toward the desirability of judicial intervention in political, social, and economic issues brought to the court.

Schwellenbach won reelection to the high court in 1952 without opposition and led the judicial ticket in total votes. In early September 1957, the judge entered a Seattle hospital for minor surgery but failed to recover. He died on September 22, 1957 of a pulmonary ailment.

Schwellenbach married Ethel Hoagland of Wisconsin in June 1918. They had a son, Baxter Ward, and a daughter, Martha Iverson. The judge belonged to Forty-and-Eight, the American Legion, Scottish Rite Masons, Phi Delta Phi, and the Episcopalian Church.

Selected References

Memorial services, *Washington Reports,* vol. 52, 2d (1958), pp. xxv-xxxiii; C. W. Taylor, *Eminent Judges and Lawyers of the Northwest* (1954), p. 55; Charles Sheldon, *A Century of Judging: A Political History of the Washington Supreme Court* (1988), pp. 101, 112, 293-303.

Elmon Scott
November 22, 1889-January 1, 1899

Born: November 6, 1853
Isle La Motte, Vermont
Died: August 31, 1921
City Attorney (1878-1881)
Pomeroy Mayor
Republican
Elected

Elmon Scott was born on a small island in Lake Champlain, the eldest of four children. In 1864, at the age of eleven, he moved with his family to a farm in Chester, south-central Michigan. Scott attended common schools, high school, and an academy in the district, and worked on a farm during summers. He began to read the law on his own while on the farm and in 1875 joined a law office in Charlotte, Michigan, to read under the supervision of a licensed attorney. The Michigan bar admitted him in 1877 and he served as city attorney for Charlotte from 1878 to 1881.

In October 1881 Scott headed west with an immigrant wagon train, $200 in his pocket. He worked on a farm near Boise, Idaho, drove an ox team in Walla Walla, Washington, and finally, upon hearing that a cousin lived in Pomeroy, moved there to open a law office in January 1882. He married Eleanor McBrearty in Pomeroy the same year. They had four children, two boys and two girls.

Voters elected Scott mayor of Pomeroy for two terms. In 1889 the Republican party placed him on its ticket in an effort to see southeastern Washington represented on the state supreme court. At that time, the *Seattle Times,* an unyielding supporter of Republican candidates, reported:

> Mr. Scott is regarded by members of the bar of the first judicial district as one of the safest lawyers among them, whose opinions are sound and his points always well fortified by authorities. He is not an advocate, but his turn of mind is eminently judicial. It is believed he will prove a learned and impartial judge.

It appeared from the paper's lukewarm endorsement of Scott that he was a legal and political unknown. Actually, he had been prominent in southeast

Washington politics. For example, in the spring of 1889 there was a special election for three delegates to the constitutional convention. The Republicans nominated Scott, but Republican Samuel Cosgrove, later to be elected governor, chose to run as a delegate under an independent label, defeating Scott. Later, in the election for the first slate of state officials in 1889, the Republicans, angry at Cosgrove's earlier repudiation of the party, chose Scott as their candidate for the supreme court, although Cosgrove had hoped for the nomination.

In October, Scott won election as one of the first judges and, at thirty-six, the youngest, on the high bench. His 33,800 votes gave him a comfortable margin of 9,224 over the nearest Democratic rival. As required by the new constitution, the five justices drew lots to determine the length of terms. Judge Thomas Anders and Scott got the three-year positions. In 1892 the Republican convention again nominated Scott and he won reelection to a full six-year term by a margin of 6,631 votes over the closest Democrat.

Perhaps Judge Scott's most readable, if not notable, opinion was his ringing dissent in the "Opium Den Case" of 1890:

> It is the one great principle of our form of government expressed throughout that soul-inspiring document, our national constitution, that the individual right of self control is not to be limited, only to that extent which is necessary to promote the general welfare... When one becomes a member of society he necessarily parts with some rights or privileges which, as an individual, not affected by his relations to others, he might retain.
>
> A body politic is a social compact by which the whole people covenants with each citizen, and each citizen with the whole people, that all shall be governed by certain laws for the common good. This does not confer power upon the whole people to control rights which are purely and exclusively private.

The courts must have a right of review or control; Scott believed there were limits to government intrusion into private behavior and the courts were primarily responsible for establishing these limits, actions of the legislature notwithstanding.

During his nearly ten years on the state's high bench, the older and more experienced men on the court overshadowed Judge Scott. In rare instances, like his dissent in the Opium Den Case, he could rise to an occasion, but most of the time he appeared satisfied to accommodate his personal views to the majority. He wrote slightly fewer than the average number of majority opinions and dissented infrequently. He agreed more with Judge Anders than with any other court members. He tended to acquiesce to the legislative version when the court confronted a constitutional question regarding the validity of a law. As a restraintist, he often joined Judge Ralph Dunbar in the few constitutional questions appealed to the high bench.

In 1890 Scott moved his family from Pomeroy to Whatcom County near what later became Bellingham. After retiring from the supreme court in 1899 at age forty-six, he practiced law in Bellingham. He won acquittal in a much-publicized trial for statutory rape in 1901 in Bellingham and continued to have a successful legal practice until 1920. That year he moved to Seattle and then San Francisco, where he died in 1921.

Selected References

Seattle Times, 12 Sept. 1889; C. S. Reinhart, *History of the Supreme Court of the Territory and State of Washington* (n.d.), p. 85; Charles Sheldon and Michael Stohr-Gillmore, "In the Beginning: The Washington Supreme Court a Century Ago," *University of Puget Sound Law Review,* vol. 12 (1989), pp. 247-284; Sheldon, "Then There Were Five: The First Washington Supreme Court," *De Novo,* vol. 3 (1989), pp. 1, 3, 6.

Morell Edward Sharp
May 28, 1970-January 11, 1971;
May 13, 1971-December 17, 1971

Born: September 12, 1920
Portland, Oregon
University of Oregon, B.A. (1942)
Northwestern University School of Law,
  LL.B. (1948)
Episcopalian
Died: October 19, 1980
Beaux Arts Councilman and Mayor
  (1952-1962)
Superior Court (1967-1970)
Consultant, U. S. Attorney General (1971)
Federal District Court (1971-1980)
Republican
Appointed (twice)

Born in Portland, Oregon, Morell E. Sharp attended public schools there and graduated from the University of Oregon in 1942. World War II interrupted his education when the army commissioned him and sent him to the Pacific theater. He served as company commander and later became regimental adjutant. He attained the rank of captain.

After the war Sharp enrolled at Northwestern University School of Law in Chicago, receiving his LL.B. in 1948. While in law school he belonged to Phi Delta Phi and was president of the student bar association, as well as a member of its board of governors. Following graduation he became counsel for the Milwaukee Railroad in Illinois. After two years in Illinois, the company assigned him to Seattle. In 1956 he left the railroad and went into private practice with the firm of Williams, Kinnear, and Sharp and then with Graham, Dunn, Johnston, and Rosenquist.

Sharp became active in the Republican party soon after moving to Seattle. He served as councilman and mayor of Beaux Arts, a small town east of Seattle, and presided over the Young Republicans of King County. In that capacity he met Daniel Evans, who would later be instrumental in Sharp's appointments to both the state and federal benches. Sharp remembered the first time he met Evans:

> [I was] president of the King County Young Republicans. The King County Republican headquarters called me one day. They said they had this young man who had just been discharged from the navy and he was interested in politics and they're going to send him over [for me] to talk with him. I remember Dan coming into the office and so, obviously, we put him to work immediately.

Although not close personal friends, Sharp and Evans became partisan allies. When King County got a new judgeship in 1967, Governor Evans appointed Morell Sharp. After only a few years on the trial bench, he became chairman of the superior court's juvenile committee and served on the executive committee of the King County Judges' Association. He was also a delegate to the National Conference of State Trial Judges, and served with the supreme court's liaison committee contemplating reforming the judicial article of the state constitution.

When supreme court Justice Frank P. Weaver resigned in 1970, Evans wanted to appoint his administrative assistant, James Dolliver, to the post. However, because of considerable resistance from the state bar association, Evans turned to Morell Sharp to fill the Weaver vacancy. Almost immediately after being sworn in, superior court Judge Charles T. Wright filed against Sharp in the upcoming supreme court election. With but the two on the ballot, the September primary would decide the outcome.

Judge Sharp had the strong backing of the Seattle-King County and Washington State Bar Associations as well as the vast majority of his superior court colleagues. The Republican party organization also helped and Governor Evans endorsed him, but to no avail. Judge Wright prevailed in the primary by more than 12,000 votes. Sharp's defeat could be attributed to a number of factors. Many, including Sharp, thought the voters confused Judge Charles Wright with popular Judge Eugene Wright, who had been on the King County Superior Court before his appointment to the federal circuit court. Labor and the Grange also worked for Wright. Finally, Judge Wright simply proved a more attractive campaigner. Judge Sharp appeared reluctant to throw himself into a public campaign. In any case, after only a few months on the state's high bench, Sharp was returned to private life.

Through his acquaintance with White House Counsel John Ehrlichman, Judge Sharp won appointment as special consultant to the U. S. Attorney General's special committee on the study of crime. He remained in that capacity until another opportunity to return to the appellate bench presented itself. This occurred when Justice Walter McGovern moved up to the federal district bench. Upon receiving the list of bar-approved candidates (which continued to include Sharp) Governor Evans promptly returned him to the supreme court. Sharp took his second oath of office a few days short of four months after having been rejected by the voters and forced to leave. The governor did not apologize for returning the judge to the bench. He said "he had no problems" with the reappointment. He continued to believe Sharp well-qualified. Sharp felt that his defeat to Wright had been due to special factors and did not constitute a rejection by the electorate. He said he "wanted to get back on the bench" and readily accepted the appointment.

Within a short time, a federal bench opening became available, and with Republican Richard Nixon in the White House, Evans recommended Sharp for the appointment. On December 17, 1971, only a year after having lost at the ballot box and a few months after his second appointment, Sharp resigned to take his oath as a federal district judge for western Washington.

Although Justice Sharp had a short tenure on the state supreme court, he left clues about his approach to appellate review. He tended to take a collective approach to decisional matters. Informal discussions worked best for him in explaining his opinions and bringing others over to his view. Comments on the passing sheets and discussions with a justice who in turn might pass comments on to a third judge indicated his collective perspective. Persuasion was his practice. His personal decisional style relied on an interesting balance between common sense and the more tangible legal factors more often associated with a trial judge than a member of a court of last resort. Sharp evaluated the facts of the case based upon his own knowledge of the law and his feeling for what was right. Then he searched for appropriate precedent to confirm his tentative conclusions. These bases for decision prevailed over information found in the attorneys' briefs or their oral arguments, the views of his brethren on the bench, and the research his law clerks provided.

Sharp believed dissents should be used to "lay the groundwork for the future." He regarded himself as a moderate concerning policy issues confronting the supreme court.

One of his former law clerks recalled:

> If anything characterized the atmosphere in the Judge's courtroom, it was his sense of humor. We remember fondly the Judge's warm but pointed wit, his wry smile, and that mischievous twinkle in his eyes; his ability to leaven serious matters with a touch of humor endeared him to us all...[However] working with the Judge was a nonstop seminar in trial conduct and strategy. We learned the value of careful and thoughtful trial preparation.

Two of his most important cases while on the federal bench concerned litigation arising from the construction of the Seattle Kingdome and the trial on racketeering charges against Pierce County Sheriff George Janovich and seven others. The U. S. Court of Appeals for the Ninth Circuit affirmed the conviction of the defendants in the Pierce County case.

Judge Sharp participated actively in a variety of court reform groups. He was a founding director of the National Center for State Courts, served on the board of editors of the journal of the American Bar Association, was a fellow of the American Bar Foundation, and a director of the American Judicature Society. His fellow judges in the Ninth Circuit chose him to be their representative at the Judicial Conference of the United States, an indication of the esteem in which they held him.

Morell and Betty Sharp were parents of two children, Laurie and John. The family was a central focus of Judge Sharp's life. Cross-country skiing, Boy Scout trips, canoe expeditions, and camping trips always involved one or another member of the family.

The judge was ill for a considerable time in late 1979 and early 1980. Surgery failed to remove a growth in his brain, and after several months of suffering he passed away on October 19, 1980.

Selected References

Memorial proceedings, *Federal Supplement,* vol. 499 (1980), pp. lvii-lxxxviii; *Seattle Times,* 22 Apr. 1979; *Seattle Post-Intelligencer,* 21 Oct. 1980. Also see Sharp's oral history interview, supreme court collection, Washington State Archives.

George Barton Simpson
September 20, 1937-January 6, 1951

Born: August 12, 1881
Pomeroy, Washington
Willamette University (1905-1906)
Willamette Law School, LL.B. (1907)
Methodist
Died: June 21, 1954
City Attorney (1915-1917)
Superior Court (1921-1937)
State Highway Commission (1951-1954)
Democrat
Appointed

George Barton Simpson was born in the small eastern Washington farming community of Pomeroy, the eldest of nine children of Thomas K. and Mary Ellen (Barton) Simpson, who farmed in that dryland area. When George was six the family moved a few miles north to Whitman County where the children attended public schools in Tekoa. In 1905, after Simpson graduated from Tekoa High School, the family moved to Salem, Oregon. George enrolled as an undergraduate at Willamette University where he excelled on the athletic field as well as in the classroom. With lawyering as his goal, he moved on to Willamette's law department and graduated with his LL.B. in 1907. Both Washington and Oregon admitted Simpson to the practice of law that year. In October, 1907 he opened an office in Vancouver, Washington, and coached the Vancouver High School football team in his spare time.

On August 8, 1911, Judge Simpson married Anita Norelius and the couple became parents to a daughter, Carol, and a son, Donald. Simpson, nominally active in Democratic politics, ran once for county prosecutor, but lost by forty-five votes. However, he won election as Vancouver City Attorney and served three terms. He was also active in the bar, serving as president of the Clark-Skamania counties association for three terms. Simpson was elected superior court judge for Clark-Skamania counties in 1920 and reelected three times, serving nearly seventeen years. His experience with juvenile matters while on the trial bench reinforced his deep concern for the problems of youth.

Simpson had applied for an appointment to the high bench when Judge Adam Beeler retired, but Governor Roland Hartley sought a Republican who could help him in his reelection effort in the more populated areas of the state. Finally,

Governor Clarence Martin, looking for a conservative Democrat, found an ideal candidate in Simpson and appointed him to the supreme court in 1937.

Simpson served twice as chief justice and was largely responsible for drafting a revision and compilation of the rules of court. With typical thoroughness, he examined the rules of virtually all state courts of last resort in preparing the draft. The resulting volume contained not only rules on appeals, but also rules for trial courts, canons of ethics, and regulations on bar admission and discipline.

During Judge Simpson's thirteen years on the supreme court he authored 362 opinions. Although always solid in his research, observers did not regard him as a creative legal scholar. He proved conservative in matters of government regulation and labor union activity. For example, in 1946 Simpson wrote an angry if not intemperate dissent, branding the federal Office of Price Administration (OPA) as a "tyrant and outlaw" that "sears, burns and destroys all it touches." The OPA had survived, in his view, only because of its "propaganda department."

In the same year, Simpson lashed out at the Communist threat to America. He warned citizens against "the inroads [Communists] are making into our way of life." Communist propaganda was "insidious, sinister and of alarming proportions... Even now [it] is seeking control of our government as a silent minority."

Judge Charles Donworth remembered one of Simpson's leading opinions upon the occasion of the court's memorial to their former colleague:

> Perhaps the most important case written by him was the unanimous *En Banc* decision in Tucker v. Brown...which is a treatise on the law of trusts. The opinion comprises 142 printed pages.... The opinion...disposed of seventy-seven legal contentions as to the various items of property and the complicated accounting problems involved and applied the applicable principles of the law of trusts.

One former law clerk recalled that Simpson was "his own man" who worked and played hard. Not given to compromising or forging majorities in troublesome cases, he was more concerned with expressing his own views than winning over others. Simpson's work schedule impressed another clerk:

> Judge Simpson was as hard a working judge in his era of any I knew. When he was writing opinions he worked night and day to get the job done. In most cases he would finish his work load weeks ahead of any other judge and prior to the next session of the Court. He at that point would go fishing and lend me to another judge to assist him in his work... With Judge Simpson I research[ed] and argued but never wrote the decision.

The judge remained somewhat aloof from his clerks and was not one to be "lobbied" by other judges, although he often consulted informally with like-minded colleagues such as Clyde Jeffers, John Robinson, and William Steinert. Simpson was very reluctant to uphold a challenge to the constitutionality of a legislative act. Precedent became his overriding measure of a correct decision. In general, Judge Simpson was one of the leading conservative-restraintists on the modern supreme court.

Simpson, Steinert, and Jeffers had all talked of leaving the high bench before the 1950 elections in order to take advantage of the new retirement law. But, as primary campaign time neared, Simpson decided to seek reelection and resign when he neared mandatory retirement age, thereby allowing the governor to appoint his successor. Since he had run unopposed in his two previous elections he did not anticipate opposition for his final term. However, Robert C. Finley filed against Simpson and, with labor and Grange backing, presented a formidable challenge. Finley had taken Judge Robinson to the November election in 1948 and had a campaign organization in place. In contrast, Judge Simpson had to build a campaign from the bottom up and his name had not been before the public to any great extent since his appointment. The Seattle Bar Association endorsed Simpson over Finley, as did virtually all other county bars. However, Simpson faced a disadvantage because of Finley's name recognition and active campaigning. Voters may have also confused Finley with the highly popular King County Superior Court Judge Howard Findlay. In any event, Finley trounced Simpson by more than 30,000 votes in the primary.

Simpson returned to Vancouver to practice law but remained quite bitter about his defeat. He felt the legal profession failed to give him the financial and organizational support he needed, and that he had been unfairly attacked by labor as well as the Catholic Church.

Simpson returned to public life when Governor Arthur Langlie appointed him to the state highway commission in 1951. Both prior and subsequent to donning the robes of judicial office, George Simpson participated in affairs concerned with youth. He was instrumental in organizing the St. Helens Council of Boy Scouts and the Vancouver Playground Association and was an active member of the Washington Children's Home. In addition, he served in many offices of the Elks, Masons, Kiwanis, and Chamber of Commerce. For his many civic activities, services, and commitment to youth, Judge Simpson received the Boy Scouts of America Silver Beaver award, the 1948 citation from the Washington Children's Home for "outstanding contributions to the care of homeless children," and the Vancouver Senior Citizen award of 1939.

Although Judge Simpson's health was failing, he continued to lead an active life. He maintained a full schedule with the highway commission, while fishing and golf filled his few spare hours. He succumbed to a heart attack in early summer of 1954 at the age of seventy-two.

Selected References

See Donald Simpson's oral history interview, supreme court collection, Washington State Archives; memorial services, *Washington Reports,* vol. 46, 2d (1955), pp. xxv-xxx; memorial services, Clark-Skamania Bar Association *Superior Court, Clark County* (31 May 1958), pp. 108.

Charles Zellender Smith

July 18, 1988-

Born: February 23, 1927
Lakeland, Florida
Florida A & M (1946-1947)
Temple University, B.S. (1952)
University of Washington, J.D. (1955)
American Baptist
Law Clerk (1955)
Deputy Prosecutor (1956-1961)
Special Assistant to U. S. Attorney General
    (1961-1964)
Municipal Court (1965)
Superior Court (1966-1973)
Law Professor (1973-1983)
Republican
Appointed

Governor Booth Gardner's appointment of Charles Z. Smith to the supreme court in the summer of 1988 was unique. First, the Democratic governor crossed over to appoint someone from the opposing party, something rarely done. Second, Judge Smith, an African American, became the first ethnic minority placed on the state's high court. Gardner hoped that from an expected middle position, Justice Smith could bring the sharply divided court closer together.

Upon his appointment, the new justice stated that he had "a mediator-conciliator type of personality," and since he knew each of the eight other justices well, he believed he could help in "reestablishing the collegiality of the court." One news account of the appointment reiterated the need for such a role:

> Now, as Governor Booth Gardner's choice Wednesday as the newest justice of the Supreme Court, [Smith] has the potential to bring a new level of balance and direction to a high court that regularly produces decisions on its toughest cases by a 5-4 margin. The closeness of tough votes has led to concern among some lawyers that the state's legal system is without a clear sense of direction.

Although his exuberant but pleasant personality indicated he could bridge ideological divisions, his varied experience suggested a strong concern for the unfortunate, underprivileged, and persecuted which would perhaps make him feel more at ease with liberal justices.

Gardner considered six strong candidates to replace Justice William Goodloe, who resigned after serving a little more than three years of his six-year term. Upon leaving, Goodloe recommended to the governor that a minority person, preferably a Democrat from eastern Washington, be selected as his replacement.

The governor had no obligation to heed the retiring justice's advice, but blacks from Washington had served on the federal bench for a number of years and it was clearly past time for them to represent the state's high bench. A Seattle Republican, Charles Smith may not have been the obvious choice, but his breadth of experience dictated the appointment.

Because of the unwritten rule in the early 1950s that Seattle law firms would not interview, and certainly not hire, a black, Smith had to look for non-traditional employment after receiving his law degree in 1955. Upon the advice of several of his law school professors, Smith applied for a clerkship with state supreme court judges and accepted an appointment with Justice Matthew Hill. The choice proved to be fortunate. Working with Justice Hill at a formative stage of his career left an indelible imprint on the young lawyer. The experience became a continual seminar in the law, ethics, and life, directed by a master teacher. Smith recalled later that "nine months working for Justice Hill...opened up the law to me in a more intense manner than three years of law school."

In 1956 Smith moved on to the King County Prosecutor's Office where he distinguished himself by successfully prosecuting labor leader Dave Beck for grand larceny. Because of his knowledge of labor union corruption and the Beck prosecution, U. S. Attorney General Robert Kennedy lured Smith away from his private practice in 1961 to serve as part of a team investigating a case against corruption in the handling of the Teamster Union pension fund. Smith brought an indictment in Chicago against then union president Jimmy Hoffa. Smith, impressed with the integrity, fair play, social consciousness, and intensity of Robert Kennedy, resigned as special assistant in the Justice Department to help Kennedy win his race for the U. S. Senate from New York in 1964. The campaign constituted Smith's single venture into the rough-and-tumble of a major campaign, although he was familiar with the give-and-take of politics.

Smith had learned his politics in King County Prosecutor Charles O. Carroll's office; his Republican affiliation came with that job. He, like every prosecutor in the office, was urged—if not required—to participate in Republican affairs and, of course, to assist in his boss's reelection. Smith joined the King County Young Men's Republican Club, chaired Lawyers for Nixon, and delivered numerous speeches for Carroll during the latter's reelection bid. However, after working in Kennedy's senate campaign, Smith no longer identified with any political party.

As soon as Smith returned to Seattle in 1965, he accepted an appointment as municipal judge—becoming the first African American to serve on the Seattle court. Governor Daniel Evans appointed him to the superior court a year later, where he served until 1973, again being the first black on the state's trial court of general jurisdiction. He won unopposed election to both the municipal and superior court benches.

In 1973 the University of Washington School of Law lured Smith away from the bench. He joined the faculty and became a tenured full professor of law and associate dean. He later served as director of clinical programs and instituted an innovative experiential legal program bringing third-year students into courtrooms to expose them to trial practice.

In 1983, with federal funds for the clinical program exhausted and the university unable to pick up the financial slack, Judge Smith took early retirement, but taught part-time in the law school. He later served the university as professor of law emeritus and as a member of the graduate faculty of the School of Social Work. Immediately upon his retirement, Smith joined with an old classmate to form the law firm of Rosenblume, Smith, and Associates in Seattle. Smith was with this firm when Governor Gardner selected him the seventy-eighth justice of the Washington Supreme Court.

Smith's background and diverse community activities greatly influenced his judging. He was born in Lakeland, Florida, in 1927, the first son in a family with four sons and four daughters. His father, an auto mechanic, was Cuban and his mother, a restaurant chef, an African American. The two separated when Smith was fourteen. But by then the family of William H. Gray, president of Florida Normal College and later president of Florida A & M University, was raising Smith. Smith attended segregated public and private schools before entering the U. S. Army in 1945. He rose to staff sergeant and served as court reporter at Fort Lee, Virginia. Upon return to civilian life in 1946, Smith continued courses at the all-black Florida A & M. When William Gray returned to Philadelphia to take over as pastor of his father's church, Smith moved too, enrolling at Temple University. In 1952 he graduated with a B.S. degree in business education and a minor in group dynamics. Gray encouraged him to enter law school rather than pursue a graduate degree in social work. As Smith recalled later, Gray told him the "law is a helping profession" and would permit him to reach into social work.

Justice Smith's public service activities reflect his earlier interest in social work. For example, he has been an officer or board member of the Puget Counseling Center, American Cancer Society, Fred M. Hutchinson Cancer Research Center, Chong-quing (China) Sister City Association, National Conference of Christians and Jews, Kawabe Memorial House, Seattle Urban League, National Association for the Advancement of Colored People, and Minoru Masuda Memorial Committee of the Japanese-American Citizens League. His involvement with church activities is extensive, including serving as president of the American Baptist Churches. He also belonged to Boys Club of Seattle, the King County Commission on Alcoholism, and at least two-dozen other service organizations, all reflecting his societal concerns.

Justice Smith has also been very involved in professional activities. A graduate of both the National Judicial College and the Naval Justice School, he served a number of years on the American Bar Association's standing committee of the federal judiciary, as well as its juvenile justice standards commission and its task force on crime. He also headed the minorities and justice task force created by the legislature to study and suggest remedies for biases in the judicial system. He remains co-chairman of the permanent minorities and justice commission.

All this suggests a person most concerned about the needs of society and the importance of law in meeting those needs. Justice Smith answers those who inquire about his ideology: "I think I am a liberal but my children think I'm conservative." He refuses to be narrowly classified:

> I don't think that intellectually I can be put in anyone's pigeon hole. I tend to get aboard what people might consider to be liberal policies...but [they] had nothing to do with trying to fit myself into...conservative or liberal [categories]... I give my personal commitment to things that I happen to believe in... If that makes me a liberal, then I'm liberal. On the other hand, because I'm so cautious, if cautious makes me conservative, then I'm a conservative.

Smith prefers to view himself as "humanitarian." Certainly his balanced, if not ambiguous, ideological view should contribute significantly in bringing together his colleagues on the court. However, his perspective regarding the court's decisional process may prove a hindrance.

Justice Smith regards the formal phases of court deliberations to be the exclusive means of reaching decisions. The oral arguments and briefs of the attorneys, facts of the case, and the lower court record, mixed with his knowledge of the law, are the factors he regards as most important to his decision-making. The work of his law clerk, the political and social context of the case, and views of his colleagues and the lower court, although to be considered, are secondary in his scale of decisional factors. Individual preparation and formal interchange among justices at post-hearing conferences constitute Justice Smith's means of convincing his colleagues of his viewpoint:

> I find that the formal around-the-table conference process is the most valuable avenue of communication. I think I would resent...lobbying a position... When I vote I have reached a firm conclusion based upon what I have read, what I have heard, and what I have reasoned, and it would take a great deal for me to flip because someone crafted a language a certain way [in a draft opinion].

Smith's voting record indicates an effort to bring the high bench together. He participated in 179 cases from his appointment until May 31, 1990. He wrote twenty-five opinions, of which eighteen were unanimous. This unanimous percentage far exceeded that of the full court.

Justice Smith tends to provide the swing vote in many split decisions, and he clearly is reluctant to dissent from a well-reasoned opinion. He refused to accept the majority's view in only two cases, one of which constituted his only written dissent. He cast a concurring vote in only two cases.

Justice Smith and Eleanor Martinez married in 1955. They had met when she moved to Seattle for her first teaching assignment, from which she recently retired. The Smiths have four children: Carlos, Michael, Stephen, and Felicia, all now adults. When the children lived at home, weekend camping trips were a frequent family activity. Now a few weeks in Hawaii to visit family—Mrs. Smith was born on the islands—permit the justice to briefly escape his busy civic and court schedule.

Selected References

Smith's oral history interview is in the supreme court collection, Washington State Archives. Also see "Profile," *De Novo*, vol. 3 (1989), p. 13; and "Man of Faith, Man of Justice," *Decision Magazine* (Sept. 1991).

Charles F. Stafford, Jr.

January 1, 1970-July 3, 1984

Born: June 24, 1918
Burlington, Washington
Whitman College, B.A. (1940)
Yale University, LL.B. (1946)
Methodist
Died: July 3, 1984
Deputy Prosecutor (1947-1953)
Superior Court (1953-1969)
Court of Appeals (1969)
Republican
Appointed

Someone once said of Chief Justice Harlan Stone of the U. S. Supreme Court that "trying to compress his meaning within the handy labels of 'conservative' or 'liberal,' had been confounded. No tag seemed to fit. Harlan Fiske Stone was a judge, a dispassionate interpreter of the law of which he was a 'well-deserved pillar.' "

Frances P. Bernat's fine biography of Charles F. Stafford concludes that Stafford, "like Stone, does not seem to fit" either liberal or conservative frameworks. "He tried to dispense dispassionate justice to the best of his ability," largely successfully because "of an idealized view of his role" as judge. For those studying his background and career, such a conclusion would not come as a surprise.

Stafford was born in the town of Burlington, Washington, the only child of Charles Sr. and Madge Marie (Davis) Stafford. His father, in the shipping business in Anacortes, Washington, managed the concerns of the Curtis-Wharf Company. Although not wealthy, the family lived securely in Anacortes. His mother, a strong believer in hard work, discipline, and education, could be described as a person exemplifying the Protestant ethic. Her father had been a Thomasite missionary in Asia. Strong-willed, proper, and well-read, she was a leading force in the community's cultural life. While his father tended to his business concerns, Stafford's mother assumed responsibility for the proper raising of her only son, surrounding him with love and security.

Although somewhat withdrawn, Stafford participated in traditional extracurricular activities. He played on the high school football team, participated in Boy Scouts, and played trumpet in the high school band. Through it all he earned good grades.

After his 1936 graduation from Anacortes High School, his mother urged him to attend Whitman College, a small private liberal arts school in Walla Walla, Washington. His mother assumed he would pursue a professional career. At Whitman he followed both a pre-med and pre-law program, but after confronting chemistry with mixed results, he concentrated on political science as the best training for law study. He widened his acquaintances by joining Beta Theta Pi social fraternity. His studies proved successful, and Stafford won a scholarship. With additional funds provided by his parents and his summer earnings as a teamster for his father's company and as a purser for the Washington state ferry lines, he concentrated on his studies during the school year, graduating in 1940 with Phi Beta Kappa honors. Yale Law School then admitted him.

Stafford excelled in law studies. In recognition of his academic success, he became a member of the law review. At New Haven he met his future wife, Gertrude Katherine "Kay" Grimm, a New Jersey native, Smith College graduate, and research assistant to a history professor at Yale. However, World War II interrupted both his romance with Kay and his study of law. He enlisted in the army in the summer of 1942. After basic training and officers' candidate school he was commissioned a second lieutenant in the U. S. Signal Corps. A week after receiving his commission, he and Kay married. Stafford served most of his military tour as a signal officer in the Aleutian Islands.

Immediately after his discharge in 1946, Stafford returned to Yale Law School and completed his legal studies within a year in an accelerated program. Although he had initially considered working with a Connecticut law firm, an acquaintance of his mother—whom she had met in Republican party activities—wrote Stafford with a counter offer, which included more money: if he, Rubin C. Younquist, succeeded in being elected Skagit County Prosecutor, he wanted Stafford as his deputy. Stafford did not know Younquist, but the opportunity to return to the West prompted him to accept. With Younquist's victory, Stafford launched his legal career.

Although Governor Arthur Langlie recruited him to run for the state legislature on the Republican ticket in 1950, Stafford declined and remained with the prosecutor's office. Two years later, Skagit County Superior Court Judge Willard L. Brickey retired and local attorneys urged Younquist to seek the post. He declined, but recommended his deputy for the trial bench seat. If elected, he would, at age thirty-four, be one of the youngest members of the state courts. After a spirited campaign against an older and well-known attorney, Don Smith, Stafford prevailed. The work of his family and friends ringing doorbells, distributing campaign literature, attending meetings, and telephoning contributed substantially to his winning majority. He was never challenged in superior court reelection bids, attesting to a general satisfaction with his work.

Although new to judging, his years with the prosecutor's office had prepared him well. Hard work filled in any voids in his background training. According to Bernat:

Stafford...spent a great deal of time...on the cases he was to hear. After his children were asleep, he would usually go back to his office and prepare for the following day. He read and reread briefs and conscientiously researched and analyzed the legal issues presented. While he never worked on Friday nights, or on Saturdays, Stafford would always go back to his office after church on Sunday to prepare for the week to come. Sunday afternoons were "sacred" hours consecrated to study of the week's docket.

One of Stafford's most controversial superior court decisions came in the *McCoy v. State* case of 1963 in which he upheld treaty-fishing rights of Native Americans. Although overturned by the state supreme court, federal courts, in the so-called Boldt decision, later vindicated Stafford's view of treaty rights. He was also especially proud of his work on the state bench-bar-press committee, established to assure voluntary observance of a balance between free press and fair trial rights.

During his tenure on the trial bench Stafford served as a *pro tempore* judge of the state supreme court, an experience he treasured. The cloistered intellectualism of appellate decision-making attracted him. On several occasions he asked Governor Daniel Evans to consider him for appointment to the state's high court, but without success. Even with support from his old friend, Speaker of the House Don Eldridge, Evans's appointments went to others.

In 1968 Washington voters approved a constitutional amendment approving an intermediate court of appeals. Governor Evans appointed Judge Stafford to one of the twelve new positions. He accepted after Evans assured him that his chances for a future high court appointment remained undiminished. Evans named him to division one of the court of appeals located in Seattle. After only four months on the intermediate court, the governor appointed Stafford to the supreme court to replace the retiring Justice Matthew Hill. Both Don Eldridge and the governor's administrative assistant, James Dolliver, who would later sit with Stafford on the high court, played key roles in the appointment. The appointment surprised Stafford, who assumed it would be some time, if at all, before promotion. He became the first judge to serve at three levels of the state's judicial system.

After an initial challenge from Superior Court Judge William Goodloe in 1970, Stafford's two following reelection bids were unchallenged. During his fourteen years on the state's high court he established a reputation as a craftsman of the law, a thorough and sometimes overly meticulous researcher with a moderate-to-conservative bent. He proved reluctant to usurp legislative prerogatives or overturn precedent. He wrote almost as many concurring as majority opinions, as he wanted to be sure the court addressed all points. He rarely dissented, believing a unified court essential in important cases. While chief justice from 1975-1977, Stafford instituted few changes and appeared reluctant to exercise the prerogatives a chief possessed. The details of administration, as well as the trappings of power and prestige, did not interest him.

Justice Stafford tended to be slightly conservative in civil liberties and economic cases. But typical of his effort to remain true to the law's dictates, he hired liberal law clerks to challenge his slightly conservative values. Bernat concluded that the justice was "neither rigid nor dogmatic in his adherence to conservative ideology." His "value system is probably better characterized as 'traditional.' " Concern for judicial restraint, carefully researched opinions, a respect for the law as an objective force, and a loyalty to the court as an institution expressed this traditionalism. According to Justice Vernon Pearson, a colleague, Stafford

> believed in a stable legal system but he didn't hesitate to change if he believed the law required it, the constitution required it, or that his value system required it. [You] can't leave your personal value system out. But you can't let your personal value system affect the application of pure legal precedent. That was the way Charles operated.

Stafford penned hundreds of opinions, his most important involving the same issue. In *Northshore School District v. Kinnear* in 1974, Stafford dissented from the majority's view that the system of financing schools through property taxes was constitutional. Stafford, in an atypical angry tone, wrote that the majority had given "birth to a legal pygmy of doubtful origin." The issue of funding public schools came before the court again in 1978 in *Seattle School District v. State.* This time Stafford forged a 6-3 majority to force the state to assume full-funding of basic education in public schools. The decision freed schools from over-reliance on the unfair system based upon local property taxes, which favored districts in well-to-do neighborhoods, and special levies, which had become an absolutely necessary, although unpredictable, source for funding basic programs. Typically, Stafford immersed himself into research of the constitutional issues involved in school funding, filling eight filing cabinets with materials in the process. His study culminated in a seventy-page majority opinion, of which he was most proud. His dissent in *Northshore* triumphed in *Seattle School District.*

Over the years Justice Stafford was active in the Methodist Church, the Young Men's Christian Association, and Boy Scouts. He presided over the Mount Vernon Rotary Club, served on the board of overseers of Whitman College—where he received an honorary LL.D. degree—and completed a term on the board of visitors of the Willamette University School of Law. He was a trustee of the Superior Court Judges' Association, a faculty member of the National College of Trial Judges, and a member of the Judicial Ethics Committee. He served on a number of judicial committees and promoted the constitutional amendment authorizing *pro tempore* judges to sit on the supreme court. He also wrote several law journal articles.

Justice Stafford treasured family life and he often regretted that the pressures of court work left less time than he desired for his wife and two daughters, Katherine and Joan. Tragedy haunted the close-knit, loving, religious family. The Staffords' first grandson died of sudden infant death syndrome in 1975. Kay suffered from cancer, fighting the painful disease bravely for years, succumbing in 1980. With encouragement from his children and friends, the justice married an old college acquaintance, Betty Greenwell, in 1981. In 1983 Justice Stafford became ill with stomach cancer. Even so, he continued to research and write opinions, several of which he penned from his hospital bed. On June 20, 1984, the Seattle-King County bar honored Justice Stafford with its prestigious Distinguished Service to the Judiciary and Public award. Betty read his acceptance speech at the ceremony, as he was too weak to attend. On July 3, 1984, Justice Charles Stafford passed away.

Selected References

Stafford's oral history interview is in the supreme court collection, Washington State Archives. Also see Frances Bernat, "Charles F. Stafford, Jr.: A Study in Judicial Behavior" (unpublished Ph.D. dissertation, Washington State University, 1987); C. W. Taylor, *Eminent Judges and Lawyers of the Northwest* (1954), p. 185; *Spokane Spokesman-Review*, 31 Jan. 1976; *Seattle Post-Intelligencer*, 4 Jy. 1984; Charles Stafford, "The Public's View of the Judicial Role," *Judicature*, vol. 52 (1968), pp. 73-77; and memorial services, *Washington Reports*, vol. 103, 2d (1984-1985), pp. xxxviii-xlviii.

William Joseph Steinert
May 23, 1932-September 12, 1949

Born: March 7, 1880
Versailles, Kentucky
Central Kentucky University, B.A. (1900)
University of Michigan, LL.B. (1905)
Presbyterian
Died: January 20, 1962
Deputy Prosecuting Attorney (1918)
Superior Court (1927-1932)
Regional Director, Office of Price Stabiliza-
    tion (1950-1952)
Republican
Appointed

William J. Steinert was born on March 7, 1880 in Versailles, Kentucky. His father, Philip Joseph, died when William was only seven years old, leaving his
mother, Katherine, with full responsibility for William and his sister. An old
friend, Dr. Cyrus Albertson, recalled the circumstances:

> They were poor, but he had a mother with great courage and conviction and faith
> and love. She went out and worked hard with her hands, and all through the life
> of this man who was our friend he had a conviction that grew with the years and
> an appreciation of the struggle that many people had to go through in order to
> make ends meet, in order that life might fulfill some of its dreams and hope.

William's mother earned money for the family as a seamstress while the children obtained what work they could. After attending public schools in Versailles,
William enrolled at age seventeen in Central Kentucky University in Richmond,
earning his B.A. degree in 1900. He taught in the normal school of S. P. Lees
Institute for two years, saving money for a legal education. In 1902 he entered
the University of Michigan Law School, graduating with a bachelor of laws in
1905. To pay back $300 borrowed to finish the last year of law school, William
worked at Speery Seed Company before beginning his law practice in Louisville
in 1906. After visiting an old classmate in Seattle during the Seattle-Yukon Exposition of 1909, Steinert decided to move there. He joined in a partnership with
Dan Earle. During World War I he served as deputy county prosecutor for King
County. Although he had affiliated with the Democratic party in Kentucky,
Steinert became a Republican in Seattle.

King County received four new superior court positions in 1926 and Steinert
applied to Governor Roland Hartley for an appointment. The governor turned

him down. With the support of several leading attorneys, he ran for one of the positions the governor had denied him. He defeated his opponent handily in the September primaries and served on the superior bench with distinction until his appointment to the supreme court in 1932.

Judge Steinert gained public prominence as presiding judge in the trial of several officers of the Puget Sound Savings and Loan Association who were accused of banking fraud. He was praised in the local press for his use of "plain English" in his instructions to a deadlocked jury. They returned a guilty verdict within a short time.

When Judge Adam Beeler resigned from the high court to run for the U. S. Senate, Governor Hartley decided to appoint the popular and respected Steinert. Hartley needed the support of King County voters in his reelection bid, and selecting a popular Seattle judge with Republican credentials would enhance his chances. But Steinert refused the initial offer. He felt that a supreme court position would isolate him from people, the profession, and his fellow judges, and he enjoyed the give-and-take of the trial bench. Also, he would have to stand for election in the September primary, giving him only a few months to organize a statewide campaign. After discussing the move with his wife "Diggy" and members of the supreme court—especially his friend and former colleague, Walter Beals—he decided against accepting the appointment. Hartley offered the position to another King County judge, who also refused. The governor returned to Steinert with a second offer and the judge accepted, largely because of persistent encouragement from supreme court members. In May 1932, Judge Steinert began a career on the state's high bench that would span seventeen years. He ran unopposed in 1932, 1938, and 1944, attesting to the esteem in which lawyers and judges held him.

In his years on the high bench, Steinert wrote 671 opinions covering sixty-seven volumes of the *Washington Reports*. He was almost universally regarded as a leading mind on the state's appellate bench. Justice Matthew Hill remarked, after a review of Steinert's decisions, that he

> was literally amazed. . . to find 40 or 50 [opinions] of which, without any hesitation and without any doubt (he) could say: "Here are the leading cases in the State of Washington;" the cases that are most cited in the briefs and the cases most cited in our opinions—what we call landmark cases.

John N. Rupp, one of the first law clerks employed by the supreme court in 1937—a practice instituted by Judge Steinert—remembered the judge's particular opinion style:

> Many of Judge Steinert's opinions were. . . admirable. But he was not afraid to go further and break new ground when he thought it sound and proper to do so. He was a scholarly man, though not pedantic in his scholarship, but sometimes he was a real pragmatist. He was not a great literary stylist nor a maker

of memorable phrases, but he had a sound straight-forward literary style and was careful to say what he meant and to say it clearly and well.

Judge Steinert had a collegial approach to court deliberations. He consulted thoroughly with his law clerk and informally with his colleagues. One law clerk remembered:

> The judge wanted to talk through an issue, to get criticisms, a fresh viewpoint, before he finally decided. He talked with other judges frequently and with me invariably.
> He rarely wrote [a dissent.] Usually tore it up if he did.
> Where there was a division in the Court, and a swing vote to be persuaded, he was diligent in attempting to win over the swing vote, to answer objections which had been raised in conference. Where there was a dissent, he tried to state the argument for the majority clearly, but he did not try to write the opinion with a view to changing the opinion of the dissenters.

Another former clerk recalled that the judge did "quite a bit of informal conferring" and tried "to get the others to agree with him or show him where he was wrong."

The judge most often directed his substantial persuasive skills toward furthering a conservative and restraintist view of the law. Steinert was reluctant to upset legislative acts and to support excessive government regulation of business enterprises. He often won over his colleagues to this conservative-restraintist approach because of his impressive research into the issues and his pleasant, but persistent, informal discussions. Actually, he could almost always count on support from fellow conservative judges George Simpson, John Robinson, and Clyde Jeffers, which meant persuading only moderates such as Beals or James Geraghty to join him. His leadership held the court together during the late 1930s and early 1940s.

Judge Steinert found the idea of law clerks, an institution then common with many state courts of appeal and the U. S. Supreme Court, attractive because of his failing eyesight and the court's increasing case load. The judge's wife acted as his "clerk" at home, reading court records and briefs. The stresses and strains of judicial office affected his heart. Many observers attributed his health problems to the circumstances surrounding the Skagit County public utility case of 1947 and the subsequent public feud between judges William Millard and Joseph Mallery. The public airing of their disagreements disturbed Steinert, who retained the manners and courtly demeanor of a Kentucky gentleman. In 1949 Steinert and his friend, Clyde Jeffers, retired from the bench.

Steinert remained fairly active in law practice after his retirement. Employed as a "lawyers' lawyer," he served as counsel for other attorneys. Called back now and then to serve as judge *pro tempore* on the King County Superior Court, he also chaired several bar association committees, served as regional director of the Office of Price Stabilization, sat on the governor's cross-sound transportation study committee, and for eight years chaired the state bar association's board of examiners. The judge's dedication and thoroughness became evident in the last few hours of his life. John N. Rupp recorded his wife's recollections:

> Mrs. Steinert told me about how the judge died. He was a member of the Board of Bar Examiners. The examination having been given, he had to grade the papers on the questions for which he was responsible. He had worked at the task for several days, with blue books spread all over the table at home. One morning she left to do some errands. He kissed her goodbye and said he was nearly through with the grading. She returned in about an hour and found him slumped in the chair, dead. Every one of the books had been carefully graded.

The judge participated in civic and fraternal affairs during his life. As president of the Fremont Business Men's Club he was instrumental in securing a public library for that Seattle neighborhood. He belonged to the Municipal League, Seattle Chamber of Commerce, Masons, Knights of Templar, Shriners, Elks, and Eagles. He was secretary of the Seattle Baseball Club for two years.

In June 1914, Steinert married Marian Augusta Miller, a teacher in the Seattle school system. The couple had no children. Judge Matt Hill paid tribute to the role "Diggy" Steinert played in the judge's life:

> We recognize that Mrs. Steinert was many times his eyes, as she read to him the briefs, and then the texts and the cases cited in the briefs. She had been his hands as well. It was her care that kept him with us over a considerable period of time.

Selected References

Tribute, *Superior Court, King County* (24 Jan. 1962), pp. 1-10; memorial services, *Washington Reports,* vol. 60, 2d (1962), pp. xvii-xxii; *Seattle Times,* 8 Jy. 1926; Kari Kisler, "William J. Steinert and the 1939 Court," Steinert file, supreme court collection, Washington State Archives.

Theodore Lamme Stiles
November 11, 1889-January 14, 1895

Born: July 12, 1848
Medway, Ohio
Amherst College, B.A. (1871)
Columbia College Department of Law, LL.B.
(1872)
Died: October 11, 1925
Washington Constitutional Convention
(1889)
President, Washington State Bar Association
(1899)
Tacoma City Attorney (1908-1916)
Republican
Elected

Theodore Lamme Stiles, one of the first five judges on the Washington Supreme Court, was the only child of Daniel J. and Maria S. (Lamme) Stiles. Born in 1848 in the small farming village of Medway, Ohio, he remained there until his mother's death in 1865. He and his father moved to Indianapolis where he assisted his father in mercantile business. His father insisted that Theodore have a liberal education, so the younger Stiles spent two years doing preparatory work at Ohio University in Athens. He then enrolled in Amherst College, Massachusetts, taking a classics course, graduating in 1871. He immediately entered Columbia College Department of Law in New York and, by taking an overload of courses, graduated in June 1872. That same year the Indiana bar admitted him and he began practice in Indianapolis.

Stiles returned to New York City in 1873 to associate in practice with Edward Jordan, former solicitor for the U. S. treasury department, and Daniel G. Thompson. He remained with the partnership until 1878 when he traveled by Union Pacific Railroad to San Francisco, then proceeded to Los Angeles and to Yuma, Arizona. There he boarded a stage coach and, after a 300 mile ordeal, arrived at Tucson, Arizona, on November 21. He practiced law in Tucson for nine years, but the opportunities of lawyering attracted him to the Pacific Northwest, where Washington statehood seemed imminent.

Judge Stiles moved to Tacoma, arriving on July 4, 1887, and established a legal practice. He married Mary Louise Duff Barbour in 1889. They had one daughter.

That same year, having displayed some interest in Republican politics, he won election as a delegate to the Washington state constitutional convention.

He played a leading role at the convention, chairing the Committee on County, Township, and Municipal Organizations and serving on the Rules, Judiciary, and Public Lands committees.

At the close of the convention, Stiles returned to Tacoma and promptly became one of the Pierce County delegates to the Republican state convention, where he served as chairman. The convention delegates felt that Tacoma, as the third largest town in Washington, ought to have one of its residents on the state's court of last resort. Accordingly, they nominated Stiles for the supreme court. He and his four other Republican brethren thrashed the Democratic opposition in the October balloting for the state's high court. In drawing lots for terms on the supreme court, Stiles selected the five-year term. He might have served another term, but to assure the renomination of fellow Tacoman, Congressman W. H. Doolittle, Stiles withdrew his name at the 1894 Republican convention. After his term ended, Stiles returned to an active law practice in Tacoma.

While on the bench Stiles authored 335 of the court's majority opinions, nearly one-fourth of the court's total of 1,187 opinions. He missed only twenty cases, dissented only sixty-seven times, and often provided the swing vote in closely divided cases. The *American Law Reports* referenced 188 of his opinions, an indication of the respect in which the profession held him. The figures alone suggest he was a leader on that first court.

Judge Stiles was an activist by the standards of the time. He proved willing to give a close scrutiny to the constitutionality of legislative enactments and, if necessary, to declare them void. In an address to the Washington State Bar Association in 1897 he expressed his view of court power:

> The courts are, and in the nature of things, must be the appellate body, and their power to review extends over the entire domain of public and private right. Once it is conceded, as it is now, universally, that a statute may be declared void as unconstitutional, there is no denying the position of judicial supremacy. Whenever the legislature enacts a law it thereby assumes and asserts it is constitutional; and whenever the court declares the contrary, the judgement of the court prevails, and there is no power except that of the people in constitutional convention that can reverse it.

In 1908 voters elected him Tacoma City Attorney and he served until 1916. In that capacity he played a decisive role in the development of the Nisqually power plant and the Green River water system, both milestones in Tacoma's growth. Throughout the time Stiles practiced law he remained active in professional organizations, serving as president of the Washington State Bar Association in 1899.

Judge Stiles developed a reputation as a scholar and as the state's leading authority on the Washington Constitution. He often presented provocative and scholarly papers at the state bar's annual conventions. One commentator noted:

During his term of office he wrote many opinions, all of them characterized by an unusual elegance and clarity of diction. He was a sound lawyer, a facile writer, an able judge. When a member of the bar reads one of his opinions he is at once impressed with the fact that he has come across the work of one of those rare beings, a lawyer with style. The literary quality of his work is unsurpassed.

Stiles belonged to the Masons and the Union Club in Tacoma. An old friend, Judge Overton Ellis, remembered his colleague:

> Judge Stiles had an active, incisive mind which was never impaired to the day of his death. Just a few days before his death [I] chanced to meet him on the street. We stood for some time discussing a legal problem in which he was much interested. I was much impressed, as always, by the clearness of his thought and the ease of his expression, and when he walked on, the thought obtruded itself: How noble a thing is a ripe old age when occupied with a keen mind and a clear heart. Both of these he possessed in a superlative degree.

Selected References

C. S. Reinhart, *History of the Supreme Court of the Territory and State of Washington* (n.d.), pp. 101-103; *Seattle Daily Times*, 17 Sept. 1889 and 21 Sept. 1889; *Seattle Post-Intelligencer*, 18 Sept. 1889; Charles Sheldon and Michael Stohr-Gillmore, "In the Beginning: The Washington Supreme Court a Century Ago," *University of Puget Sound Law Review*, vol. 12 (1989), pp. 247-282; W. C. Wolfe, *Sketches of Washingtonians* (1906), p. 286.

Warren Winfield Tolman

May 11, 1918-September 20, 1937

Born: December 7, 1861
Kendall County, Illinois
Northwestern University Law School, LL.B.
 (1888)
Baptist
Died: May 15, 1940
State Senate (1901-1905)
Democrat
Appointed

Warren Tolman was born on a farm about two miles from Yorkville, Illinois, approximately fifty miles southwest of Chicago. He spent the first few years of his life on farms until the family moved to Geneva, Illinois, in 1866. His father briefly owned a grocery store before becoming an agent for a company selling illustrated family Bibles. Tolman's education began in public schools in Geneva, but the family moved back to a farm near St. Charles, Illinois, after one year. Four years later they moved to another farm between Batavia and Aurora, Illinois. Warren's farm work left little time for school. In the fall in 1874 he went to public school in Aurora, hoping to become a Baptist preacher, but he remained in high school only one year.

In 1877 Tolman's father traded the Illinois farm for land in Nebraska. Warren worked in a greenhouse in Batavia until joining his father. After his father's death in 1878, Warren managed the Nebraska family farm for four seasons before leaving for Chicago. Tolman worked in a farm machine factory, a carpet factory, and a creamery, interspersed with jobs as a carpenter, a farm hand, a railroad brakeman, and a well digger. Finally, in March 1886, he made the decision to seek a career in law. Judge Tolman later recalled these early days in a family scrapbook:

> Went to E. B. Preston & Co. in the fall having in the meantime in March 1886 determined to study law, registered as a student in the office of my cousin Edgar B. Tolman. In March 1887 I made up my mind that the way to become a lawyer was to give up all other occupations so I went into Edgar's office and since that time I have lived by the law alone. In the fall of '87 I entered the senior class of the law school of Northwestern University of Chicago and graduated with the

class of 1888 being admitted to the bar after examination before the Appellate Court at Springfield May 17th, 1888. Let my viscissitudes [*sic*] and uncertainties before I finally found my occupation be a lesson to you to determine as early as possible what your vocation is to be and then be content to begin at the bottom and stick to it until you reach the top. As soon as I graduated the firm became Tolman & Tolman and so continued for about 18 months when on the death of James R. Doolittle, Jr. we consolidated with the firm of Doolittle & McKey under the name of Doolittle, McKey & Tolman.

Tolman's initial practice with the large Chicago law firm proved unsatisfying because, in his words, the nature "of the business forced [me] to be a sort of managing clerk," which kept him "from going into court." He left the firm in April 1890, forming a partnership with an old classmate, Charles B. Simons. With careful management and hard work he began to prosper, but his wife's health deteriorated, prompting them to move to Spokane in October 1892 to avoid Chicago's harsh winters. He joined Millard T. Hartson in the law firm of Hartson and Tolman, barely making ends meet financially. In 1895 he formed a partnership with Mark F. Mendenhall, but a year later went into sole practice, developing a stable clientele and some financial independence. In 1899 Herbert L. Kimball joined Tolman, a partnership that lasted seven years.

Tolman's judicial career began with a temporary stint as acting municipal judge in 1897. His activity in the Democratic party brought him recognition that same year when he served as chairman of the city convention. The next year he became chairman of the Spokane County convention and served as permanent chairman of the county central committee for two years. In 1900 Tolman won election to the state senate for a four-year term. Beginning with the 1901 session, Tolman gained recognition as minority floor leader in the senate and later as chairman of the Democratic caucus of both houses. He also chaired the eastern Washington caucus of both parties in both houses. Perhaps his greatest contribution, however, came with his work on behalf of a state railroad commission.

Strong sentiment existed in eastern Washington for legislative regulation of freight rates to reduce costs of shipping wheat to the Seattle and Tacoma ports. Convinced the legislature had neither the time nor the expertise for setting rates and disclosing railroad abuses, Tolman advocated establishing an independent commission to protect the public interest. The Republicans introduced their version of the commission, but insisted that it be appointed by a Republican-dominated board. Unable to win passage of his bill, Tolman led the fight against the Republican legislation. The 1901 session failed to approve a commission bill, but Tolman's efforts gained him considerable respect from both sides of the legislative aisle. In subsequent legislative sessions Tolman proved instrumental in gaining approval of a railroad commission whose members the governor appointed. He successfully argued for an anti-gambling bill and supported other progressive legislation. His colleagues often consulted him on parliamentary procedure and looked to him as leader in many legislative struggles.

Tolman also gained recognition for his fight against a highly partisan reapportionment plan introduced at the last minute by the Republicans. One account of the legislative struggle described Tolman's efforts:

> At the beginning of the session the Republicans introduced a bill for the apportionment of the state into legislative districts, which was a mere skeleton. From time to time thereafter they caucused until they agreed upon the details of the bill and signed up two-thirds of the legislators in both the senate and house to pass the bill, and to pass it over the governor's veto if necessary. The result of the Republican caucus was presented to the state senate at the hour of convening one morning, with a report from the committee recommending that it be made a special order of business for thirty minutes later, and be considered until passed, to the exclusion of other business. Mr. Tolman took the floor in opposition to the committee report, although two-thirds of the senate, being the Republican members, were pledged in writing to pass the bill. He succeeded by a straightforward appeal to their sense of fair play, in gaining twenty-four hours in which to prepare his points in opposition to the bill. The next day when it came on for final action he spoke from the time of convening at 10 o'clock in the morning until 4 o'clock in the afternoon, with only thirty minutes for luncheon and that, too, after the senate, about noon, brought in a rule forbidding further debate. He offered a minority report for the recommitment of the bill to the committee; offered a substitute for the bill; and then, one by one, offered a hundred and thirty-six different amendments to the bill, each one of which was germane; and in private conversation by the opposition, his points were all admitted to be well taken. His fight on that occasion was so conducted as to bring him the good will and admiration of his opponents, the congratulations of most of those who witnessed it and favorable newspaper comment throughout the state.

Although Democrats applied considerable pressure on Tolman to seek the party's nomination for governor in 1904, he chose to return to full-time law practice and did not seek reelection to the senate. Elected a member of the Spokane school board between 1903 and 1906, he also served as a member of the Washington state commission to the 1904 St. Louis Exposition. In 1905 Governor John R. Rogers appointed him to consult with organizers of the Lewis and Clark Exposition to be held in Portland that year.

In 1906 the Democrats nominated Tolman as one of their candidates for the state supreme court, an honor he apparently did not seek. He was resoundingly defeated by the dominant Republican candidates. In 1910 he again received the party's endorsement, and the nonpartisan league convention formally nominated him. He ran as an independent to protest the Republican's reintroduction of partisanship to supreme court judge elections. Again, the Republicans dominated, turning back Tolman in his lackluster effort.

In 1914 Tolman mounted an extensive campaign for Congress from the Fifth District. The campaign emphasized his contribution to instituting the railroad commission, his progressive leadership in the legislature, and his commitment to the principles of Woodrow Wilson's "New Freedom." He failed to gain the Democratic nomination despite his apparent popularity.

Curiously, Tolman, reluctant to campaign for election to the supreme court, eagerly sought appointment to the same post. A realistic view that under the earlier partisan system a Democrat stood very little chance of winning probably explained his election reluctance. But with Democrat Ernest Lister in the governor's mansion, Tolman stood a good chance of appointment. Tolman had strongly supported Lister and was a leader in the governor's wing of the party. When Judge Overton Ellis resigned from the supreme court in May 1918, the governor selected Warren W. Tolman to fill the vacancy. In the 1918 election Tolman edged Walter French in the primary and ran unopposed in November. Tolman garnered the most votes of all the candidates in 1920, ran unopposed in 1926, and won a close and hard-fought race in 1932.

Tolman's liberalism, evident from his legislative voting, carried over to his judicial decisions. In workers' injury cases, criminal appeals, and government regulation disputes, he tended toward a liberal position. He often wrote more opinions than his colleagues, suggesting that his view tended to prevail in conference and during opinion circulation. He had a moderate dissent record. He served one term as chief justice in 1925. In 1937, after nearly twenty years on the state supreme court, he decided not to run again. Justice Tolman retired under the new judicial retirement act which provided that "any Supreme Court or Superior Court judge who has served for ten years and believes he is incapacitated from duty may apply for retirement." His retirement pay amounted to one-half of his $7,500 annual salary.

Upon leaving the bench Tolman and his wife left immediately for California for an indefinite stay. Failing health confined Tolman to a hospital for several months during the early part of 1940. He died suddenly at home after a visit with his family on May 15, 1940.

Tolman married Maude Ingersoll of Chicago in April, 1889. She was active as vice president of the Olympia Women's Club and was a moving force in the state association of the Daughters of the American Revolution. The Tolmans had one daughter and a son.

Selected References

N. W. Durham, *History of Spokane and the Inland Empire,* vol. 3 (1912), pp. 481-485; W. C. Wolfe, *Sketches of Washingtonians* (1906), p. 292; "Reminiscences of Nancy Burns Tolman," Tolman papers, Manuscripts, Archives and Special Collections, Washington State University Library.

Robert F. Utter
December 20, 1971-

Born: June 19, 1930
Seattle, Washington
Linfield College (1948-1950)
University of Washington, B.S. (1952)
University of Washington, LL.B. (1954)
Baptist
Deputy Prosecutor (1955-1957)
Juvenile Court Commissioner (1959-1964)
Superior Court (1964-1969)
Court of Appeals (1969-1971)
Republican
Appointed

Robert Utter's maternal grandparents were long-time residents of New Plymouth, Idaho. His father's parents owned a small farm and country grocery store near Boise. Utter's father, John M., was a successful insurance salesman and executive with Equitable Life Insurance of Iowa. His mother, Besse, died when Robert was five. His father later remarried, and both he and his new wife actively participated in the Baptist Church. Religion played a significant role in the life of Robert and his two younger brothers, Tim and Fred.

Born in 1930 in Seattle, Robert attended public schools there, graduating from West Seattle High School in 1948. He attended Linfield College in Oregon for two years, majoring in business, then transferred to the University of Washington to continue his studies in English and political science. Under the early entry program then common with law schools, Utter enrolled in the university's law school and won his B.S. degree after successfully completing the first year of legal training. He was awarded his LL.B. in 1954.

Immediately after graduation, Judge Matthew Hill of the Washington Supreme Court hired Utter as a law clerk. He remembers his year with the court and Judge Hill with fondness. Hill involved the young clerk in an ongoing seminar in law, life, morals, and politics quite beyond the narrow legal issues confronting the court. The experience, although for but a year, provided Utter with a lingering taste for appellate judging.

Utter had several opportunities after his year of clerking, but the King County Prosecutor responded first with an attractive offer. After a year-and-a-half with the King County office, Utter joined the Seattle law firm of Rummens, Griffen,

Short, and Cressman in 1957. Trial, corporate and civil law, wills, estates, and probate work occupied him during his short stay with the firm, but legal practice thus far had not provided him with the satisfaction he had anticipated:

> I grew a little dissatisfied with the social utility of the practice of law and received a call from a superior court judge whom I had tried cases a number of times before, asking me if I cared to serve full-time as a commissioner of juvenile court.

The appointment meant a fifty percent salary cut, but as commissioner, Utter felt perhaps the law and courts could be brought to bear in a positive way to deal with the troubles of young people. He remained with the King County Juvenile Court until 1964 when, upon the urging of members of the King County bench, he ran for and was elected to the superior court. He gained reelection to the trial post in 1968, and, because of his prior experience as juvenile commissioner and his deep interest in the problems of young people, his superior court colleagues chose him to preside over the state juvenile court committee.

Legal professionals and members of the judiciary regarded Utter as a competent and bright jurist, and his off-bench activities added considerably to his image. He served as a member of the board of deacons of the First Baptist Church of Seattle and was a founder and president of both Big Brothers of Seattle and Job Therapy, Inc. He served on the boards of Friends of Youth, the Seattle Day Nursery, and the Little School. He was also vice president of the Metropolitan Board of Directors of the Greater Seattle Young Men's Christian Association. For his many contributions to the Seattle community, the Junior Chamber of Commerce named him Seattle's outstanding young man for 1964 and the Washington Congress of Parent-Teacher Associations awarded him a lifetime membership.

In 1968 Washington voters approved a constitutional amendment instituting an intermediate court of appeals, and authorizing the governor to appoint the initial twelve judges. Judge Utter's reputation as a civic-minded jurist, his efforts on behalf of young people, his short-lived Republican activities while on the King County Prosecutor's staff, and bar association approval led Governor Daniel Evans to appoint him to the new Washington Court of Appeals, division one, located in Seattle. He won election to the post the next year, running unopposed for a full six-year term.

Justice Morell Sharp resigned from the state supreme court in December 1971, and Governor Evans quickly appointed Judge Utter to the vacancy. At forty-one, he became one of the youngest jurists to serve on the state's high bench. Utter had not been a close associate of the governor, but his reputation as a civic activist weighed heavily in his favor: "I think I had been on the bar list for [several years]. Although I had not been an active party member... I had, through civic projects in Seattle, been involved with some of the people who worked closely with the Governor's office." With only Justice Robert Finley representing the

King County region on the supreme court, Utter's appointment brought some representational balance to the high bench.

Utter has built a solid reputation on the supreme court as an innovative jurist, creatively mixing elements of conservatism with liberalism, defying common ideological designation. On the one hand, he is a constitutional intentionist, usually associated with conservative restraintists: the intent of the framers of the state constitution should be determined and applied in constitutional cases despite the demands of the current situation. In a number of such decisions the freedoms given individuals exceed those granted by the U. S. Supreme Court. For example, Utter maintains that the founders intended in Article 1, Section 7 of the Declaration of Rights to protect the private affairs of persons and, consequently, to place greater restrictions on the intrusions of the state into one's privacy than the Bill of Rights of the U. S. Constitution requires with its absence of direct reference to the right of privacy.

On the other hand, his historical analysis of the meaning of the state constitution leads him to fear not only governmental but also private transgressions into individual freedom. State action is not a requisite for court intervention, according to the justice's version of the state's fundamental law. Thus, his conservative intentionist reading of the constitution often leads to liberal results. Such an apparent confusion of ideological labels lends credence to Utter's contention that when applied to him the labels are "too confining because they don't describe the dynamics of what you're working with. . . I believe that my views are really constantly evolving."

The high bench is, of course, a multi-member court which needs a majority of the nine to decide. To forge a majority—and perhaps unanimity—requires compromise and persuasion. A justice often must relinquish a favored position to be part of the majority. In a sense, that justice loses his or her identity in the process. However, dissenting opinions help the justice to retain or regain his or her individuality. Often to understand a dissent is to understand its writer.

Justice Utter has not been reluctant to dissent from his colleagues. He has separated from the majority in more than ten percent of cases. He explained his motivations and, in the process, revealed some of his view of his role on the court:

> I dissent for two purposes. Sometimes when I feel. . .the court is flatly wrong. It is not a question of philosophy but just simply a question of misunderstanding the law or the issues. I will write that dissent with the hope that I can convince a majority of the court that I am right. . .[I'll also write] dissents where [I] feel the law hasn't quite reached that point yet but you need to express that view so sometime in the future other judges looking at the question may understand there are at least two viewpoints.

In 1980, with some citizens and prosecuting attorneys disturbed by the court's apparent "permissiveness" regarding criminal appeals, Justice Utter found himself challenged for the first time at the ballot box. Kitsap County Prosecutor

Dan Clem conducted a vigorous law and order campaign but Utter, with the endorsement of the Seattle Police Officer's Guild, State Labor Council, and the Seattle and state bar associations, prevailed in the primary by more than 200,000 votes. He ran unopposed in 1986.

Justice Utter has earned a national reputation for his scholarly applications of state constitutional law. In 1991 he was elected president of the American Judicature Society, a 20,000 member national organization dedicated to improving the administration of justice. As a scholar and practitioner of "new judicial federalism" he has been invited to submit law review articles, has given lectures, and has been appointed a "visiting scholar" at law schools. He regularly teaches a well-attended state constitutional law course at the University of Puget Sound Law School. Utter takes what has been called the "dual sovereignty" method in applying state constitutional provisions to challenged laws:

> Courts applying the dual sovereignty model always evaluate both federal and state provisions in the course of their decisions, even when the decision rests firmly on state grounds. This type of analysis reflects the policies underlying our federal system by making available the maximum protections both levels of government offer to citizens.

The dual method provides greater state constitutional protections to state citizens and, as Utter argues, it can also nourish the federal constitution with innovative ideas developed by state judicial review. But the method might also invite review by a skeptical U. S. Supreme Court if there is a heavy infusion of federal law in the decisional formula. The design of "dual sovereignty" however, allows the best of both federal and state constitutional law to creatively resolve fundamental issues.

The justice's decisional style varies with the issues and the particular voting line-up at the conference. He neither avoids consultation with colleagues nor depends upon coalition building. A former law clerk, commenting on the justice's style, said:

> Justice Utter falls somewhere between the types of judges who employ a collective style and those who employ an individual style. He does not have frequent conferences with other justices after the official conference (as do some of the judges)... He also does not totally isolate himself from the other judges... Rather, he adopts a careful mixture of the styles. During the official conference, he does of course interact with the other judges. Then, when the opinions... are circulated, he may in certain cases draft and circulate legal memoranda to the other judges to discuss specific issues further. In this manner, he can circulate his analysis and views to all of the other judges, without encountering the problems of partial group discussions that arise when judges discuss the case with other individual judges or groups.

The justice confirmed his eclectic style:

It depends upon what the sense of the court is from the initial conference. If the court has agreed, no matter how difficult the case is, I'll work it through myself. If there is a serious division and the court has focused on areas of policy questions, I'll take a rough draft to two or three persons who have expressed concerns in an area before I circulate it, and say "Does this meet the concerns you have?"

Utter often shared his views with Justices Charles Horowitz and Vernon Pearson while they were on the high bench. He prefers one-on-one informal and cordial discussions on legal and policy issues which permit him to give some direction to an often-divided high bench.

Serving as chief justice between 1979 and 1981, Utter took special interest in establishing a judicial qualifications commission (later known as the judicial conduct commission), responsible for disciplinary actions against violators of the *Code of Judicial Conduct*. The idea of an independent watchdog commission did not sit well with some judges and justices, but with the chief justice's endorsement the voters approved the commission as an amendment to the state constitution in 1982. Chief justices traditionally are responsible for devising ways for attacking the court's backlog. Mostly by example, Utter encouraged his colleagues to file opinions early. Although not obligated to take any opinion assignments as chief, he continued to carry a full assignment load. Under his leadership the output of written opinions increased from 150 in 1978 to 203 in 1980.

Utter takes the resolution of legal disputes, especially those involving constitutional issues, as intellectual challenges. He has admitted that "I probably would find myself involving the court more in change than . . . in other areas that can be more clearly defined." New and changing resolutions are to be sought, but they should be blended with precedents and history for a satisfying resolution to the issues before the court.

Utter married another Seattle native, Betty Stevenson, whom he had met at Linfield College. They became the parents of three children: Kim, Kirk, and John. The justice is an accomplished ocean sailor and a pilot. He holds a single and multi-engine airplane license and also an instrument rating.

Selected References

Utter's oral history interview is in the supreme court collection, Washington State Archives. Also see *Washington State Bar News* (Feb. 1971), pp. 7-23 and (Dec. 1979), pp. 13-19; *Washington State Judicial Newsletter* (Jan. 1979), pp. 1-2; *Seattle Post-Intelligencer,* 23 Mar. 1979 and 31 Aug. 1980; *Seattle Times,* 6 Apr. 1979; *Seattle Times/Post-Intelligencer,* 21 Oct. 1984; *Atlanta Daily,* 24 Jy. 1990; and *Tacoma Morning News Tribune,* 22 Aug. 1990.

Frank Parks Weaver
May 21, 1951-May 21, 1970

Born: March 17, 1904
Greensburg, Pennsylvania
University of Michigan, B.A. (1926)
University of Washington, LL.B. (1928)
Lutheran
Died: November 19, 1983
Law Professor (1928-1949)
Dean, Gonzaga Law School (1945-1948)
Republican
Appointed

Frank Parks Weaver was born March 17, 1904 in Greensburg, Pennsylvania, a community of about 8,000 residents thirty miles southeast of Pittsburgh. He was the son of Amos Pool Weaver, a blacksmith and farrier, and Oma (Parks) Weaver. Frank attended Greensburg public schools until age sixteen, when he joined what he called a "working boys corps" at Mercersburg Academy. The first year he waited tables, and the next two he was "in charge of chapel" where he "kept the chairs straight, the hymnals in place, opened and closed the doors, and did such errands as the headmaster wished." In 1922 Frank became the first "working boy to be graduated as president of the senior class."

Encouraged by his uncle, Samuel Pool Weaver, Frank enrolled at the University of Michigan, intending to study law. He competed on the varsity debating team, served as head manager of the basketball squad, and won election to Phi Beta Kappa. After graduating with a degree in history, Frank took the first year of law study at the University of Michigan School of Law, then transferred to the University of Washington School of Law. By his third year there Frank gained election to the Order of Coif and was a member of law review. In 1928 he received his LL.B. and joined his uncle's law firm in Spokane.

Although only a few months out of law school, Frank was hired as professor of law at Gonzaga Law School where he remained until 1949. He served as secretary and then dean of the school while carrying on an active private practice. The Spokane Bar Association recognized his leadership in the profession by selecting him as president in 1946.

Weaver had always been interested in politics, but more as an observer than a participant. In 1932, a disastrous year for Republicans, he was soundly thrashed running for the state legislature. It was his first and last contested race.

His efforts on behalf of Gonzaga Law School, legal acumen, bar endeavors, geography, and partisan activities all coalesced in 1951 when Governor Arthur B. Langlie appointed him to the high court. In later years he recalled the occasion:

> My appointment came as a bolt of lightning. Spokane County, the second most populous, was not represented on the Court. The Spokane Bar Association thought it should be represented. I was their "fair haired boy."
>
> What the politics involved were, I do not know nor do I care. I had carried some "water to the elephant." I was a delegate to the Republican National Convention in 1944. I was a personal friend of Thomas E. Dewey, the [presidential] nominee. He was also a friend of Governor Langlie. Whether this had anything to do with my original appointment, I do not know.

As one might expect, there was more involved in the appointment. One Monday morning the soon-to-be judge was surprised by a lead article in the *Spokane Spokesman-Review* advocating his appointment to the state's high bench. He talked to his wife, Margaret, about the possible appointment. Margaret, daughter of former Governor Marion Hay, responded favorably: "When I was two years old, the voters kicked me out of Olympia in 1912. If my husband can take me back, I'm ready to go." Weaver recalled other details of the appointment:

> Having made a decision to be interested, I wrote three letters: the first to the president of the state bar association indicating my interest in being included in the recommended list to the Governor; the second letter was to Governor Langlie that if I were on the list, I would be pleased if he would consider my qualifications; the third letter was to Thomas E. Dewey in New York... I knew that he and Langlie had become good friends. I told him of my ambitions.

A few weeks later Governor Langlie offered him the job.

On May 21, 1951 Frank Weaver began a judicial career that spanned exactly nineteen years. He wrote 531 opinions covering forty volumes of the *Washington Reports*. Never challenged in four reelection campaigns, Weaver attributed his lack of opposition to his many years as law professor:

> I had approximately 700 former law students throughout the state. They were Democrats, Republicans, Independents, Socialists, Catholics, Protestants, and agnostics but they were all in "my corner." I would file at the earliest opportunity and within an hour we were aboard our 28′ sloop heading north to the Canadian Gulf Islands... I saw to it that the vacation was publicized. My campaign expenses for four times was $55.00 – $20.00 for an ad in a local paper; the rest for stationery which I am still trying to use up.

Precedent always served as the starting point for any decision Judge Weaver rendered. But he subjected precedent to three tests. First, he evaluated the reputation of the opinion writer. Next, he consulted the legal principle "to check up on precedent." Finally, he examined the "prospective [policy] consequences of the rule under consideration." This was what some scholars have referred to as "the grand style," and U. S. Supreme Court justices Holmes, Brandeis, and

Frankfurter, among others, practiced it. It was a tradition of restraint mixed with the felt necessity of the times. Accordingly, Weaver insisted:

> The policy making departments of state government under the constitution are the executive and legislative branches. This does not include the judiciary. The ultimate purpose of the highest appellate court in any jurisdiction is to decide the questions of *law* that are brought before it for decision. There are times, of course, when the policy making power must be used when the question involved is one of judicial administration and the control of the courts. When a Supreme Court goes beyond this it is in the realm of "dictum" and advisory opinions.
> The theory [of *stare decisis*] should not be ignored. The theory is the foundation of continuity and consistency in our jurisprudence. It is necessary for our stability of the law. If precedent is clearly wrong it is wrong and not just wrong at times... If the reason for the precedential rule no longer exists by reason [of] changing social and economic conditions, the precedent should not be ignored—it should be overruled and a new rule developed that meets present conditions.

Justice Weaver refused to view the supreme court's decisional process from a political perspective. Once conference discussions had concluded and the tentative vote been taken, "politics" ceased. Here was his theory:

> When I have been assigned to write an opinion for the Supreme Court when a majority agreed tentatively with my conclusion, I became the constitutional judge to proffer a written opinion to the court for consideration.
> My distribution of the opinion I wrote was not a circulating of a draft opinion; it was my offer of my decision... expressing a conclusion a majority had expressed as a tentative conclusion.
> The other justices had not given up a bit of their judicial power. They still had six alternatives: (1) sign my opinion, (2) write "I concur in the results," (3) write their own concurring opinion, (4) sign "I dissent," (5) write their own dissent, [or] (6) sign a dissent written by another.

Choosing representative opinions from over 500 in a nineteen-year span is difficult. However, Judge Weaver had some favorites. He remembered with obvious delight the circumstances of one 1952 case, *First National Bank v. Tiffany*. He had been on the bench only a few months:

> I recall one case written by [Tom] Grady dealing with the right of possession of land during the year of redemption after mortgage foreclosure... It was signed by a majority before it came to me, next to low man in circulation...
> I had taught mortgages [at Gonzaga] for 19 years... I wrote a concurring opinion... based upon my teaching and experience and it was put in circulation starting at the top again and darned if it didn't reach me signed also by all judges except Grady. Which opinion to file?
> An *en banc* conference was called by the [chief justice]. It developed into a Gaston and Alphonse affair. Grady said, "I will withdraw my opinion." "No," I replied, "I will withdraw mine." Every time I opened my mouth I'd get a gentle kick in the shins from long-legged [Ralph] Olson from across the table. I finally shut up and my opinion was published concurred in by all.

It was really my first important opinion and did much to establish me as fitted for the job.

Weaver also proudly remembered his opinion in *Adams v. Cullen,* although he did not realize its importance until more than twenty years after he penned it. After retirement, in 1980, the justice visited his daughter Sarah, a second year law student at the University of Oregon. School officials invited him to her real property class, a subject Weaver had taught for twenty-three years at Gonzaga. The class used "a new combined text-case in the American Casebook Series... The lead case to be dissected and digested [by the class] was *Adams v. Cullen*...written by an unknown Justice by the name of Weaver."

Frank admitted that *Adams*

> was not a great opinion but it did establish the law [of precedent in real estate] in Washington... But had I written it any other way I could imagine about 700 of my former students saying "That isn't what the old goat taught me in law school." I thought the case was buried in 1954. I was flabbergasted to find it resurrected...twenty years later in the most recent [law school] textbook and in my daughter's class.

Weaver was not reluctant to express indignation at obvious inequities in the law and to work toward correcting them. In *Pier 67 Inc. v. King County* in 1970, a case dealing with the method of valuation of a leasehold interest on state- or federal-owned tax exempt land for the purpose of county taxation, he argued that "the 'robber-barons' leasing state owned property had been cheating the state, especially King County, out of millions [in] taxation." He worked over a month researching, studying, writing, and rewriting to eliminate the favoritism. He admitted that: "I may have been wrong but I was not in doubt."

Weaver's most satisfying case was *Yelle v. Kramer* in 1974, four years after he officially left the bench. The case confronted the issue of whom should prevail in setting salaries of elected officials: the people through the initiative process or the legislature. Because their salary increases were at stake, the entire supreme court disqualified itself and appointed nine retired judges as the first full *pro tempore* supreme court in state history. Frank acted as chief justice. The dispute brought together nine devoted judges who volunteered because they felt they were needed. Judge Weaver worded it this way:

> Another question that has been asked is: Why did we consent to act?... When the fire bell rings, the old horses who were put out to pasture when they were supplanted by the fire engines, stomp around. I think that spirit is in our souls also... I know that we all feel a deep obligation first to our state and second to the administration of justice.

His colleagues honored him by asking him to write the majority opinion. In upholding the power of the initiative process, his "grand style" became evident. In response to the contention of petitioners that constitutional restraints do not apply to initiatives, Frank displayed impatience tempered with foresight:

[We] fear, should we fail to answer the issue raised, it would be interpreted as silent approval of the bizarre theory advanced by *amicus*---

He and his principal would have us burke the constitution and its heretofore judicial interpretation applying to initiatives...

We reject the contention... To do otherwise would be a recognition that we have an initiative process "governed by men not by law." Nothing in this opinion is to be interpreted as opening a Pandora's box, releasing a runaway, uncontrolled initiative process.

Weaver regarded *Yelle* as a milestone because it proved that the law can resolve a highly volatile political issue: law and politics are not mutually exclusive.

Weaver gained appointment once again as *pro tempore* chief justice in 1982. It was his proudest moment. The occasion was the swearing-in ceremony of new members of the Washington bar, among whom was Sarah, the fifth member of the Weaver family to join the profession. Frank remembered the occasion with obvious pleasure and pride:

She stood on the same spot I stood 54 years ago when I was sworn in and on the same spot each of her [three] brothers stood when I swore them in. It was a banner day in the Weaver family history. It closed a cycle and continued an era.

Justice Weaver and his first wife, Margaret Hay, married in 1933. They had four children: Alan, Parks, Marion, and Sarah, all of whom became lawyers. Margaret Weaver died in 1963 and Justice Weaver later married Katherine Allard, who had served many years as his administrative assistant.

In May 1970, exactly nineteen years after his appointment, Weaver retired from the high bench. He had struggled with a drinking problem and friends persuaded him to leave the court before the malady affected his work. In retirement the justice moved to Lacey, near Olympia. His continued interest in the law and in politics was reflected in his reading and, as fate would have it, in his writing. His appointment as chief justice of the *pro tempore* court in the *Yelle* case prompted his recording the experience in a book published in 1980 entitled *Politicians, Judges and the People.* Failing health forced his move to a nearby convalescent home, where he died in 1983.

Selected References

Weaver's oral history interview is in the supreme court collection, Washington State Archives. Also see the Weaver papers, same collection; Charles Sheldon and C. Wade, "Frank Parks Weaver: A Short Biography," *Gonzaga Law Review,* vol. 19 (1983-1984), pp. 219-230; Sheldon, "The Washington Supreme Court: What it was Like Thirty Years Ago," *Gonzaga Law Review,* vol. 19 (1983-1984), pp. 231-263; memorial services, *Washington Reports,* vol. 101, 2d (1984), pp. xxx-xxxviii; and Sheldon and Weaver, *Politicians, Judges and the People* (1980).

John Stanley Webster
November 20, 1916-May 11, 1918

Born: February 22, 1877
Cynthiana, Kentucky
University of Michigan School of Law, LL.B.
  (1899)
Christian Disciples
Died: December 24, 1962
Prosecuting Attorney (1902-1907; 1907-1909)
Superior Court (1909-1916)
U. S. House of Representatives (1919-1923)
Federal District Court (1923-1939)
Republican
Appointed

John Stanley Webster was born in northern Kentucky about fifty miles from the Ohio border. His father, John Bascom Webster, fought on the side of the Confederacy in the Civil War, but his mother, Lucinda Landrum (Anderson), had been sympathetic toward the Union. Thus the family avoided political discussions. Webster had two sisters and a brother. He attended public schools and then Smith's Classical School for Boys before entering the University of Michigan School of Law in 1897. Upon graduation in 1899 he returned to Cynthiana, Kentucky, to practice law.

In 1902, at the age of twenty-five, voters elected Webster to a four-year term as prosecuting attorney of Harrison County, Kentucky. His relentless prosecution of feuding families in the region drained his health, prompting his move to a stump farm near Spokane. While at the University of Michigan, Fred C. Pugh, later prosecuting attorney for Spokane County, became a close friend. Upon learning of Webster's move to the region, Pugh persuaded him to serve as his deputy. Webster spent the next two years as Pugh's chief trial lawyer and developed a reputation for hard work and tough prosecutions. Within two years–on September 12, 1908–he gained appointment as superior court judge at the age of thirty-one, the youngest judge then on the Washington bench. That year he married Gertrude Lathrum of Spokane. They had no children.

Webster served on the superior court bench for eight years, resigning to run for the supreme court vacancy created by Judge Frederick Bausman's resignation in 1916. He swamped his single opponent in the September primary and ran unopposed on the November ballot.

Bausman had announced in July that he would resign immediately after the September primary, allowing Governor Ernest Lister to "appoint the high man as [his] successor, taking for granted...that the high man would...be perfectly agreeable to the governor." Some confusion existed as to exactly when Webster would assume his seat as a result of his November victory. A 1911 law mandated that a successful supreme court candidate "shall not qualify until the second Monday in January, succeeding his election." At the same time, Article IV, Section 3 of Washington's constitution simply stated that judges serve out their terms until the "election and qualification" of their successors. This constitutional provision meant that Webster could assume his place on the bench thirty days after the November balloting, when official election results were certified. Attorney General W. V. Tanner advised the governor that the constitutional version prevailed and Webster could take office by December. Rather than selecting someone else to serve only three weeks, Lister appointed Webster.

Webster served from November 20, 1916 until May 11, 1918. He resigned to conduct a successful congressional campaign, unseating eastern Washington incumbent C. C. Dill by more than 2,000 votes. Some question arose over his eligibility for a congressional seat. Article IV, Section 15 of the Washington constitution stated that judges are ineligible for "any other office or public employment" during the term for which they were elected. Judge W. W. Black had been disqualified for nomination as a gubernatorial candidate in 1912 because of the provision. However, Webster's defenders correctly pointed out that that section of the constitution could apply only to other state offices and not to federal positions.

Webster won election to two subsequent terms in the U. S. House of Representatives. He resigned on May 8, 1923 to accept an appointment to the federal district bench when President Warren Harding elevated Frank Rudkin to the U. S. Court of Appeals. At the age of forty-six, J. Stanley Webster had returned to that area of public service which he most enjoyed. In a 1923 letter to Senator James Hamilton Lewis, Webster wrote:

> I found myself constantly yearning to get back to the wool sack, where definite questions are presented for consideration; where definite rules and processes are available in their solution; where politics and expediency are laid aside, and one's efforts are directed solely to making the award to him whose cause is just. Moreover, the independence prevailing in the Federal Judiciary is especially gratifying to me, for after all, the sole end of the courts as tribunals of justice is the enforcement of the law, uniformly and impartially, without regard to persons or places or the opinions of men.

Webster had other opportunities for government service. Some suggested him as a possible candidate for the U. S. Supreme Court as well as for the U. S. Court of Appeals. In 1927 supporters made a serious attempt to persuade Webster to seek the Republican nomination for governor. The judge would have none of it. In a letter to his old congressional colleague, Representative Clarence F. Lea, Webster made it clear that he had no desire to return to politics:

> I regretted to give up my friends in Washington, but my inclination always has been toward judicial work. The harassments and annoyances of politics wear me out, and I was anxious to be into a new field and under a new environment.

On August 24, 1939, Webster resigned from the federal bench for health reasons. However, he remained active in private and public endeavors. He served as president of the Western International Baseball League in 1940-1941 and enjoyed his hobby of breeding and showing championship Boston terriers. He returned shortly to the federal bench to serve on an interim basis until Chief Justice Samuel Driver of the state supreme court gained confirmation to the federal district bench.

While serving on the state trial bench, Webster was instrumental in recruiting a faculty for the newly organized Gonzaga Law School, and school officials persuaded him to teach a course for the first two years of the school's existence. With much justification, Judge Webster could be regarded as the "father" of Gonzaga Law School.

While on the supreme court, Webster displayed an eloquent but terse opinion-writing style and seldom dissented. An old friend, Benjamin H. Kizer of Spokane, described Webster's style:

> Though he was engaged in the private practice of the law only until he was 25, a period of barely 3 years, Judge Webster's whole nature and his life were wrapped up in the law. He had a photographic memory. Lawyers practicing before him were repeatedly amazed, often dismayed by his ability, at the close of a long trial, to have him quote verbatim critical testimony of witnesses. After a single reading of an important case, he could quote from memory passages from the opinion that, in his view, were of prime importance. This natural endowment was increased by his intense nature, his ability to give the closest attention to all that went on in the courtroom. This intensity of nature was part of his fiery temperament, as a true Kentuckian.
>
> Essentially, Judge Webster was an idealist about his work as a jurist. As he grew older in judicial work, he tended more and more to withdraw from social life, so that no man could say that he was influenced by friendship. He gave his whole life to the duties of a jurist, and all the ardor of his nature was expended in matching up to that ideal of strict impartiality.

Kizer provided further insights into the character of John Stanley Webster:

> He had an unequalled gift of eloquence that never smelled of the lamp. It flowed from him, seemingly, as spontaneously, as fluently as common-places do from less gifted mortals. Those listening to him for the first time were generally carried away by his remarkable gift of utterance. In addition he had the voice, the presence, the bearing of a great man. Nor was there anything shallow or insincere about that eloquence. On the contrary, it was evident that his eloquence was the product of a first-rate fast-travelling mind that was continuously active.

He was no less fascinating in private conversation. He was the prince of story-tellers, and there seemed no limit to their number, their variety, their originality and their charm, enriched by a play of wit and humor that were unforgettable. Thus, whether men listened to him on the platform, in the courtroom or in private converse, the listener was sure to be deeply impressed by this highly gifted, deeply attractive personality.

Washington Supreme Court Justice Frank P. Weaver recalled arguing a case before Judge Webster when he presided over the federal bench in Spokane:

His lightning-like mind encompassed an intelligent appreciation and understanding of the facts, and the controlling questions of law involved, with a rapidity that confounded counsel.

I soon learned, when examining a witness, to keep one eye on the witness and the other eye on Judge Webster. He had two unconscious characteristics: one — he would tap a finger — the other — he would rock in his chair.

Counsel was not in trouble the *moment* either of these two things happened; but he was on the brink. They were danger signals that counsel was, in the court's opinion, wasting time.

The situation then posed a problem for counsel: it called for a delicate balance between keeping the judge happy and getting the jury informed.

A case tried before Judge Webster met the highest standards ever devised for the administration of justice.

His precise and eloquent command of the English language — after all, he was from Kentucky — made his instructions to the jury, not only an epitome of law and justice, but a composition of literary beauty.

Selected References

Webster papers, Manuscripts, Archives, and Special Collections, Washington State University Library; memorial services, *Washington Reports,* vol. 52, 2d (1963), pp. xvi-xxiv; *Congressional Record,* vol. 109 (28 Jan. 1963), p. 1003; *Spokane Spokesman-Review,* 20 Aug. 1939 and 21 Aug. 1939.

William Henry White
June 3, 1900-January 14, 1901;
March 20, 1901-October 7, 1902

Born: May 28, 1842
Wellsburg, Virginia
Vermillion Institute (1860-1862)
Protestant
Died: April 29, 1914
Probate Judge (1868-1871)
Prosecuting Attorney (1876-1878)
Territorial Legislature (1878-1880)
U. S. Attorney (1885-1889)
Democrat
Appointed/Elected

Although he served on the supreme court only two years, William Henry White established many firsts: the first judge appointed by a governor to fill a vacancy; the first elected to a short term; the first appointed to a temporary vacancy; the first to return to the high bench after having previously served; and the first Democrat.

White traced his Scotch-Irish ancestry in America back to the Revolutionary War. His parents, Thompson and Sarah, had moved from Pennsylvania to Virginia, where William was born. Thompson operated flour and saw mills in Wellsburg, Virginia, and became a staunch Unionist and Republican at the outbreak of the Civil War. The younger White received his education from private schools, including the Vermillion Institute at Hayesville, Ohio. But he left at age fifteen to serve with the Ohio Volunteer Infantry in the War Between the States. Because of a serious battle wound, he returned to civilian life to teach school in Ohio and then to study law under the supervision of Judge Joseph H. Pendleton. The West Virginia bar admitted White in 1868. He then won election as recorder and probate judge of Brooke County, Ohio, as a Democrat. He rejected the Republicans because of disagreement over reconstruction, the impeachment of President Andrew Johnson, and loyalty oaths required in West Virginia. In 1871 he moved to Seattle. Because of the 1873 economic depression, White moved back east in a vain search of better opportunities for practicing his profession.

In 1874 he returned to Seattle, resumed his law partnership with Colonel Charles H. Larrabee, and threw himself into local politics. According to a Seattle Bar Association memorial:

Mr. White took an active part in politics. He had been the leader of the progressive wing of the Democratic party, and because of his aggressiveness, eloquence and power he had become popularly known as "War Horse" White. He was chairman of the Democratic state delegation at the National Convention in 1896 that nominated William J. Bryan for President... He was the foremost orator of his party in the territory and state... His activities as a lawyer and citizen made him a prime factor in the upbuilding of Seattle.

In 1876 voters elected him prosecuting attorney for the Third Judicial District. Two years later he entered the lower house of the territorial legislature and served as chairman of the Judiciary Committee. He also served as Seattle City Attorney and narrowly missed being elected the territory's delegate to Congress in 1884. In 1885 President Grover Cleveland appointed White U. S. Attorney for Washington Territory.

While U. S. Attorney, White played a leading role in the 1885 Seattle Chinese riots. A mob of whites forced Chinese residents out of their homes and herded them onto a steamer headed for San Francisco. White arrived on the scene and ordered the police to break up the mob, which they refused. According to one account, White then "cursed the police as cowards and ordered the mob to disperse. They didn't. They jeered him and he cursed them, too." He, the mayor, and sheriff called out the home guard, bringing the situation under control and allowing the Chinese to return to their homes. White won grand jury indictments against the riot leaders, although, much to his disappointment, all won acquittal.

Although "War Horse" White was better known for his partisan activities prior to his short tenure on the high bench, he quickly joined in the court's deliberations and wrote his share of opinions. He rarely dissented from his colleagues, even though he was probably the most progressive among them. White was never hesitant in political or judicial matters. His opinions often reflected his boldness. For example, in *Palmer v. Laberee,* White wrote that courts "cannot correct what they deem excesses in legislation," but if enactments threatened such fundamental provisions of the state constitution as the right of contract they become "obnoxious to all constitutional restriction, and should not be upheld." He and his colleagues then promptly invalidated the law.

William White was a tall, imposing figure, which enhanced his considerable public-speaking talents. As the Seattle bar's memorial described, his "physical form and proportions [made] so striking a figure that it would not be hyperbole to describe him as an Apollo." White, sure of his politics and daring in his advocacy, did not easily change his views.

White married Emma McRedmond in June 1898, and they became parents of Martha, Dorothy, and Ruth. The city of Redmond was named after Emma's father, and the Whites' 320-acre estate became the Redmond golf course and their home the club house. White was an active Mason, a commander of the Stevens Post, Grand Army of the Republic, and a member of the Sons of the American Revolution.

Selected References

W. C. Wolfe, *Sketches of Washingtonians* (1906), p. 302; *Seattle Post-Intelligencer,* 23 Apr. 1976; Washington State Bar Association *Proceedings* (1914), pp. 232-236; H. K. Hines, *History of Washington* (1893), pp. 532-533.

William Henry Williams
January 8, 1979-January 13, 1985

Born: April 27, 1922
University of Idaho, B.A. (1948)
Gonzaga University Law School, LL.B.
  (1950)
Congregational
Deputy Prosecutor (1951-1954)
Superior Court (1958-1979)
Democrat
Elected

On May 14, 1984, after only six years, Washington State Supreme Court Justice William H. Williams announced he would retire at the end of his term. Previously, Williams hinted he would run for a second term. Some thought he would serve a couple of years, resign, and allow Democratic Governor Booth Gardner to fill his vacancy. But Williams believed election to be a contract with voters to complete a term. The chief justice's tenure of six years on the Washington State Supreme Court and twenty-one on the Spokane County Superior Court made him the state's senior judge. In announcing his retirement Williams explained, "After this many years in public service, my wife, Ruth, and I would like to have some time of our own to do those things we've always wanted to do."

William Henry Williams spent his earliest years on a family farm located between Fairfield, Washington, and Plummer, Idaho. The uncertain nature of farming forced his father to seek more secure employment, and he began working for the Washington Water Power Company during the off-season while farming during the summer. In 1926, when William was four years old, his father moved the family to Opportunity, Washington, nine miles east of Spokane, to work full time as an electrician for the power company. He remained there until his retirement in 1953. Except for a brief period in a real estate office, the justice's mother never worked outside the home.

In 1933 the Williams family moved to Spokane's south hill. Judge Williams attended public schools—first Roosevelt Elementary and then Lewis and Clark High School. In his senior year Bill started boxing at the Young Men's Christian Association. His prowess gave the young man an opportunity for a college education at the University of Idaho, one of the nation's boxing power-houses. The boxing coach arranged part-time employment for Williams, and his investment paid off when Williams won the Pacific Coast intercollegiate boxing championship in only his second year of collegiate competition.

The future judge entered an advanced Reserved Officers Training Corps pro-gram at the university, but discomforting thoughts of commanding an infantry unit prompted him, on the day before he was to be sworn in as an army officer, to travel to Fairchild Air Force Base, near Spokane, and enlist in the U. S. Army Air Corps. Within a couple of months he entered flight training school. Later, the air corps assigned Williams to the Eighth Air Force in England as a B-24 bomber pilot and he flew twenty-six combat missions.

In 1946 Williams returned to the University of Idaho to resume work on his B.A. degree in political science. Athletics again drew his attention. After guid-ing his intramural football team to victory, Williams joined the university's var-sity squad and played quarterback in the last four games of the 1946 season. The next year, while completing his first year of law school, he started at quarterback for the university's team. Although he had never lived in the Spokane suburb, his passing prowess earned him the title of "The Hillyard Rifle." Bill played on the West squad of the East-West Shrine football game on New Year's day 1948.

For William H. Williams, the practice of law had been a life-long goal. Two men – his father and his father's high school Latin teacher, Charles Greenough – had planted the seeds of this ambition. Williams therefore transferred to Spokane's Gonzaga Law School to complete his legal training. His grades were only aver-age, but he completed the four-year program in only two-and-a-half years.

After graduation, Jack Dean, a 1950 graduate of Gonzaga Law School and later Williams's law partner, drew Williams into Democratic partisan politics. Dean would later serve as Williams's campaign manager in races for the superior court and the state supreme court. But in 1952, Jack Dean managed the Spokane area election bid of Democratic gubernatorial candidate Hugh Mitchell and asked Williams to help. Republican Arthur Langlie trounced Mitchell, but the Dean-Williams "machine" gained valuable experience. Williams then managed the suc-cessful political campaign of a friend for sheriff. Albert Rosellini approached Wil-liams and Dean to manage his Spokane gubernatorial effort in 1956. The campaign brought the future judge and the new governor together in a lasting friendship. In recognition of his partisan efforts, Democrats elected Williams a state com-mitteeman from Spokane County in 1957.

The law, however, prevailed over partisan politics. Williams worked for Spo-kane County Prosecutor Hugh Evans and soon developed a reputation as a talented trial lawyer. Shortly after joining the prosecutor's office, Williams felt financially secure enough to begin family life. He married in November 1951 and his first daughter was born in 1953. The marriage ended in divorce in 1954.

Williams's second marriage to Ruth, a Spokane nurse, proved longer-lived. Six months after their marriage, she retired from nursing and focused her energies on homemaking and raising their family. The couple had three daughters and two sons.

Williams and Dean formed a general practice partnership when Williams left the prosecutor's office. As Dean later described it, "We starved together with dignity." Williams handled most of the trial work.

In 1958, Judge Carl Quackenbush retired from the Spokane County Superior Court. In part because Williams had managed the governor's Spokane campaign, and because the Spokane Bar Association placed Williams first on its list of recommended attorneys, Rosellini selected him to the superior court vacancy.

Judge Williams served on the superior court bench for twenty one years, becoming one of the most respected members of the state's trial bench. His colleagues honored him when they elected him to the board of trustees of the Washington State Judges Association and later selected him as its president. He was a no-nonsense, yet compassionate jurist. Because of his straightforward and firm sentencing practices, the judge became known around the inmate population of the state prison as "Walla Walla Williams."

He was particularly proud of two practices he introduced while serving as senior judge on the trial bench. The first was a *pro tempore* judge system; the second, a weekly brown-bag lunch where he and his colleagues discussed administrative problems and shared thoughts on matters of mutual concern. Gradually, a strong group identity emerged out of what previously had been six separate judicial operations. This latter innovation typified Williams's practice of informally consulting with colleagues and attempting to bring together a number of independently minded judges toward a common goal.

In 1978 Williams's old friend from the Washington Supreme Court, Orris L. Hamilton, another east-sider, urged Williams to consider running for the supreme court seat he would soon relinquish. Williams, honored by Hamilton's suggestion, liked life as it was and politely but emphatically turned down his friend's offer. Justice Hamilton phoned again in two weeks, and persuaded Williams to reconsider. This time Williams admitted he was tempted, but remained noncommittal. The odds that someone from the east side could win an election to the supreme court seemed very low. But Williams thought his two major opponents—Keith Callow and Francis Holman—both from Seattle, would split the western vote in the September primary. With enough Democratic and labor support Williams could be a credible candidate in November. Williams outpolled his three opponents in the primary. In the general election he faced his old friend and fellow superior court jurist, Holman. He won a narrow election victory, 386,244 votes to Holman's 365,721.

While serving on the trial bench, most people perceived Walla Walla Williams as being firmly on the side of law enforcement. On the supreme court,

Williams appeared to abandon his previous hard line views, especially in search and seizure cases. He believed "the Bill of Rights was written to protect people against their government; the price of liberty is that some get away." Justice Williams warned that "law enforcement agencies must also follow the law; if you do not follow the law, be prepared to suffer the consequences." However, once convicted by scrupulously gathered evidence, guilty parties could expect little sympathy from the judge.

One observer saw Williams as "philosophically in the middle" of supreme court jurists. Williams's close friend and colleague, Justice Hugh Rosellini, also saw him as a moderating influence on the court. As a superior court judge, Williams gained credit for strengthening the cohesiveness of that bench. But each member of the supreme court was working to capacity, and there was no time for leisurely reconciliation of issues. Williams became particularly bothered by the vast amount of reading required. During court terms, a table in his chambers supported a mountain of briefs, memos, and records waiting to be read carefully and thoughtfully. The chief justice readily admitted he was not the speed reader that some of his colleagues were, but he managed to complete his work.

Williams accepted dissent as a critical part of the supreme court's decisional process. To him, the most important function of drafting dissenting opinions was to win over a majority. In his six years on the court he wrote thirty-one dissents, seventeen of which proved compelling enough to become majority opinions. These figures point to the power of dissent, and the persuasiveness of Williams.

After four years as an associate justice, Williams inherited the responsibilities of chief justice in 1983. Although he was not required to write opinions, Chief Justice Williams chose to write a few each term, including an occasional dissent.

In his six years on the high bench, Williams became instrumental in moving the court slightly toward the liberal side of the political spectrum. He most often found himself aligned with moderate-to-liberal justices. He often cast the swing vote in close cases, making him a powerful court member. Each time Williams wrote an opinion, he had a high probability of retaining or getting a majority.

In a February 1984 interview, Chief Justice Williams admitted that

> being a public servant is not easy. It's frustrating to me sometimes. There's too high an expectation of what we can do. Changing society is not our role constitutionally. At the same time, we come out with things that we are required constitutionally to do that dissatisfy people.

Bill Williams felt his greatest accomplishment on the high court was to help revitalize the state constitution by basing decisions on that fundamental law rather than the United States Constitution. In retirement, Williams sat as *pro tem* judge at all levels of the Washington court system and did occasional work for federal courts in Spokane. He still retains a desk in Jack Dean's law office.

Selected References

See the Williams oral history interview, supreme court collection, Washington State Archives and the Jack Dean oral history interview, same collection. Also see *Spokane Spokesman-Review,* 20 Jy. 1978, 29 Oct. 1978, and 26 Feb. 1984; *Seattle Post-Intelligencer,* 11 Feb. 1979 and 15 May 1984; Moscow *Palouse Empire News,* 27 Nov. 1981; and *Yakima Herald-Republic,* 23 Je. 1983.

Charles Thomas Wright
January 11, 1971-November 6, 1980

Born: March 7, 1911
Shelton, Washington
College of Puget Sound (1928-1932)
University of Washington (1932-1934)
Episcopalian
Died: November 6, 1980
Acting Prosecuting Attorney (1942-1945)
Superior Court (1949-1971)
Republican
Elected

Justice Charles Thomas Wright was a soft-spoken, quiet, and gentle man. Deeply religious, he viewed the world in simple fundamental terms. He and his wife Helen put into practice their Christian virtues. According to a close friend:

> His deep religious faith. . .translated into a concern for the less fortunate of our people, made him and his wife. . .almost a one-family United Good Neighbors. While they had no children of their own, they raised and cared for a number of foster children, and over the years shopped and delivered necessities for an untold number of families who were in need.

Wright had an impressive heritage. His grandfather, Henry J. Whitney, was Washington's first surgeon, practicing in Davenport before moving to Cashmere to continue his practice and supervise fairly extensive fruit orchard holdings. His grandmother, H. Josephine Whitney, a talented artist and one of the first women fully qualified as a physician in the western United States, practiced with her husband.

D. F. Wright, Charles's father and Josephine's son from a previous marriage, chose to practice law. He earned both LL.B. and LL.D. degrees from Drake University, and gained admittance to the bar in Iowa and Washington. Prior to his law studies, he had been a professional photographer with his own studio in Davenport. He opened a law office in Davenport in 1900, moved to Coulee City in 1905, and then went to Shelton in 1907, where he practiced until 1914, when he won election to the superior court. Charles's mother, Fanna Bell (Streator) Wright, also earned LL.B. and LL.M. degrees, passed the bar in Iowa and Washington, and became one of the first women lawyers in the state. Active in a national organization for women lawyers, she had practiced law for a time with her husband in Davenport, but after moving to western Washington concentrated on raising the family. She soon became a leading figure in Shelton's civic life. The elder Wrights mostly observed rather than participated in partisan affairs, although D. F. Wright had avidly followed William Jennings Bryan. After election to the superior court bench in 1914, he withdrew entirely from partisan activity.

Charles Thomas, born on March 7, 1911 in Shelton, attended public schools there and in Olympia, and the College of Puget Sound in Tacoma from 1928 to 1932. He left without graduating to attend the University of Washington School of Law. His parents had wanted Charlie to study medicine, but he chose law. In 1934 he withdrew from the university to study law under his father. After being admitted to the Washington bar in 1937, he practiced in Union and Shelton, first by himself, then in 1945 in the partnership of Wright and Malloy. After one year he returned to sole practice, where he remained until appointed to the superior court bench in 1949. His practice involved work with insurance companies, banks, the Mason County Public Utility District and general law for individuals. During World War II Wright served as acting prosecuting attorney for Mason County. He also invested in and managed real estate holdings and had Christmas tree and timber interests, as well as oyster beds in Hood Canal.

Charles considered himself an activist in Republican politics prior to his appointment to the trial bench. He ran for the state legislature four times between 1936 and 1942, each time surviving the primaries but never claiming victory in the November balloting. The Twenty-fourth District, encompassing Clallam, Jefferson, and Mason counties, remained a Democratic stronghold throughout the period. Even so, his campaigning stood him in good stead in his later supreme court races. Although his sympathies lay with the Republicans, after his appointment to the bench, Judge Wright always recorded his party affiliation as "independent."

After thirty-four years on the Mason-Thurston County Superior Court, Judge D. F. Wright announced his retirement in 1949. Governor Mon C. Wallgren promptly appointed son Charles to the vacancy. At age thirty-seven he began a career on the bench that would span thirty-one years. At his death in 1980, Judge Wright was the second most senior jurist in the state.

As trial judge for Thurston County—which included Olympia—Charles, like his father, heard some of the most political cases in the state. Whenever the state was involved in litigation, the Thurston County Superior Court very likely heard the case. While on the trial bench, Judge Wright served as president of the Superior Court Judges' Association and edited its newsletter, *Washington Court Commentaries*. He also chaired the committee on the improvement of the administration of justice.

Despite the security he enjoyed on the superior court bench—he was challenged only twice in his six reelection attempts, and in both bids won handily—Judge Wright actively sought appointment to the state's supreme court. In 1963 he informed Governor Albert Rosellini of his availability. The governor responded that although he considered Judge Wright highly qualified he had "pretty well made a determination" to place Frank Hale, a Democrat, on the bench. Likely, Wright's earlier Republican activities placed him low on the Democratic governor's appointment priorities.

Throughout the 1960s, Wright's name remained on the appointment list but in 1970 he made it known that should a supreme court appointment evade him, he would file for election to the post. When Governor Daniel Evans appointed Morell Sharp, Wright promptly filed for his spot and solicited financial and organizational support from other superior court judges, trial court clerks, state notables, and many members of the legislature. Initially he planned to challenge Chief Justice Robert Hunter, but supporters persuaded him to take on Republican Justice Sharp. The state bar association overwhelmingly endorsed Sharp, who also had the public support of Governor Evans and the Republican party. Even so, Wright defeated the incumbent by more than 12,000 votes.

Some observers attributed Wright's victory to the fact that he had the same last name as Eugene Wright, a popular King County Superior Court judge before being appointed to the U. S. Circuit Court of Appeals. Although admitting the possibility of such name confusion, Charles pointed out that he had been on the state bench for over twenty-one years and was "probably as well-known statewide" as Eugene Wright. Through his own efforts, those of labor, and the Grange, Wright defeated an incumbent, the first time that had happened in over twenty years.

Again without the endorsement of the legal profession, he turned aside the challenge of popular King County Superior Court judge and former prosecutor, Lloyd Shorett, in 1972, narrowly winning a full six-year term on the court. Shorett focussed on Wright's record as a superior court judge rather than his two years on the supreme court: "I am running against Wright because he was about as bad a procrastinator when he was on the superior court as we have had." Wright demonstrated his ability to attract voters in his first two supreme court campaigns, and in 1978 he won reelection without opposition.

After his 1970 election victory, Wright summarized his view of judging. He proudly accepted the label of "strict constructionist" in constitutional matters. He favored capital punishment as a deterrent against crime: "I think a man might think twice before he shot a policemen if he knew he might hang for it." He also believed taxpayers should have the benefit of the doubt in any conflict with government. Private property was, in his view, a vested right. Later, he came under criticism for being nearly five-years delinquent in paying his own property taxes.

In a 1971 address to the western district of the State Association of Counties, Justice Wright revealed his views of many contemporary issues. Sinister forces threatened local government and brought local elected officials into disrepute. "All you have to do is see the slurring remarks in the news media time after time about legislators and Congressmen to know what I mean," he said. So-called "progressive thinkers," Indian activists, "agitators," and "Communists" were to blame. County officials ought not to adopt a civil service program for county employees:

> Civil service has laudable purposes, but by the same token it takes control of the people that are serving the public, the people that are coming in contact with the public and it takes control away from the electorate.

As a lifetime member of the National Rifle Association, he also warned against those who would "disarm the people." Taxation policies would destroy self government. He condemned the centralizing of government in Olympia and Washington, D.C. Local government ought to be strengthened, for there "everything is in plain sight. We don't have scandals like the Pentagon Papers in local government." Even so, the "enforcement of the criminal law" must be flexible. A misguided and confused youth should not be subject to the same standards as a person with a criminal record.

Justice Wright worked closely with his law clerks. According to one of his former clerks, the judge "could always be reached during the noon hour (we talked on almost a daily basis at noon). He enjoyed an educational interchange about upcoming cases... Judge Wright was refreshingly unpretentious, unthreatening and one of the kindest men I have ever met." However, his decisional style remained individual in the sense that he tended not to consult on a regular basis with other members of the bench. One of his campaign ads noted that:

> Charles Wright is OPPOSED to the view... that the members of the Supreme Court ought to be considered a 'team.' He believes that every case should be weighed on its merits, INDEPENDENTLY by each member of the Supreme Court and that no judge on the basis of his own affiliations should ever be for or against any person or group of persons.

This independent perspective came partially from his reserved and somewhat withdrawn personality and also from the fact that, although close friends with all other members of the bench, he parted from their moderate-to-liberal views regarding law and order and property issues. Thus, although not a habitual dissenter—he wrote 125 majority and thirty-three concurring or dissenting opinions—he often found himself isolated on these issues. He would draft dissents if they "might lay the groundwork for the future" and win over some votes to his viewpoint. But he also felt compelled to "write it as I see it despite the majority." Although well-liked and respected by other members of the bench, Justice Wright provided no leadership. But he did not intend to be the court's conscience.

While serving as chief justice in 1978 and 1979, court delay became his special concern. He argued that much of the delay could be eliminated by giving more discretion to trial judges:

> Delay is certainly one of the major causes of dissatisfaction with the judicial process. . . . I feel a great deal can be done by placing enough power in the trial judges to eliminate the wholly unmeritorious cases. The means are now available by summary judgment, and similar proceedings, if only the appellate courts would support the trial judges in the use of those means.

After a period of failing health, suffering from diabetes and heart trouble, Justice Wright passed away on November 6, 1980 at the age of sixty-nine. Chief Justice Robert Utter, in a tribute to Wright, said, "He was always concerned about the little person and about injustice and fairness. His opinions and personal life reflected this concern."

Selected References

See Wright's oral history interview, supreme court collection, Washington State Archives. Also see memorial services, *Washington Reports,* vol. 95, 2d (1981), pp. xxxvii-liii; *Seattle Post-Intelligencer,* 7 Nov. 1980; *Shelton-Mason County Journal,* 12 Aug. 1971; C. W. Taylor, *Eminent Judges and Lawyers of the Northwest* (1954), p. 375; and Charles Sheldon, "An Interpretation of the Judicial Process: The Washington Supreme Court as a Small Group," *Gonzaga Law Review,* vol. 13 (1977), pp. 97-139.

Appendix

Law Clerks
Washington State Supreme Court

Name	Term	Judge
	1937-1938	
John N. Rupp		Steinert
Robert Reid		Robinson-Geraghty
Ernest H. Campbell		Holcomb
		Tolman
		Simpson
	1939	
Robert Reid		Robinson-Geraghty
William Lowry		Steinert
Ernest H Campbell		Beals-Simpson
Charles I. Stone		Simpson
	1940	
Jack H. Jaffee		Simpson
Max Kaminoff		Steinert
Robert Reid		Robinson-Geraghty
Lamar N. Ostrander		Beals-Jeffers
William Blevens		
	1941	
Kenneth A. Cox		Steinert
Robert Reid		Robinson
Lamar N. Ostrander		Beals-Jeffers
Frank W. Foley		Beals-Driver
	1942	
Robert E. Stoeve		Steinert
Nona B. Fumerton (Cox)		Beals-Jeffers
Robert Reid		Robinson
Esther Jane Johnson		Beals
	1943-1944	
Mary Ellen Krug		Beals
Robert Reid		Robinson
	1945-1946	
Filis L. Otto		Steinert
Robert Reid		Robinson

Name	Term	Judge
	1947	
Gordon E. Blechschmidt		Hill
M. Bayard Crutcher		Steinert
Robert Reid		Robinson
George Bonneville		Simpson
John F. Dore		Connelly-Millard
	1948	
Richard White		Mallery
Daniel C. Blom		Beals
David B. Hallin		Schwellenbach
Norman B. Nelson		Steinert
Robert Reid		Robinson
Richard E. Callahan		Hill
Donald C. Blair		Simpson
William J. Millard, Jr.		Millard
	1949	
Tyler C. Moffett		Beals
John H. Kirkwood		Mallery
George H. Davies		Hill
John C. Lombard		Hamley
Will L. Lorenz		Schwellenbach
William A. Roberts		Donworth
John S. Robinson, Jr.		Robinson
Jeff D. Miller		Grady
Charles L. Sayre		Steinert
	1950	
Tyler C. Moffett		Beals
William A. Roberts		Donworth
Warren Chan		Hamley
Edmund J. Jones		Simpson
Burroughs B. Anderson		Mallery
Dave C. Hutchison		Grady
Leo H. Frederickson		Schwellenbach
John Robinson, Jr.		Robinson-Finley
James Truman Johnson		Hill
	1951	
Cleary S. Cone		Donworth
Jo Ann Gunn (Locke)		Beals
Pat Townsend (Long)		Finley
Larry White		Hamley
William L. Stephens		Hill

Name	Term	Judge
	1952	
James Dolliver		Hamley
W. Willard Jones		Donworth
Edward W. Hautanen		Finley
John T. Slater		Olson
Robert J. McNichols		Grady
Don L. Holman		Hill
Herbert Legg		Mallery
Art J. Hutton, Jr.		Weaver
James Connelly		Schwellenbach
	1953	
Gordon F. Crandall		Hamley
Tom R. Garlington		Finley
Robert S. Day		Schwellenbach
John A. Westland, Jr.		Weaver
Robert Manley		Mallery
Keith Callow		Hill
Richard W. Buchanan		Donworth
Joanne Bailey Wilson		Rosellini
Charles R. Olson		Olson
	1954	
Donald N. Olson		Schwellenbach
John K. Pain, Jr.		Schwellenbach
Elvin J. Vandeberg		Weaver
Newman L. Dotson		Hamley
Myrtle R. Kvangnes		Mallery
E. Glenn Harmon		Donworth
Robert F. Utter		Hill
Dan R. Olson		Olson-Ott
Joanne Bailey Wilson		Rosellini
Richard W. Bartke		Finley
Robert DeGrief Skidmore		Hill
	1955	
Gordon C. Swyter		Finley
Joel A. Rindal		Ott
Elbert R. Browder		Weaver
John A. Gose		Hamley
Charles Z. Smith		Hill
John K. Pain, Jr.		Schwellenbach
Joanne Bailey Wilson		Rosellini
Myrtle Kvangnes		Mallery
Joseph E. Brennan		Donworth

Name	Term	Judge
	1956	
Joanne Wilson		Rosellini
Theodore R. Fournier, Jr.		Donworth
Robert F. Hauth		Schwellenbach
Irwin L. Treiger		Finley
Robert E. Dixon		Ott
Craig P. Campbell		Donworth-Foster
Joseph J. Roller		Foster
Howard A. Anderson		Weaver
Jerome Shulkin		Hill
Myrtle Kvangnes		Mallery
	1957	
Josepy J. Roller		Foster
Joanne Wilson		Rosellini
William L. Dwyer		Donworth
Robert J. Doran		Hunter
C. Duane Lansverk		Finley
Theodore A. Roy		Ott
James E. Kennedy		Mallery
Gordon L. Walgren		Hill
Marcus M. Kelly		Weaver
Theodore Fournier, Jr.		Finley
	1958	
Joanne Wilson		Rosellini
Robert J. Hall		Donworth
James E. Kennedy		Mallery
Robert T. Carter		Hill
Rembert Ryals		Finley
Richard M. Montecucco		Hunter
Robert L. Harris		Weaver
William H. Fraser		Ott
Gilbert C. Valley		Foster
Bennett Feigenbaum		Weaver
	1959	
Joanne Wilson		Rosellini
Duane S. Stookey		Donworth
Robert T. Kennedy		Ott
Donald J. Horowitz		Foster
James A. Alfiere		Hunter
Phillip Holmes Austin		Finley
Victor V. Hoff		Ott
Matthew E. Brislawn		Mallery
Theodore O. Torve		Hill
Bennett Feignebaum		Weaver

Name	Term	Judge
	1960	
Matthew E. Brislawn		Mallery
Joanne Wilson		Rosellini
Timothy R. Clifford		Finley
John F. Colgrove		Weaver
Charles E. Siljeg		Ott
Frank J. Woody		Hunter
Ronald J. Bland		Donworth
James G. Leach		Hill
John F. Coleman, Jr.		*
Thomas E. Headrick		Foster
	1961	
Joanne Wilson		Rosellini
Robert Baronsky		Hunter
Joseph A. Mallery, Jr.		Mallery
Frank J. Owens		Ott
Lloyd W. Peterson		Finley
Angelo Petruss		Weaver
Harding T. Roe		Hill
Alan G. Sumberg		Foster
Peter D. Francis		Donworth
	1962	
Joanne Wilson		Rosellini
Stephen S. Bassett		Foster-Hale
Henry Haas		Ott
David D. Hoff		Weaver
James R. Irwin		Hill
John E. Iverson		Hunter
Larrie E. Elhart		Donworth
Edward B. Mackie		Finley
Robert Baronsky		Hunter
	1963	
Odine H. Husemoen		Donworth
Joanne Wilson		Rosellini
Samuel A. Weaver		Weaver
Jay A. Whitfield		*
Charles B. Cooper		Finley
Hobart S. Dawson		*
Thomas L. Dempsey		Ott
Bradford M. Gierke		Hill

Name	Term	Judge
	1963 (Continued)	
Louis L. Barokas		*pro-tempore*
Thomas R. McMillen		Hale
John E. Murray		⋆
John G. Schultz		Hunter
Edmond Neal King		Hamilton
	1964	
Joanne Wilson		Rosellini
Samuel A. Weaver		Weaver
Paul James Codd		Ott
Morris G. Shore		Hamilton
Edward L. Meuller		Donworth
Matt M. M. Sayre		Hunter
Kenneth L. Schubert, Jr.		Finley
David L. Scott		Hale
Bruce A. Butcher		*pro-tempore*
Juseph H. Gordon, Jr.		Hill
Lembhard B. Howell		⋆
Patrick W. Crowley		Hamilton
	1965	
Joanne Wilson		Rosellini
William Wayne Baker		Hunter
Lawrence P. Gill		Hale
Camden M. Hall		Hamilton
Stephen J. Bean		Weaver
Howard J. Coleman, Jr.		Hill
R. Graham Cross		Ott
Joe Keith Dysart		Finley
Edward L. Meuller		Donworth
David G. Metcalf		*pro-tempore*
Merle E. Wilcox		*pro-tempore*
Ronald J. Meltzer		*pro-tempore*
	1966	
Joanne Wilson		Rosellini
John M. Wolfe		Donworth
Frank P. Weaver, Jr.		Weaver
William Ronald Hulen		Hamilton
C. Raymond Eberle		Hill
William M. Gingery		*pro-tempore*

Name	Term	Judge
	1966 (Continued)	
Thomas J. Heye		Ott
Duncan A. Bayne		Hale
Peter E. Paget		*pro-tempore*
Stephen P. Ryder		Hunter
Stephen A. Crary		Finley
	1967	
Joanne Wilson		Rosellini
Paul W. Whelan		*pro-tempore*–Finley
Dennis D. Yule		Hill
James C. Middlebrooks		Neill
Bruce M. Pym		Finley
Roger M. Leed		Hunter
James E. Allen, Jr.		★
James H. Allendoerfer		Hamilton
Frederick W. Fleming		McGovern
James A. Grutz		*pro-tempore*
Faye Collier Kennedy		Finley
Bruce M. Cross		Weaver
Michael E. Donohue		Hale
Arther H. Ward		*pro-tempore*
Edmund J. Jones		Finley
	1968	
Joanne Wilson		Rosellini
Robert I. Betts		Hill
Howard R. Eddy		Finley
John S. Fattorini, Jr.		*pro-tempore*
Stanbery Foster, Jr.		Hale
Charles K. Grosse		Weaver
Mark G. Honeywell		Ott
Thomas A. Clark		Hamilton
Roger Leed		Hunter
James Anthony Kramer		Hill
Charles W. Lean		Neill
Linda Lee Dawson (Watkins)		*pro-tempore*
Dennis J. LaPorte		Hunter
Frederick W. Fleming		McGovern
	1969	
Joanne Wilson		Rosellini
Gerald K. Mooney		Neill
Eugene C. Routh		Finley
Bruce D. Erickson		McGovern

Name	Term	Judge
	1969 (Continued)	
Fred Caruso		*pro-tempore*
David E. Rhea, Jr.		*pro-tempore*
Michael L. Cohen		Weaver-Sharp
William E. Cullen, Jr.		Hamilton
Charles J. DeLaurenti		Hunter
C. Robert Wallis		Hale
Paul L. Stritmatter		Hill-Stafford
	1970	
Richard J. Langabeer		Hunter
Gary M. Cuillier		Hamilton-Hunter
Edward F. Schaller, Jr.		Hunter-Wright
Clifford Stilz, Jr.		Finley
Ralph D. Pittle		Hamilton
Robert L. Gunter		McGovern
Tim Weaver		Sharp-Hamilton
Bart G. Irwin		Stafford
Joanne Wilson		Rosellini
C. Robert Wallis		Hale
Gerald K. Mooney		Neill
	1971	
Joanne Wilson		Rosellini
Gary M. Cuillier		Sharp
Brian D. Leahy		Hamilton
Robert M. McIntosh		Finley
Thomas J. Taylor		Hunter
Phillip D. Noble		Sharp
Earl R. McGimpsey		Stafford
Norman J. Ericson		Wright
Tim Martin		Neill
Darrell Syferd		Utter
Gerald K. Mooney		Neill
C. Robert Wallis		Hale
	1972	
Keith L. Kessler		Finley
Ronald L. Coleman		Stafford
David Kader		Utter
G. Tim Martin		Neill-Brachtenbach
Brian Leahy		Hamilton
Robert Wallis		Hale

Name	Term	Judge
	1972 (Continued)	
Joanne Wilson		Rosellini
Norman J. Ericson		Wright
Terry McCarthy		Hunter
	1973	
Tracy Rosellini		Hale
A. Peter Parsons		Finley
Frank L. Dacca		Hunter
John A. Hoglund		Hamilton
Joseph D. Puckett		Stafford
Michael E. Andrews		Utter
Curtis Lee Brooke		Hale
C. Robert Wallis		Hale
Joanne Wilson		Rosellini
Norman J. Ericson		Wright
G. Tim Martin		Brachtenbach
	1974	
Curtis Lee Brooke		Hale
Joanne Wilson		Rosellini
Nick Phillips		Hale
Kerry D. Kidman		Finley
Andrew C. Bohrnsen		Hunter
Anne L. Ellington		Hamilton
James E. Ryan		Stafford
Drake Charles		Wright
Tim K. Ford		Utter
Donovan R. Flora		Brachtenbach
Arthur A. Butler		Horowitz
	1975	
Sally E. Mathiasen		Stafford
Bryan Fischnaller		Finley
Richard Klobucher		Hunter
Joseph McMonigle		Hamilton
Richard J. Fink		Utter
Drake Charles		Wright
Gregory C. Abel		Brachtenbach
Richard A. Paroutaud		Horowitz
Leonard J. Nelson, III		Stafford
Joanne Wilson		Rosellini
Susan Hammer		Dolliver

Name	Term	Judge
	1976	
Karen Dobson		Hunter
Dave Lombard		Hamilton
Brian Tollefson		Wright
Stephen Oliver		Utter
Kenneth K. C. Webster		Brachtenbach
Timothy Osborne		Horowitz
Susan Hammer		Dolliver
Sally Mathiason		Stafford
Joanne Wilson		Rosellini
	1977	
Lucy Isake		Hamilton
Kate Julin		Stafford
Greg Adams		Utter
Bruce Buskirk		Brachtenbach
Ellen Dial		Horowitz
Gayle Bush		Dolliver
Bill Lynn		Hicks
Brian Tollefson		Wright
Joanne Wilson		Rosellini
	1978	
Gini McGown		Utter
Pat Youngblood		Stafford
Arnie Braafladt		Wright
Ellen Dial		Horowitz
Chris Meserve		Dolliver
Kerry Radcliffe		Hicks
Lynn DuBey		Williams
Simon Klevansky		Utter
Joanne Wilson		Rosellini
Joseph Schickich		Brachtenbach
	1979	
Randy Hertz		Utter
Joan Elgee		Utter
Joanne Wilson		Rosellini
Pat Marshall		Stafford
Arnie Braafladt		Wright
Jeff Haley		Brachtenbach
Catherine Smith		Horowitz
Lori Nelson		Dolliver
Brian MacRitchie		Hicks
Sue Jones		Williams

Name	Term	Judge
	1980	
Robert Spitzer		Brachtenbach
Timothy Dowling		Brachtenbach
Robert Cole		Stafford
Michael Helgren		Utter
Alan Osaki		Dolliver
Sue Jones		Williams
Irene Bronstein		Dore
Janet Gray		Dimmick
Joanne Wilson		Rosellini
	1981	
Bertha Fitzer		Brachtenbach
Heidi Sachs		Brachtenbach
Joanne Wilson		Rosellini
Janet Gray		Stafford
John Phillips		Utter
Bill King		Dolliver
James Horne		Williams
Sherrie Bennett		Dore
Carol Wardell-Mack		Dimmick
Mark Lewington		Pearson
	1982	
Sherrie Bennett		Dore
Bertha Fitzer		Rosellini
Carl Gunn		Utter
James Horne		Williams
Mark Lewington		Pearson
Joe Mentor		Dolliver
Elizabeth Pike		Stafford
Michael Reynvaan		Brachtenbach
Heidi Sacks		Brachtenbach
Carol Wardel-Mack		Dimmick
	1983	
Mathew Fick		Williams
Ida Leggett		Williams
Bertha Fitzer		Rosellini
Steve Helgeson		Rosellini-Dore
Heather Huston-Reeve		Utter
Mark Ebert		Brachtenbach
Carrie McIntosh		Brachtenbach

Name	Term	Judge
	1983 (Continued)	
Karen Sly		Dolliver
Paul Burns		Dore
Chirstina Corder		Dimmick
Robert Casey		Pearson
Tad Sowers		Pearson
	1984	
Sylvia Luppert		Williams
Mary Fiarhurst		Williams
Steve Helgeson		Rosellini
Jeannie Kroum		Rosellini-Dore
Paul Parker		Utter
Kathryn Frank		Utter
Terese Richmond		Brachtenbach
Cheryl French		Brachtenbach-Dimmick
Peter Goldman		Dolliver
Sal Mungia		Dore
Cheryl Bleakney		Dimmick
Cindy Burdue		Pearson
Karin Nyrop		Pearson-Andersen
Frankie Adams Crain		Andersen
	1985	
Cheryl Bleakney		Dolliver
Peter Goldman		Dolliver
Paul Parker		Utter
Kathryn Frank		Utter
Terese Richmond		Brachtenbach
Cheryl Frence		Brachtenbach-Durham
Steve Helgeson		Dore
Sal Mungia		Dore-Goodloe
Cindy Burdue		Pearson
Karin Nyrop		Pearson-Andersen
Janice Creim		Andersen
Mark Clausen		Callow
Lisa Knirk		Callow
Mary Fairhurst		Goodloe
Howard Coleman		Durham
	1986	
Craig Shuman		Dolliver
John McLean		Utter
Camille Gearhart		Utter-Callow

Name	Term	Judge
	1986 (Continued)	
Charles Maduell		Brachtenbach
Dee Brookings		Brachtenbach-Pearson
Steve Helgeson		Dore
Stuart Horwich		Dore
Charlie DeJong		Pearson
James McNeill		Pearson
Carole Breitenbach		Andersen
Greg Trautman		Andersen-Durham
John Karna		Callow
Cameron Comfort		Callow
Mary Fairhurst		Goodloe
Richard Thuman		Goodloe
Ingrid Hollund		Durham
	1987	
Carol Hunting		Dolliver
Sanford Pitler		Utter
Reiko Cushman		Utter
Duane Thurman		Brachtenbach
Helen Benson		Brachtenbach
Zera Holland		Dore
Stuart Horwich		Dore
Misty Mondress		Pearson
Alice Leiner		Pearson
Carole Breitenbach		Andersen
Jim Tierney		Andersen
Greg Trautman		Callow
Alice Wright		Callow
Cameron Comfort		Goodloe
Lauren Marshall		Goodloe
Ingrid Hollund		Durham
Rick Neidhardt		Durham
	1988	
Nan Thomas		Pearson
Margaret Dore		Pearson
Rebekah Ross		Utter
Mark Olsen		Utter
Duane Thurman		Brachtenbach
Helen Benson		Brachtenbach
Michael Ryan		Dolliver

Name	Term	Judge
	1988 (Continued)	
Jessica Porter		Dolliver
James Tierney		Dore
Kyron Huigens		Dore
Carole Breitenbach		Andersen
Heidi Irvin		Andersen
Kathy Gerla		Callow
Deborah Carstens		Callow
Kim Comfort		Goodloe
Alice Wright		Goodloe
Jeff Chasnow		Durham
Rick Neidhardt		Durham
	1989	
Brad Steiner		Pearson
Stacy Cole		Pearson
Susan McClelland		Utter
Mark Olsen		Utter
Daniel Compton		Utter
Michael Targett		Brachtenbach
Helen Benson		Brachtenbach
Brenda Turner		Dolliver
Elizabeth Petrich		Dore
Kyron Huigens		Dore
Carol Breitenbach		Andersen
Mary Lobdell		Andersen
Russell Brine		Andersen
Mathew Edwards		Callow
Peter Marchel		Callow
Jeff Chasnow		Durham
Rick Neidhardt		Durham
Monica Fernandez		Smith
	1990	
Kathy Stockman		Callow
Ron Sergi		Callow
Kara Larsen		Utter
David Driesen		Utter
Helen Bensen		Brachtenbach
Mary Sue Wilson		Brachtenbach
Mimi DesJardins		Dolliver
Liz Petrick		Dore

Name	Term	Judge
	1990 (Continued)	
Joan Marchioro		Dore
Barbara Zanzig		Dore
Carole Breitenbach		Andersen
Nan Thomas		Andersen
Connie Dillon		Durham
Gregory Tolbert		Durham
Caroll Rusk		Smith
Nancy Hoodecheck		Smith
Mark Kamitomo		Guy
	1991	
Kate Walsh		Dore
Millie Dooris		Dore
Osler McCarthy		Dore
Bruce Brown		Utter
Coleen O'Connor		Utter
Helen Bensen		Brachtenbach
Tommy Prudhomme		Brachtenbach
David Ericksen		Dolliver
Alicia Ramos		Dolliver
Nan Thomas		Andersen
Sheila Huber		Andersen
Connie Dill		Durham
Shelly Crocker		Durham
Artee Young		Smith
Anthony Keating		Guy
Clark Shores		Guy
Rick Neidhardt		Johnson
Donna Matsumoto		Johnson

* = Assigned to no particular judge

Bibliography

The Washington Supreme Court has been the focus of only a few studies. Consequently, most sources on its personnel, practices, and impact are rare and diverse first-person accounts. Only three other secondary works have focused on the high bench. Charles Sheldon's *A Century of Judging: A Political History of the Washington Supreme Court* (1988) constitutes a full-length, comprehensive study of the state's high bench from its beginnings to the 1980s. C. S. Reinhart, who served as the second clerk of court from 1891 to 1934, published his *History of the Supreme Court of the Territory and State of Washington: With Reminiscences of the Author* in the 1930s. This 148-page book contains brief anecdotal accounts of all judges who sat on the high bench to 1931 and includes some photos. Copies of this privately published volume are available in large research libraries. Arthur S. Beardsley's yet unpublished manuscript entitled "The History of the Bench and Bar in Washington: 1850-1900," is a monumental work covering territorial days and early years of statehood. It contains accounts of trials and profiles of attorneys and judges for the state's supreme and superior courts as well as the federal territorial and district benches. Copies of the manuscript are located in the University of Washington Law School Library and the Supreme Court Library in Olympia. The State Archives in Olympia not only has a copy of the manuscript in its supreme court collection, but also retains copies of the author's notes, historic photos Beardsley collected over the years, and earlier drafts of the work.

Much of the information about recent members of the state's court of last resort gathered for this volume comes from personal interviews with the justices, their law clerks, family members, and acquaintances. Copies of the taped interviews are available in the supreme court collection of the State Archives. The following justices were interviewed, often several times: Joseph A. Mallery, Matthew W. Hill, Frank P. Weaver, Hugh B. Rosellini, Richard B. Ott, Robert T. Hunter, Orris L. Hamilton, Frank Hale, Marshall A. Neill, Walter T. McGovern, Charles F. Stafford, Morell E. Sharp, Charles T. Wright, Robert F. Utter, Robert Brachtenbach, James M. Dolliver, Floyd V. Hicks, William H. Williams, Fred H. Dore, Carolyn R. Dimmick, Vernon R. Pearson, James A. Andersen, Keith M. Callow, William C. Goodloe, Barbara Durham, Charles Z. Smith, Richard P. Guy, and Charles W. Johnson. Also interviewed were supreme court clerk Jack Champagne, reporter of decisions Robert F. Jones, court commissioner Joan Smith Lawrence, and court bailiff David Webster.

Family and friends of the following were interviewed, tapes of which are available at the State Archives: George B. Simpson, Samuel M. Driver,

Thomas E. Grady, Robert C. Finley, Charles F. Stafford, John S. Robinson, and Ralph O. Olson.

The private papers of Robert Finley, Robert Hunter, William Goodloe, Frank Weaver, John Stanley Webster, Orris Hamilton, Samuel Driver, Charles Wright, Charles Smith, and Joseph Mallery proved helpful for the study and are available in either the State Archives or Manuscripts, Archives and Special Collections at Washington State University Library. The Manuscripts Division of the University of Washington Library has an extensive collection of materials relating to Frederick G. Hamley.

I surveyed former law clerks to the justices, beginning with two of the first three who served in 1937—John N. Rupp and Ernest H. Campbell—through the class of 1984, by means of a mailed questionnaire. A total of 166 responded and more than fifty of these were also interviewed. Again, the taped interviews and questionnaires are part of the supreme court collection in the State Archives.

Finally, the author's files on each of the justices, containing microfiche copies of accounts of the justices published in the *Seattle Times* and *Post-Intelligencer,* correspondence with the jurists, clerks, and acquaintances, copies of some of their published works, newspaper clippings, and drafts of biographies, constituted sources often consulted for this study. These files also are part of the WSU and State Archives collections.

Two Ph.D. dissertations reveal much about two jurists and the courts upon which they served: Orman Vertrees, "Mr. Justice Hugh J. Rosellini: A Study of his Reference Groups and Washington Supreme Court Voting Record," and Frances P. Bernat, "Charles F. Stafford, Jr.: A Study in Judicial Behavior." Both studies are available in the dissertation collection in the WSU Library.

A few short autobiographical and biographical accounts of several high court justices have appeared. See Sheldon and C. Wade, "Frank Parks Weaver, A Short Biography," *Gonzaga Law Review,* 19 (1983-1984), pp. 219-229; Alan Gallagher, "The Fighting Judge: Justice William H. Pemberton," *Washington State Bar News,* 43 (1989), pp. 15-21; Dave James, "Just Call Me Joe," *Eagle Magazine* (Sept. 1945), pp. 12-15; George Morris, "Herman D. Crow," Washington State Bar Association *Proceedings* (1915), pp. 179-181; Stephen Chadwick, "The Recollections of Stephen James Chadwick," *Pacific Northwest Quarterly,* 55 (1964), pp. 111-118; James Dolliver, "Charles Horowitz: A Memoir," *Washington Law Review,* 56 (1981), pp. 167-170; Seattle Bar Association, "Memorial to the Late Judge William H. White," (13 Je. 1914); "In Memoriam: William H. White," Washington State Bar Association *Proceedings* (1914), pp. 232-236; Don Duncan, "Forgotten Man's Widow Waits," *Seattle Times,* 21 Je. 1965; Mack Gose, "Presidential Address," Washington State Bar Association *Proceedings* (1915), pp. 121-130; Robert Hunter, "The Practice of Law in the Early Days of Grand Coulee, 1935-1946," *Pacific Northwest Forum,* 3 (1988), pp. 3-17; Hunter, "The Practice of Judging with the Superior and Supreme Courts of Washington, 1946-1976,"

Pacific Northwest Forum, 2 (1989), pp. 2-23; Mike Sprouse, "Honorable Fred Dore, Alumnus of the Year," *Seattle University News,* 13 (1989), pp. 1-2; and Hilda Bryant, "Bicentennial Biographies: William Henry White," *Seattle Post-Intelligencer,* 23 Apr. 1976.

A number of justices have written about the court and their views regarding the court's work. See Jessie Bridges, "Presidential Address," Washington State Bar Association *Proceedings* (1909), pp. 159-168; Bridges, "Log Booms on Navigable Rivers," Washington State Bar Association *Proceedings* (1906), pp. 189-195; Charles Horowitz, "Values and Decision Making: Some Observations on the Role of Non-legal Factors in the Appellate Process," *Washington Appellate Practice Handbook,* 3 (1990), pp. 1-16; Hugh Rosellini, "Crises in the Courts," *Gonzaga Law Review,* 3 (1968), p. 8; Robert Brachtenbach, "Mechanics of Supreme Court Decision-Making," *Washington State Bar News,* 8 (1972), pp. 8-11; Overton Ellis, "The Court's Work," Washington State Bar Association *Proceedings* (1914), pp. 179-185; John Mitchell, "Address," Washington State Bar Association *Proceedings* (1921), pp. 172-176; Frank Rudkin, "The Court's Work," Washington State Bar Association *Proceedings* (1906), pp. 170-173; Frederick Hamley, "Condensation of Remarks to Ninth Circuit Law Clerks School: 1970-71-72," *Federal Rules Decisions,* 63 (1972), pp. 478-487; and Emmett Parker, "American Law Institute," Washington State Bar Association Proceedings (1923), pp. 66-71. Frederick Bausman authored three books on European affairs. Under the pen name "Aix" he wrote *Adventure of a Nice Young Man* (1908) and later, under his own name, *Let France Explain* (1923) and *Facing Europe* (1926). Joseph Mallery published several political tracts during the depression: *Dated Producers Money: A Plan to Induce Production and Compel Consumption,* (1932) and *Public Receivers: A Plan for Universal Employment,* (1933).

Justice Robert Utter has written a number of articles in *Washington State Bar News* which shed light on the courts and his thinking: "Let's Really Get Tough on Crime," (1971), pp. 7-8, 21-23; "Can Washington Afford an Elected Judiciary?" (1972), pp. 5-7,28-29; "The Forgotten Man," (1972), pp. 7-8,27-28; "The State of the Judiciary, 1979," (1979), pp. 13-18; "Statement of Philosophy," (1979), pp. 14-15; and "Some Things Never Change...," (1984), pp. 28-29. Also see his "Selection and Retention–A Judge's Perspective," *Washington Law Review,* 48 (1973), pp. 839-846; and the article he coauthored with Judge James Cameron, "Let Us Create a Judicial Services Corporation," *Judges' Journal* (1979), pp. 39-43. See also "Justice Dore Expresses Optimism to New Attorneys," *Gonzaga Law Review,* 21 (1985-1986), pp. 337-343. Frank Weaver coauthored with Sheldon, *Politicians, Judges and the People* (1980). Justice William Goodloe published a number of patriotic pamphlets and model constitutions. See, for example, *The Bill of Rights and My Responsibilities* (1977); *The Mayflower Compact: A Document of Freedom* (1979); and *The Constitution of the United Republics of Africa* (1989). In 1976 he published *Jury Selection Manual for Bench and Bar.*

Judge Theodore Stiles began a tradition of jurists writing on legal subjects beyond their official opinions. See his "Legislative Encroachments upon Private Rights," Washington State Bar Association *Proceedings,* 59 (1899), pp. 59-75; "Should this State Permit Corporations to Own and Vote Stock in Other Corporations?" Washington State Bar Association *Proceedings,* (1904), pp. 140-152; and "The Constitution of the State and Its Effects Upon the Public Interest," *Washington Historical Quarterly,* 4 (1913), pp. 281-287.

Justice Charles Horowitz has a long listing of articles, beginning when he was a student and law review editor at the University of Washington and continuing after his retirement from the high bench. Volume 56 of the *Washington Law Review* (pp. 163-178) is dedicated to Justice Horowitz and has a bibliography of his many articles. See also his "Legal Justice, Values and Appellate Decision-Making," *Gonzaga Law Review,* 18 (1982-1983), pp. 633-664.

Robert Finley's writings are also revealing. See, for example, his "Some Observations on the Law and the Nature of the Judicial Process," *Washington Law Review,* 35 (1960), pp. 1-36; "Miscellaneous Observations In Re the Law and The Judge Function," *Louisiana Law Review,* 25 (1965), pp. 467-490; "Constitutional Responsibility and Authority for Court Administration," *Journal of the American Judicature Society,* 47 (1963), pp. 30-34; "Judicial Administration: Who Is on Trial—The Police? The Courts? Or the Criminally Accused?" *Journal of Criminal Law, Criminology and Police Science,* (1966), p. 238; "Judicial Administration: What is This Thing Called Legal Reform?" *Columbia Law Review,* 65 (1965), pp. 569-592; "Upgrading Court Organization and Administration: A Small Blueprint for a Big Job," *Duke Law Review* (1965), pp. 322-328; "Bare Bones of Court Reform," *St. Louis University Law Journal,* 13 (1968), p. 171; and "Remodeling the Judiciary," *Trial,* 5 (1969), p. 10.

Justice Robert Utter has written extensively on constitutional issues. See his "The Right to Speak, Write, and Publish Freely: State Constitutional Protection Against Private Abridgment," *University of Puget Sound Law Review,* 8 (1985), pp. 157-194; "Freedom and Diversity in a Federal System: Perspectives on State Constitutions and the Washington Declaration of Rights," *University of Puget Sound Law Review,* 7 (1984), pp. 491-525; "Swimming in the Jaws of the Crocodile: State Court Comment on Federal Constitutional Issues when Disposing of Cases on State Constitutional Grounds," *Texas Law Review,* 63 (1985), pp. 1025-1050; "Survey of Washington Search and Seizure Law," *University of Puget Sound Law Review,* 9 (1985), pp. 1-205; "Survey of Washington Search and Seizure Law: 1988 Update," *University of Puget Sound Law Review,* 11 (1988), pp. 411-657; "Interpreting State Constitutions: An Independent Path," 15 *Intergovernmental Perspective* 30 (1989), pp. 30-32; and "State Constitutional Law, the United States Supreme Court, and Democratic Accountability: Is There a Crocodile in the Bathtub?" *Washington Law Review,* 64 (1989), pp. 19-49. Also see Utter and Sanford Pitler, "Presenting a State Constitutional Argument: Comment on Theory and Technique," *Indiana Law Review,* 20 (1987), pp. 635-677.

See also Fred Dore, "On Modernization of State Government," *Report, Joint Interim Committee of Facilities and Operations (1965);* Robert Brachtenbach, "Public Policy in Judicial Decisions," *Gonzaga Law Review,* 1 (1985-1986), pp. 1-19; and James Dolliver, "Condemnation, Credit and Corporations in Washington: 100 Years of Judicial Decisions—Have the Framers' Views Been Followed?" *University of Puget Sound Law Review,* 12 (1989), pp. 163-196; "Law as a Profession: Will it Survive," *Gonzaga Law Review,* 26 (1990-1991), pp. 267-275; "The American Experiment," *Gonzaga Law Review,* 22 (1986-1987), pp. 301-305; and "The Washington Constitution and 'State Action': The View of the Framers," *Willamette Law Review,* 22 (1986), pp. 445-458.

Aside from the standard biographical and *Who's Who* works, the State Archives houses gubernatorial papers containing files on supreme court appointments and candidates. The Northwest collections at both the State Library and the University of Washington have card files on many of the early jurists. *Washington Reports, Federal Reporter* (federal district), and *Federal Reports* (federal circuit courts) publish memorials shortly after members or former members of the state's high bench have passed away. Earlier, the Washington State Bar Association's *Proceedings* contained memorial addresses.

An often neglected source is the published opinions of the justices reported in *Washington Reports,* located in any attorney's office and all county law libraries. These written opinions explaining the rulings of the jurists reveal much about individual jurists and their decision-making styles.

Finally, the King County and Washington Supreme Court law libraries also contain copies of the briefs filed by attorneys in each of the court's cases, and the supreme court clerk's office and the State Archives retain a file on each case, including recordings of each of the oral arguments, copies of lawyer's written briefs, motions, and court opinions. Not to be ignored are the files in the Public Disclosure Commission on campaign contributions and spending for all candidates for the supreme court since 1973.

A great body of material is available for research on the eighty justices who helped make history for the State of Washington. However, until very recently, most of these sources have been scattered about the state in private and public collections. Hopefully, the supreme court collection with the State Archives will bring together many of the sources and provide students and scholars with the sources needed to develop an understanding of the crucial role the justices of the Washington Supreme Court play.

Name Index

Case Index

Subject Index

computers and court records, 95
Constitution of the U.S.: amendments, 8-9, 10, 12, 16, 19, 20, 21-22; discussed, 8-9, 18-19, 166, 327
Constitution of Washington State: amendments, 38, 51-52; convention, 31-33, 135, 326; discussed, 1-12, 17, 20, 27, 47
Constitutional Conventions, 31-33, 135, 168, 221, 326
contestedness in judicial races, 29-31, 33, 36, 38, 40-42, 56
Corporate Counsel, 84, 89, 122, 158
Council of Chief Judges of Courts of Appeal, 103
Council of Chief Justice's Coordinating Committee, 277
Court Administrator's Office, 149
Court Commissioner's Office, xi, 53
Court of Appeals (federal), 197, 298
Court of Appeals (state): division one, 75, 103, 128, 138, 319, 334; division two, 275; mentioned, xi, 38, 39, 52, 214, 226
Cowlitz County, 242
Cynthiana, Ky., 343

Dakota Constitutional Convention, 168
Dalles, The, Oreg., 135
decision-making deliberations on supreme court, ix, 47-56
Declaration of Rights (state), 1-2, 20, 21, 22
Democratic Council, 106
Democratic Party, 17, 33, 38, 67, 68, 293, 348
Department of Ecology (state), 209
Department of Efficiency (state), 159
Department of Forestry (state), 114
Department of Labor and Industries (state), 114, 179
Department of Social and Health Services (state), 179
DePauw University, 97
District Courts, 114, 138 *see also* U.S. District Court
Douglas County, 132, 224, 228, 258, 299
Duke University, 145

Earlham College, 182, 279
Eastern Washington Natural Gas, 127
elections of supreme court judges, 27, 29-42
Electric Service and Supply Company, 97
Ellensburg, Wash., 218, 219, 297
Emergency Unemployment Relief Commission, 159
endorsement and judicial appointments, 33-34, 39
Ephrata, Wash., 226, 228, 229, 299
equal protection provisions, 17-18
Equal Rights Amendment, 216
Everett, Wash., 118

Federal Alcohol Control Administration, 146
Federal Courts Study Commission, 103
Federal Housing Administration, 146
First Baptist Church, 334
First National Bank, Pomeroy, 171
First Realty Corporation, 123
Florida A & M University, 314
formalism, 8, 12, 14-17, 22
Franklin County, 191, 297
Fusionist Party, 158, 183, 211, 221

Garfield County, 171
General Insurance Company, 163
Genesee Wesleyan Seminary, 256
George Washington University, 86
Georgetown University, 126, 129, 132, 140, 146, 158, 250, 253
Goldendale, Wash., 135, 282
Gonzaga College/University, 108, 110, 140, 179, 245, 277, 338-339, 345, 351
Governor's Safety Conference, 78
Grand Coulee, Wash., 224
Grand Coulee dam, 196, 299
Grange, the, 37, 226, 243, 244, 252, 280, 293, 295
Grant County, 224, 228, 299
Grays Harbor County, 67, 97
Grays Harbor Railway and Light Company, 97
Great Depression, 17, 36, 185, 187, 293
Great Northern Railway Company, 168, 288
gubernatorial appointments of judges, 27, 32-35, 37-39
Guthrie Industries, 179

Harrison County, Ky., 343
Harvard Law School, 7, 80
Highway Patrol, 159
Hillsdale College, 154
Hoquiam, Wash., 67

Idaho Territory, 220
Indiana University, 86
Industrial Workers of the World 77, 236
Institute of Judicial Administration, 194
Island County, 265

Jamestown College, 273, 274
judges *see* Supreme Court; judges' names
Judicial Arbitration and Mediation Services, 104
Judicial Conduct/Qualifications Commission, 232, 277, 337
Judicial Conference of the U. S., 307
Judicial Council, x, 131, 152, 175, 235, 277
Judicial Ethics Committee, 320
judicial federalism, 19-22